Automating Microsoft® Windows Server® 2008 R2 with Windows PowerShell® 2.0

Automating Microsoft® Windows Server® 2008 R2 with Windows PowerShell® 2.0

Matthew Hester
Sarah Dutkiewicz

WILEY

Wiley Publishing, Inc.

Acquisitions Editor: Agatha Kim
Development Editor: Dick Margulis
Technical Editor: Sarah Dutkiewicz
Production Editor: Liz Britten
Copy Editor: Kim Wimpsett
Editorial Manager: Pete Gaughan
Production Manager: Tim Tate
Vice President and Executive Group Publisher: Richard Swadley
Vice President and Publisher: Neil Edde
Book Designer: Franz Baumhackl
Proofreader: Word One, New York
Indexer: Jack Lewis
Project Coordinator, Cover: Katie Crocker
Cover Designer: Ryan Sneed
Cover Image: © Petrovich9 / iStockPhoto

Dear Reader,

Thank you for choosing *Automating Windows Server 2008 R2 with Windows PowerShell 2.0*. This book is part of a family of premium-quality Sybex books, all of which are written by outstanding authors who combine practical experience with a gift for teaching.

Sybex was founded in 1976. More than 30 years later, we're still committed to producing consistently exceptional books. With each of our titles, we're working hard to set a new standard for the industry. From the paper we print on, to the authors we work with, our goal is to bring you the best books available.

I hope you see all that reflected in these pages. I'd be very interested to hear your comments and get your feedback on how we're doing. Feel free to let me know what you think about this or any other Sybex book by sending me an email at nedde@ wiley.com. If you think you've found a technical error in this book, please visit http://sybex.custhelp.com. Customer feedback is critical to our efforts at Sybex.

Best regards,

Neil Edde
Vice President and Publisher
Sybex, an Imprint of Wiley

To Deb, my strength and heart, thank you so much for all of your unwavering love and support. I would not be who I am today without you. I love you.

To Nicole, Mitchell, and Caitlin, thank you for teaching me the meaning of grace. I love you all very much.

—Matt

To Kevin, my wonderful husband who survived my talks about PowerShell from a developer's perspective while writing, offered suggestions when I needed another person's real-world IT perspective, and has been very supportive of me through my "wrediting" process.

—Sarah

ACKNOWLEDGMENTS

Being able to write this book has been a blessing, and I could not have done it without a lot of top-notch help. First, I would like to thank my fabulous technical editor and coauthor, Sarah, for going on this journey with me. Sarah, your knowledge and insight are inspiring. Thank you for making sure this book is rock solid. Second, I would like to thank Dick Margulis. Dick, you truly are an editor extraordinaire who I have thoroughly enjoyed working with. I hope I did not drive you to nutty with all of my "great new features." Thank you, sir. Lastly, a huge thanks to Agatha Kim not only for giving me my first opportunity to write a book but also for encouraging me to write this book. Thank you so much for your guidance and support over the past few years.

Matt

I would like to thank my IT friends for encouraging me and inspiring me as I explored many of the topics in this book. Thanks to Jay R. Wren, my tech editor for the appendixes. As always, Jay made sure I didn't stray technically and inspired new changes. Thanks to all of our editors at Sybex, and especially thanks to Dick Margulis, our development editor, who shepherded us when we got carried away. Most of all, I would like to thank my awesome coauthor and great friend, Matt Hester, for the many commas and "great features" that I had to cut out while tech editing, the laughs throughout the process, and the advice when it came to writing the appendixes. Matt inspired me to create the term wrediting—writing and editing, as I had originally been set as a tech editor for Chapters 1–12 and later was added as a coauthor. It has been a great adventure, and I look forward to more adventures with Matt!

Sarah

ABOUT THE AUTHORS

Matt Hester is a seasoned Information Technology Professional Evangelist for Microsoft. Matt has been involved in the IT Pro community for more than 15 years. Matt is a skilled and experienced evangelist presenting to audiences nationally and internationally. Prior to joining Microsoft, Matt was a highly successful Microsoft Certified Trainer for more than eight years. After joining Microsoft, Matt has continued to be heavily involved in IT Pro community as an IT Pro Evangelist. In his role at Microsoft, Matt has presented to audiences in excess of 5,000 and as small as 10. Matt has also written four articles for *TechNet* magazine, and his first book was *Microsoft Windows Server 2008 R2 Administration Instant Reference*. Matt is a movie buff with a massive DVD collection; he also runs marathons and dreams of joining the PGA tour. Matt cites his father as his role model: "The older I get, the smarter he gets." Funny how that works.

Sarah Dutkiewicz is a seasoned technology professional and has been working in a variety of technologies for more than eight years. Sarah's well-rounded background includes roles in technical support, desktop support, database administrator, system administrator, and professional developer. Sarah's true passion comes from developing and writing code. Currently Sarah develops for a Cleveland, Ohio–based company, focusing mostly on ASP.NET development and improving processes using various .NET solutions. Sarah is currently a Microsoft MVP in Visual C# and is deeply passionate about the technical community. Sarah's many community activities include blogging, running a technical community website, planning events, and speaking at regional and national conferences.

CONTENTS AT A GLANCE

TABLE OF CONTENTS

INTRODUCTION

PowerShell is a scripting language built into Windows Server 2008 R2 servers. PowerShell is designed to help you perform routine and repetitive tasks in a scriptable fashion. PowerShell helps alleviate many of the time-consuming and tedious tasks administrators have had to do in the past. You may have used various scripting technologies over the years to accomplish these tasks; however, in PowerShell 2.0, you have a better tool than you have ever had when working with Microsoft environments. PowerShell 2.0 was launched with the release of Windows 7 and Windows Server 2008 R2. You can now leverage tons of new built-in capabilities to help make administering your server easier. It is quickly growing to become the scripting tool of choice for Microsoft operating systems and applications. In many cases, PowerShell has replaced former command prompt tools or has been incorporated into new tools. PowerShell provides a common language you can use to manage any of your Microsoft infrastructure that supports PowerShell scripting.

Who Should Read This Book

This book is for anyone who wants to learn more about PowerShell, from novices to scripting aficionados. If you are looking to learn PowerShell for the first time or if you are looking to learn how to manage Windows Server 2008 R2 with PowerShell, then this book is for you. Whether you are an IT administrator, developer, scriptaholic, or anyone else with an interest in PowerShell, you will find something in this book to help you use PowerShell to save you time. This book is designed to allow you to use PowerShell to meet your everyday business needs.

What You Will Learn

In this book you will learn the foundation behind PowerShell and how to work with this powerful scripting language. This book covers four main things:

▶ The foundation of PowerShell from the smallest components to how to create your own scripts and a lesson in syntax and grammar. The foundation you build here will enable you to work with PowerShell regardless of the operating system or application.

▶ How to practically apply PowerShell to your Windows Server 2008 R2 servers. Topics include server essentials tasks such as backup to management of Active Directory and many other Windows Server 2008 R2 server roles and features.

▶ The foundation of how to incorporate PowerShell into your application development environment and how to take PowerShell to the next level.

▶ The new capabilities of PowerShell 2.0. Throughout the chapters in this book you will see many of the new built-in capabilities of PowerShell 2.0, from new commands in Active Directory management to new functions such as remoting.

At the end of each chapter, you will get to practice what you have learned and try PowerShell with exercises designed to reinforce what you saw in the chapter. Most importantly, this book will jump-start your learning of PowerShell. Once you learn the essentials provided in the book, you can apply your knowledge to leverage PowerShell not only in Windows Server 2008 R2 but also in other Windows operating systems and applications such as Microsoft Exchange Server and Microsoft SharePoint Server, as well as anywhere else you find PowerShell.

What Is Covered in This Book

Automating Microsoft Windows Server 2008 R2 with Windows PowerShell 2.0 is organized to provide you with the knowledge to be successful with PowerShell.

Chapter 1: What Is PowerShell, and Why Do You Need It? talks about the importance of learning PowerShell not only for IT professionals but also for application developers. You will also see many of the new tools in PowerShell 2.0.

Chapter 2: Installing and Configuring PowerShell 2.0 focuses on installing and configuring PowerShell 2.0, including other Microsoft operating systems besides Windows Server 2008 R2 and Windows 7.

Chapter 3: PowerShell Grammar Lesson breaks down the PowerShell language to its smallest parts. This chapter provides the background to cmdlets and how you can work with them.

Chapter 4: Aliases, Functions, and the Pipe, Oh My! shows how to create shortcuts for your commands, called aliases. You will also learn the power of functions, which give you the ability to create your own custom commands. You will also see how to tie PowerShell commands together with the pipe (|).

Chapter 5: Creating Your Own Scripts focuses on creating and writing your own scripts by combining your PowerShell commands.

Chapter 6: Remoting with PowerShell 2.0 shows how to use the new PowerShell 2.0 capability of being able to create remoting sessions and run PowerShell commands remotely.

Chapter 7: Server Essentials in PowerShell shows how to use PowerShell to perform daily server administrative tasks such as backing up your server as well as unlocking other data stores directly with PowerShell.

Chapter 8: Managing Active Directory with PowerShell takes a look at the new built-in commands for working with Active Directory with PowerShell.

Chapter 9: Managing Desktops with PowerShell shows how to manage your desktops via Group Policy and how to manage Group Policy with PowerShell.

Chapter 10: Managing IIS Web Server with PowerShell discusses how you can use PowerShell to manage your web servers in Internet Information Services (IIS).

Chapter 11: PowerShell and Deployment Services shows how to work with Windows Deployment Services (WDS) and the free Microsoft Deployment Toolkit (MDT) to deploy operating systems for your organization. The MDT has native PowerShell support and allows you to build custom deployment images for your environment.

Chapter 12: PowerShell and Virtualization gives you a brief tour of Hyper-V, Microsoft's virtualization platform, and how you can manage it with PowerShell.

Appendix A: Solutions to Exercises gives the answers for the end-of-chapter exercises.

Appendix B: Developing at a Command Prompt discusses choosing between the Integrated Scripting Engine (ISE) and the command prompt and establishes a foundation for working with objects in PowerShell.

Appendix C: Providing for PowerShell discusses the built-in providers and provides a basic example for creating your own provider in PowerShell.

Appendix D: Custom Cmdlets and Functions discusses how to create your own cmdlets and functions, allowing you to extend PowerShell to meet your needs.

Appendix E: Packaging PowerShell Extensions discusses how to work with modules and how to create your own custom module.

Appendix F: Building Your Own GUI with PowerShell discusses the options for creating a graphical user interface (GUI) from scratch in PowerShell and shows examples for getting started in creating a GUI.

How to Contact the Author

We welcome feedback from you about this book or about books you'd like to see from us in the future. You can reach us by writing to Matt at raid78@msn.com or Sarah at sarah@sadukie.com or by contacting us on our blogs at http://blogs.technet.com/matthewms or http://codinggeekette.com. You can also follow Sarah on Twitter as @sadukie.

For more information about our work, please visit our websites at http://blogs.technet.com/matthewms and http://codinggeekette.com.

Sybex strives to keep you supplied with the latest tools and information you need for your work. Please check its website at www.sybex.com, where we'll post additional content and updates that supplement this book if the need arises. Enter **Automating Microsoft Windows Server 2008 R2 with Windows PowerShell 2.0** in the Search box (or type the book's ISBN—**9781118013861**), and click Go to get to the book's update page.

What Is PowerShell, and Why Do You Need It?

HERE ARE THE TOPICS COVERED IN THIS CHAPTER:

T professionals have been looking for ways to automate and perform tasks in a consistent manner for years. There have been many techniques and technologies — from simple batch files to third-party tools — to accomplish the tasks. Some IT professionals have gone the extra step and learned developer languages, such as Visual Basic or JavaScript, to give their scripts more power.

A majority of these tools were not integrated into the Microsoft environment. More importantly, the documentation for these tools to accomplish common administrative tasks was not readily available. As part of its effort over the years to improve the scripting environment, Microsoft developed PowerShell to overcome the challenges of previous scripting languages.

PowerShell provides a common language you can use throughout your Microsoft infrastructure. You will spend less time on manual repetitive tasks by scripting these tasks with PowerShell. PowerShell is used in a number of scenarios, including system administration and software development. PowerShell is ideal for remote management, reporting, automation, and administration.

This book focuses on learning this powerful scripting language with real-world examples and ways to perform common, everyday tasks. Tasks such as backing up servers, maintaining web servers, analyzing your environment, and many more can benefit from PowerShell. Step-by-step instructions in the chapters that follow show you how you can make PowerShell work for you.

The book is divided into two sections. In the first few chapters, you will build the foundation of your PowerShell knowledge. You will learn the basics of a building block known as a *cmdlet* (pronounced "command-let") and how to read script. The second section of the book focuses on administrative tasks you can perform in Windows Server 2008 R2. Although the book is geared to working on a Windows Server 2008 R2 setup, the foundational knowledge provided in the book allows you to leverage PowerShell regardless of the target Windows operating system. The goal is to demystify PowerShell for you so you can use it in your day-to-day tasks.

This chapter gives an overview of PowerShell and why it is important.

Why PowerShell?

If you have been working in a Microsoft environment for the past few years, you may have seen or heard about PowerShell. You may even remember its original code name, Monad. It may have been discounted as "yet another scripting language" and put aside to look at later. You may have even thought, why reinvent the wheel?

In other words, your environment was running smoothly, you were busy, and you had no time to learn the language. You may have decided to wait to see whether there would be a version 2 and whether Microsoft was really serious about this language. Well, here we are with version 2, and PowerShell is getting better than ever. Microsoft and communities such as `http://powershellcommunity.org/` are creating native PowerShell commands and providers as well as the documentation for scripts to make your everyday work with PowerShell even easier. So, you are not in this alone. The community is growing and vibrant!

The initial project Monad debuted in June 2005. In April 2006, Microsoft announced that Monad's name would be PowerShell, and PowerShell Release Candidate 1 was released. PowerShell 1.0 was released in November 2006. It was well received in the community, and with its integration into the Windows environment, this became a new language for administrators to work with. In 2009, version 2 of PowerShell was released and built into Windows 7 and Windows Server 2008 R2. PowerShell 2.0 is also available for free download for systems newer than Windows XP SP3. Chapter 2 discusses how to install the tools on older, supported operating systems.

Overview of PowerShell

What is PowerShell?

- ► PowerShell is an extensible automation engine from Microsoft.
- ► PowerShell is a command-line shell and task-based scripting technology that provides you with enhanced remote management and automation of system administration tasks.

PowerShell can look like Figure 1.1, and it can look like Figure 1.2.

What can it do?

PowerShell enables you to perform via scripts virtually any task you can do in the GUI for your local or remote Windows operating systems and your computers. With PowerShell, you can script and automate your day-to-day administrative tasks.

- ► Do you need to get a list of all the computers on the network and create a report on the service pack level for each operating system?
- ► Do you need to check to make sure that all the users in the domain are complying with the corporate password policy?
- ► Do you need to start a service on 500 computers?
- ► Do you need to add 100 user accounts to your domain?

▶ Do you need to collect all the critical and error events from the event logs of all your servers?

FIGURE 1.1   This is PowerShell.

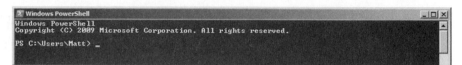

FIGURE 1.2   This is PowerShell too.

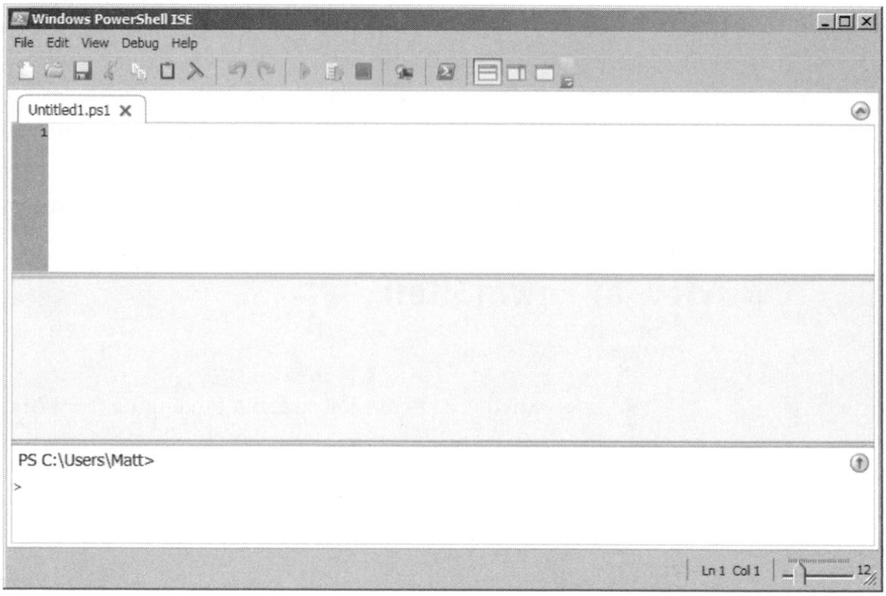

PowerShell can do that.

Once you learn the language, you should be able to perform these tasks faster than you have in the past.

By integrating PowerShell scripts into your environment, you can automate many of the time-consuming, monotonous tasks required of system administrators. If you look at tasks such as some of the previous examples that gather and parse large amounts of information, it may take a long time to do them manually. These types of tasks are perfect candidates for PowerShell scripting.

PowerShell includes numerous system administration utilities, consistent syntax and naming conventions, and improved navigation for common management data, such as the registry, certificate store, and Windows Management Instrumentation (WMI). WMI is a core technology for Windows system administration, because it exposes a wide range of information in a uniform manner. PowerShell includes a cmdlet that allows you to interface with WMI objects, enhancing your ability to do real work.

But isn't PowerShell just a command-line tool? Yes, it is a command-line tool, but in most cases PowerShell can accomplish all the tasks that graphic management tools can.

PowerShell is built upon a robust architecture that includes the following:

- ► A script parser that processes language constructs, such as scripts, predicates, and conditionals

- ► A pipeline processor, which manages intercommand communication using pipes (|)

- ► A command processor, which manages command execution, registration, and associated metadata

In addition to those processors, the shell can also manage session state and has an extended type system, which exposes a common interface for accessing properties and methods independent of the underlying object type. Lastly, PowerShell includes a robust error handler for managing error exceptions and error reporting.

The Power Behind PowerShell

PowerShell is built around an object-oriented language that lets you manage your Windows infrastructure. It provides an interface and programming environment that allows users and administrators to access and set system properties through .NET objects and single-function command-line tools called cmdlets. Cmdlets are the building blocks for PowerShell scripts. Chapter 3 explores cmdlets and the core PowerShell syntax.

The scripting language manipulates objects (not text) using the .NET Framework and the .NET common language runtime. PowerShell is built on top of, and is integrated with, the Microsoft .NET Framework. It accepts and returns .NET objects, allowing for robust scripting that interfaces seamlessly with many line-of-business tools.

This is the main reason PowerShell is more than just a console application. It is a robust scripting environment that supports a full range of logical program control, including simple conditional statements and complex switch statements using regular expressions to parse conditions. Scripts can be used independently or in conjunction with other scripts, with .NET Framework or COM objects, or even in code. PowerShell enables easy access to COM and WMI to provide an environment for local and remote Windows systems.

In many cases, a majority of the built-in roles and services (such as IIS or Active Directory) that you may run on your Windows Server 2008 R2 server have PowerShell providers and cmdlets to manage them. For example, the PowerShell Provider for Internet Information Services (IIS) 7.5 allows you to easily automate routine and complex IIS 7.5 administration tasks, such as creating websites and managing configuration and runtime data by using PowerShell. Chapter 10 shows how to work with PowerShell and your websites.

All of the other major applications running on a Windows Server 2008 R2 server, including Microsoft Exchange Server, Microsoft SQL Server, and Microsoft SharePoint Server, have built-in support for PowerShell. (Exchange Server was the first major server application to get full support for PowerShell.) The SQL Server 2008 PowerShell snap-in supports more complex logic than Transact-SQL scripts, allowing SQL Server administrators to build robust administration scripts not only for server administration but also to extend the power of SQL databases. PowerShell in some cases is also replacing existing tools for the command prompt management of a server. With SharePoint Server, PowerShell is gradually replacing the stsadm tool, which has been the main tool for command prompt administration for SharePoint servers.

What About the Learning Curve?

One of the many benefits of PowerShell is that the learning curve to get started with it is minimal. If you already know scripting languages, you have a good base for working with PowerShell. Whether you have a background with command prompt tools for Microsoft or non-Microsoft operating systems such as UNIX, PowerShell lets you build on your existing command prompt knowledge. Throughout this book, you will see many examples of PowerShell that look similar to techniques you have used in other shells. PowerShell includes single-function tools such as cd, copy, and dir that you are familiar with from the Windows command interface. You can also recognize these other PowerShell functions from a UNIX background, such as ls or man.

If you have a UNIX administration background, you are familiar with the term *shell*. A shell provides a powerful, flexible, and scriptable command-line experience that allows you to perform any administrative task that you can perform using the console. The difference between using the shell and the PowerShell console is that the PowerShell is ideally suited to repetitive tasks. PowerShell is not a text-based shell but a console. PowerShell has a substantial number of built-in commands that provide you with a powerful tool set for script-based administration.

The formatting for commands that use the .NET Framework, COM objects, and WMI are slightly different from other scripting technologies, but in general those commands are simpler in PowerShell. If you are not familiar with scripting techniques, the base set of cmdlets is easy to learn, as you'll see throughout this book. PowerShell provides an intuitive scripting language specifically designed for day-to-day administrative of servers.

Cmdlets really showcase the intuitive nature of PowerShell. Cmdlets have a verb-noun structure, so they are somewhat self-describing. For example, here is a simple cmdlet that returns the current system date and time:

```
Get-Date
```

Your results will look similar to Figure 1.3.

FIGURE 1.3   A simple cmdlet

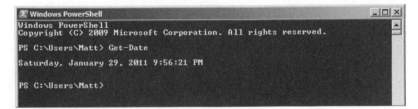

The cmdlets can also get more complex. In this book, you will start with the building blocks and get more in depth. Cmdlets can be used independently or scripted together to create a powerful automation application. Lastly, the language also provides a self-service help system, allowing you to learn the language quickly. Chapter 3 will show you how to get help by using the `Get-Help` cmdlet.

What's New in PowerShell 2.0?

With the launch of PowerShell 2.0, Microsoft began to take a deeper look into this language. With PowerShell being built into operating systems, IT administrators took notice. You may have been asking this question: "How can I leverage PowerShell in my environment, and where do I start?"

Microsoft wanted to make PowerShell 2.0 more enterprise-friendly so IT administrators everywhere could run, learn, and share PowerShell easily from within the GUI. PowerShell also had to be made to run safely and securely.

One of the new features in PowerShell 2.0 that allows IT administrators throughout the world to use PowerShell more easily is called *internationalization*. Internationalization enables PowerShell scripts to display messages in the language specified by the UI language setting on the user's computer. Under the hood, this features queries the operating system of the user to determine what language is being used. This lets PowerShell display the appropriate language.

Microsoft added more than 50 cmdlets for the core PowerShell sessions. Although those new cmdlets are important, Microsoft also addressed many of the server roles on Windows Server that did not have native PowerShell cmdlets in PowerShell 1.0. One of the key roles on Windows Server 2008 R2 that got new cmdlets was Active Directory (AD). Managing AD with PowerShell 1.0 was a challenge. There were no built-in cmdlets, so you had to know how to work with LDAP in script. Chapter 8 takes a look at the new PowerShell cmdlets you can use to manage your AD environment. Chapter 8 will also show you a couple of new features — Recycle Bin and managed service accounts — you can manage only in PowerShell.

PowerShell in the Enterprise

PowerShell 2.0 provides several new capabilities to make the tool more enterprise-friendly. For example, running PowerShell commands on remote computers in PowerShell 1.0 was not built in. A lot of administrators started remote desktop sessions to run PowerShell commands. This was one of the challenges that was addressed in PowerShell 2.0.

Remoting uses the WS-Management protocol and the Windows Remote Management (WinRM) service that implements WS-Management in Windows. This protocol is a standard-based, firewall-compatible communications protocol. Chapter 6 covers remoting and shows you how to configure and work with PowerShell remoting.

Key to working with remoting is another new concept in PowerShell 2.0 called *sessions*. A session is the environment where you run PowerShell commands. Every time you start PowerShell, a new session is created. You can even create a new session in your existing session for a local or remote computer.

The session cmdlet uses a parameter called `ComputerName`. This allows you to specify the remote computer you want to start the PowerShell session on. For example, the following cmdlet would create and enter a new PowerShell session on Server2:

```
Enter-PSSession  -ComputerName Server2
```

Your results will look similar to Figure 1.4.

FIGURE 1.4   Remote session

Another key addition to PowerShell 2.0 is the ability to create and run background jobs. After you start a background job, you are returned almost immediately to your interactive PowerShell session. This allows you to continue to do work in your PowerShell session, and at any time you can see the status of your background jobs. The following command starts a command in the background to get the existing services:

```
Start-Job -name Services -scriptblock (Get-Service)
```

To see the status of background jobs you started in your PowerShell session, you would run the following command:

```
Get-Job
```

Your results will look similar to Figure 1.5.

FIGURE 1.5   Background jobs

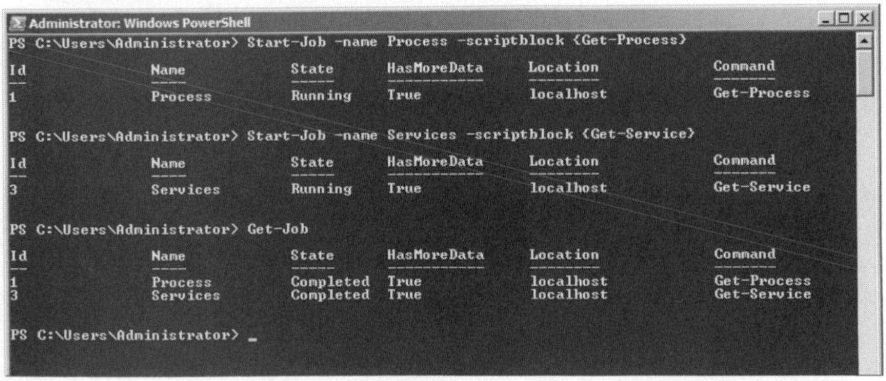

PowerShell with a GUI

There was no built-in GUI in PowerShell 1.0, so you had only the command console for your PowerShell session. There were third-party tools you could use, such as PowerGUI (`http://powergui.org/index.jspa`).

With PowerShell 2.0, Microsoft added new features to take advantage of the GUI. The following are two of the main ways you can use PowerShell's GUI features:

► Integrated Scripting Environment (ISE)

► `Out-GridView`

The ISE shown in Figure 1.2 is a new GUI front-end application console for PowerShell. However, the primary benefit of the ISE is to create, edit, and debug PowerShell scripts. The ISE provides an easy-to-use, syntax-highlighted way to work with your scripts, as shown in Figure 1.6.

FIGURE 1.6   ISE with a script

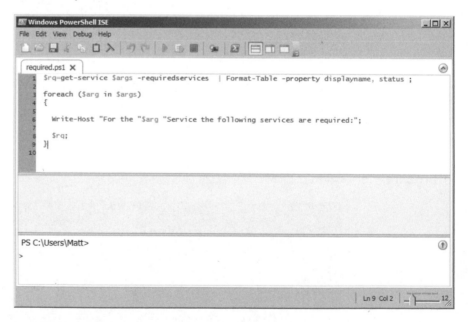

There are debugging tools built in to PowerShell 2.0. Scripts are created in many different tools, from the ISE to Notepad, and scripters have used a variety of debugging tools with PowerShell. The new debugging features allow you set breakpoints on the following:

- Lines

- Columns

- Variables

- Commands

If you are using the debugger with your scripts, you can step into, over, and out of the scripts, and you can even display the call stack, often with a single keystroke. There are cmdlets to work with the debugger. You can also display the values of variables and run standard commands in the debugger.

The ISE makes it easy to interact with the debugger. Figure 1.7 shows the Debug menu.

FIGURE 1.7   ISE's Debug menu

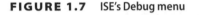

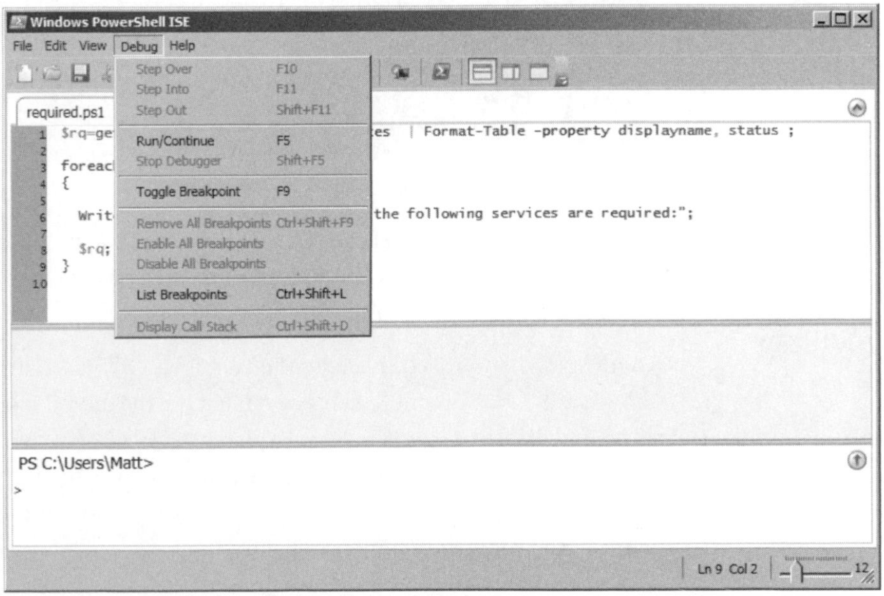

You can also access the debugger in your PowerShell sessions. You can set breakpoints using the Set-PSBreakpoint cmdlet, and you can list your breakpoints with the `Get-PSBreakpoint` cmdlet for any of your PowerShell scripts. Figure 1.8 shows an example of a debugging session from the PowerShell console.

FIGURE 1.8 Debugging session in PowerShell

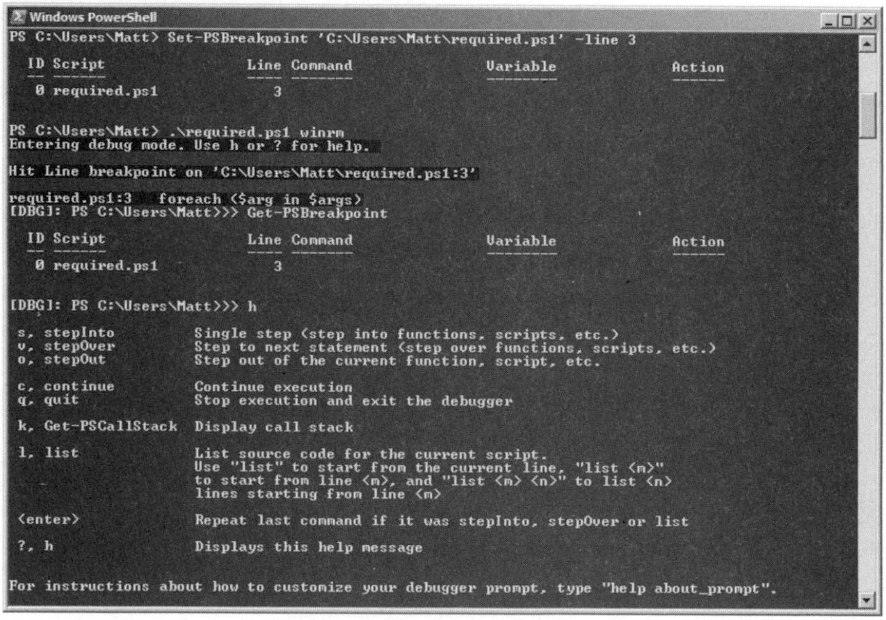

To learn more about the ISE, see Chapter 2 and Chapter 5. Chapter 2 shows you how to install the ISE, which may not be installed by default. Chapter 5 shows how to use this tool when working with PowerShell scripts.

Another way PowerShell leverages the Windows GUI is with the output cmdlet `Out-GridView`. This cmdlet allows you to take the output from a PowerShell command and display it in a Windows Explorer–style window, which not only displays your data but also allows you some interaction such as sorting and quickly filtering the data. For example, if you ran the command `Get-Process | Out-GridView`, your results would look similar to Figure 1.9.

You can click any of the column headings in the `Out-Gridview` window, and the content will be sorted. You can also quickly filter the data by either adding criteria or typing in the Filter text box. Chapter 4 takes a look at the `Out-GridView` cmdlet as well as other ways to work with data from your PowerShell commands.

FIGURE 1.9   Out-Gridview

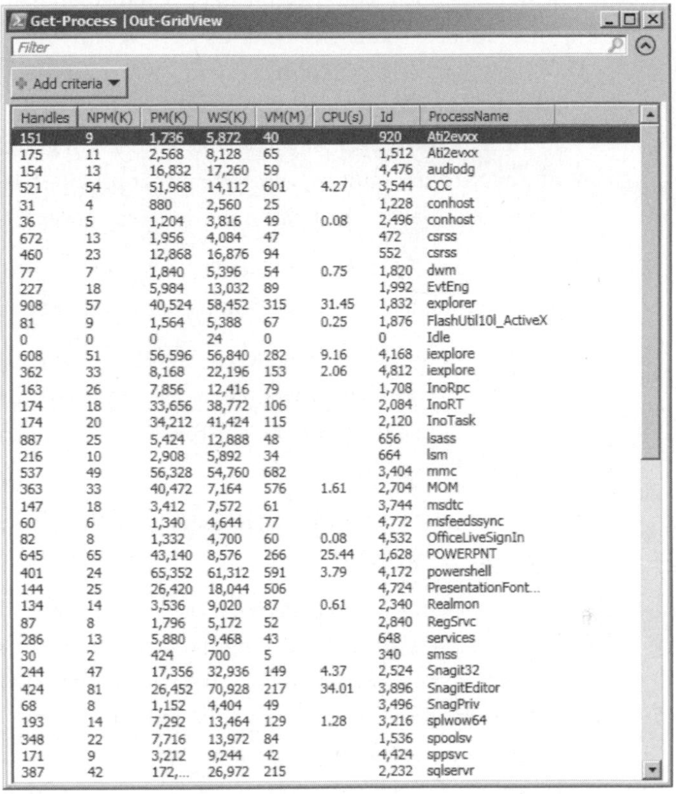

```
Get-Process | Out-GridView                                    _ □ ×
Filter                                                         🔍 ⊙
⊕ Add criteria ▼
```

Handles	NPM(K)	PM(K)	WS(K)	VM(M)	CPU(s)	Id	ProcessName
151	9	1,736	5,872	40		920	Ati2evxx
175	11	2,568	8,128	65		1,512	Ati2evxx
154	13	16,832	17,260	59		4,476	audiodg
521	54	51,968	14,112	601	4.27	3,544	CCC
31	4	880	2,560	25		1,228	conhost
36	5	1,204	3,816	49	0.08	2,496	conhost
672	13	1,956	4,084	47		472	csrss
460	23	12,868	16,876	94		552	csrss
77	7	1,840	5,396	54	0.75	1,820	dwm
227	18	5,984	13,032	89		1,992	EvtEng
908	57	40,524	58,452	315	31.45	1,832	explorer
81	9	1,564	5,388	67	0.25	1,876	FlashUtil10l_ActiveX
0	0	0	24	0		0	Idle
608	51	56,596	56,840	282	9.16	4,168	iexplore
362	33	8,168	22,196	153	2.06	4,812	iexplore
163	26	7,856	12,416	79		1,708	InoRpc
174	18	33,656	38,772	106		2,084	InoRT
174	20	34,212	41,424	115		2,120	InoTask
887	25	5,424	12,888	48		656	lsass
216	10	2,908	5,892	34		664	lsm
537	49	56,328	54,760	682		3,404	mmc
363	33	40,472	7,164	576	1.61	2,704	MOM
147	18	3,412	7,572	61		3,744	msdtc
60	6	1,340	4,644	77		4,772	msfeedssync
82	8	1,332	4,700	60	0.08	4,532	OfficeLiveSignIn
645	65	43,140	8,576	266	25.44	1,628	POWERPNT
401	24	65,352	61,312	591	3.79	4,172	powershell
144	25	26,420	18,044	506		4,724	PresentationFont...
134	14	3,536	9,020	87	0.61	2,340	Realmon
87	8	1,796	5,172	52		2,840	RegSrvc
286	13	5,880	9,468	43		648	services
30	2	424	700	5		340	smss
244	47	17,356	32,936	149	4.37	2,524	Snagit32
424	81	26,452	70,928	217	34.01	3,896	SnagitEditor
68	8	1,152	4,404	49		3,496	SnagPriv
193	14	7,292	13,464	129	1.28	3,216	splwow64
348	22	7,716	13,972	84		1,536	spoolsv
171	9	3,212	9,244	42		4,424	sppsvc
387	42	172,...	26,972	215		2,232	sqlservr

PowerShell Has Something for Everyone

PowerShell has something for everyone, from IT professionals to developers to the casual scripter. PowerShell is a tool that can save you time and show you a new way to automate a task that was previously difficult or impossible. Unlocking PowerShell to meet your needs always starts with the basics.

Before you can dive into PowerShell to meet your particular interest or business, you need a solid foundation in PowerShell. You need to know the basics of installing PowerShell and of reading and writing PowerShell scripts. That way, you can build your knowledge for many other aspects of PowerShell. Whether your focus is IT administration or development, you need the basics.

PowerShell needs to be installed on any system you want to be able to manage with PowerShell. PowerShell can be installed on many Microsoft operating systems (including XP mode on Windows 7). There are third-party PowerShell add-ons for non-Microsoft operating systems. Knowing what systems you want to manage allows you to determine which is the best path to deploy PowerShell. Chapter 2 focuses on the proper way to enable and install PowerShell.PowerShell has a robust and easy-to-use built-in help system that provides descriptions of the various cmdlets, as well as examples in most cases.

After PowerShell has been installed, you can learn to read the language. When you see a command like the following, you should understand what it does:

```
Get-ADObject -SearchBase "CN=Deleted Objects,↵
DC=your domain name,DC=Com" -Filter {lastKnownParent ↵
-eq "OU=marketing,DC=deploy,dc=com"} -includeDeletedObjects↵
| Restore-ADObject
```

This command restores deleted users from the marketing organizational unit (OU) in the deploy.com domain.

You can then begin to combine multiple commands into one script. You need to know how to shorten those commands and unlock many of the other administrative aspects of PowerShell. Working with scripts involves combining the tasks in the proper order and saving them in one file. There are websites that have PowerShell script repositories, and you can leverage the work of another PowerShell administrator. PowerShell also protects you from rogue PowerShell scripts and allows only those scripts that are safe and secure

In Chapters 3–5, you will learn to master the basics. You will be able to break the previous command down into its smallest parts so commands like these do not scare you away from PowerShell. You will see how easy the language can be used to perform complex tasks.

What's in It for IT Professionals?

With Windows Server 2008 R2, you can install many roles and features to provide functionality to your infrastructure. From Active Directory to Hyper-V to IIS to Deployment Services, you can perform day-to-day administration with PowerShell.

After you learn the basics of the language, you need to put PowerShell in practice. When you install the features on your Windows Server 2008 R2 server, nearly all of them have their own set of PowerShell commands and functions to perform a variety of tasks specific to the particular role or feature.

Beginning with basic installation of the roles and features on your server, PowerShell can be used to perform these functions for your full and core Windows Server 2008 R2 servers. Performing and scheduling a task such as a backup can be quickly created in a PowerShell script and tied to the Task Scheduler.

PowerShell can provide a consistent approach to the daily maintenance of servers. In some cases, PowerShell may be the only utility you can use. This is the case with the Active Directory Recycle Bin and managed service accounts, two features in Windows Server 2008 R2 Active Directory.

IIS provides another scenario for IT professionals to use PowerShell. With PowerShell, you can work with the core configuration to manage sites and work with web applications. This allows you to manage and quickly maintain web farms.

As an IT professional, you want PowerShell to be consistent when you work on various tasks or when you download third-party tools. This is where you see the pervasiveness of PowerShell. For example, when you download the Microsoft Deployment Toolkit (MDT), this free tool has built-in PowerShell cmdlets.

What makes PowerShell a unique tool set is the strong community following the language. In some cases, Microsoft did not provide cmdlets for a Windows Server 2008 R2 server role. Yet you can find third-party ones with an Internet search. This is the case with Hyper-V. With PowerShell 2.0, there are no built-in cmdlets to support working with Hyper-V, and you may have to use WMI to work directly with Hyper-V via PowerShell. However, the PowerShell community has created a dedicated provider for managing Hyper-V in PowerShell, making it easier than having to use WMI to accomplish the same tasks.

Chapters 7–12 focus on many of the daily workloads you may encounter when you manage a Windows Server 2008 R2 server with PowerShell. These chapters will show how to install server components; how to manage IIS, Hyper-V, and Active Directory; and how to use many other roles and features you will find in Windows Server 2008 R2.

What's in It for Developers?

Although this book does focus on some of the IT professional and administrative tasks performed on Windows Server 2008 R2 servers, there is a side of PowerShell that developers can work with, making it that much more powerful and beneficial in your workplace. PowerShell is another development platform you can use to automate many tasks via code. After you have the foundational knowledge presented throughout this book, looking at the programmatic side of PowerShell will allow you to take PowerShell to another level.

PowerShell provides you with a lightweight (when compared to Visual Studio or other developer tools) programmatic interface. Many of the applications utilizing PowerShell have a core set of APIs accessible with PowerShell. There are features that were designed in PowerShell 2.0, such as transactions, geared to be used in code.

For those who are new to development and unfamiliar with the basic concepts of objects and properties, Appendix B explores objects and properties from a PowerShell perspective.

It may seem odd to develop on the command prompt. PowerShell has many tools to be able to extend the language into your developers' code. The ISE allows you to create full and robust scripts using PowerShell, with some familiar keyboard commands from Visual Studio. Not only does PowerShell have the tools, but it also has been designed to write your own advanced functions and cmdlets using programmatic logic and constructs at the command prompt. Appendix D covers working with advanced functions and cmdlets.

Being able to program with PowerShell allows you to create and work with your own providers. There are many providers built into your systems, but you may have a particular scenario where there is a gap and PowerShell does not have a tool set to help you. You can create your own custom providers, like the developers did for Hyper-V. These providers allow you to access data stored inside data stores such as the registry environment variables and certificate stores easier than former methods with a command line. Appendix C provides a guide for creating custom providers. PowerShell also provides the necessary tools and framework to be able to deploy the custom tools you create in your infrastructure. In PowerShell v1.0, these were called *snap-ins*; in PowerShell 2.0, *modules* make this even easier to do. Appendix E explains how to work with existing snap-ins and how to create your own.

Lastly, you can create GUIs in PowerShell. Whether you want to take advantage of Windows Presentation Foundation (WPF), with the separation of design and code, or continue the look of legacy applications with Windows Forms (WinForms), PowerShell allows you to work with both of these technologies. Although it is relatively easy to work with GUI technologies in PowerShell, there are also some tools to make this easy process even easier. Appendix F explores creating GUIs in PowerShell.

EXERCISE 1: INVENTORY YOUR SCRIPTS

Take an inventory of the tasks you are currently using scripts to perform. By the end of the book you should be able to take the script or scripts you are currently using and convert them to PowerShell.

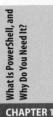

What Is PowerShell, and Why Do You Need It?

CHAPTER 1

CHAPTER 2

Installing and Configuring PowerShell 2.0

IN THIS CHAPTER, YOU WILL LEARN TO:

As you will learn throughout this book, PowerShell is a great tool, and the new version, PowerShell 2.0, has some exciting features to offer. In fact, many Microsoft roles and servers, such as Microsoft Exchange and Microsoft SharePoint, require PowerShell to be installed on the server.

Knowing how to install PowerShell 2.0 is an important skill and is sometimes necessary to enable many key functions you may need to use in your infrastructure. For example, you can access the Active Directory recycle bin easily only via PowerShell. (You will learn more about the recycle bin in Chapter 8.)

Installing PowerShell 2.0 is straightforward, and you can install it on several different operating systems. You can even install PowerShell in XP mode on your Windows 7 client systems. One of the key aspects of installing PowerShell correctly is the systems you install it on. You will need to install PowerShell 2.0 on administrative consoles, the systems from where you manage and monitor your infrastructure. In addition to those systems, you will also need to install PowerShell on the system that you want to manage with PowerShell.

PowerShell 2.0 has one key prerequisite, and that is the .NET Framework. Since PowerShell is based on the .NET Framework, you need to make sure you have the framework installed. Specifically, to enable the core functionality of PowerShell, you need the Microsoft .NET Framework 2.0 with Service Pack 1. Depending on what new features of PowerShell 2.0 you are leveraging, you may also need to install the Microsoft .NET Framework 3.51. For example, the Integrated Scripting Environment is an enhancement that provides a graphical user interface for PowerShell 2.0, but it requires the Microsoft .NET Framework 3.51 server feature to be installed in order for it to function.

This chapter describes how to install PowerShell 2.0, the prerequisites, and some additional features you may need to make PowerShell 2.0 hum in your environment.

Configure PowerShell 2.0 on Windows Server 2008 R2

PowerShell 2.0 is already built in on newer Microsoft systems. Specifically, Windows 7 and Windows Server 2008 R2 (except the Server Core installations) already have PowerShell 2.0 installed and ready to use. In those cases, you can start using the tool right away.

Even though you do not need to install PowerShell 2.0 on Windows 7 and Windows Server 2008 R2, you need to do some configuration to unlock the full power of PowerShell 2.0 on both operating systems. On a Windows 7 system, all of the tools for PowerShell 2.0 are located in the Accessories folder in the Start menu. Select Start ➢ All Programs ➢ Accessories ➢ Windows PowerShell to find them, as shown in Figure 2.1.

FIGURE 2.1   Windows 7 PowerShell

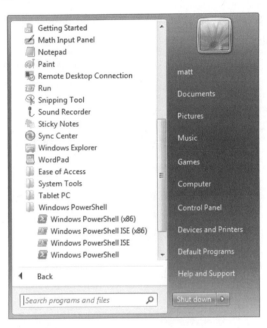

On Windows Server 2008 R2, you may want to install the Integrated Scripting Environment (ISE). The ISE provides a graphical user interface (GUI) for interacting with PowerShell 2.0. The GUI provides you with an easy-to-use interface for creating, troubleshooting, and working with PowerShell 2.0 scripts. (In Chapter 5, you will learn more about the ISE.)

PowerShell 2.0 (and the ISE, once it's enabled) on Windows Server 2008 R2 is located in the same location as on Windows 7. You can find the PowerShell 2.0 tools by selecting Start ➢ All Programs ➢ Accessories ➢ Windows PowerShell.

In the next section, you will learn how to install the ISE on your Windows Server 2008 R2 servers.

Installing and Configuring PowerShell 2.0

CHAPTER 2

Install the ISE on Windows Server 2008 R2

To install the ISE on Windows Server 2008 R2, you need to add this feature via Server Manager:

1. On the Windows Server 2008 R2 server where you want to install the ISE, open Server Manager.

2. In the tree on the left, click Features.

3. In the Features Summary pane, click Add Features.

   The Add Features Wizard appears.

4. Scroll down the list to find Windows PowerShell Integrated Scripting Environment (ISE), as shown in Figure 2.2.

FIGURE 2.2   Adding Windows PowerShell ISE

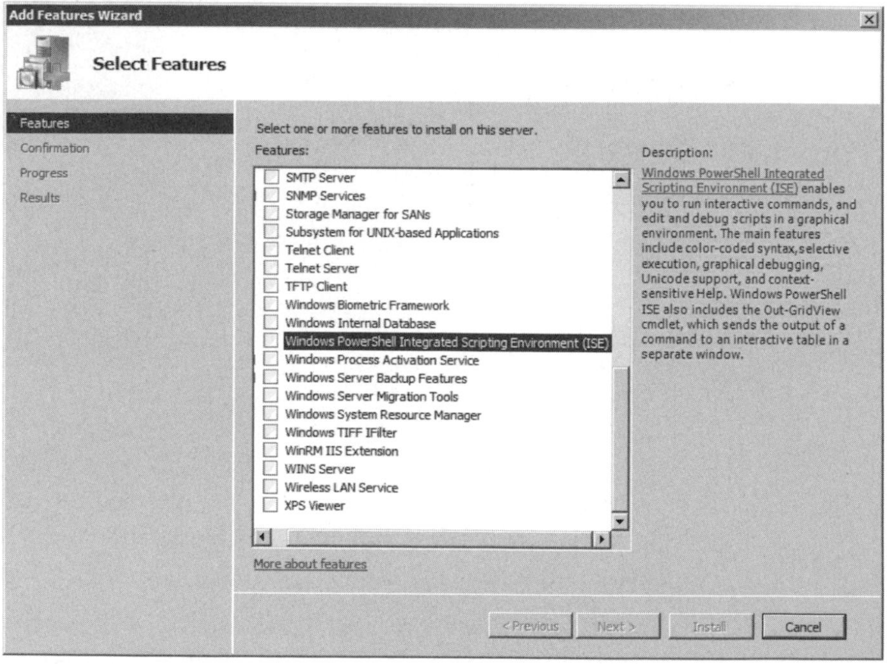

5. Select Windows PowerShell Integrated Scripting Environment (ISE). If this is the first time you are working with your Windows Server 2008 R2 server, you also need to install the Microsoft .NET Framework 3.51 feature, as shown in Figure 2.3.

FIGURE 2.3   .NET Framework 3.51 features

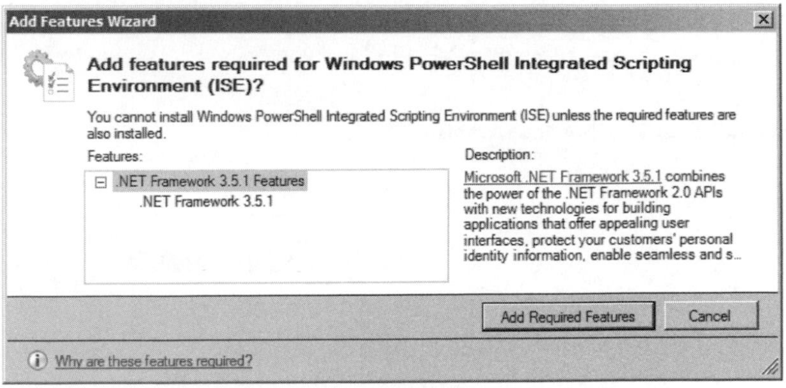

6. If you see the message shown in Figure 2.3, then click Add Required Features. You are returned to the Add Features Wizard.

7. Click Next, and confirm your installation selections. Your screen should look like Figure 2.4. Click Install.

FIGURE 2.4   Feature confirmation

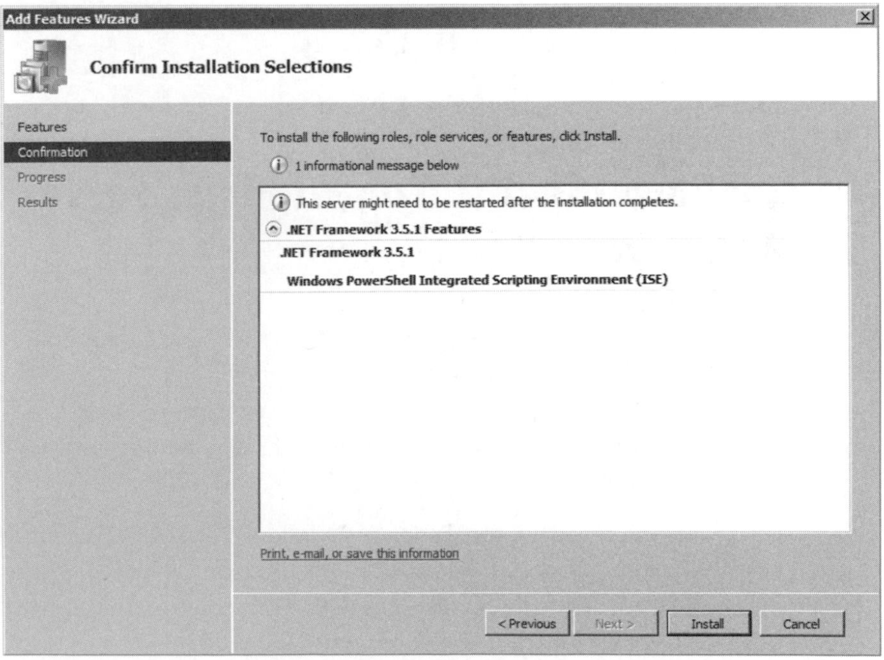

8. Review the installation results, and click Close.

After you have installed the ISE, you can find it by selecting Start ➢ All Programs ➢ Accessories ➢ Windows PowerShell, as shown in Figure 2.5.

FIGURE 2.5   ISE on the Start menu

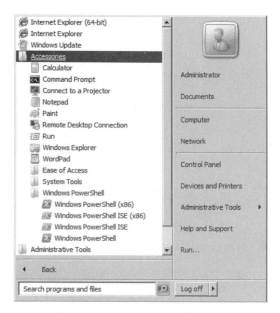

Install PowerShell 2.0 on Windows Server 2008 R2 Core

One of the exciting additions to the Server Core installations of Windows Server 2008 R2 is the support for the .NET Framework. This enables all kinds of capabilities on a Server Core installation that in previous versions were not possible. One of the best scenarios is that you can now run PowerShell 2.0 on Server Core installations.

Unlike the full installations of Windows Server 2008 R2, the Server Core installations do not have PowerShell 2.0 already installed. So, you need to install PowerShell 2.0, as well as the .NET Framework, on the Server Core installations by hand. Note that Server Core installations do not support the ISE, because Server Core installations lack a GUI.

In this section, you will learn how to install PowerShell 2.0 on a Server Core installation. You will use the Deployment Image Servicing and Management (DISM) tool commands to install the necessary components to enable PowerShell 2.0. DISM is the common tool used to install any of the features or roles on any Windows Server 2008 R2 Server Core installation. Whether you want to install Hyper-V or IIS, you will use DISM.

Before you begin to install any features on your Windows Server 2008 R2 servers, though, you should check to see what features are currently enabled on the server. To see what features are installed, run the following command from the server's command console:

```
DISM /Online /Get-Features
```

You will see results similar to Figure 2.6.

Installing and
Configuring
PowerShell 2.0

CHAPTER 2

FIGURE 2.6   Features on Windows Server 2008 R2 Server Core

```
Administrator: C:\Windows\system32\cmd.exe

Feature Name : QWAVE
State : Disabled

Feature Name : NetFx2-ServerCore
State : Disabled

Feature Name : NetFx2-ServerCore-WOW64
State : Disabled

Feature Name : NetFx3-ServerCore
State : Disabled

Feature Name : WCF-HTTP-Activation
State : Disabled

Feature Name : WCF-NonHTTP-Activation
State : Disabled

Feature Name : NetFx3-ServerCore-WOW64
State : Disabled

Feature Name : MicrosoftWindowsPowerShell
State : Disabled

Feature Name : MicrosoftWindowsPowerShell-WOW64
State : Disabled

Feature Name : ServerManager-PSH-Cmdlets
State : Disabled

Feature Name : BestPractices-PSH-Cmdlets
State : Disabled

Feature Name : PeerDist
State : Disabled

Feature Name : Microsoft-Hyper-V
State : Disabled

Feature Name : VmHostAgent
State : Disabled

Feature Name : CertificateServices
State : Disabled

Feature Name : SMBHashGeneration
State : Disabled

Feature Name : ServerMigration
State : Disabled

Feature Name : ServerCore-WOW64
State : Enabled
```

Install .NET Framework Support on Windows Server 2008 R2 Core

The feature you are specifically looking for in order to support PowerShell 2.0 is NetFx2-ServerCore. If NetFx2-ServerCore is not shown as enabled when you look at the installed features, run the following command to enable it:

```
DISM /Online /Enable-Feature ↵
/FeatureName:NetFx2-ServerCore
```

Depending on the types of commands or scripts you need to run on your server, you may need to support 32-bit; if you do, you will also need to run this command:

```
DISM /Online /Enable-Feature ↵
/FeatureName:NetFx2-ServerCore-WOW64
```

Install PowerShell 2.0 on Windows Server 2008 R2 Core

After you have installed the NetFx2-ServerCore feature, you then can install PowerShell 2.0 on your Server Core installation. To install PowerShell 2.0 on your Windows Server 2008 R2 Server Core installation, run the following command:

```
DISM /Online /Enable-Feature ↵
/FeatureName:MicrosoftWindowsPowerShell
```

If you run the command on your Windows Server 2008 R2 Server Core installation and you get an error message with error code 50, as shown in Figure 2.7, it means either you did not install the .NET Framework or it did not install correctly. Repeat the installation of the .NET Framework in the previous section to complete the installation of PowerShell 2.0.

FIGURE 2.7   PowerShell 2.0 error 50

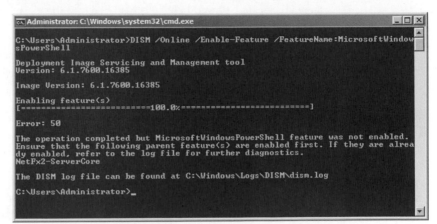

Just like with the .NET Framework, you may need to support 32-bit PowerShell on your server. If so, run the following command:

```
DISM /Online /Enable-Feature ↵
/FeatureName:MicrosoftWindowsPowerShell-WOW64
```

Once PowerShell 2.0 has been successfully installed on your server, you should see a screen similar to Figure 2.8.

FIGURE 2.8   PowerShell 2.0 installed on a Server Core installation

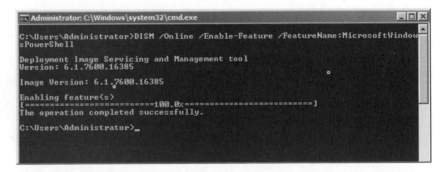

Once you have installed PowerShell 2.0 on your server, you may be wondering where it is located. PowerShell 2.0 is installed into the `%windir%\system32` directory.

To test PowerShell on your Server Core installation, you can start PowerShell and verify it has been installed correctly. To start Windows PowerShell, run the following command:

```
C:\windows\system32\windowspowershell\v1.0\PowerShell.exe
```

POWERSHELL DIRECTORY V1.0

When you work with PowerShell on your systems, you will probably wonder why you are running PowerShell out of the v1.0 directory. There is no need to worry; you are actually getting PowerShell v2.0, not v1.0. To verify you are running PowerShell v2.0, you can run this simple command in a PowerShell session:

$Host.Version

After you run the command, you will see the major version listed as 2, which verifies you are running PowerShell 2.0.

Figure 2.9 shows the result of running the command. Notice the PS before the command prompt.

FIGURE 2.9   PowerShell on Windows Server 2008 R2 Server Core

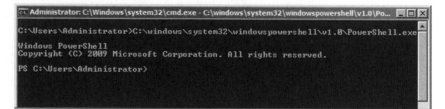

Once you have started a PowerShell session, you can run a quick test to make sure PowerShell is running correctly. Run the following command, which displays basic system information about your Windows Server 2008 R2 Server Core installation:

```
Get-WMIObject Win32_ComputerSystem
```

Once you are finished with your PowerShell session and you want to return the command shell of the Server Core installation, type **exit** at the PowerShell session, and your PowerShell session will end.

If you will be using PowerShell frequently on your Windows Server 2008 R2 Server Core system, you may want to add the PowerShell directory to the path statement of the server. To do that, run the following command on your Server Core installation at the command prompt of the server. This modifies the local path, and you will no longer need to navigate to the PowerShell directory to run PowerShell.

```
path=%path%;C:\windows\system32\windowspowershell\v1.0\
```

Install PowerShell 2.0 on Other Operating Systems

When you look at your entire infrastructure, most likely you will find an assortment of server and client operating systems. You may be wondering whether you can install PowerShell 2.0 on these systems. Chances are the answer is yes, because PowerShell 2.0 is supported on the following operating systems:

Windows Server 2008 with Service Pack 1

Windows Server 2008 with Service Pack 2

Windows Server 2003 with Service Pack 2

Windows Vista with Service Pack 2

Windows Vista with Service Pack 1

Windows XP with Service Pack 3

Windows Embedded POSReady 2009

Windows Embedded for Point of Service 1.1

The ability to run PowerShell 2.0 on legacy operating systems and platforms in your infrastructure means you can leverage PowerShell 2.0 to manage your environment. However, unlike with Windows 7 or Windows Server 2008 R2, PowerShell 2.0 is not built into these legacy operating system, so you will need to install it. In this section, you will learn how to set up the prerequisites for PowerShell 2.0 and how to install it on other operating systems, including Windows XP mode on Windows 7.

Set Up the Prerequisites

Windows PowerShell 2.0 requires the Microsoft .NET Framework 2.0 with Service Pack 1. If you try to install the Windows Management Framework — the package that contains PowerShell — and you receive the message shown in Figure 2.10, then you need to install the .NET Framework 2.0 Service Pack 1.

FIGURE 2.10 .NET Framework error

You can do a quick Internet search for the framework, or you can find the version for your operating system (x86 or x64) at the following locations.

You can download the x86 framework here:

```
www.microsoft.com/downloads/en/details.aspx?FamilyID=79bc3b77-
e02c-4ad3-aacf-a7633f706ba5&displaylang=en
```

You can download the x64 version of the framework here:

```
www.microsoft.com/downloads/en/details.aspx?FamilyId=029196ED-
04EB-471E-8A99-3C61D19A4C5A&displaylang=en
```

After downloading the package, double-click the file to run the setup process to install the .NET Framework 2.0. After you double-click the file, you will see a screen similar to Figure 2.11. When the screen appears, click Install and wait for the installation to complete. The installation may take a few minutes.

FIGURE 2.11 Installing the Microsoft .NET Framework 2.0 with Service Pack 1

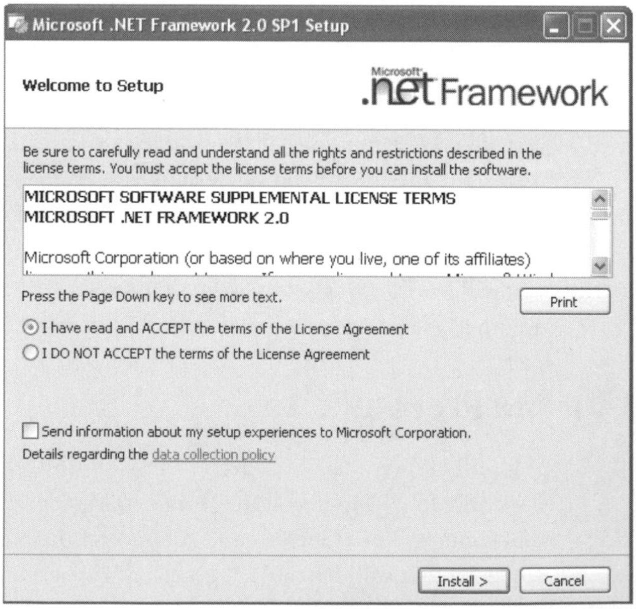

ISE REQUIREMENTS ON POWERSHELL SYSTEMS

If you want to have the ISE installed on your other PowerShell systems, you will need to install the .NET Framework 3.5 Service Pack 1. (You will learn more about the ISE in Chapter 5.) You can download the required component here:

`www.microsoft.com/downloads/en/details.aspx?familyid=AB99342F-5D1A-413D-8319-81DA479AB0D7&displaylang=en`

Obtain and Install PowerShell 2.0

After you have the Microsoft .NET Framework 2.0 with Service Pack 1 installed, you can install PowerShell 2.0.

The Windows Management Framework contains three components, listed in Table 2.1. You can download the Windows Management Framework files here:

`http://support.microsoft.com/kb/968929/en-us`

TABLE 2.1   Windows Management Framework components

Component	Description
Windows Remote Management (WinRM) 2.0	This is the Microsoft version of the WS-Management Protocol. WinRM 2.0 allows for interoperability between different hardware and operating systems. It is designed to be secure and easy to work with on firewalls. It allows PowerShell remoting.
Windows PowerShell 2.0	This is the scripting language that this book is about.
Background Intelligent Transfer Service (BITS) 4.0	This is a file transfer service that allows background file transfers (usually updates or other client-side packages are examples of how BITS is used) to occur quickly and securely to client-side systems. The transfers are typically done in the background. For our discussion on PowerShell, it is not necessary to download this component.

Windows Management Framework is available for download at `http://support.microsoft.com/kb/968929/en-us`.

The main component you need is PowerShell 2.0, of course, and since the WinRM component provides support for PowerShell 2.0 remoting, you'll want to download it too. (You will learn more about remoting in Chapter 6.) The Windows Management Framework is broken down into two downloads:

▶ Windows Management Framework Core, which includes WinRM 2.0 and Windows PowerShell 2.0

▶ Windows Management Framework BITS, which includes BITS 4.0

You need to download and install only the Windows Management Framework Core. On the download page, select the appropriate package for the operating system on which you are installing PowerShell 2.0. The packages you will find on the Windows Management Framework website are similar to Figure 2.12.

FIGURE 2.12   Download

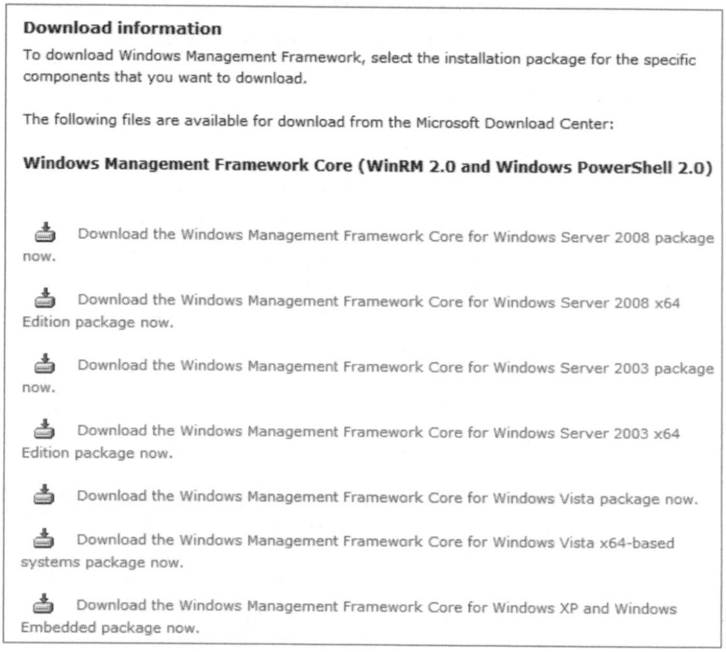

After you have downloaded the appropriate file to your system, you are ready to begin the installation.

1. Double-click the Windows Management Framework file you downloaded, and you will see a screen similar to Figure 2.13. Review the welcome screen, and click Next.

2. Read the license agreement, click I Agree, and then click Next.

3. Review the summary screen, and then click Finish.

Once PowerShell 2.0 is installed, you will find it in the same place as on other operating systems, at Start ➢ All Programs ➢ Accessories ➢ Windows PowerShell. Figure 2.14 shows an example of PowerShell installed on an x86 version of Windows XP with SP 3.

FIGURE 2.13   Windows Management Framework installation

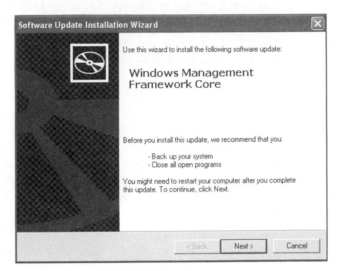

FIGURE 2.14   Windows XP and PowerShell

A QUICK NOTE ON WINDOWS XP MODE AND POWERSHELL

One of the great application compatibility additions to Windows 7 is Windows XP mode. Windows XP mode is a free download for Windows 7 and provides a fully functional 32-bit version of Windows XP. The version installed in Windows XP is Service Pack 3, so the operating system is ready to install PowerShell.

You might think since this is XP mode, you will have to perform the special installation steps to get PowerShell 2.0 installed and configured on the Windows XP mode virtual system. In truth, you do not; you can perform the installation the same way you did in this section. You will need to install the Microsoft .NET Framework 2.0 with Service Pack 1 and install the Windows Management Framework Core package. Here you can see the beginning of the Windows Management Framework Core installation on Windows XP mode:

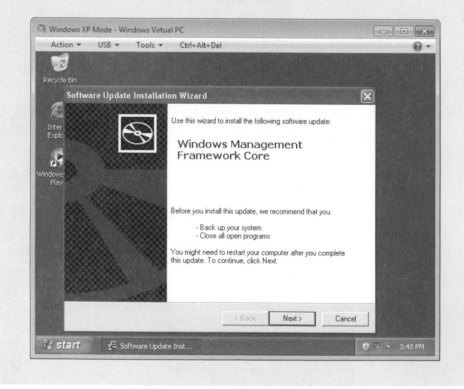

If you're using Windows Vista, you may not need to download the files from the Microsoft website; chances are, you already have the PowerShell tools available to you via Windows Update. Figure 2.15 shows the Windows Update dialog box on a Windows Vista system.

FIGURE 2.15   Windows Vista PowerShell

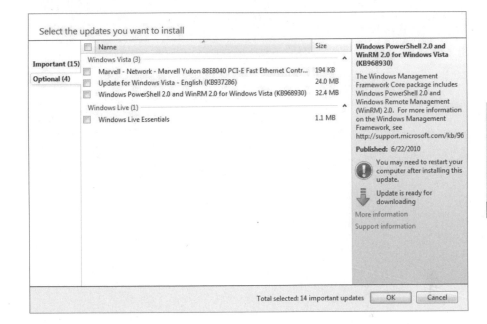

Notice that the listing for KB968930, for Windows PowerShell 2.0 and WinRM 2.0 for Windows Vista, is available as an optional update. To install the update, select the option, and click OK.

There will be some special configurations you will have to do to get remoting to work properly, but they will be discussed in Chapter 6.

EXERCISE 2: INSTALLING POWERSHELL

In this exercise, you will need a test system or a system you are willing to install PowerShell on. Install PowerShell in Windows XP mode on a Windows 7 system.

PowerShell Grammar Lesson

IN THIS CHAPTER, YOU WILL LEARN TO:

PowerShell 2.0 is a powerful language, having immense capabilities for you and your environment. Almost anything you can do in the interface of your Windows operating systems, you can do with PowerShell 2.0. When you look at the vast array of things you can accomplish with PowerShell 2.0, learning the language may seem daunting, maybe even impossible. I am here to tell you that anyone can learn to read, write, and — if they really want to — speak this great language. However, speaking PowerShell 2.0 in your local supermarket may garner some odd looks or stares, especially if you say something like this:

```
new-alias -name w -value get-wmiobject -description ↵
"quickwmi alias" -option ReadOnly
```

This line does not have anything to do with spies or getting a new identity. You should look at the example as a puzzle you can learn from. Like any language you may have learned in the past, you have to break PowerShell down into the individual components in order to understand it. You have to start with the easiest parts first and then build from there. Once you learn to break the language into its smallest components it will be easier to work with and understand.

In this chapter, you will learn how to break down the syntax for PowerShell 2.0. This will give you the necessary building blocks to begin leveraging this powerful scripting tool, and by the end of this chapter, you will be able to start reading and writing your own commands. In this chapter, you will also learn how to fish for the answers in PowerShell 2.0 by using the built-in help system.

This chapter also covers how to get even more commands in PowerShell 2.0 by working with the modules you have installed on your server. Modules can be extremely useful for the different workloads you may have installed on your server; for example, there are modules for Active Directory, IIS, and many other roles. Learning how to work with PowerShell 2.0 and the modules for these roles gives you the administrative flexibility to manage your environment.

Break Down PowerShell: A Lesson on Cmdlets

Cmdlets (pronounced "command-lets") are the building blocks for all your PowerShell 2.0 scripts. Building and writing cmdlets will allow you to start learning this language.

Hundreds of cmdlets are built into PowerShell 2.0, and as you install more roles on your Windows Server 2008 R2 server, you will get even more cmdlets to leverage.

In this section, you will look closely at the basics of PowerShell 2.0 cmdlets and command syntax.

A basic cmdlet looks like this:

```
Get-Service
```

Like all cmdlets, `Get-Service` is constructed from a verb and a noun and may have some parameters. The verb (`Get`) and noun (`Service`) are separated by a hyphen, and it doesn't contain any spaces.

Learn the Verbs

Learning some of the basic verbs of PowerShell 2.0 will help you see the possibilities of what you can accomplish in PowerShell 2.0. As in any language, verbs convey action or doing something. In PowerShell, this is no different, and most of the verbs of the cmdlets are straightforward to understand and use. Table 3.1 describes some of the more common verbs you will likely be using in PowerShell 2.0.

TABLE 3.1   Common verbs in PowerShell 2.0

Verb	Description
Get	The `Get` verb is useful when you want information about something on your system, such as a service, a variable, or permissions. `Get` is also combined with other cmdlets, usually via the pipe (|) symbol (which you will learn more about in Chapter 4), so you can perform more actions on the items that are returned with the `Get` command.
Set	The `Set` command lets you define the value for something on your system. You can set permissions, locations, or the values of variables. `Set` is useful when you are working with functions. (You will learn more about functions in Chapter 4.)
Out	`Out` is the verb that lets you output data from PowerShell 2.0 into a variety of resources. Typically you use the `Out` verb to take the data you received from PowerShell 2.0 and use it in another form for analysis. For example, you might want to create a comma-delimited file to use in Excel. (You will learn more about the `Out` verb in Chapter 4, where you will look at using PowerShell to output to various forms of data.)
Start	`Start` is a straightforward verb that allows you to start services currently not running. You will use `Start` when you are working with services, process, websites, and so forth.
Stop	`Stop` is another common verb allowing you to stop services, process, websites, and so forth.
Restart	The `Restart` verb is for when you want to do a simple recycle of services or other transactions.
Add	`Add` is useful in a lot of areas in PowerShell 2.0, such as adding a user to Active Directory, joining a domain, or doing other functions. (You will see some great examples of the `Add` verb in action in Chapter 8, where you will see how you will use PowerShell 2.0 with Active Directory.)

PowerShell Grammar Lesson

CHAPTER 3

Table 3.1 lists just a few of the verbs you will use as you learn PowerShell 2.0. I am sure throughout your adventures in PowerShell 2.0 that you will use plenty more. Note that when you learn the core purpose of a verb, it has that same function across the various nouns in PowerShell 2.0.

Learn the Nouns

Nouns (or objects, as you might sometimes see them referred to) are the things you are looking to find out more about, do something to, or just learn from inside PowerShell. When you look at the nouns by themselves, they really do not do much. Nouns are also typically unique to a role or aspect of the system. There are some common nouns, but as you become familiar with PowerShell, you may also find plenty of other nouns that you use on a daily basis.

In PowerShell 2.0, the nouns are, with a few exceptions, always singular. Even when you want to look at multiple objects, the noun you use is still singular. For example, if you are looking to learn about all the services running on your server, you run the following cmdlet:

```
Get-Service
```

and *not* the following, which is incorrect:

```
Get-Services
```

Table 3.2 describes some of the nouns you may encounter when working with PowerShell 2.0.

TABLE 3.2   Common nouns

Noun	Description
Command	This is quite possibly the most useful noun you will encounter in PowerShell. Command, when combined with the Get verb, allows you to list all of the commands in your particular PowerShell session. This lets you learn PowerShell quickly. (See the "Help Yourself with PowerShell" section in this chapter to see the Command noun in action.)
Computer	You can use Computer to add computer accounts to domains, modify access control lists, or even specify a computer you want to have PowerShell affect.
PS…	PowerShell 2.0 also has some great self-servicing administrative tools you can leverage to work with PowerShell. A noun that begins with PS normally lets you work with the PowerShell engine and gives you control over your PowerShell environment.
Service	This is the noun you use to interact with the services on your system, including when you start, stop, or restart any service.

> ## A LONG UNIQUE NOUN
>
> One of my favorite nouns is `ADDomainControllerPasswordReplicationPolicy`, because it is one of the longest nouns! In my opinion, it is the PowerShell equivalent of supercalifragilisticexpialidocious. This particular noun allows you to work with a read-only domain controller's (RODC's) password replication policy.

Put Verbs and Nouns Together: Cmdlets

Now that you have taken a look at the two big building blocks — verbs and nouns — it is time to see what happens when they're combined to form a cmdlet. Cmdlets are the result of adding a hyphen (-) between a noun and a verb. This little hyphen makes all the difference in PowerShell and allows you to begin to learn the syntax. In this section, you learn some of the common cmdlets that are built into PowerShell. (If you want to learn how to create your own cmdlets, check Appendix D.)

Although learning the verbs and nouns is very useful, you have probably realized that on their own they really do not do much of anything. It is combining the two that allows you to begin to unlock the magic and power of PowerShell. Table 3.3 describes some common cmdlets and explains how they can help you.

TABLE 3.3 Common cmdlets

Cmdlet	Description
Get-Command	This cmdlet lists all the commands at your disposal in your current session. Along with Get-Help (which you will learn in this chapter), Get-Command is a great way to see what is possible in your PowerShell session.
Get-Service	This cmdlet shows you all the services on your current system and can help you find out how to work with your services on your systems. Related to this cmdlet, you can use Start-Service, Stop-Service, and Restart-Service to manipulate the services running on your servers.
Add-Computer	You can use this cmdlet if you need to be able to join a computer to a workgroup or a domain. Use this command instead of going through the GUI when you want to join a domain.
Get-Member	This command is a must-have to take PowerShell to the next level. Developers can use it to learn more about the programming side of PowerShell. In PowerShell you are not dealing with text; rather, you are dealing with .NET objects. Get-Member helps you learn about these objects by listing the type, properties, and methods of the objects you are dealing with. This is helpful when coming to grips with how to use a particular object.

PowerShell Grammar Lesson

CHAPTER 3

Figure 3.1 shows how you can use `Get-Member` to list the `Get-Service` resultant object's properties. The returned object is of the .NET type `System .ServiceProcess.ServiceController`. Note here that the pipe (|) operator is used to bring in the results of a command to the `Get-Member` cmdlet. This is an example of PowerShell pipelining, which you will learn more about in Chapter 4.

FIGURE 3.1   `Get-Service | Get-Member`

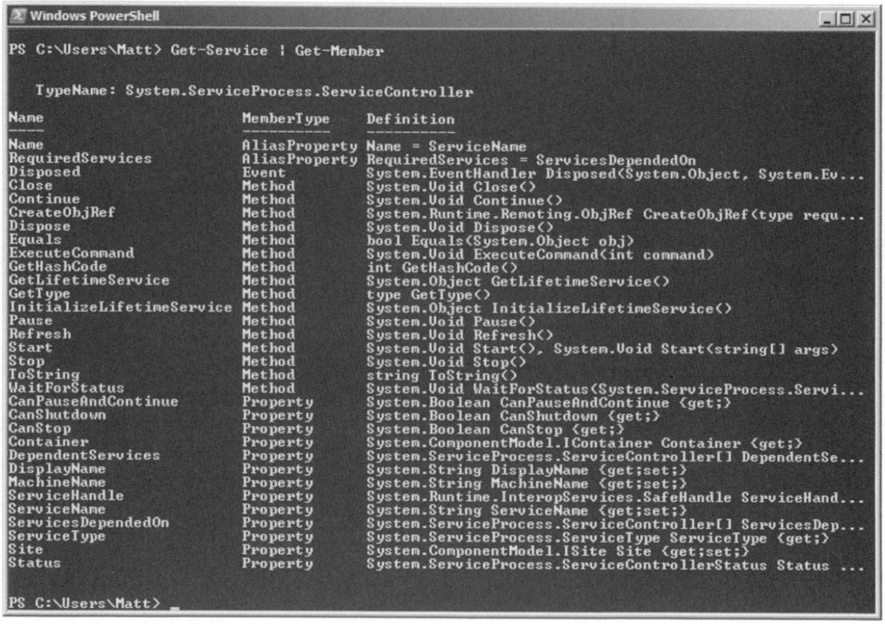

Use Parameters

Parameters give you control over cmdlets when they are run. When you execute cmdlets, you get a set of results, and these results contain the properties and their values from the nouns of your cmdlets. Parameters allow you to control what properties are returned in the resulting table for your command. In a sense, they extend the power of your cmdlets, giving you even more flexibility in how you work with PowerShell and the results it gives you.

Parameters allow you to be more specific in how your cmdlets run and what you see as a result. You can sort, remove, or even output specific properties and their values by modifying the parameters. You will learn more about how to work with outputting data in Chapter 4. Parameters are unique to the nouns in your cmdlets, and to see what parameters are available for a particular cmdlet, you can just run the cmdlet. The default results normally show you some of the parameters available but not all. You can ask the built-in help to see all the parameters available (see "Help Yourself with PowerShell" in this chapter). Figure 3.2 shows how to use the -name parameter to find just the names of services with NET in their names. The cmdlet used for the figure is Get-Service -name "*NET*".

FIGURE 3.2   **Get-Service** with the **-name** parameter

When you work with parameters, you usually use a hyphen (-) to precede the parameter in your cmdlet. In Figure 3.2, the -name parameter was explicitly specified in the cmdlet. You do not always need to include the actual parameter name in your cmdlet. Some parameters are positional, which means if you know the order of the parameters, you do not have to use them explicitly by name. You could have run the previous Get-Service example without the -name parameter, Get-Service "*NET*", and it would have yielded the same results because the name parameter can be used in position for this command.

Keep two important things you in mind with positional parameters. First, with positional parameters you have to know the exact position they need to be in when you write your command to use them. Second, not all parameters are positional; some are named parameters instead. This means you have to specify them explicitly to use them. Figure 3.3 shows both types.

PowerShell Grammar
Lesson

CHAPTER 3

FIGURE 3.3   Named and positional parameters

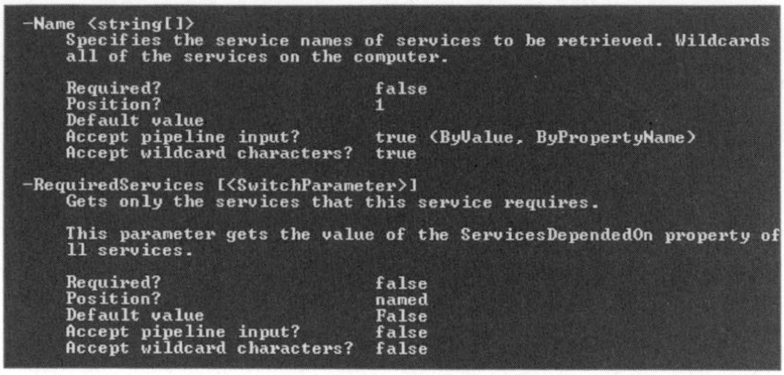

```
-Name <string[]>
    Specifies the service names of services to be retrieved. Wildcards
    all of the services on the computer.

    Required?                          false
    Position?                          1
    Default value
    Accept pipeline input?             true (ByValue, ByPropertyName)
    Accept wildcard characters?        true

-RequiredServices [<SwitchParameter>]
    Gets only the services that this service requires.

    This parameter gets the value of the ServicesDependedOn property of
    ll services.

    Required?                          false
    Position?                          named
    Default value                      False
    Accept pipeline input?             false
    Accept wildcard characters?        false
```

As you can see, the Name parameter has to be in position 1, and RequiredServices is a named parameter.

To see the requirements for your parameters, you leverage the built-in help system with the -full parameter. Figure 3.3 was the result of this command:

```
Get-Help Get-Service -full
```

Positional parameters help cut down on typing and sometimes can help with reading the cmdlets. For example, look at this cmdlet:

```
Get-Service -name RemoteAccess -RequiredServices
```

The output of this cmdlet will show you the required services for the RemoteAccess service. This cmdlet could have also been written as follows:

```
Get-Service RemoteAccess -RequiredServices
```

Figure 3.4 shows the results of this cmdlet.

FIGURE 3.4   Positional parameter

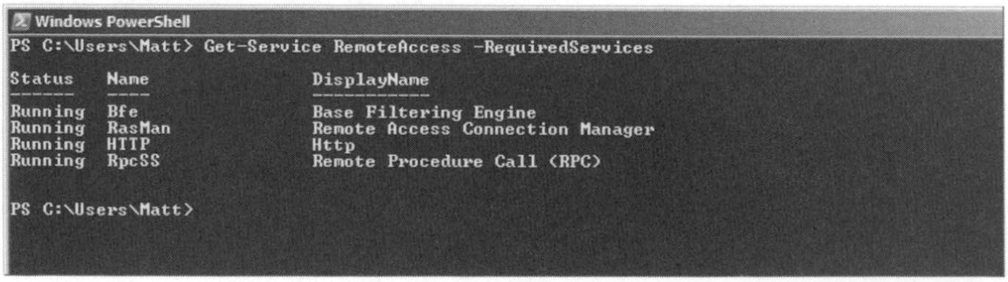

```
Windows PowerShell
PS C:\Users\Matt> Get-Service RemoteAccess -RequiredServices

Status     Name                DisplayName
------     ----                -----------
Running    Bfe                 Base Filtering Engine
Running    RasMan              Remote Access Connection Manager
Running    HTTP                Http
Running    RpcSS               Remote Procedure Call (RPC)


PS C:\Users\Matt>
```

When you are first learning to use PowerShell, I caution against using the positional nature of parameters. You will be able to troubleshoot and read your cmdlets much easier if you specify all the parameters by name.

As your knowledge grows with PowerShell, positional parameters can provide a quicker way to work with PowerShell.

Use Wildcards

To further work with parameters, PowerShell supports the use of wildcards. If you have worked with any command prompt environment in the past, you will find the wildcards to be similar to other languages. If you are new to command prompts and PowerShell, wildcards provide a quick and easy way to find things you are looking for if you are not quite sure of the exact name or spelling. Also, you can use wildcards to save on typing. Table 3.4 describes the wildcard characters and their uses.

TABLE 3.4   PowerShell wildcards

Wildcard	Usage
*	Matches any character starting where you placed the *. For example, if you typed h*, you would find anything that started with the letter *h*.
?	Matches a single character in the position of the ?. For example, m?tt could return *matt*, *mitt*, or any other character in the position of the ?.
[]	Allows you find a range of or a certain character. For example, [k-s]arah could return *karah*, *marah*, or *sarah*. Or you could be more specific with [osu]rocks, which could result in *orocks*, *srocks*, or *urocks*.

Figure 3.5 shows the Get-Command s* cmdlet. As you can see, this returns just the commands beginning with the letter s.

Notice, however, what happens when you use the Get-Command *s. It shows all the services that have the letter s in the name. In Figure 3.6, you can see this in action.

FIGURE 3.5 Wildcard after letter

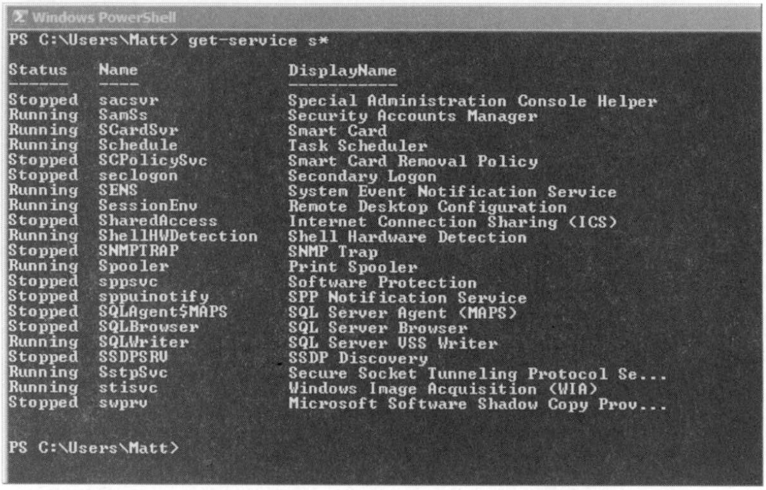

```
Windows PowerShell
PS C:\Users\Matt> get-service s*

Status   Name               DisplayName
------   ----               -----------
Stopped  sacsvr             Special Administration Console Helper
Running  SamSs              Security Accounts Manager
Running  SCardSvr           Smart Card
Running  Schedule           Task Scheduler
Stopped  SCPolicySvc        Smart Card Removal Policy
Stopped  seclogon           Secondary Logon
Running  SENS               System Event Notification Service
Running  SessionEnv         Remote Desktop Configuration
Stopped  SharedAccess       Internet Connection Sharing (ICS)
Running  ShellHWDetection   Shell Hardware Detection
Stopped  SNMPTRAP           SNMP Trap
Running  Spooler            Print Spooler
Stopped  sppsvc             Software Protection
Stopped  sppuinotify        SPP Notification Service
Stopped  SQLAgent$MAPS      SQL Server Agent (MAPS)
Stopped  SQLBrowser         SQL Server Browser
Running  SQLWriter          SQL Server VSS Writer
Stopped  SSDPSRV            SSDP Discovery
Running  SstpSvc            Secure Socket Tunneling Protocol Se...
Running  stisvc             Windows Image Acquisition (WIA)
Stopped  swprv              Microsoft Software Shadow Copy Prov...

PS C:\Users\Matt>
```

FIGURE 3.6 Wildcard before letter

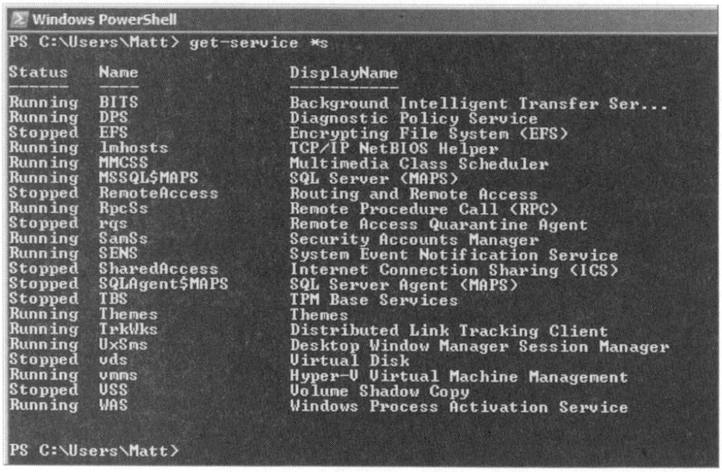

```
Windows PowerShell
PS C:\Users\Matt> get-service *s

Status   Name               DisplayName
------   ----               -----------
Running  BITS               Background Intelligent Transfer Ser...
Running  DPS                Diagnostic Policy Service
Stopped  EFS                Encrypting File System (EFS)
Running  lmhosts            TCP/IP NetBIOS Helper
Running  MMCSS              Multimedia Class Scheduler
Running  MSSQL$MAPS         SQL Server (MAPS)
Stopped  RemoteAccess       Routing and Remote Access
Running  RpcSs              Remote Procedure Call (RPC)
Stopped  rqs                Remote Access Quarantine Agent
Running  SamSs              Security Accounts Manager
Running  SENS               System Event Notification Service
Stopped  SharedAccess       Internet Connection Sharing (ICS)
Stopped  SQLAgent$MAPS      SQL Server Agent (MAPS)
Stopped  TBS                TPM Base Services
Running  Themes             Themes
Running  TrkWks             Distributed Link Tracking Client
Running  UxSms              Desktop Window Manager Session Manager
Stopped  vds                Virtual Disk
Running  vmms               Hyper-V Virtual Machine Management
Stopped  VSS                Volume Shadow Copy
Running  WAS                Windows Process Activation Service

PS C:\Users\Matt>
```

Understand Properties

There are two parts to properties in PowerShell: property names and property values. Names are the column headings in your output data, and property values are the values. For example, in Figure 3.7, you see the `Get-Service` cmdlet. The property names for this example are Status, Name, and DisplayName. The property values are the listing of the results under the names.

FIGURE 3.7   Properties

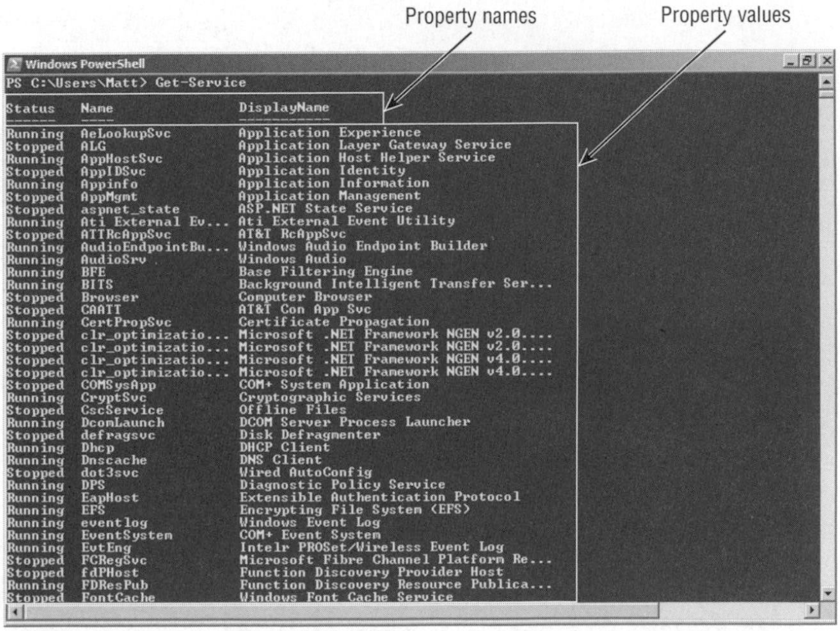

Although you cannot directly use properties in your PowerShell commands, you can manipulate what properties are displayed in the output of your PowerShell cmdlets by working with the parameters for a particular command. For example, when you run the command Get-Service, you get some of the properties displayed. If you want to control what is displayed, you may need to take advantage of the other parameter names to control what results you see, as you can see in this example:

```
Get-Service RemoteAccess -RequiredServices
```

Even though you do not see RequiredServices in the property names, the property values are filtered, showing only the required services. You will see in Chapter 4 how you can further control the results and how the properties are used to give you the results you want. In Appendix B, you will learn how to do even more with properties and create your own custom objects and properties.

A WORD ON CASE FOR POWERSHELL

Although PowerShell 2.0 is a sensitive language in terms of spelling and syntax, it is mostly case insensitive. When you are looking at help files or other forms of online documentation, you see a mixed-case pattern, with the beginning of every word in the cmdlet being capitalized. In the documentation, you will see the `Get-Service` cmdlet written like this:

```
Get-Service
```

However, the following three versions of this cmdlet will do the same thing:

```
get-service
GEt-sErVIce
GET-SERVICE
```

You can type the cmdlet in all lowercase, or you can write your cmdlets in mixed case. They will all do the same thing. Although I do not recommend all uppercase: while it does make the PowerShell cmdlets stand out, it makes it harder to troubleshoot.

Although PowerShell is not case sensitive, PowerShell is still very much spelling and syntax sensitive. There is no IntelliSense to help with spelling, but tab completion can be very helpful if you struggle with spelling.

Help Yourself with PowerShell

To start building your PowerShell knowledge, you need to learn some commands. Maybe you think you will discover what you need to know by pressing F1 for help. But in a command prompt, pressing the F1 key does not get you much. So, how do you ask for help in PowerShell? You use a cmdlet, of course! The cmdlets and parameters in the section show you how to leverage the powerful built-in help system.

Learn How to Help Yourself

To be successful with Windows PowerShell, you need to learn how to help yourself. Fortunately, PowerShell provides tools to help you do that. You can use two commands to find more information about commands and, more importantly, how to use them. The following two cmdlets will allow you to access PowerShell's built-in help system:

```
Get-Command
Get-Help
```

When you run the Get-Command cmdlet, you see a list of the currently loaded cmdlets and functions on your Windows system. You can also run the Get-Command cmdlet to learn which commands work with certain objects.

Suppose you want to use PowerShell to work with the services on a particular server or system but you are not sure of the available cmdlets for doing this. To find out, use the following command:

```
Get-Command *-service
```

This displays all the commands you can run against the services running on your system, as shown in Figure 3.8.

FIGURE 3.8   `Get-Command *-service`

So, now that you know what commands you can use against the service object, what is the proper syntax for those commands? This is where the Get-Help cmdlet comes in. By itself, the Get-Help cmdlet, by default, gives you a generic help listing on how to use Get-Help. In other words, it gives you help on help.

However, the true benefit of the Get-Help cmdlet is when you run it in context. When you use the Get-Command and Get-Help cmdlets in conjunction, you can unlock any information you need to learn PowerShell, including the proper syntax and usage needed to work with PowerShell cmdlets.

Looking back to the previous example for services, let's say you want to learn how to properly stop a service. When you run the following cmdlet, you can learn more about the proper process for stopping a service:

```
Get-Help Stop-Service
```

This cmdlet gives you the general information about what the `Stop-Service` cmdlet does, how to use it, and any possible parameters that can be used with the cmdlet. You may need more information on the command or even examples of the cmdlet in action. No need to go search the Internet just yet. The PowerShell help system can provide you with even more information with the three following switches you can apply to your cmdlets. Switches in PowerShell are much like the switches used in DOS commands. They are different than parameters because they do not accept any arguments. Much like a light switch, the switch is either on (included in the command) or off (omitted from the command). An example of a switch in PowerShell is the Force switch, which tells a command to bypass roadblocks and just run. In the case with help you can use the switches to display different forms of the help system:

-example   If you learn by viewing examples, you would run the following cmdlet to see a list of examples of the cmdlet in action:

```
Get-Help Stop-Service -examples
```

I find the `-examples` switch extremely useful, if not the most useful. When you use it, as you can see in Figure 3.9, you get real examples to be able to learn a cmdlet from. This helps slim down the learning curve for PowerShell. Ideally, you have that little reverse engineer inside of you that can take a script and retrofit it for your particular environment. The `-examples` switch was key to unlocking PowerShell for me when I first started using the tool.

-detailed   To see even more detailed information about the cmdlet you are looking at using, run this cmdlet:

```
Get-Help Stop-Service -detailed
```

-full   To see more technical information about the cmdlet you are running, run the following cmdlet. This cmdlet also shows you all the additional parameters and how they are used with the cmdlet. The `-full` switch provides an exhaustive explanation of the cmdlet.

```
Get-Help Stop-Service -full
```

You can use the `-example`, `-detailed`, and `-full` switches with virtually all the cmdlets in PowerShell. This provides a consistent approach to how you can learn to use PowerShell. However, depending the command, sometimes the results for the -detailed and -example switches will be identical.

FIGURE 3.9 PowerShell examples

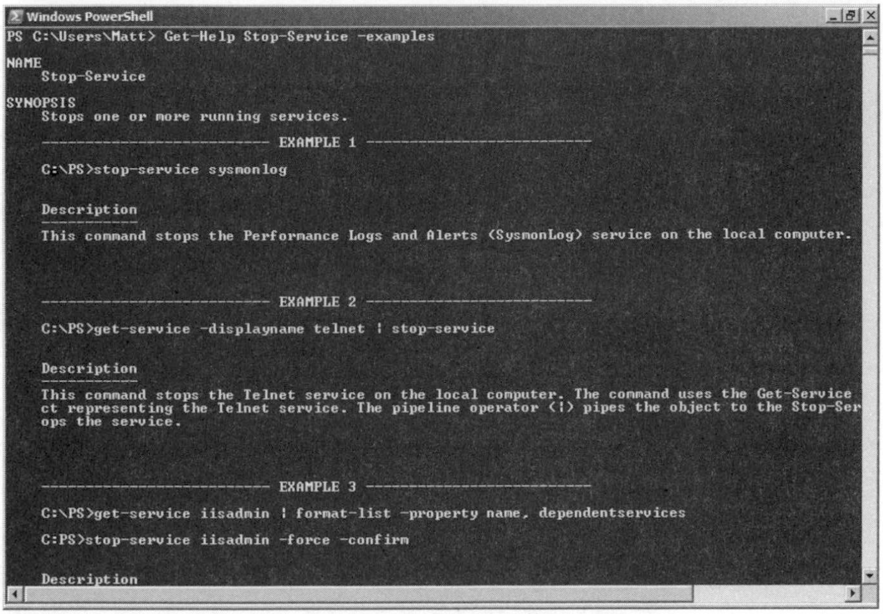

PowerShell provides other ways to get even more information about how to run commands. You can get help on a keyword that is used in the commands. For example, you could use the following cmdlet to learn more about the service keyword:

```
Get-Help service
```

Although the results for this cmdlet may look the same as the Get-Command *-service cmdlet you ran earlier, this cmdlet actually provides other areas that you can investigate with the help system. Additionally, the help system lets you query based on the topic you are interested in. Inside PowerShell are several help files built into the PowerShell interface. These are traditional-style help files you can quickly access. To get a full listing of the available topics, you can run this cmdlet:

```
Get-Help about
```

To explore one of the about topics, it is a matter of just asking PowerShell. For example, what if you wanted to learn more about parameters and how they are used in PowerShell? You would run this cmdlet:

```
Get-Help about_parameters
```

This last cmdlet offers a great example of working with the help system in PowerShell. Normally when you start looking at the information contained in the about help files, there will be several screens of information generated when you access the file. This will require you to scroll back up through the window to see all the information. Fortunately, the help system has an alternative to viewing multiple pages. If you want to have a break at each page so you read the information before you move to the next page, you use the `help` command instead of the `Get-Help` command. When you use the `help` command, you have to press a key to move to the next page of information. For example, notice the difference in the scrolling behavior between the running the previous cmdlet for looking at parameters vs. running the following cmdlet, which is shown in Figure 3.10:

```
Help about_parameters
```

FIGURE 3.10   **Help about_parameters**

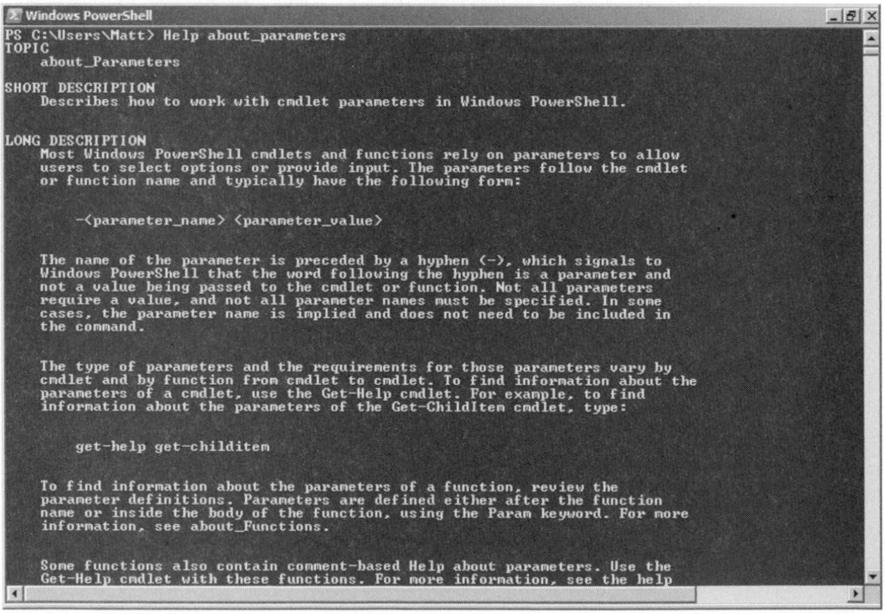

You can also get help with various levels of detail about cmdlets and parameters you are interested in. For example, if you run the following cmdlet, you will learn more about the `ComputerName` parameter used in the `Get-Service` cmdlet, as shown in Figure 3.11:

```
Get-Help Get-Service -Parameter ComputerName
```

FIGURE 3.11   `ComputerName Parameter` help

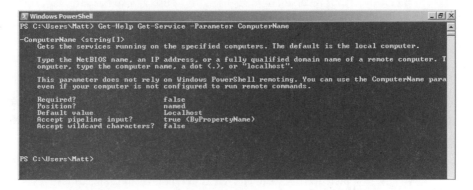

Use Tab Autocomplete

PowerShell is spelling sensitive, and commands sometimes can have really long names. Look at the noun `ADDomainControllerPasswordReplicationPolicy`. Trust me: No one really wants to type in that name. So, what do you do? You cheat a little, by using a great built-in tool.

The tool you can use to save you misspellings and cramped fingers is called tab autocomplete. To use tab autocomplete, you just need to know a portion of the noun you want to use in your cmdlet. Suppose you remember that a command started with `Get-Web` but can't remember which cmdlet you were working with. You could start typing **Get-Web** and then use the Tab key to cycle through all commands that start with `Get-Web`.

Another built-in tool that saves you typing and repeating previous commands is a tool you may be familiar with if you have previously used DOS. You can use the DOSKey behavior of recalling commands by pressing the up arrow to cycle you through previous commands you have typed in.

Leverage Online Resources

The PowerShell community has built several great online resources for help. The following are the online locations where I go when I am looking for assistance in PowerShell:

Scripting with Windows PowerShell   Chances are this site has a script for a task similar to what you are trying to do, which makes it a great resource for you to put your reverse-engineering skills to use. It also has sample scripts for the many different areas PowerShell can manage, including scripts for Exchange, SharePoint, Windows, and many other areas in the script repository. Scripting with Windows PowerShell takes the `Get-Help -Examples` cmdlet to the next level. See `http://technet.microsoft.com/en-us/scriptcenter/powershell.aspx`.

The PowerShell Guy   What I like about this blog is that Marc (aka the PowerShell guy) always seems to have great insights into PowerShell. See `http://thepowershellguy.com/blogs/posh/default.aspx`.

PowerTab   This is for the mini-developer in you. PowerTab takes the tab autocomplete feature to an entirely different level of usage. This gives even clearer insight into PowerShell commands when you hit the Tab key to help create your scripts. See `http://powertab.codeplex.com`.

Hey, Scripting Guy! Blog   The Microsoft scripting guys have answered all sorts of scripting questions for various scripting languages, including PowerShell. The PowerShell answers range from how to build custom functions to how to work with WMI and Active Directory. Developers and IT pros should be able to follow their answers easily. See `http://blogs.technet.com/b/heyscriptingguy`.

PowerShellCommunity.org   Is a solid community website where you can find more examples and custom PowerShell tools that are built by the PowerShell community. They also have a fun feature called the random cmdlets, where they show a random cmdlet with a definition.

See `http://powershellcommunity.org`.

Of course, you can always use a search engine to help find what you need.

Use Even More Commands with Modules

This section gives you even more cmdlets to learn and use. By default when you open your PowerShell window and run the `Get-Command` cmdlet, you see only the commands available to you at the time. Typically these are the core functions of PowerShell, and depending on your system or what roles are installed on your Windows Server 2008 R2 server, you may have only a few cmdlets to take advantage of.

The additional commands are stored in role-specific features called *modules*, and almost every Windows Server 2008 R2 server role has a set of dedicated cmdlets for that specific role. This section tells you how you can find out which modules are available to you on your server, how to bring them into your PowerShell session, and how to begin using them.

Use and Understand Modules

A module is an installable package for your system that contains several different cmdlets, functions, aliases, and various other capabilities that extend PowerShell's capabilities. Even though you can create your own custom modules (discussed in Appendix E), typically from an IT administration standpoint PowerShell modules are installed onto your server as you install roles or other pieces of software onto your Windows Server 2008 R2 servers. You can think of modules as mini-toolboxes providing you with specific tools to use PowerShell to administer roles on your system.

As I've said, modules are specific to the installed role or software; in other words, they are designed for that role. In the case of Microsoft Windows Server 2008 R2 server roles, the Microsoft product groups create modules specific to roles you can install on the servers. In Windows Server 2008 R2 and PowerShell 2.0, this is relatively new. Although you could maintain and work with most roles on a server, in PowerShell 1.0 it was not intuitive or easy. With PowerShell 2.0, these new modules, which make working with roles such as Active

Directory easier, are typically installed onto your system when you install the role on the server.

There are usually a couple of ways to access these modules. One common way is to load the shortcut for the PowerShell module for the role you want to administer. These are PowerShell shortcuts and are typically stored in administrative tools. In Figure 3.12, you can see the shortcut for the Active Directory module for PowerShell.

FIGURE 3.12   Active Directory module for Windows PowerShell

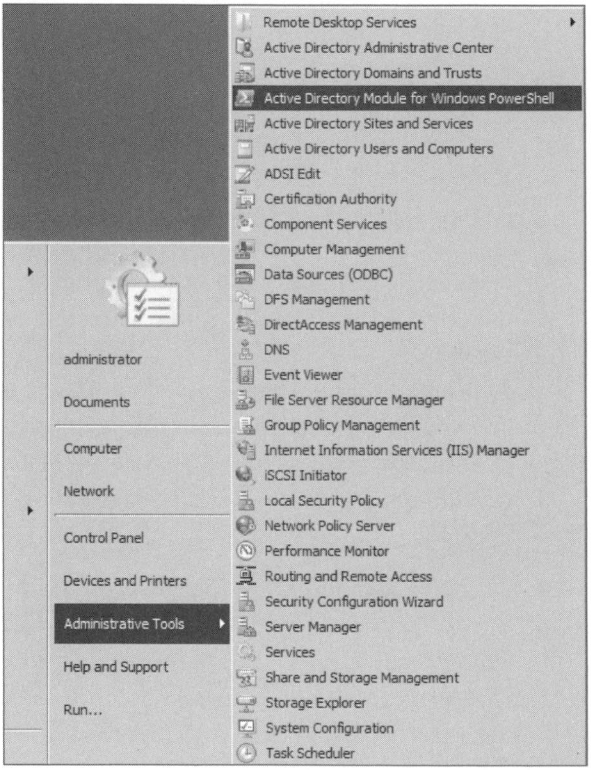

When you load these specialized shortcuts, you automatically load the module for that specific role or software. So, you will have access to those specific cmdlets, but you will not have access to other modules, because they are not currently loaded.

If you want to launch PowerShell with all the available modules loaded for you so all the cmdlets that you can use on your system are available and ready to be used, you can load the Windows PowerShell modules shortcut, which you also will find in the Administrative Tools group, as shown in Figure 3.13.

FIGURE 3.13   Windows PowerShell modules

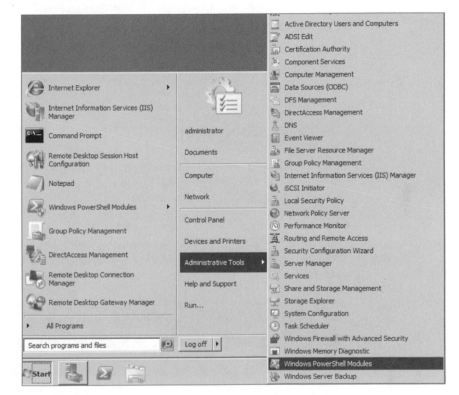

Using this shortcut is a quick and easy way to have all your modules loaded when you start a PowerShell session. It essentially loads all the available and installed modules on your server with one click of a mouse button. Another way to load the modules in one fell swoop is to load just the contents of the module for that specific role or software.

You can learn more about the basics of modules by running this cmdlet:

```
Get-Help about_modules
```

In the next section, you will see how to import and work with the modules on your system.

Get to Know Your Modules

Picture this: you have opened your PowerShell session on a Windows Server 2008 R2 server you just inherited as part of your administrative workload, and you wonder what is available to you to work with in PowerShell. You know you may have more than what `Get-Command` shows you. So, how do you find out which modules are loaded and which modules you can load? The answer to that starts with this cmdlet:

```
Get-Module
```

LOADING ALL MODULES INTO AN EXISTING POWERSHELL SESSION

You may already be in an existing PowerShell session and want to load all the installed modules on your server at once. You can do that easily. In your running PowerShell session, run the following built-in function, and it will load all the available modules for you:

```
ImportSystemModules
```

When you run this command, you will see the modules loading in your PowerShell session.

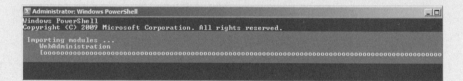

This loads the modules only temporarily, and when you exit the session, the modules will not be automatically loaded for the next session.

When you run Get-Module by itself, it displays all the modules currently loaded into the PowerShell session. Your results will look something like Figure 3.14.

FIGURE 3.14   Get-Module

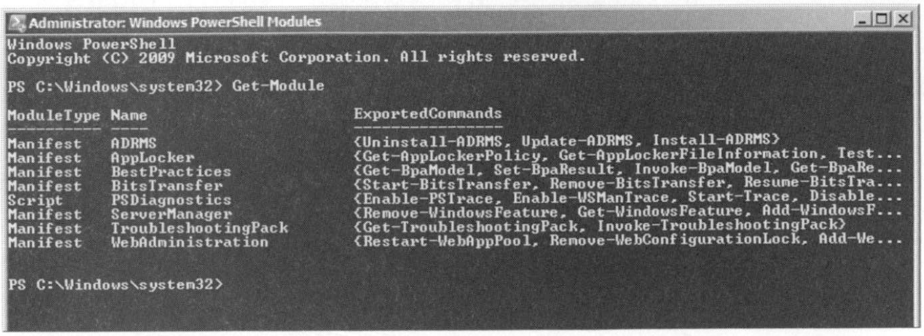

If you run the Get-Module cmdlet and you get blank results, that means you do not have any modules currently loaded into your session. To see what modules you have available to be loaded into your current PowerShell session, add the -ListAvailable parameter to the Get-Module cmdlet. Figure 3.15 shows an example of Get-Module -ListAvailable.

FIGURE 3.15   Get-Module -ListAvailable

PowerShell Grammar Lesson

CHAPTER 3

When you see the list of modules available to you after you run the `Get-Module -ListAvailable` cmdlet, take note of the spelling and the names of the modules you can import, because the names of the modules are not supported by tab auto-complete. Knowing the names of the modules available gives you a sense of what roles are installed on your system, as well as giving you enough information to load those cmdlets for your use.

Once you know what module or modules you want to load and use in your PowerShell session, use the `Import-Module` cmdlet to bring the new module and cmdlets into your PowerShell session. For example, if you wanted to use the cmdlets for the Windows Server 2008 R2 Best Practices Analyzer (BPA) system utility, run this cmdlet:

```
Import-Module -Name BestPractices
```

If you want to see what new cmdlets are now available after that, run the following cmdlet:

```
Get-Command -Module BestPractices
```

When you are done using the modules and you are finished with your PowerShell session, close the PowerShell console. If you are not done with your PowerShell session and just want to remove the module, you can use the `Remove-Module` cmdlet to perform the reverse of the import command and remove PowerShell modules from your current session.

Create a Custom PowerShell Shell

As you work with modules, you may come to a point where you want to have only certain modules loaded or have PowerShell look and feel a certain way every time you start a PowerShell session. You can accomplish this in two ways. The first way to load only the module for your PowerShell shell is to create a shortcut that loads a PowerShell session and add a command to the shortcut target that loads the module you want to have automatically loaded. For example, to load the System modules, use this shortcut target path:

```
%SystemRoot%\system32\WindowsPowerShell\v1.0\powershell.exe ↵
-NoExit -ImportSystemModules
```

SECURITY ACCESS AND SCRIPTS EXECUTION

Some modules may require you to run your PowerShell session as an administrator. If that's the case, follow these steps:

1. Right-click the PowerShell icon on your taskbar or in your Start menu.

2. Select Run As Administrator.

3. If you are prompted by User Account Control, click Yes to continue.

Some scripts and modules do not load into PowerShell by default; in these cases, you'll receive an error saying the execution of scripts is disabled on the system. To get by this error, you can run the following cmdlet from an administrative PowerShell session:

```
Set-ExecutionPolicy RemoteSigned
```

Chapter 5 explains more about the security protecting your PowerShell environment.

Although the first method is quick and dirty, it does not offer the greatest degree of usability and flexibility. The second way uses a concept in PowerShell called a *profile*.

Profiles offer a great deal of flexibility and customization to your PowerShell sessions. You can think of a profile as a customizable startup script for PowerShell. A profile can affect multiple users and multiple shells. Essentially the contents of all profiles are the same. However, the name of the profile and location where the profile file is stored and created determine the impact a profile you create has on your system. There are only two filenames to use for profiles:

profile.ps1   This file affects all shells.

Microsoft.PowerShell_profile.ps1   This file affects only the PowerShell shell, the base command prompt.

Likewise, you can store the profiles in one of two locations:

%windir%\system32\WindowsPowerShell\v1.0   This location affects all users.

PowerShell Grammar
Lesson

CHAPTER 3

%UserProfile%\My Documents\WindowsPowerShell This location affects only the current user.

Table 3.5 summarizes the four types of profiles you can have.

TABLE 3.5 PowerShell profiles

Scope of profile	Profile filename	Path for
All users and all shells	profile.ps1	%windir%\system32\ WindowsPowerShell\ v1.0\
All users, but only to the Microsoft .PowerShell shell	Microsoft.PowerShell_ profile.ps1	%windir%\system32\ WindowsPowerShell\ v1.0\
Only current user and affects all shells	profile.ps1	%UserProfile%\ My Documents\ WindowsPowerShell\
Only current user and the Microsoft.PowerShell shell	Microsoft.PowerShell_ profile.ps1	%UserProfile%\ My Documents\ WindowsPowerShell\

When you first start using PowerShell on your system, there are no profiles on the system. First you need to create the profiles; then you will be able to edit them. Creating profiles is a straightforward process, but you need to know the location and filename that is currently configured on your system. To see what the current profile path is on your system, you can use a default variable; to see the value, type the following command in a PowerShell session:

```
$profile
```

This variable returns the current directory and current file location for your profile. By default when you first load PowerShell, there is no profile created. You need to create the file to store the commands for your profile. To create your profile, run this cmdlet:

```
New-Item -Path $profile -ItemType File -force
```

After the command is run, you will see results similar to Figure 3.16.

FIGURE 3.16 Creating a profile

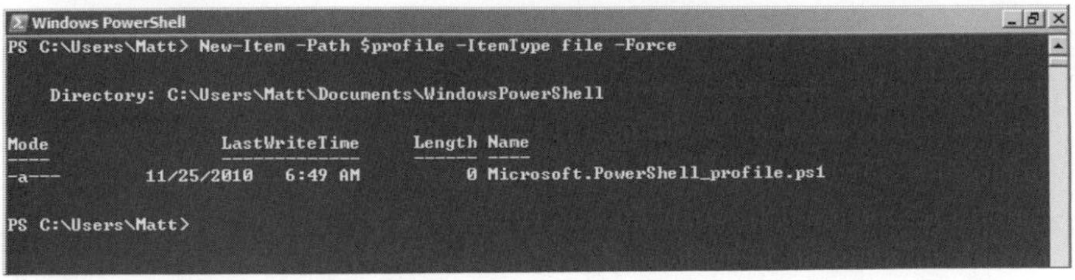

The -force value on the end creates the necessary directories and files if they do not currently exist. By default this creates a script file called Microsoft .PowerShell_profile.ps1 in the %UserProfile%\My Documents\ WindowsPowerShell directory. So, this profile affects only the current user for the current shell.

If you want to change the scope of the profile on your system, copy the file to one of the two locations, and rename it to meet your needs. You could also include the path and name of the file in the New-Item cmdlet to create the file in the location you want to have. For example, this command would create a profile affecting only the current user but for all the shells:

```
New-Item -path "$env:UserProfile\My Documents ↵
\WindowsPowerShell\profile.ps1" -itemtype file -force
```

When you create the profile, it will be a blank profile. It is up to you to determine what modules you want to put in the profile. You just need to edit the profile and add the modules or commands you want to preload. You can use Notepad, or any other favorite PowerShell editor you prefer, to edit the profile. You can either open Notepad in your PowerShell session or open the file directly via Windows Explorer and modify the file. In this example, you can see how to use PowerShell to begin editing the profile. Run the following command:

```
notepad $profile
```

Once Notepad opens, you can put in the commands that you want to preload into your PowerShell session. In this section, you saw how to use the Import-Module command to bring modules into PowerShell. You can see an example of a profile in Notepad in Figure 3.17.

PowerShell Grammar
Lesson

CHAPTER 3

FIGURE 3.17   Sample profile

If you run the command and you see an error, like the one displayed in Figure 3.18, then you need to make sure your file has been created and is in the proper location.

FIGURE 3.18   Notepad error

What makes profiles so flexible is that you can put any PowerShell command in the profile you want to preload into your environment, allowing PowerShell to open with the location you set, or modules loaded, or anything else you would like to specify about the default behavior of PowerShell. This allows you to have the values you want to have every time you load PowerShell.

EXERCISE 3: CREATE A POWERSHELL PROFILE

In this exercise, you get to work with profiles, modules, and a basic command. Create a profile that will load the Active Directory and IIS modules automatically on your system. Then run a command to verify the IIS and Active Directory modules have been properly loaded.

Aliases, Functions, and the Pipe, Oh My!

IN THIS CHAPTER, YOU WILL LEARN TO:

This chapter covers three important tools to add your own style to PowerShell: aliases, functions, and the pipe (|) operator.

Aliases provide a way to shorten long cmdlets, saving you typing. More importantly, aliases allow you to use your former command prompt knowledge and put it to use inside a PowerShell session.

Functions let you take PowerShell to an entirely new level. They extend the concept of aliases and can take advantage of the power of the .NET Framework.

The pipe symbol allows you to tie multiple cmdlets together into one line of script. You will learn the basics of using the pipe symbol and how combining cmdlets with the pipe symbol lets you quickly control and format the output from your PowerShell commands.

Use Aliases

Aliases are shortcuts that let you shorten commands in PowerShell. The following command is an example of an alias:

```
dir
```

You are most likely thinking that this is the directory command from your command shell in Windows or from your DOS background. However, PowerShell does not have a cmdlet called `dir`; it does have the alias `dir`, which accomplishes the same task as a directory list. When you type the alias in PowerShell, you get a listing of the directory, as shown in Figure 4.1.

If you come from a Unix or open source background, you may be familiar with the `ls` command. Just as with `dir`, PowerShell does not have a native cmdlet for `ls`, but it has an alias for it.

There are two main reasons why PowerShell uses aliases. First, aliases allow you to leverage existing command prompt knowledge. By providing aliases like `dir` and `ls`, PowerShell allows you to use commands you might already know and get through some of the basics very quickly and easily. The `dir` and `ls` aliases also illustrate another important concept of aliases. A cmdlet can have more than one alias associated with it. For example, the `dir` and `ls` aliases are for the cmdlet `Get-ChildItem`. Just for good measure, there is another alias for `Get-ChildItem`, which is `gci`. This is not as common as `dir` and `ls`, but all three perform the same command. And if you wanted another alias for `Get-ChildItem`, you could create one.

FIGURE 4.1 dir

GETTING HELP WITH ALIASES

In Chapter 3 you learned about the built-in help system. You can also use the `Get-Help` cmdlet to find help about aliases. When you run `Get-Help` with an alias like `dir` or `ls`, you get the help entry for `Get-ChildItem`. This is useful not only for determining how the alias works but also for determining what cmdlet the alias is associated with.

Second, aliases allow for customization. You can create your own aliases to help reduce the length of some existing cmdlets. In Chapter 3, you saw that there is a potential for cmdlets to be quite long, such as any cmdlet using the noun `ADDomainControllerPasswordReplicationPolicy`. It would be simpler if you could shorten that to `ADDCPRP`, wouldn't it? You can use aliases to do just that.

Use Built-in Aliases

More than 130 aliases are built into PowerShell, ready for you to use. To get a list of the aliases in your PowerShell session, run the following cmdlet:

```
Get-Alias
```

You will see results similar to Figure 4.2.

FIGURE 4.2   Get-Alias

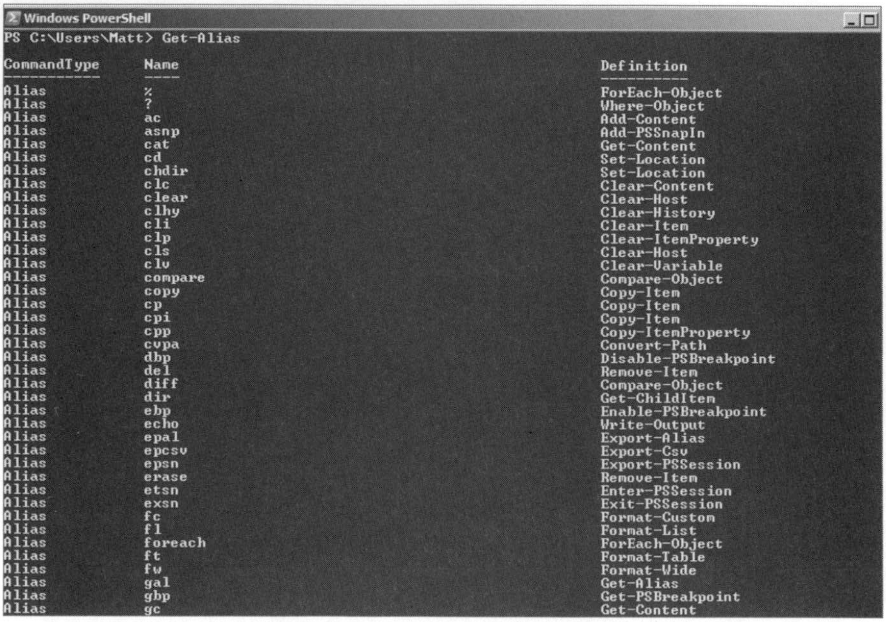

Table 4.1 describes some of the built-in aliases and their corresponding cmdlets.

TABLE 4.1   Common aliases

Alias	Cmdlet	Description
cd chdir sl	Set-Location	Changes the current directory for your PowerShell session.
kill spps	Stop-Process	Stops a running process.
copy cp cpi	Copy-Item	Allows you to copy files, subdirectories, and so on.
gcm	Get-Command	Lists all the cmdlets currently available in the PowerShell session.
man	Get-Help	If you are from a Unix background, this is your version of help, and in PowerShell you may be happy to see this alias.

The `Get-Alias` output shows not only a list of the currently loaded aliases but also the corresponding cmdlets they are associated with. By the way, the alias for the `Get-Alias` cmdlet is `gal`.

If you used PowerShell 1.0, these aliases look the same, and in most cases, all the aliases in PowerShell 1.0 have found a place in PowerShell 2.0.

Create Your Own Aliases

One of the great things about aliases is that you can create your own. The ability to create your own aliases will allow you to have PowerShell work in a way you are familiar with. By creating and using aliases, you can make your PowerShell commands easier to read and use. The trick with creating your own aliases is remembering they are there.

You can create aliases for a wide variety of purposes in PowerShell. You will most likely create aliases for cmdlets. However, you can create aliases for functions, scripts, files, executables, and other aspects in your environment that you may want to use in a PowerShell session.

If you find yourself constantly repeating the same cmdlets, then those commands are perfect candidates for aliases. If you find the need to reference the same drive and directory for PowerShell output, these are also great candidates for aliases. You need to discover the need for the aliases so you can effectively leverage them.

Creating aliases is a straightforward process. You can use either of two cmdlets to actually create the alias:

```
New-Alias
Set-Alias
```

Although you can use both cmdlets to create aliases, there is one main difference between the two. You can use the `Set-Alias` cmdlet to create an alias or change an existing alias in your PowerShell session. This lets you change the value of an alias. You can use the `Set-Alias` cmdlet only on aliases that are not read-only. For example, if you wanted to change the `si` alias (which by default is an alias for `Set-Item`) to `Get-Command`, you would see an error message similar to Figure 4.3, because the `si` alias is a read-only alias.

Aliases, Functions, and the Pipe, Oh My!

CHAPTER 4

FIGURE 4.3   Set-Alias error

The New-Alias cmdlet just creates a new alias. You should consider using this cmdlet whenever creating a new alias so that you do not accidentally overwrite an existing alias. However, the Set-Alias command provides a great resource if you need to change one of the aliases you have made for the PowerShell session.

Both cmdlets have the same two parameters: an alias name and the command element for which you want to create the alias. For example, if you wanted to create an alias for the Get-Random cmdlet, which gets a random number or a random item from a list, you could use one of the following two commands:

```
New-Alias rand Get-Random
Set-Alias rand Get-Random
```

Both cmdlets create the alias rand for the PowerShell session. So when you type rand in your PowerShell session, you actually call the Get-Random cmdlet. Figure 4.4 shows an example of the rand alias.

FIGURE 4.4   rand alias

Let's take this example a bit further to illustrate the difference between New-Alias and Set-Alias. Use the New-Alias in the following command:

```
New-Alias rand Get-Command
```

You will get the error message shown in Figure 4.5. The reason you get the error is because you have already created the rand alias.

Aliases, Functions, and
the Pipe, Oh My!

CHAPTER 4

FIGURE 4.5   rand alias error

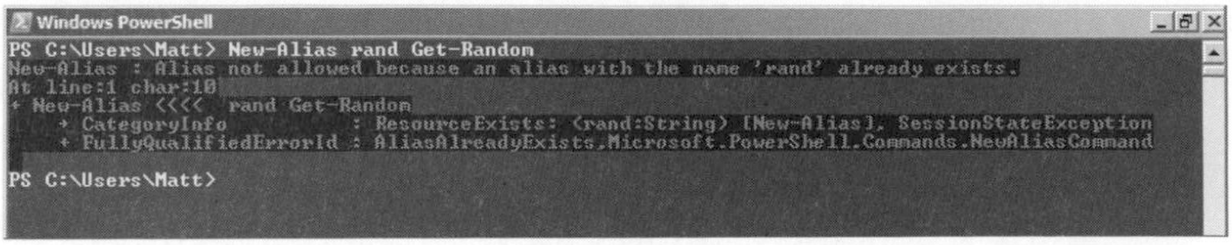

Alternatively, use Set-Alias in the following command:

```
Set-Alias rand Get-command
```

You will not get an error message, and your screen may look like the screen in Figure 4.6. As you can see, the Set-Alias cmdlet overwrote the existing alias for the PowerShell session.

FIGURE 4.6   Set-Alias rand overwrite

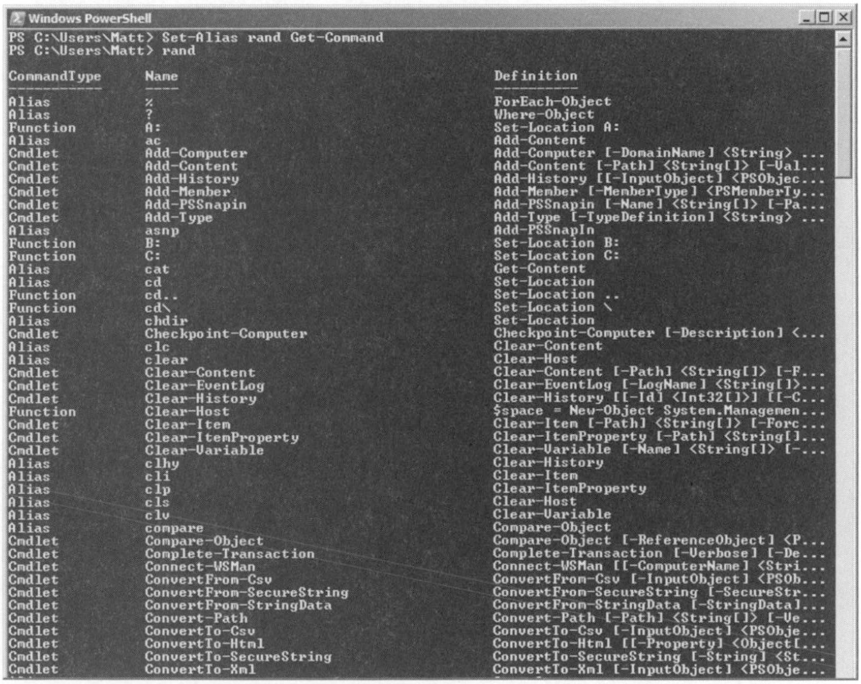

So again, when creating aliases, you want to consider using New-Alias rather than Set-Alias to avoid accidentally overwriting any existing aliases in your current PowerShell session.

Make Aliases Permanent

When you create aliases, they are used only for the current session. It does not matter whether you use Set-Alias or New-Alias; the aliases you create with those two cmdlets are for the existing PowerShell session. If you close your PowerShell session and later try to run aliases you created in it, then you will most likely see what's shown in Figure 4.7.

FIGURE 4.7   Aliases not loaded

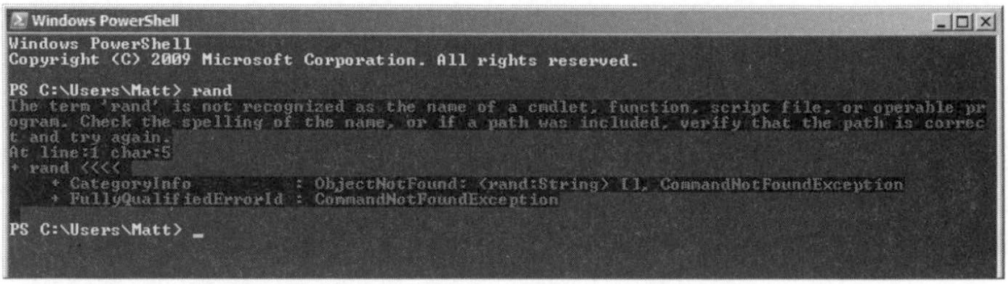

This is a standard error message (you may see it even when you misspell commands), but in this example, it means the rand alias does not exist.

In this section, you will learn how to keep from having to rebuild your aliases. There are a couple of ways to be able to take your aliases with you, in other words, make them permanent.

One method allows you to export your aliases to a text file and then reimport them into an existing PowerShell session. The export/import method allows your aliases to travel with you. You can place the exported text file on a USB stick or removable drive. You can even email it to yourself. To export your aliases in your current PowerShell session, run the following command:

```
Export-alias -path aliases.csv
```

This command exports your existing aliases into the file called aliases.csv in the current directory. You can use your own filename and put the file in whatever directory you want. You should always export the aliases to .csv so you can read and import them easily into a spreadsheet program such as Microsoft Excel. If you export them to a .txt file, you may not be able to easily read the results. Figure 4.8 shows aliases in a .txt file.

WORKING WITH FILE EXTENSIONS

When you export the aliases using extensions, you can easily work in other programs such as Notepad or Excel. The extensions are not needed if you need to reimport the files into a PowerShell session.

FIGURE 4.8 Looking at aliases in Notepad

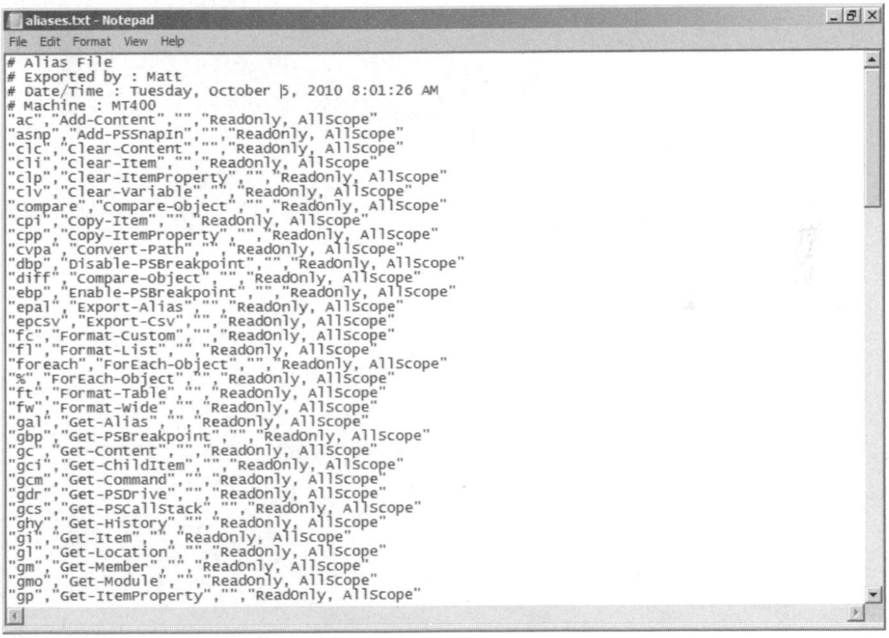


```
# Alias File
# Exported by : Matt
# Date/Time : Tuesday, October 5, 2010 8:01:26 AM
# Machine : MT400
"ac","Add-Content","","ReadOnly, AllScope"
"asnp","Add-PSSnapIn","","ReadOnly, AllScope"
"clc","Clear-Content","","ReadOnly, AllScope"
"cli","Clear-Item","","ReadOnly, AllScope"
"clp","Clear-ItemProperty","","ReadOnly, AllScope"
"clv","Clear-Variable","","ReadOnly, AllScope"
"compare","Compare-Object","","ReadOnly, AllScope"
"cpi","Copy-Item","","ReadOnly, AllScope"
"cpp","Copy-ItemProperty","","ReadOnly, AllScope"
"cvpa","Convert-Path","","ReadOnly, AllScope"
"dbp","Disable-PSBreakpoint","","ReadOnly, AllScope"
"diff","Compare-Object","","ReadOnly, AllScope"
"ebp","Enable-PSBreakpoint","","ReadOnly, AllScope"
"epal","Export-Alias","","ReadOnly, AllScope"
"epcsv","Export-Csv","","ReadOnly, AllScope"
"fc","Format-Custom","","ReadOnly, AllScope"
"fl","Format-List","","ReadOnly, AllScope"
"foreach","ForEach-Object","","ReadOnly, AllScope"
"%","ForEach-Object","","ReadOnly, AllScope"
"ft","Format-Table","","ReadOnly, AllScope"
"fw","Format-Wide","","ReadOnly, AllScope"
"gal","Get-Alias","","ReadOnly, AllScope"
"gbp","Get-PSBreakpoint","","ReadOnly, AllScope"
"gc","Get-Content","","ReadOnly, AllScope"
"gci","Get-ChildItem","","ReadOnly, AllScope"
"gcm","Get-Command","","ReadOnly, AllScope"
"gdr","Get-PSDrive","","ReadOnly, AllScope"
"gcs","Get-PSCallStack","","ReadOnly, AllScope"
"ghy","Get-History","","ReadOnly, AllScope"
"gi","Get-Item","","ReadOnly, AllScope"
"gl","Get-Location","","ReadOnly, AllScope"
"gm","Get-Member","","ReadOnly, AllScope"
"gmo","Get-Module","","ReadOnly, AllScope"
"gp","Get-ItemProperty","","ReadOnly, AllScope"
```

If you want to read the file, open it in Excel or another spreadsheet program. To do that, complete the following steps:

1. Open Microsoft Excel, and browse to the directory where the alias file is stored. Make sure you are browsing for all files. Select the file you want to open, and click Open.
2. You may see a screen similar to Figure 4.9. This is the Text Import Wizard in Microsoft Excel 2007.

FIGURE 4.9   Text Import Wizard

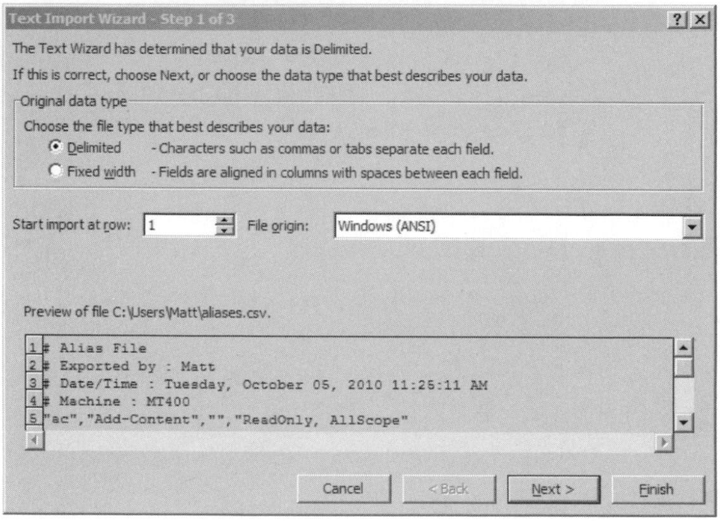

3. Click Next.

4. Select Comma as the delimiter, as shown in Figure 4.10, and then click Next.

FIGURE 4.10   Comma delimiter

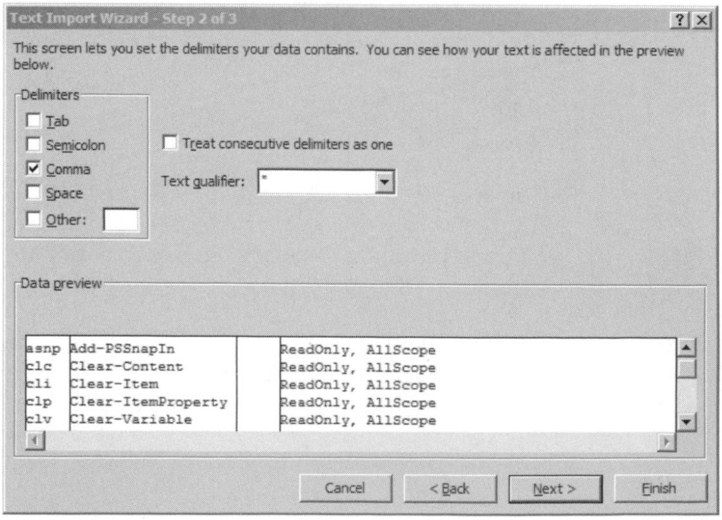

5. Click Finish to view your file, as shown in Figure 4.11.

FIGURE 4.11   Aliases file in Excel

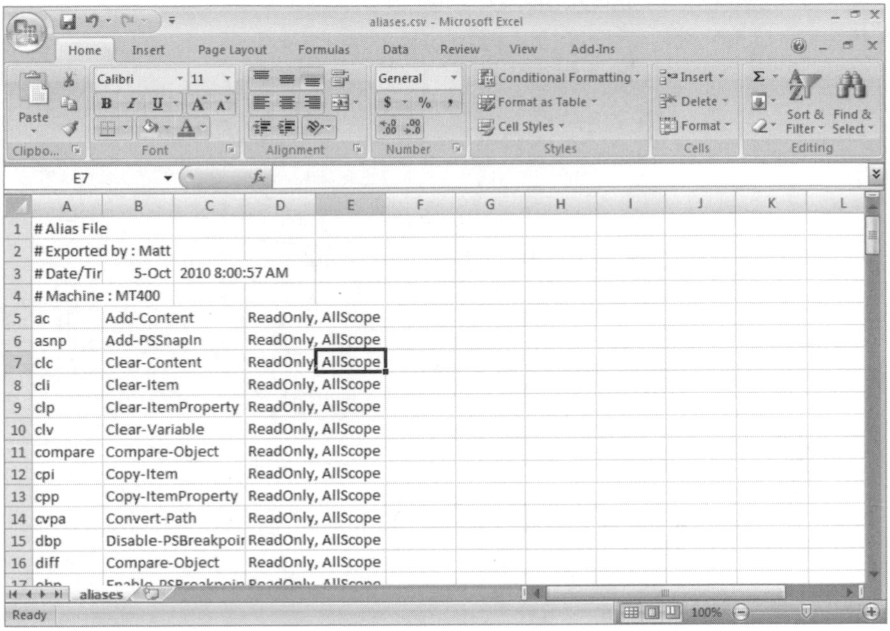

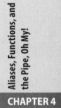

As you can see, the alias file is easier to read in Microsoft Excel. Although you normally would not do this, it sometimes helps to look at the file structure so that you can make changes or additions to this file to control what aliases you import into your PowerShell session.

When you want to import the files into your PowerShell session, run the following command:

```
Import-Alias -path aliases.csv
```

The first time you run this file, you may see a screen similar to Figure 4.12.

Although you may be inclined to panic with all the error messages on your screen, there is no need to do so. The repeated error messages show that you tried to import aliases overtop existing aliases in your current PowerShell session. There are a couple of ways to handle the error messages. The first way is to ignore the message and just go on with your PowerShell work. The other way is to delete all the built-in PowerShell aliases in the exported file, leaving only your custom aliases.

FIGURE 4.12   **Importing existing aliases**

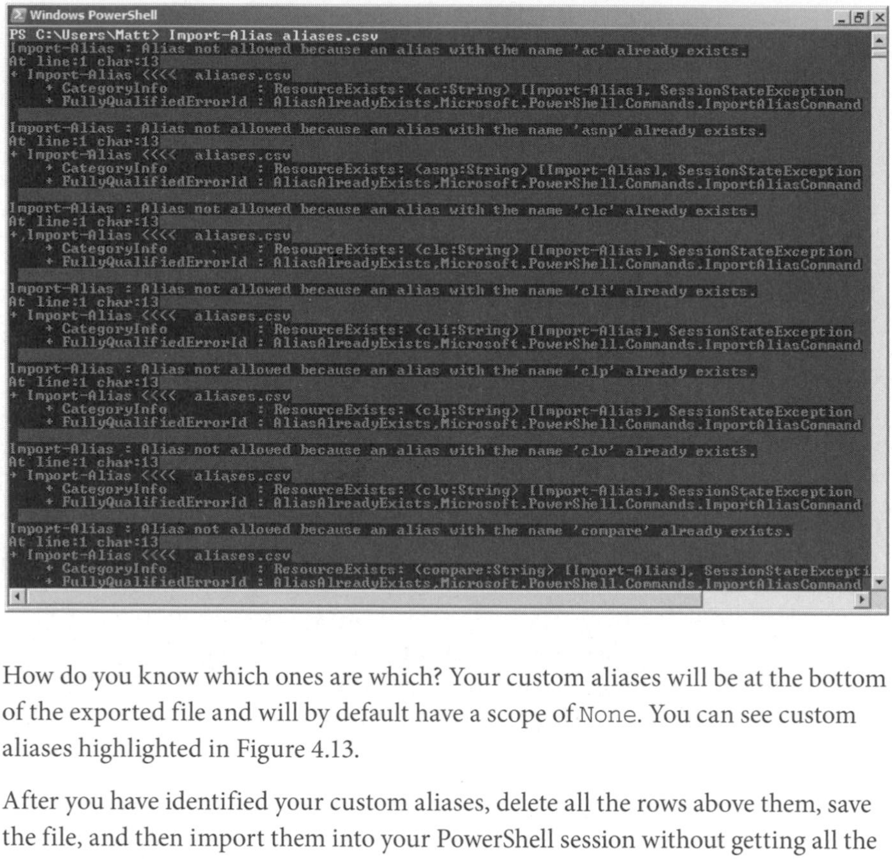

How do you know which ones are which? Your custom aliases will be at the bottom of the exported file and will by default have a scope of None. You can see custom aliases highlighted in Figure 4.13.

After you have identified your custom aliases, delete all the rows above them, save the file, and then import them into your PowerShell session without getting all the error messages.

The second, preferred method to make your aliases permanent is to modify the profile for your local system. By modifying the profile with your aliases you will be assured they are at your fingertips every time you start a PowerShell session on the system you created the custom profile on. The advantage to the export/import method discussed earlier is that the file you create is more portable. Having a simple .csv or .txt file on a portable drive, or even emailed to yourself, makes your custom aliases easily transferable to other PowerShell systems.

FIGURE 4.13   Custom aliases

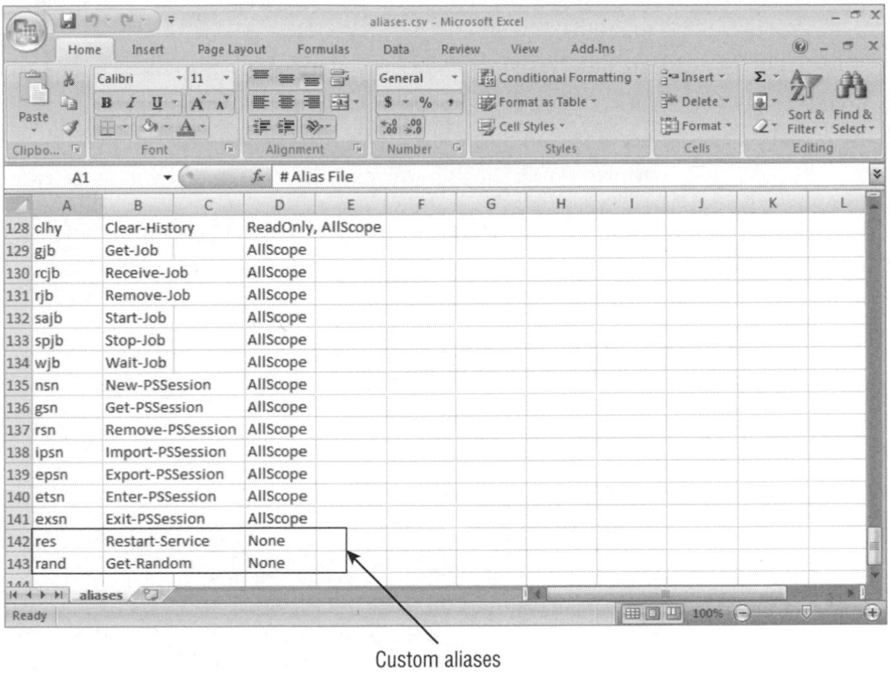

Custom aliases

In Chapter 3, you learned how to modify the profile for a PowerShell session. Once you have opened and modified the profile, then it is just a matter of including the appropriate `New-Alias` or `Set-Alias` commands to have the aliases you need at your fingertips.

Use Functions

Another powerful aspect to working with PowerShell is the ability to work with functions. Functions go hand in hand with aliases in certain aspects but also offer a lot of additional power. The additional power behind functions is their ability to accept and pass parameters.

In this section, you will see some of the basics of functions. You will get a brief introduction to the built-in functions and an overview of how to create customized functions to perform tasks in PowerShell.

Understand Functions

Functions provide another way to save time in the PowerShell environment. Functions extend the power of aliases by being able to accept parameters or other blocks of PowerShell script into a single command. You can then pass parameters into the command that allow you to have the functions not only perform scripting but also perform PowerShell scripting within the context you set by using the parameters.

One of the limitations of aliases is that you cannot create an alias with any parameters in it. For example, if you ran the following command:

```
New-Alias setd Set-Location D:
```

you would receive an error message, similar to Figure 4.14.

FIGURE 4.14   Alias with parameters error

As you can see, aliases cannot be created with additional parameters. In other words, aliases are a great way to shorten base PowerShell cmdlets, but functions allow you to not only shorten up cmdlets but also include any parameters or additional properties you want to set as part of your PowerShell commands.

PowerShell has several built-in functions. In fact, you probably have used a PowerShell function and did not even know it. Here is an example of a built-in PowerShell function:

```
D:
```

Again, you are probably thinking you have to run that command or a variation of that command (C:, E:, or even Z:) to change your drive letter to whatever drive you specified before the colon. The actual cmdlet that is performed when you run the command is this one:

```
Set-Location D:
```

So, like aliases, functions provide another built-in tool, allowing you to leverage your existing command prompt knowledge.

Use Existing Functions

To list all the default functions in your PowerShell session, you can run the following command:

```
Get-ChildItem -path function:
```

You will see a screen similar to Figure 4.15.

FIGURE 4.15 Listing of functions

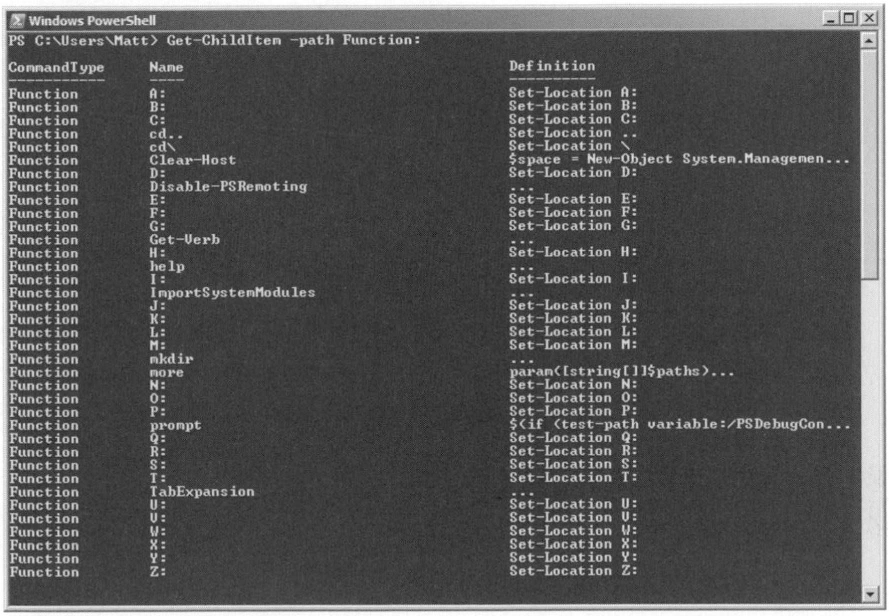

```
Windows PowerShell
PS C:\Users\Matt> Get-ChildItem -path Function:

CommandType     Name                          Definition
-----------     ----                          ----------
Function        A:                            Set-Location A:
Function        B:                            Set-Location B:
Function        C:                            Set-Location C:
Function        cd..                          Set-Location ..
Function        cd\                           Set-Location \
Function        Clear-Host                    $space = New-Object System.Managemen...
Function        D:                            Set-Location D:
Function        Disable-PSRemoting            ...
Function        E:                            Set-Location E:
Function        F:                            Set-Location F:
Function        G:                            Set-Location G:
Function        Get-Verb                      ...
Function        H:                            Set-Location H:
Function        help                          ...
Function        I:                            Set-Location I:
Function        ImportSystemModules           ...
Function        J:                            Set-Location J:
Function        K:                            Set-Location K:
Function        L:                            Set-Location L:
Function        M:                            Set-Location M:
Function        mkdir                         ...
Function        more                          param([string[]]$paths)...
Function        N:                            Set-Location N:
Function        O:                            Set-Location O:
Function        P:                            Set-Location P:
Function        prompt                        $(if (test-path variable:/PSDebugCon...
Function        Q:                            Set-Location Q:
Function        R:                            Set-Location R:
Function        S:                            Set-Location S:
Function        T:                            Set-Location T:
Function        TabExpansion                  ...
Function        U:                            Set-Location U:
Function        V:                            Set-Location V:
Function        W:                            Set-Location W:
Function        X:                            Set-Location X:
Function        Y:                            Set-Location Y:
Function        Z:                            Set-Location Z:
```

A lot of the functions listed in Figure 4.15 should look familiar if you have used a command prompt environment. You may also notice some other functions that you have not seen in the list before. Functions, like aliases, provide a transition point into PowerShell. Table 4.2 explains a few built-in functions.

TABLE 4.2   Built-in functions

Function	Description
Get-Verb	Allows you to find all the verbs in your PowerShell session, which is useful when you are trying to find all the cmdlets available with a particular verb.
TabExpansion	Provides the ability for tab autocomplete to work in your PowerShell sessions. This function has also been greatly improved to help not only with cmdlets but also with file and directory locations, among other capabilities.
Clear-Host	A fancy way to run CLS — and another example of being able to carry over previous knowledge from the command prompt. Additionally, CLS is an alias for this function.

As you can see, functions assist in the everyday usage of PowerShell.

Create Your Own Function

Functions are easy to create. They have three basic components:

- ► Function: This is the marker for the beginning of a function definition; it can also be used to modify existing functions or rename functions.

- ► Function name: This is the name of the function you are creating.

- ► Script block: This is where you put all of your cmdlets and PowerShell script with parameters; in other words, it's where you do all the work and logic of the function.

So, the basic syntax for creating a function is as follows:

```
Function (function name) {Script block}
```

In the following example, you will create a function that will show you all the existing functions on your system. This example will give you a quick peek into how functions operate.

```
Function Get-Function { Get-ChildItem -path function: }
```

As you can see, this function calls the command you saw earlier in this chapter.

One last note on functions: like aliases, functions are not permanent. If you want a function to be permanent, you have to edit the profile for PowerShell. In Chapter 3, you learned how to modify the profile for a PowerShell session. Just like other commands you included in the profile, you can put your custom functions in the profile as well, like so:

```
Function Get-Function { Get-ChildItem -path function: }
```

In this section, you just scratched the surface of working with functions in PowerShell. For more information and to see some of the power behind functions, refer to Appendix D.

Work with the Pipe Operator

Up until this point, you have been using simple commands to get information out of PowerShell. In this section, you will learn how to tie cmdlets together by using the pipe (|) operator.

By using the pipe operator, you can string multiple commands together into one line of PowerShell script. This not only lets you make your PowerShell scripts simple to write but more importantly makes it easy to have consistent commands.

Some of the things you can do with the pipe operator include recovering users from Active Directory, finding all the services that are currently running, or sorting your output list from a PowerShell command.

Use the Pipe Operator to Combine PowerShell Cmdlets

Piping commands together is called *pipelining*. Pipelining allows you to take the output from one command and pass it to the next command, essentially becoming input for the next command. This is also very similar to using | more, which you may have used at the command prompt; like the pipe at the command prompt, | more will help avoid scrolling through output from a PowerShell command. For example, the following command lets you show the services on your system sorted by their status, including the name of the service, any required services, and the status of the service:

```
Get-Service | Sort-Object -property status | ↵
Format-Table -property name, requiredservices, status
```

Notice the object-based nature of the language, which allows you to work with any of the parameters from a particular object. This allows parameter binding, which is key to working with the pipe operator. Little scripting effort is required when you tie commands together. The pipe routes information automatically and correctly into the right parameters, offering a consistent experience with little work on your part.

Aliases, Functions, and the Pipe, Oh My!

CHAPTER 4

Control PowerShell Output

Commands that are used with the pipe operator typically fall in one of the following categories:

► Formatting — making the output look the way you want to see the information

► Sorting — organizing your data further

► Redirecting output to a file or other output mechanism

► Filtering using the `Where-Object` cmdlet

Let's take a look at another example using `Get-Service`:

```
Get-Service | Format-List
```

The `Format-List` cmdlet is piped the output from the `Get-Service` cmdlet. This causes the output to be formatted in a list. You can see an example of this output in Figure 4.16. As a comparison, if you run just the `Get-Service` cmdlet, the output may look like Figure 4.17.

FIGURE 4.16   `Get-Service | Format-List`

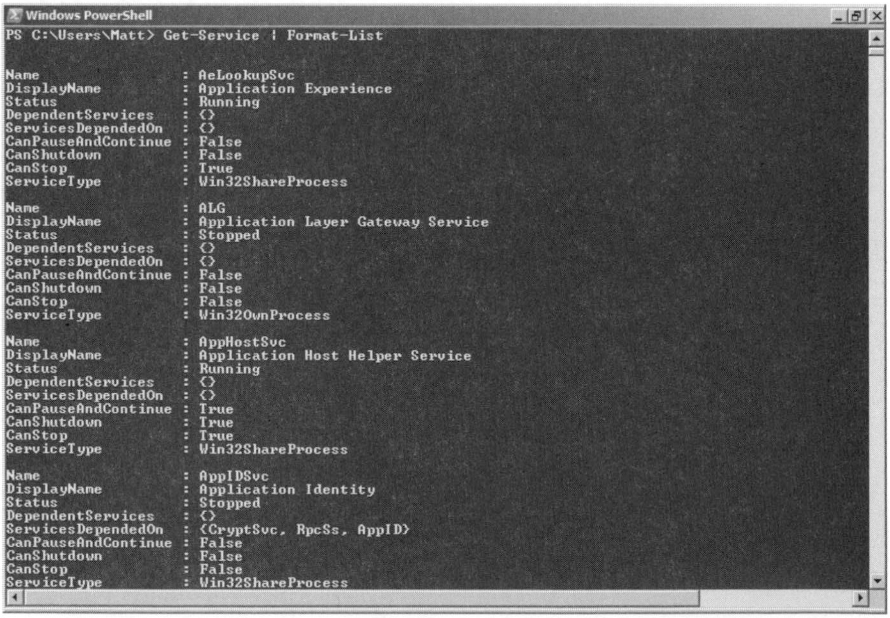

FIGURE 4.17   Get-Service

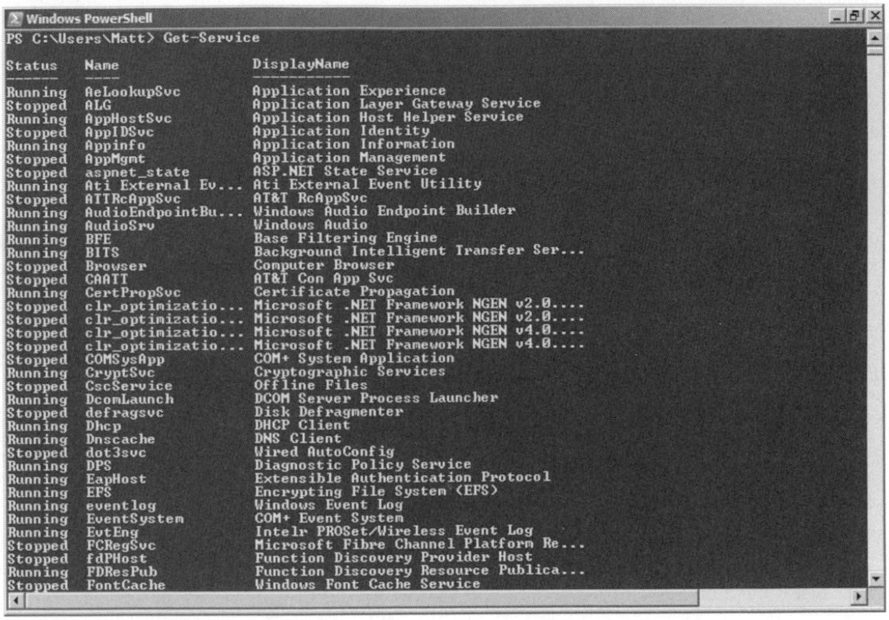

There are also other format cmdlets to format the output in tables and grids. The sorting cmdlet works like the format cmdlets in that its input is piped in from a separate cmdlet. Take a look at Figure 4.18.

```
Get-Process | Sort-Object -Property handles
```

The Sort-Object cmdlet takes a property parameter specifying the property to sort on—handles, in this case.

Another set of utility cmdlets are those that deal with output redirection. The following example redirects the output of Get-Service to a file rather than writing out the services list to the PowerShell environment. Figure 4.19 shows the resulting services.txt file.

```
Get-Service | Out-File -FilePath C:\temp\services.txt
```

The FilePath parameter of the Out-File cmdlet specifies the file path where you want the output to be saved.

Aliases, Functions, and the Pipe, Oh My!

CHAPTER 4

FIGURE 4.18 `Sort-Object`

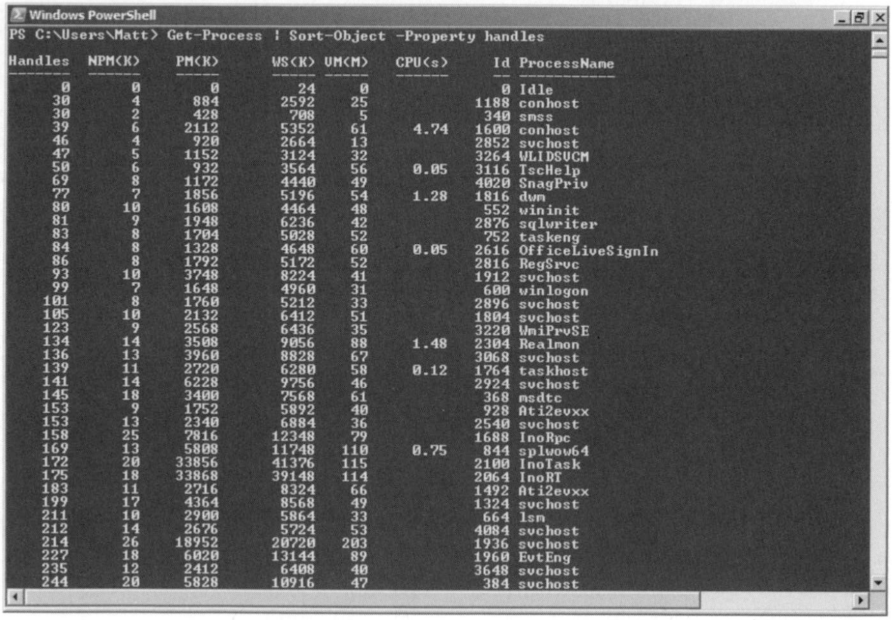

```
Windows PowerShell
PS C:\Users\Matt> Get-Process | Sort-Object -Property handles

Handles  NPM(K)    PM(K)      WS(K) VM(M)   CPU(s)     Id ProcessName
-------  ------    -----      ----- -----   ------     -- -----------
      0       0        0         24     0               0 Idle
     30       4      884       2592    25            1188 conhost
     30       2      428        708     5             340 smss
     39       6     2112       5352    61     4.74   1600 conhost
     46       4      920       2664    13            2852 svchost
     47       5     1152       3124    32            3264 WLIDSVCM
     50       6      932       3564    56     0.05   3116 TscHelp
     69       8     1172       4440    49            4020 SnagPriv
     77       7     1856       5196    54     1.28   1816 dwm
     80      10     1608       4464    48             552 wininit
     81       9     1948       6236    42            2876 sqlwriter
     83       8     1704       5028    52             752 taskeng
     84       8     1328       4648    60     0.05   2616 OfficeLiveSignIn
     86       8     1792       5172    52            2816 RegSrvc
     93      10     3748       8224    41            1912 svchost
     99       7     1648       4960    31             600 winlogon
    101       8     1760       5212    33            2896 svchost
    105      10     2132       6412    51            1804 svchost
    123       9     2568       6436    35            3220 WmiPrvSE
    134      14     3508       9056    88     1.48   2304 Realmon
    136      13     3960       8828    67            3068 svchost
    139      11     2720       6280    58     0.12   1764 taskhost
    141      14     6228       9756    46            2924 svchost
    145      18     3400       7568    61             368 msdtc
    153       9     1752       5892    40             928 Ati2evxx
    153      13     2340       6884    36            2540 svchost
    158      25     7816      12348    79            1688 InoRpc
    169      13     5808      11748   110     0.75    844 splwow64
    172      20    33856      41376   115            2100 InoTask
    175      18    33868      39148   114            2064 InoRT
    183      11     2716       8324    66            1492 Ati2evxx
    199      17     4364       8568    49            1324 svchost
    211      10     2900       5864    33             664 lsm
    212      14     2676       5724    53            4084 svchost
    214      26    18952      20720   203            1936 svchost
    227      18     6020      13144    89            1960 EvtEng
    235      12     2412       6408    40            3648 svchost
    244      20     5828      10916    47             384 svchost
```

FIGURE 4.19 `Out-File`

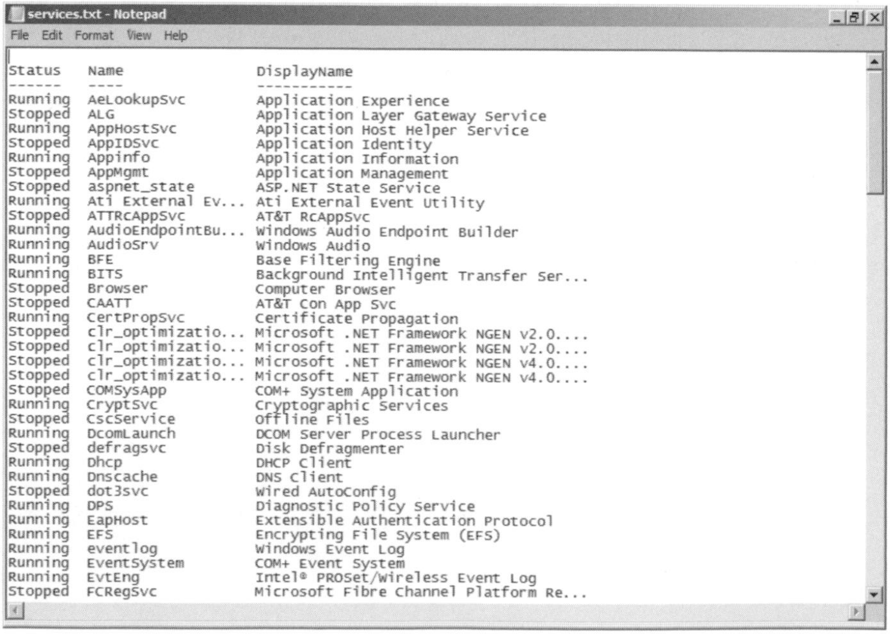

```
services.txt - Notepad
File  Edit  Format  View  Help

Status   Name               DisplayName
------   ----               -----------
Running  AeLookupSvc        Application Experience
Stopped  ALG                Application Layer Gateway Service
Running  AppHostSvc         Application Host Helper Service
Stopped  AppIDSvc           Application Identity
Running  Appinfo            Application Information
Stopped  AppMgmt            Application Management
Stopped  aspnet_state       ASP.NET State Service
Running  Ati External Ev... Ati External Event Utility
Stopped  ATTRcAppSvc        AT&T RcAppSvc
Running  AudioEndpointBu... Windows Audio Endpoint Builder
Running  AudioSrv           Windows Audio
Running  BFE                Base Filtering Engine
Running  BITS               Background Intelligent Transfer Ser...
Stopped  Browser            Computer Browser
Stopped  CAATT              AT&T Con App Svc
Running  CertPropSvc        Certificate Propagation
Stopped  clr_optimizatio... Microsoft .NET Framework NGEN v2.0....
Stopped  clr_optimizatio... Microsoft .NET Framework NGEN v2.0....
Stopped  clr_optimizatio... Microsoft .NET Framework NGEN v4.0....
Stopped  clr_optimizatio... Microsoft .NET Framework NGEN v4.0....
Stopped  COMSysApp          COM+ System Application
Running  CryptSvc           Cryptographic Services
Stopped  CscService         Offline Files
Running  DcomLaunch         DCOM Server Process Launcher
Stopped  defragsvc          Disk Defragmenter
Running  Dhcp               DHCP Client
Running  Dnscache           DNS Client
Stopped  dot3svc            Wired AutoConfig
Running  DPS                Diagnostic Policy Service
Running  EapHost            Extensible Authentication Protocol
Running  EFS                Encrypting File System (EFS)
Running  eventlog           Windows Event Log
Running  EventSystem        COM+ Event System
Running  EvtEng             Intel® PROSet/Wireless Event Log
Stopped  FCRegSvc           Microsoft Fibre Channel Platform Re...
```

FINDING CMDLETS FOR YOUR VERBS WITH THE POWER OF THE PIPE

When working with Get-Command, you may get a long list of results. However, suppose you want to narrow the commands to a subset of a particular verb. In this case, you could use the pipe operator with the Get-Verb function and Get-Command to list all the commands for a particular verb.

For example, if you just want to find all the commands that go with the Format verb, you would run this command:

```
Get-Verb Format | Get-Command
```

The Get-Verb function lets you find any commands if you know the verb you are looking for, and you pipe it into the Get-Command cmdlet.

Aliases, Functions, and the Pipe, Oh My!

CHAPTER 4

Format PowerShell Output

Table 4.3 describes the four main cmdlets you can use to help format data in your PowerShell commands.

TABLE 4.3   Format cmdlets

Cmdlet	Usage
Format-List	Lets you control what properties are displayed in a list view when you run PowerShell cmdlets.
Format-Wide	Creates a wide table in the form of columns; displays one property for the objects returned in your cmdlet. This is similar to the command prompt command dir /w.
Format-Table	Outputs data into a table format, typically the default view for outputting data.
Format-Custom	Allows you to leverage custom views defined by XML. There is a lot of customization to be done in creating your own view. In Appendix D, you will see a little bit more on how to create a custom view.

Let's take a look at the format cmdlets in action. To be effective with the format cmdlets, you need to know the property names for the particular object you are working with. You may recall the Get-Member cmdlet mentioned in Table 3.3 in Chapter 3. When you run Get-Member for a particular cmdlet, it displays not only programmatic methods for the cmdlet but the properties as well. When you are looking for properties to use in formatting your output, you can see them in the results of Get-Member. Figure 4.20 shows the properties for the Get-Service cmdlet.

FIGURE 4.20   Get-Service|Get-Member

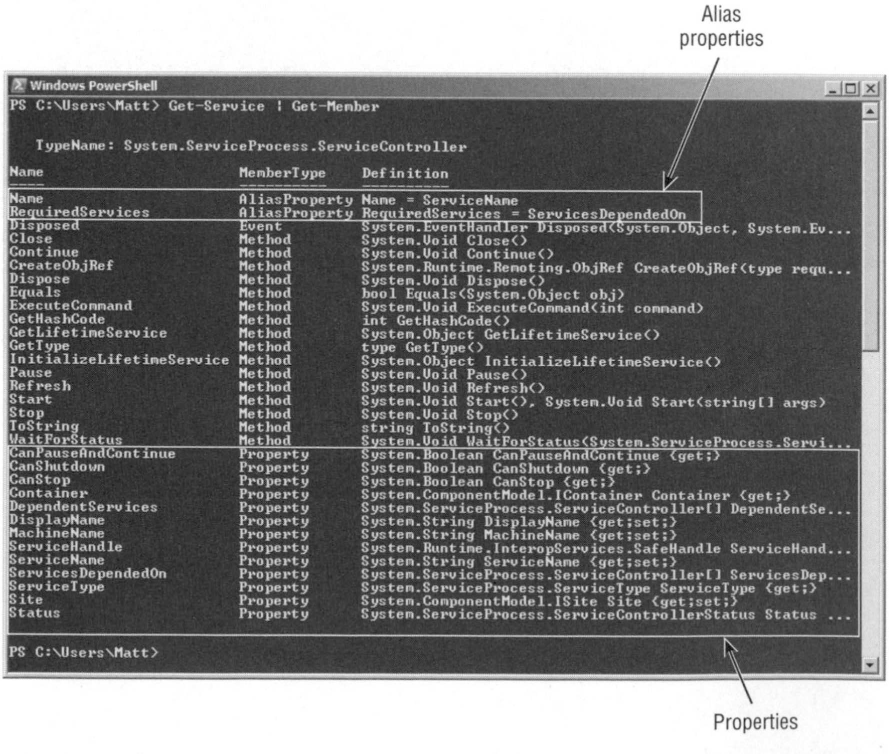

Alias properties

Properties

After you know what properties to use, it is just a matter of plugging the correct names into the `-property` parameter of the `Format-List` cmdlet. You can also have alias properties. For the `Get-Service` cmdlet, there are two alias properties, `name` and `requiredservices`, which can be used for `ServiceName` and `ServiceDependsOn`, respectively. When you use multiple property names, separate them with a comma. For example, if you wanted all the required services for each service on your machine, you would run this command (Figure 4.21 shows the output):

```
Get-Service | Format-List ↵
-property displayname, requiredservices
```

FIGURE 4.21   `Format-List` with properties

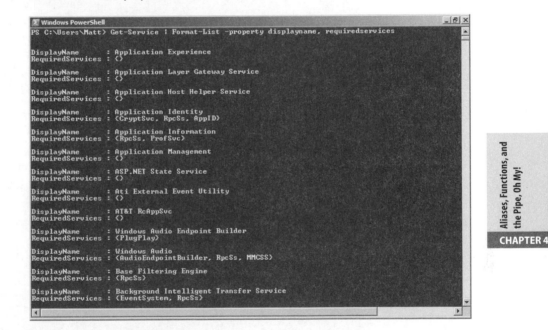

The property names also work in the `Format-Table` cmdlet. Figure 4.22 shows the output of the following command:

```
Get-Service | Format-Table ↵
-property displayname, requiredservices
```

The results of the `Format-List` and `Format Table` commands are the same; it is the formatting that is different. Choosing which cmdlet you use really becomes a matter of preference. These two cmdlets are the most common formatting cmdlets you will use in PowerShell.

FIGURE 4.22 Format-Table with properties

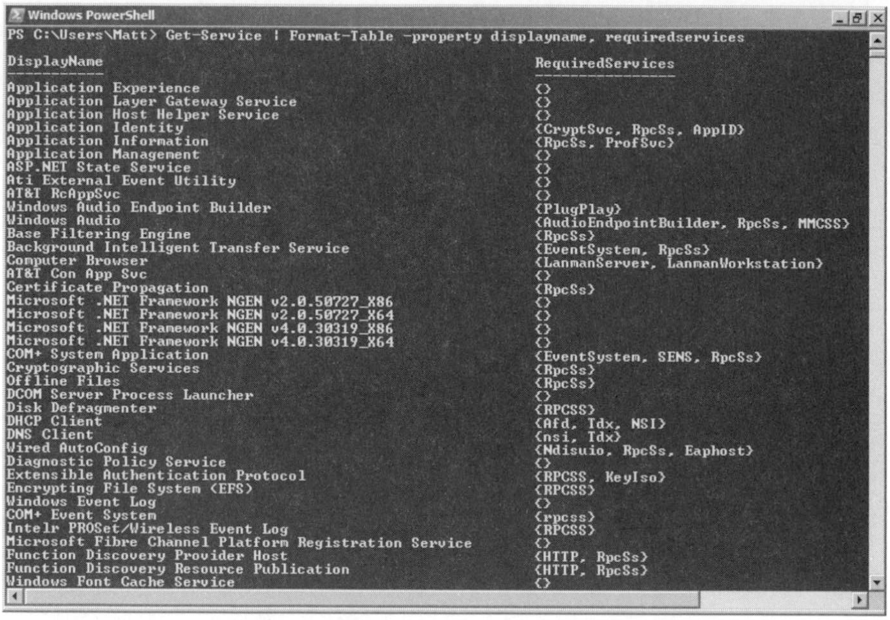

The Format-Wide cmdlet, while not used for the previous commands, can be very useful when looking at files and directories. The following example shows why Format-Wide is a good formatting option when you want to display a list spanning multiple columns (see Figure 4.23):

```
dir | Format-Wide -column 3
```

FIGURE 4.23 Format-Wide

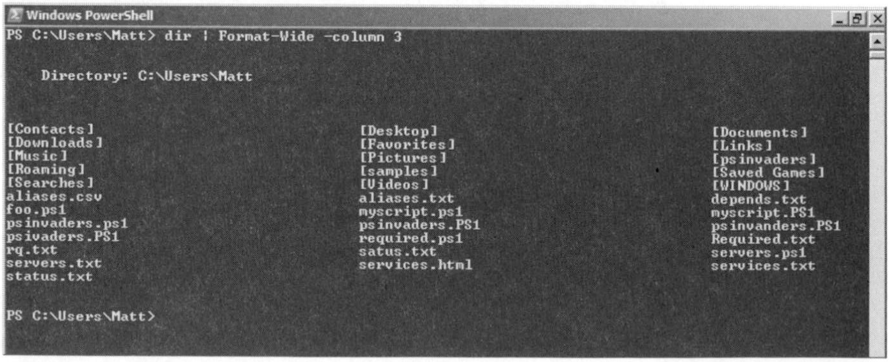

Sort PowerShell Output

There is only one cmdlet you will need to know how to use for sorting your data. The `Sort-Object` cmdlet can take a few parameters. As with the format cmdlets, you need to know the properties of an object in order to sort on them with `Sort-Object`. If you want to sort the list of services by their status, run this command:

```
Get-Service | Sort-Object -property status
```

To sort this list so the running services are listed first, change the sort order with this command:

```
Get-Service | Sort-Object -property status -descending
```

When using the `Sort-Object` cmdlet in conjunction with the format cmdlets, make sure the `Sort-Object` cmdlet precedes the format cmdlets. This is a good situation to use `| more`. Notice how the behavior of the output changes, when you run the same command with the `| more`:

```
Get-Service | Sort-Object -property status -descending | more
```

It makes scrolling through the data easier. You can scroll the output either one page at time by pressing the spacebar or one line at a time by pressing the Enter key.

Redirect PowerShell Output

The results of almost any PowerShell command can be redirected to a file. You can redirect your output into many different types of file formats, including CSV, HTML, and, yes, even the GUI. Table 4.4 shows the types of output you can use for your PowerShell cmdlets.

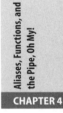

Aliases, Functions, and the Pipe, Oh My!

CHAPTER 4

TABLE 4.4   Out cmdlets

Out cmdlets	Description
Out-Default	Sends the output to the default output formatter. This can be useful when debugging PowerShell scripts. By default, this is to the PowerShell shell. This really is just a placeholder and does not directly impact output.
Out-File	Lets you output the results of a PowerShell command to a file.
Out-Gridview	Lets you output the results to a sortable, filterable grid.
Out-Host	Displays the results in the PowerShell session. This is the default output option for most cmdlets.
Out-Null	Deletes the output instead of displaying it.
Out-Printer	Sends output to a printer on your server.
Out-String	Lets you output the results to an array of strings. This is particularly useful for setting up variables for scripting operations.

The most common cmdlets when outputting data are `Out-File` and `Out-Gridview`. Sending the output of a cmdlet to a file is as simple as knowing where you want to save the file. If the file does not exist, the `Out` cmdlets create it for you.

You can control the format by combining the `Out` cmdlets with the `Format` cmdlets, giving you the same control over the formatting for your redirection as you do for your regular output. Although you do not have to place the `Out` cmdlet at the end of the command string, you will want to place the command at the end of the string to make it easy to follow. The following is an example of outputting the data to a file:

```
Get-Service | Format-Table -property displayname, ↵
requiredservices |Out-File Required.txt
```

You can control the sort of the data by piping the `Sort-Object` into the command as follows:

```
Get-Service | Sort-Object -property status | Format-Table ↵
-property displayname, requiredservices, status |Out-File status.txt
```

You can see what this command and its output look like in Figure 4.24.

FIGURE 4.24   Sort and **Format** and **Out**

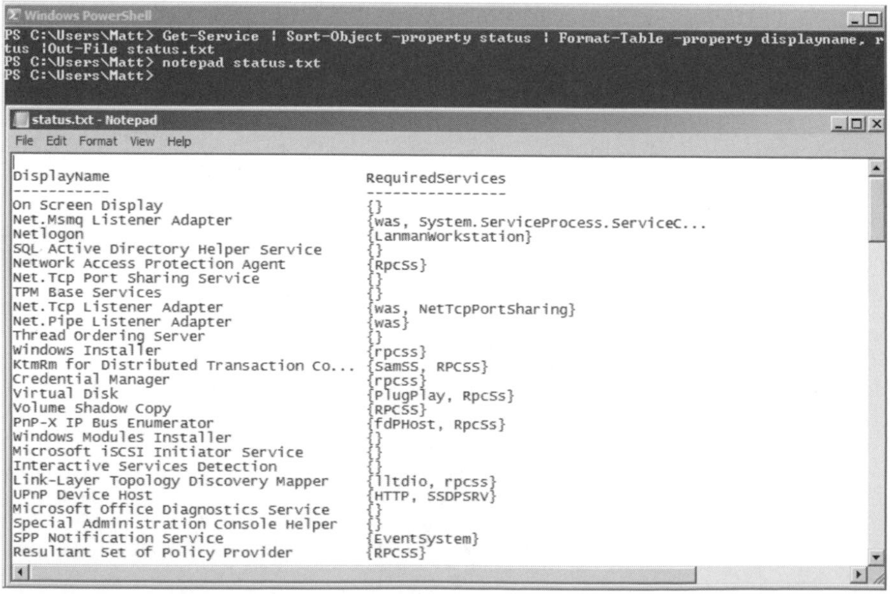

As you begin to working with output data to your files, one of the invaluable parameters for the `Out-File` cmdlet is the `-Append` parameter. When you output data to files, by default without the -Append parameter, you overwrite the existing data in the file. With the -Append parameter, you add data to the end of the existing file. If the file does not exist and you still use the -Append parameter, a new file is created automatically.

PowerShell 2.0 has a new Out cmdlet called Out-GridView, which takes the output of a PowerShell command and places it in a GUI window. There is one requirement: Out-GridView requires Microsoft .NET Framework 3.5 with Service Pack 1 to be installed on the system. This output option provides a great way to interact with PowerShell data if you do not want to make a file.

If you find yourself creating output files, looking at the data quickly, and then deleting the files, you may find the Out-GridView cmdlet to be a time-saver. Not only does it provide a nice GUI for you to see the data, but you can also filter and sort your data quickly and easily. It is similar to working with a Windows Explorer window.

In Figure 4.25, let's look at Get-Service again, this time in a grid view.

```
Get-Service | Out-GridView
```

FIGURE 4.25   Out-Gridview

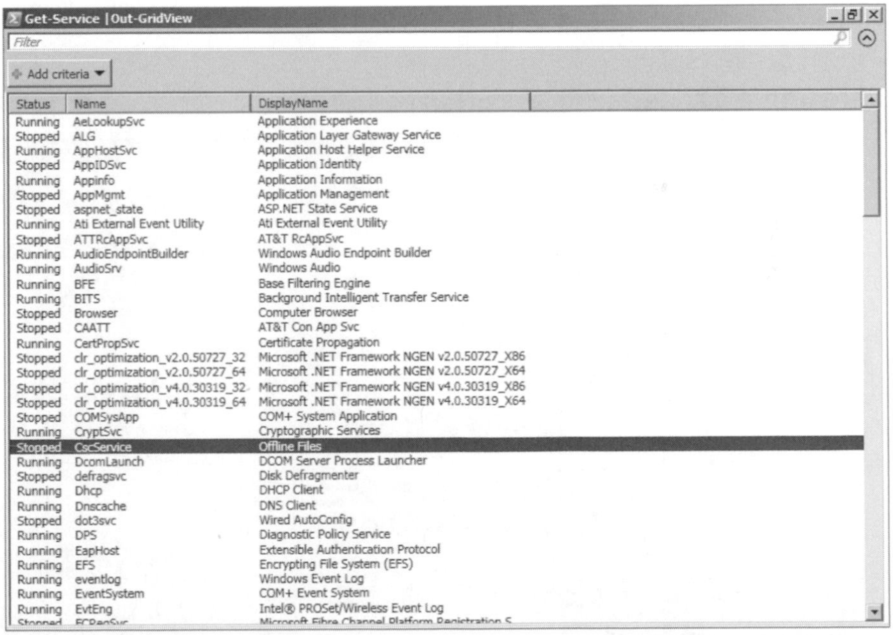

You can quickly sort the list by clicking the respective column heading. The Add Criteria button allows you to filter data based on the properties you are currently viewing in the window.

Do not use the format cmdlets when using `Out-Gridview`. If you try to run the `Format` cmdlets with the `Out-GridView` cmdlet, like in the following command, you will see a screen similar to Figure 4.26.

```
Get-Service | Format-Table -property displayname, ↵
requiredservices, status |Out-File Required.txt
```

FIGURE 4.26 **`Out-GridView` error**

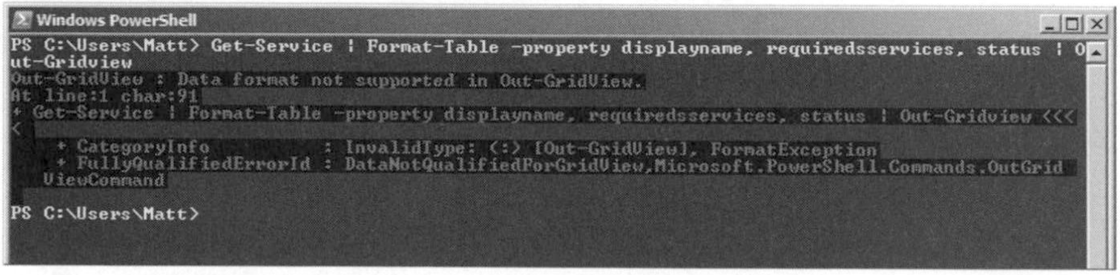

What if you want to add properties, such as `requiredservices`, to the `Out-Gridview`? You can do this with the `Select-Object` cmdlet. Using the previous example, the following would look like Figure 4.27 if you used `Out-Gridview`:

```
Get-Service | Select-Object -property DisplayName, ↵
name, requiredservices, status |Out-GridView
```

FIGURE 4.27 **`Out-GridView` with additional properties**

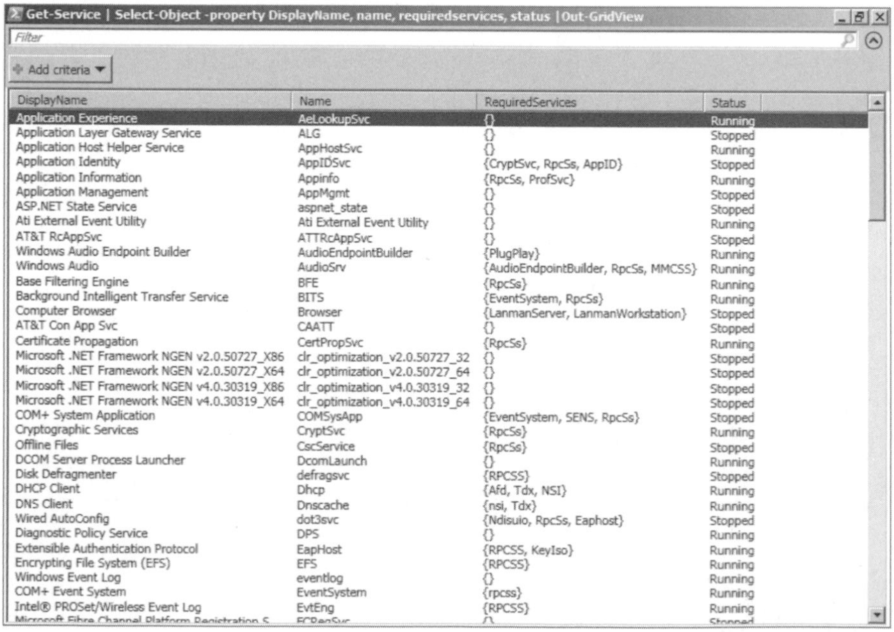

DisplayName	Name	RequiredServices	Status
Application Experience	AeLookupSvc	{}	Running
Application Layer Gateway Service	ALG	{}	Stopped
Application Host Helper Service	AppHostSvc	{}	Running
Application Identity	AppIDSvc	{CryptSvc, RpcSs, AppID}	Stopped
Application Information	Appinfo	{RpcSs, ProfSvc}	Running
Application Management	AppMgmt	{}	Stopped
ASP.NET State Service	aspnet_state	{}	Stopped
Ati External Event Utility	Ati External Event Utility	{}	Running
AT&T RcAppSvc	ATTRcAppSvc	{}	Stopped
Windows Audio Endpoint Builder	AudioEndpointBuilder	{PlugPlay}	Running
Windows Audio	AudioSrv	{AudioEndpointBuilder, RpcSs, MMCSS}	Running
Base Filtering Engine	BFE	{RpcSs}	Running
Background Intelligent Transfer Service	BITS	{EventSystem, RpcSs}	Running
Computer Browser	Browser	{LanmanServer, LanmanWorkstation}	Stopped
AT&T Con App Svc	CAATT	{}	Stopped
Certificate Propagation	CertPropSvc	{RpcSs}	Running
Microsoft .NET Framework NGEN v2.0.50727_X86	clr_optimization_v2.0.50727_32	{}	Stopped
Microsoft .NET Framework NGEN v2.0.50727_X64	clr_optimization_v2.0.50727_64	{}	Stopped
Microsoft .NET Framework NGEN v4.0.30319_X86	clr_optimization_v4.0.30319_32	{}	Stopped
Microsoft .NET Framework NGEN v4.0.30319_X64	clr_optimization_v4.0.30319_64	{}	Stopped
COM+ System Application	COMSysApp	{EventSystem, SENS, RpcSs}	Stopped
Cryptographic Services	CryptSvc	{RpcSs}	Running
Offline Files	CscService	{RpcSs}	Stopped
DCOM Server Process Launcher	DcomLaunch	{}	Running
Disk Defragmenter	defragsvc	{RPCSS}	Stopped
DHCP Client	Dhcp	{Afd, Tdx, NSI}	Running
DNS Client	Dnscache	{nsi, Tdx}	Running
Wired AutoConfig	dot3svc	{Ndisuio, RpcSs, Eaphost}	Stopped
Diagnostic Policy Service	DPS	{}	Running
Extensible Authentication Protocol	EapHost	{RPCSS, KeyIso}	Running
Encrypting File System (EFS)	EFS	{RPCSS}	Running
Windows Event Log	eventlog	{}	Running
COM+ Event System	EventSystem	{rpcss}	Running
Intel® PROSet/Wireless Event Log	EvtEng	{RPCSS}	Running
Microsoft Fibre Channel Platform Registration S...	FCRegSvc	{}	Stopped

You can also send data directly to a printer in your environment. The Out-Printer cmdlet is easy to use. If you want to send the output of any of your cmdlets to the default printer, append | Out-Printer on the end of your command. If you do not specify the printer name, PowerShell uses the default printer on your system. For example, if you want a printout of the services on your server, run the following command:

```
Get-Service | Out-Printer
```

You can also specify the printer by name as well as UNC names for network available printers. Out-Printer also has a built-in alias lp, which you can leverage.

Filter PowerShell Output

Understanding how the Where-Object cmdlet works is key to understanding PowerShell's powerful filtering capabilities. You need to understand a couple of key concepts about the Where-Object cmdlet. First you need to be familiar with the automatic variable $_. This automatic variable refers to the current object on the pipeline. If you want to learn more about automatic variables, use Help about_automatic_variables.

Second, you need to know a little bit about the comparison operators to use with Where-Object. Table 4.5 describes the comparison operators. Each operator begins with a hyphen. You can also learn more about the operators by running the following command:

```
Help about_Comparison_Operators
```

The Where-Object command provides many useful abilities to track down and query different aspects of the PowerShell environment. For example, the following command shows just the stopped services on your system:

```
Get-Service | Where-Object {$_.Status -eq "Stopped"}
```

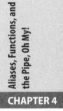

Aliases, Functions, and the Pipe, Oh My!

CHAPTER 4

TABLE 4.5   Comparison operators

Operator	Definition
-eq	Equals, used for finding identical values; you have to know the exact values of the parameters for the objects you are looking at
-ne	Not equals, includes different values; as with -eq, you need to know what you're looking for
-gt	Greater than

(continues)

TABLE 4.5   *(continued)*

Operator	Definition
-ge	Greater than or equal to
-lt	Less than
-le	Less than or equal to
-like	A matching operator that uses the * wildcard operator
-match	A matching operator that uses regular expressions, with the automatic variable $Matches
-contains	Allows you to see whether an identical value exists in a list of values
-notlike	Allows you to identify the value that does not match
-notmatch	Allows you to find the values of a string that do not match your criteria
-notcontains	Allows you to identify the values in a list that do not contain your matching criteria

Figure 4.28 shows an example of the output of this command.

FIGURE 4.28   Where-Object with a pipe operator

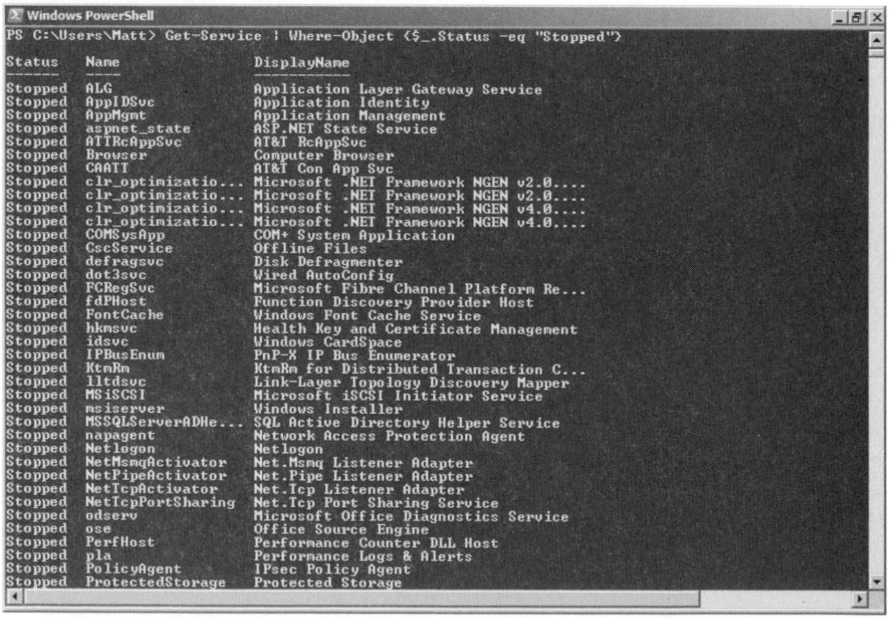

Notice the use of the common variable preceding the name of the property you are looking to query. This is just a simple example of the Where-Object cmdlet.

However, this cmdlet can become powerful and sometimes complex when you are looking for specific objects. You will see a few examples in Chapter 8, when you begin working with Active Directory objects. You will be able to use `Where-Object` to work with the LDAP nature of Active Directory.

EXERCISE 4: CREATE YOUR OWN ALIAS

In this exercise, you will practice working with aliases, functions, and the pipe operator. Write a PowerShell command that does the following:

▶ Lists running services of your server

▶ Determines what services are dependent on those services

▶ Displays service name, status, and dependent services in a table format in a text file

Create either an alias or a function for the command you just created.

Aliases, Functions, and
the Pipe, Oh My!

CHAPTER 4

Creating Your Own Scripts

IN THIS CHAPTER, YOU WILL LEARN TO:

I n the first few chapters, you saw some of the basics of the PowerShell language. You also learned how to tie cmdlets together with the pipe operator. Now, you will be able to take PowerShell to another level by tying in logic. So in this chapter we will take a look at the question: To script or not to script?

You can create scripts for several different purposes, including, but not limited to, populating Active Directory, backing up the servers in your infrastructure, and deploying web applications. In the "Create Your Own Scripts" section, you will see how PowerShell works with scripts and how to create your own basic scripts.

The key to being successful with scripts is in the order of handling them:

> First, find the need.

> Second, write the script.

> Finally, test your script.

Writing scripts is putting together the cmdlets in the proper order, with the necessary logic to do your bidding. Testing is running the script and seeing whether it does the job you want it to do. However, when you run scripts, you may run into security issues; in the "Understand Security and PowerShell Scripts" section of this chapter, you will see how to work with the built-in security of PowerShell and how to run your scripts safely and securely.

When you write scripts, you can use tools you may have used in the past to create scripts, such as Notepad, or you can use new tools such as the Integrated Scripting Environment (ISE). In the "Work with the GUI and the Shell" section of this chapter, you will see how you can leverage this new tool in PowerShell.

Create Your Own Scripts

The question at the beginning of this chapter really is not simply to script or not to script; rather the question really is what to script, what not to script, and how to do it.

Although you can create a script to accomplish virtually anything, you do not need to script everything. When you begin to take a look at what to script, look at really one basic idea: is the task something you are doing repeatedly? If you find yourself doing repetitive tasks, then those are perfect candidates for a PowerShell script. The advantage of working with a PowerShell script is summed up in one word — consistency.

PowerShell is not case sensitive, but it is spelling sensitive, and syntax is always important. You have probably misspelled a word or two or missed a comma, space, or other special character while writing a batch file. Scripts give you a custom, homegrown administrative tool, allowing you to perform tasks quickly and consistently in your environment.

PowerShell Scripting Overview

PowerShell scripts are structured similarly to batch files you may have written in the past. In terms of power and potential, they are closer to VBScript files, which you also may have worked with. You may be thinking then, why don't I just keep using my VBScript files? When you begin to look at PowerShell, you will notice it is tuned to do things that VBScript may not have been able to accomplish. In fact, you can do many things in PowerShell with less work and complexity than with VBScript, and one of the nice constructs of the PowerShell language is that it is similar in nature to VBScript syntactically. This makes converting your VBScript scripts into PowerShell fairly straightforward.

Microsoft has released the VBScript-to-Windows PowerShell Conversion Guide. You can find it here:

```
http://technet.microsoft.com/en-us/library/ee221101.aspx
```

You will want to keep in mind a few things as you get into scripting. First, PowerShell scripts should have the .ps1 extension in their filenames. This makes identifying the scripts very easy. As you may recall from Chapter 3, profiles also have the .ps1 extension. Although they are used as configuration files, they are scripts that are designed to run when you start a PowerShell session. This is similar to when you place programs in your Startup folder in Windows. By default, the .ps1 extension for PowerShell scripts are associated with Notepad. So, you can still use Notepad to create and write your scripts, as you may have done with batch files in the past. Although you can still use Notepad, you should check out the "Work with the GUI and the Shell" section later in this chapter to learn about an alternative way to writing scripts.

Another thing to keep in mind when creating scripts is that your scripts can have parameters. When you use parameters in your scripts, you have more control over those parameters. Parameters are space-delimited when you call your custom script.

Creating Your Own Scripts

CHAPTER 5

For example, if you wanted to write a script and pass the `Server1` and `Server2` parameters into the script, your command would look like this:

```
myscript.ps1 Server1 Server2
```

When you start creating and working with scripts, you may realize that you have several custom scripts you cannot live without on your Windows Server 2008 R2 servers. One of the built-in advantages of PowerShell, as shown in Chapter 3, is modules. Multiple scripts can be grouped into modules, and modules make it easier for you to distribute your custom scripts throughout multiple environments. If you remember this last tidbit, it will make it that much easier to reuse your scripts.

Create a PowerShell Script

So, how do you create a script? It's simple:

1. Open Notepad.

2. Type in these two lines:

```
Get-Process
Get-Service | Where-Object {$_.Status -eq "Running"}
```

3. Select File ➤ Save As, and put a `.ps1` extension on the end of the filename.

Although the script does not do a whole lot — the script returns the running processes and services on your current server — it shows how easily you can create scripts. This script would save the time of typing in the commands.

When you choose to write a script, it really can be that simple — put your cmdlets in order, save the file with a `.ps1` extension, and you are ready to go. However, scripts in PowerShell can be a lot more powerful than the previous example. You can accomplish many things in PowerShell scripts. You can create GUIs with PowerShell, you can create advanced functions you can pass parameters to, and you can write simple scripts to make sure you are in the proper directory on a server to copy files. (Although you will be able to begin writing your own scripts in this section, you should not expect to be able to write a full-fledged GUI in PowerShell. If you want to take writing scripts further, check out the appendixes. Specifically, check out Appendix F and how PowerShell can be used to create a full-fledged GUI.)

The next few sections give you the logical building blocks to help you write more advanced PowerShell scripts. However, this chapter is covering these building blocks at a high level. If you want to get more in depth with custom scripts, take a look at the appendices.

Variables in Scripts

Being able to use variables inside PowerShell scripts is extremely valuable. Windows PowerShell supports strongly typed variables; however, you do not have to declare the variable's type before populating it. This makes it easy when you are writing your scripts. When you use variables in Windows PowerShell, they will always begin with a dollar sign ($), and you set their value with the equal sign (=). You can also use dynamically typed variables; you create one by referencing it or by assigning a value to it.

DYNAMIC AND STATIC VARIABLES IN POWERSHELL

Variables in PowerShell are dynamic in nature, which means they adjust to the way the variable is used for the type of data used in the variable. If the variable needs to be an integer or string value, PowerShell variables are able to adjust to that need on the fly. Although this works for many situations in your scripts, there may be times you want to control the variable and make it a static variable. You can explicitly assign the variable type by bracketing the type. If you wanted to declare a variable to be an integer, it would look like this:

```
$i = [int] "456"
```

You can assign variables to many types by simply preceding the value by the type, surrounded by [ ].

Using variables allows you to quickly assign values and even cmdlets in your scripts with just a little scripting. For example, if you wanted a variable to reference the output of the get-service cmdlet, you would write this:

```
$serve=get-service
```

PowerShell also offers a built-in variable, $args. The $args variable is a default storage location for the parameters passed to your scripts. Suppose you have a PowerShell script called servers.ps1 and you run the following command:

```
servers.ps1 server1 server2 server3
```

The $args variable automatically gets the array (server1, server2, server3). This lets you use loops and perform functions on the parameters as a collection. Also, $args is a zero-based array, so in the previous example, the storage number for each of the variables would be as follows:

```
$args[0] server1
$args[1] server2
$args[2] server3
```

Creating Your Own Scripts

CHAPTER 5

To see how the $args variable works, here is a simple piece of script you can use to display the values and the count of the values in the $args variable:

```
Write-Host "Num Args:" $args.Length;
foreach ($arg in $args)
{
  Write-Host "Arg: $arg";
}
```

If you named this script servers.ps1 and entered the following command, you would get results similar to Figure 5.1:

```
servers.ps1 server1 server2 server3
```

FIGURE 5.1   **$args**

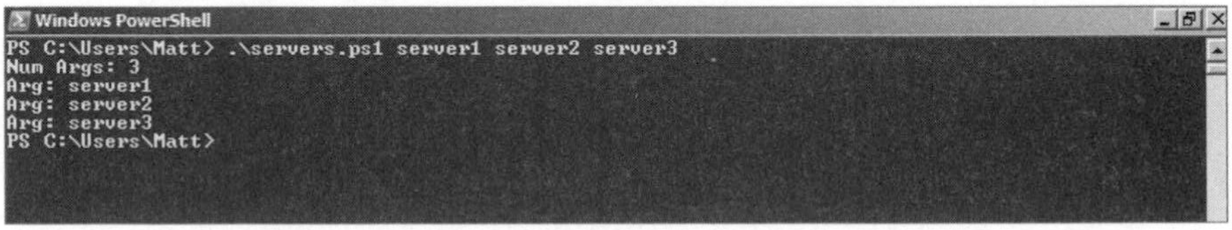

When running these commands, you may run into a security issue with the scripts. The default message from PowerShell you may receive prevents you from running scripts. You can adjust the settings of PowerShell session on your system by adjusting the remote execution policy. The "Understand Security and PowerShell Scripts" section of this chapter shows how to use the scripts securely and avoid the error messages.

Logic in Scripts

You can use operators to increment your loop index so you do not get your PowerShell script stuck in the loop. You can use three types of operators to get you through your loops — arithmetic, assignment, and unary operators, as described in Table 5.1.

One of the fundamental tools you will need when you are creating scripts is the ability to loop. Looping gives you access to more advanced scripting techniques and procedures. Specifically, looping gives you flow control through your PowerShell script. Looping allows you to set conditions and repeat code while those conditions are met.

TABLE 5.1   Common logic operators

Type of operator	Operator	Usage
Arithmetic		
	+	Addition.
	–	Subtraction.
	*	Multiplication.
	/	Division.
	%	Returns the remainder of a division operation or modulus, for example `7%4 = 3`.
Assignment		
	=	Allows you to set the value of a variable to a specific value. If you are going to increment this variable, make sure you know the proper starting number. For example, `$v=10` sets the value to 10.
	+=	Increases the value of the variable by the specified value or will append to the value. For example, if `$v = 10`, then `$v+=5` results in `$v = 15`.
	–=	Decreases the value by a specified value. For example, if `$v = 10`, then `$v-=5` results in `$v = 5`.
	*=	Multiplies the value of the variable by a specific value. For example, if `$v = 10`, then `$v*=5` results in `$v = 50`.
	/=	Divides the value of the variable by a specified value. For example, if `$v = 10`, then `$v/=5` results in `$v = 2`.
	%=	Divides the value of the variable by a specified value and assigns the remainder to the variable. For example, if `$v = 10`, then `$v%=5` results in `$v = 0`.
Unary		
	++	Increments the value of an integer. For example, if `$v = 10`, then `$v++` results in `$v = 11`.
	– –	Decrements the value of an integer variable. For example, if `$v = 10`, then `$v--` results in `$v = 9`.

Table 5.2 describes some of the different types of looping functions in PowerShell.

TABLE 5.2 Common logic statements

Command	Usage	Syntax
If	Evaluates an expression and executes a block of script if the expression is true.	`if (<test1>){<code_block1>}`
If Else	Evaluates an expression and executes one block of code if the expression is true and a different block of code if the expression is false.	`if (<test1>){<code_block1>} else {<code_block2>}`
If Elseif Else	Evaluates an expression and executes one block of code if the expression is true but tests another expression if the first expression is false. Multiple `Elseif` clauses can be included.	`if (<test1>){<code_block1>}` `elseif (<test2> {<code_block2>}` `else {<code_block3>}`
For	Runs a script block based on a conditional test. It will loop for as many iterations you indicate.	`for (<init>; <condition>; <repeat>){<code_block>}`
ForEach	Allows you to perform a set of tasks on each item as your script goes through a collection of items.	`foreach ($<item> in $ <collection>){<code_block>}`
While	Runs a loop with a command block while a certain condition is true. This is great when you want to make sure tasks are being performed until completion. The condition is tested before each iteration of the script.	`while (<condition>) {<code_block>}`
Do-While	A variation of the `While` loop. Runs a command block at least once before checking whether the condition is true and continues to run until the condition is returned as false.	`Do {<code_block>} while (<condition>)`

All the statements in Table 5.2 use code blocks or scripting blocks. These blocks are surrounded by curly braces and contain a series of statements. Scripting blocks allow you specify actions inside your scripts. In this way, you can repeat a sequence of tasks if certain criteria is met.

Sample of a ForEach Loop

Suppose you want to know how your environment variables are configured and want to list them in the format Name: Value. Use the following command:

```
Get-ChildItem -path env: | ForEach-Object ↵
  { Write-Host $_.Name ":" $_.Value }
```

Figure 5.2 shows the results.

FIGURE 5.2   ForEach example

This shows an example of the environment variable provider. Providers are another tool making administration tasks easier to script. You will learn more about providers in Appendix C. Providing for PowerShell.

Sample of Script

Here is an example of a script that displays all the required services for the names of the services you provide to the script:

```
$rq=get-service $args -requiredservices  | Format-Table ↵
-property displayname, status;

foreach ($arg in $args)
{

  Write-Host "For the "$arg "Service the following services↵
  are required:";

  $rq;
}
```

The following statement shows results similar to Figure 5.3.

```
required.ps1 winrm netlogon plugplay
```

FIGURE 5.3   Sample script output

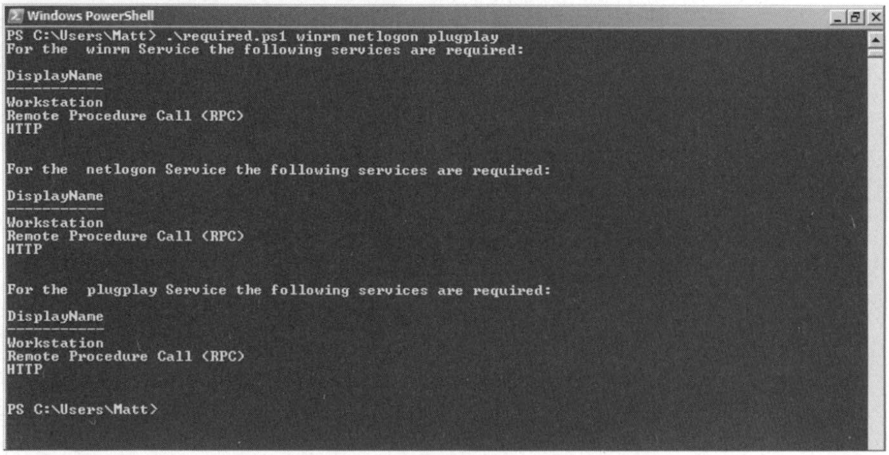

In the script, notice the use of the $args variable to capture all the services listed in the command. PowerShell steps through each item in the $args array, and when the array is empty, the script ends.

Run Your Scripts

How do you run a script? Call the script by name and path. So, if you have a script called myscript.ps1 located in the c:\users directory, use the following command to run the script:

```
c:\users\myscript
```

The .ps1 extension does not need to be included in the command. However, it is acceptable to use it, if you prefer.

When you are already in the directory where the PowerShell script resides, you may be inclined to just type the name of the script file you want to run, the way you may have run batch files or other executables. However, when you try to run the script in the directory, you see a screen similar to Figure 5.4.

FIGURE 5.4   Script error

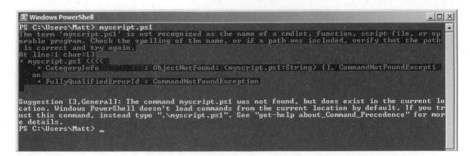

You can avoid this error by referencing the full path or by using the shortcut path notation of . \ to indicate the current directory. For example, from the c:\users directory, you can run the myscript.ps1 script with the following command:

    .\myscript.ps1

Tab autocomplete works with PowerShell script files. So, just like cmdlets, you do not have to always remember how to spell the scripts you want to run. If you use tab auto-complete in the same directory where the script resides, it will put in the . \ for you.

When you run your scripts, you may encounter security issues preventing your scripts from running. To learn more about how to handle security and your scripts, see the "Understand Security and PowerShell Scripts" section in this chapter.

Find Scripts

In Chapter 3, you saw the basics of the help system, as well as some online resources. One of the resources worth mentioning again is the script repository on the Microsoft TechNet website:

http://gallery.technet.microsoft.com/ScriptCenter/en-us/

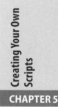

Creating Your Own
Scripts

CHAPTER 5

When you visit the website, you will see it contains scripts for several different languages, including Visual Basic, Python, Kixtart, and — of course — PowerShell. You can filter the scripts on the site to display just the PowerShell scripts (see Figure 5.5).

FIGURE 5.5   Scripting repository for PowerShell

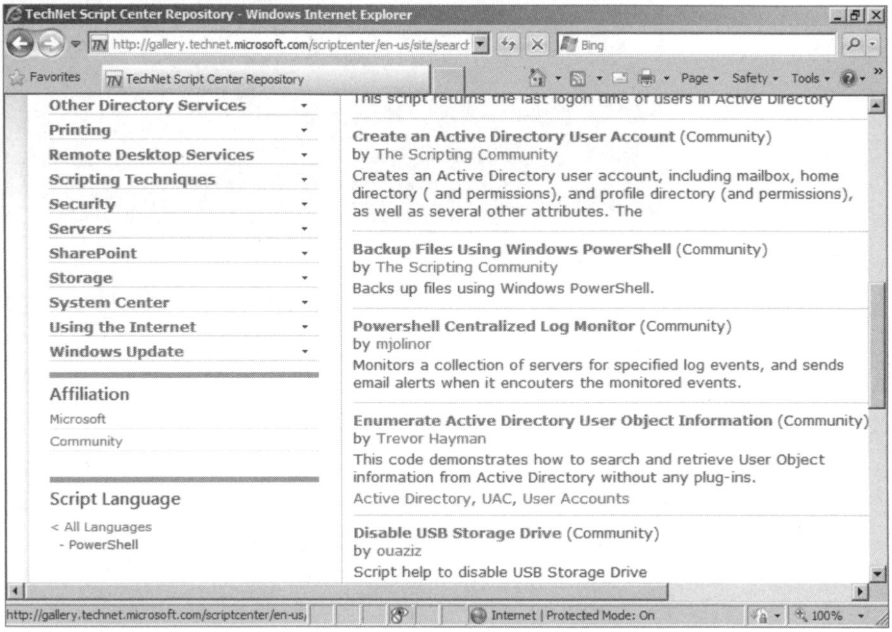

Understand Security and PowerShell Scripts

One key to working with scripts is understanding the security underlying PowerShell. The security is designed to protect you and prevent malicious scripts from running on your system. Not all scripts are bad; however, PowerShell by default thinks so and will prevent scripts from running. You can see the default message from PowerShell in Figure 5.6 when it prevents you from running scripts.

This error message was also mentioned in Chapter 3, when working with profiles. Although profiles are technically configuration files, they do have a .ps1 extension for the file and are treated as scripts. By default, like other scripts, they do not run. In this section, you will see how the scripting policy works and understand how to work with PowerShell to ensure not only that your scripts run but that they run safely and securely.

FIGURE 5.6   Denied access

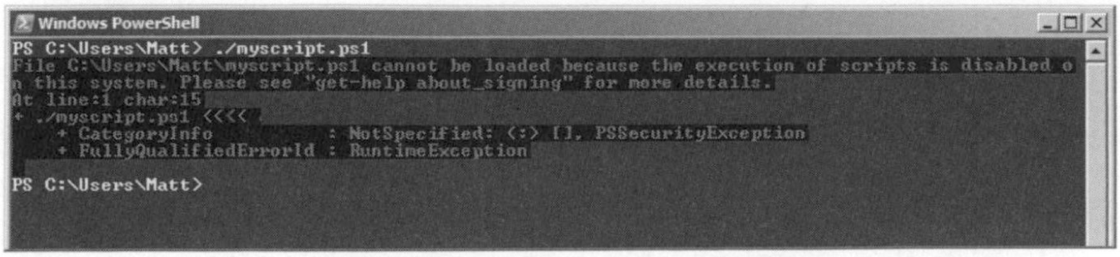

Work with Default Execution Policy of Scripts

By default, PowerShell prevents unsigned scripts from running on your system, because the default execution policy for running scripts on your PowerShell systems is set at the restricted level. There are four types of execution policy for scripts on your system, listed in Table 5.3.

TABLE 5.3   Execution policy settings

Setting	Description
Restricted	This is the default execution policy for PowerShell on your system. It prevents all scripts from running on your system, including profiles and other PowerShell files.
AllSigned	This requires all scripts — local and remote — to be digitally signed by a trusted publisher. If they are signed, then the scripts will run as planned. In the "Understand Digital Signing" section of this chapter, you will get a brief introduction to signing scripts.
RemoteSigned	This allows scripts that are local on your system to run without having to be signed; however, scripts that have been downloaded or are remote still have to be digitally signed before they are allowed to run.
Unrestricted	This allows any script to run on your server. This is not a recommended setting for any scenario other than testing, because this can open the security door on your servers for unwanted and unsecured PowerShell scripts.

Although the Unrestricted execution policy poses a big security risk for your system, it does offer one piece of security. If you download a script file from the Internet, you have to approve it before it is allowed to run on your system. When you run this type of script, you see a message similar to Figure 5.7.

The message lets you determine whether the script should run; by default, the script is not allowed to run. As the administrator of the system you have to take action. You control whether this script is allowed to run. If you choose to not run the script, you see a message similar to Figure 5.8.

Creating Your Own Scripts

CHAPTER 5

FIGURE 5.7   Unrestricted prompt

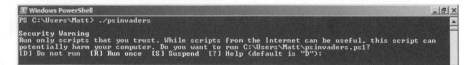

FIGURE 5.8   Unrestricted denied script

Understand the RemoteSigned PowerShell Execution Policy

RemoteSigned is by far the most common execution policy setting on systems running PowerShell. Although this can pose a security risk to your server, it may not be as bad as you think. For the PowerShell script to be local, the script needs to be created on the system on which you want to run the PowerShell script. If you download a script from the Internet, it will be denied if the script is not digitally signed. So, this really gives you control over which scripts are allowed to run on your server. Ideally, it would be great if all of your PowerShell scripts were signed, but sometimes that may not be the most realistic approach.

When you download a file from the Internet, you need to find out what the RemoteSigned execution policy checks to see whether the script can run. If you got the file via a browser or an email client, like Microsoft Outlook, look at the zone identifier stream. This value indicates whether the file will be able to run.

To determine the value, you can also use the zone identifier parameter for the script. You can use Notepad to view the value of the zone identifier parameter to determine whether the script will be considered to be remote and not allowed to execute. For example, to find out the zone identifier for a script called `myscript.ps1`, run the following command in the directory where the script resides (you can see the output in Figure 5.9):

```
notepad myscript.PS1:Zone.Identifier
```

FIGURE 5.9 Zone identifier

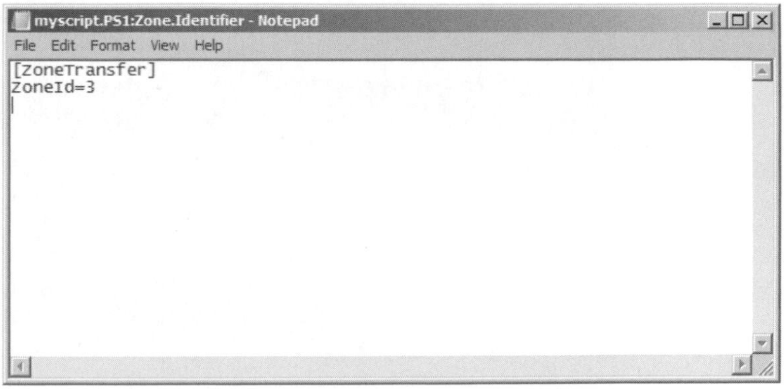

If the value is greater than or equal to 3, the script is considered to be remote and will abide by your policy. After you have reviewed the zone identifier for the script, if you choose to, you can modify the value in Notepad to allow the script to be run. Normally, you would change the value to 2 and save the value; however, the zone identifier can be any of six values:

NoZone	−1
MyComputer	0
Intranet	1
Trusted	2
Internet	3
Untrusted	4

Don't modify the value of the script unless you trust the location or person you got the script from. You don't want to compromise the security of your environment.

Set the PowerShell Execution Policy

When you start working with PowerShell scripts, you need to know how to work with the execution policy for your system. You can change the execution policy either via the PowerShell cmdlet `Set-ExecutionPolicy` or via the registry.

Before you set your policy, determine what the current policy is for your PowerShell environment. To do that, run the following cmdlet:

```
Get-ExecutionPolicy
```

Creating Your Own Scripts

CHAPTER 5

Your results will look similar to Figure 5.10.

FIGURE 5.10   `Get-ExecutionPolicy`

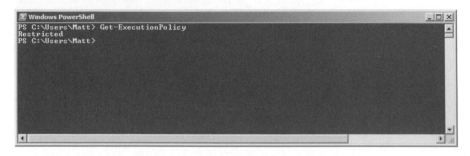

To change the execution policy for your system with PowerShell, use the
`Set-ExecutionPolicy` cmdlet. The first time you try to run the `Set-ExecutionPolicy` cmdlet, you may see a screen and message similar to
Figure 5.11.

FIGURE 5.11   `Denied Set-ExecutionPolicy`

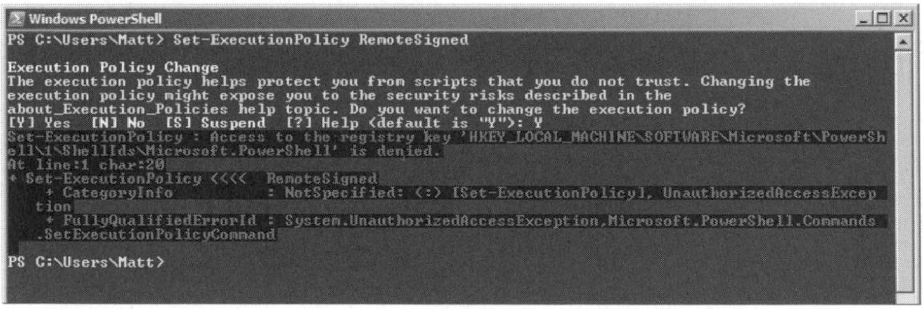

To set the execution policy via PowerShell, load an administrative PowerShell
session. To run a PowerShell session as an administrator, follow these steps:

1. Right-click the PowerShell icon on your taskbar or in your Start menu. If
   you right-click the icon on your taskbar, you will see a screen similar to
   Figure 5.12.

FIGURE 5.12   Taskbar context menu

2. Select Run As Administrator.

3. If you are prompted by User Account Control, click Yes to continue.

When the PowerShell session launches, you will see a screen similar to Figure 5.13. Notice the administrator indicator in the title bar of the PowerShell window.

FIGURE 5.13   PowerShell administrator session

Administrative
PowerShell session

```
Administrator: Windows PowerShell
PS C:\Windows\system32> _
```

Once you are in the administrator PowerShell session, you can then set your execution policy by running the Set-ExecutionPolicy cmdlet. Based on what you want to set your policy to, put in one of the four parameters — Restricted, AllSigned, RemoteSigned, or Unrestricted — after the cmdlet. If you wanted to set your execution policy to RemoteSigned, for example, run the following command:

```
Set-ExecutionPolicy RemoteSigned
```

When you run the cmdlet, you are given a warning and prompted to accept the change. You should see a message similar to Figure 5.14.

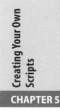

Creating Your Own Scripts

CHAPTER 5

FIGURE 5.14 `Set-ExecutionPolicy` prompt

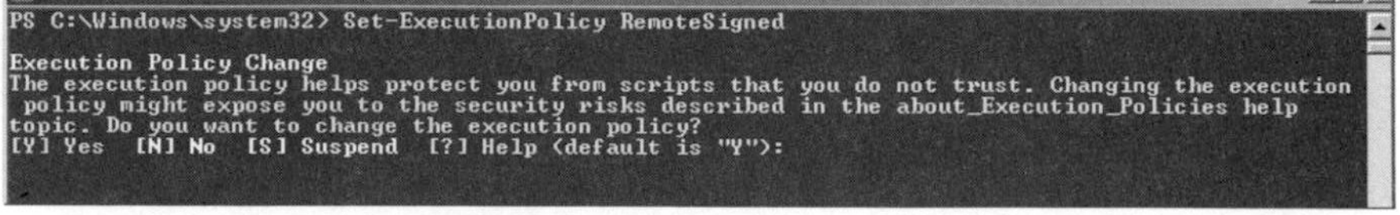

```
Administrator: Windows PowerShell                                    _ 8 x
PS C:\Windows\system32> Set-ExecutionPolicy RemoteSigned

Execution Policy Change
The execution policy helps protect you from scripts that you do not trust. Changing the execution
 policy might expose you to the security risks described in the about_Execution_Policies help
topic. Do you want to change the execution policy?
[Y] Yes  [N] No  [S] Suspend  [?] Help (default is "Y"):
```

To finalize your policy, type **Y** to accept your policy setting. Now you are ready to run the scripts according to your new policy.

Another way to modify the execution policy is by modifying the registry directly. You need to be an administrator of the server to get registry access. The registry key that you need to modify is HKEY_LOCAL_MACHINE\SOFTWARE\Microsoft\ PowerShell\1\ShellIds\Microsoft.PowerShell.

WARNING Make sure you back up your registry and your system prior to modifying the registry. Modifying the registry can cause unwanted errors, including system errors, that may require reinstallation.

1. Click Start.

2. Place your cursor in the Search Programs And Files input box, or click the Run command, depending on your operating system.

3. Type **regedit**, and click OK.

4. In the User Account Control dialog, click Yes.

5. Navigate to HKEY_LOCAL_MACHINE\SOFTWARE\Microsoft\ PowerShell\1\ShellIds\Microsoft.PowerShell.

6. Modify the ExecutionPolicy key with the value you want to set for your PowerShell. As with the Set-Execution cmdlet, use one of the four values: **Restricted**, **AllSigned**, **RemoteSigned** or **Unrestricted**. You can see this entry in Figure 5.15.

FIGURE 5.15   Execution Policy in the registry

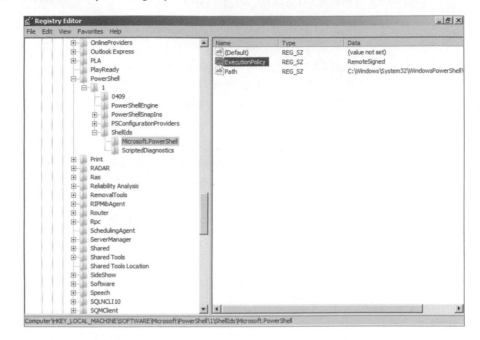

7. When you are finished making your change, close the Registry Editor.

This is a PowerShell book, and you can also modify the registry with PowerShell. You do not really need to run regedit directly. You can also use providers. You will see in Chapter 7 how to work with the registry with PowerShell, and you can find more details on providers in Appendix C.

1. Open PowerShell in administrator mode.

2. Run the following command:

```
Set-ItemProperty -path ↵
HKLM:\SOFTWARE\Microsoft\PowerShell\1\ShellIds↵
\Microsoft.PowerShell -Name "ExecutionPolicy" ↵
-Value "RemoteSigned"
```

Creating Your Own
Scripts

CHAPTER 5

Understand Digital Signing

Digital signing PowerShell scripts lets you ensure the scripts have been validated from a trusted authority or a trusted third party. So even though it can provide an additional layer of agitation to go through the process of creating or finding digitally signed scripts, it is worth the protection the signed scripts provide. At the end of the day, it is worth your time to have your scripts digitally signed and, more importantly, use scripts that are digitally signed in your environment.

Digital signing requires a Class III Authenticode Code-Signing Certificate, which you can get in a variety of ways. You need a certificate authority (CA) to get the certificates needed for digitally signing your PowerShell scripts. You can use an internal CA, a commercial CA (such as VeriSign or Thawte), or even a self-signed certificate. If you use a self-signed certificate, it is valid only for the computer you create the certificate on.

Although understanding digital certificates is important, you will need to determine how you want to accomplish this in your environment. Installing your own CA or getting a third party can lead you down a complex process in order to make sure your certificates are properly signed. If you are going to sign your own PowerShell scripts and want to learn more about the process, you will find the built-in help extremely useful. To access the signing help, run this command:

```
help about_signing
```

Work with the GUI and the Shell

Notepad is the down-and-dirty, quick-and-easy tool to create scripts, but you may not want to use Notepad all the time. PowerShell 2.0 introduces a new GUI to work with scripts called the Integrated Scripting Environment (ISE).

ISE is a great tool providing you with a much-needed upgrade to Notepad when you want to work with scripts. In this section, you will learn how to work with the ISE and how to use it to troubleshoot and work with your scripts.

Understand What the ISE Is

In Chapter 2, you saw how to install the ISE on a Windows Server 2008 R2 system. The server platform is the only instance where you may want to install the ISE. The ISE is already installed on Windows 7; it is just a matter of opening the tool. In either Windows Server 2008 R2 or Windows 7, you can find the tool by selecting Start ➤ Accessories ➤ Windows PowerShell.

You can see what the ISE looks like in Figure 5.16.

FIGURE 5.16   The ISE

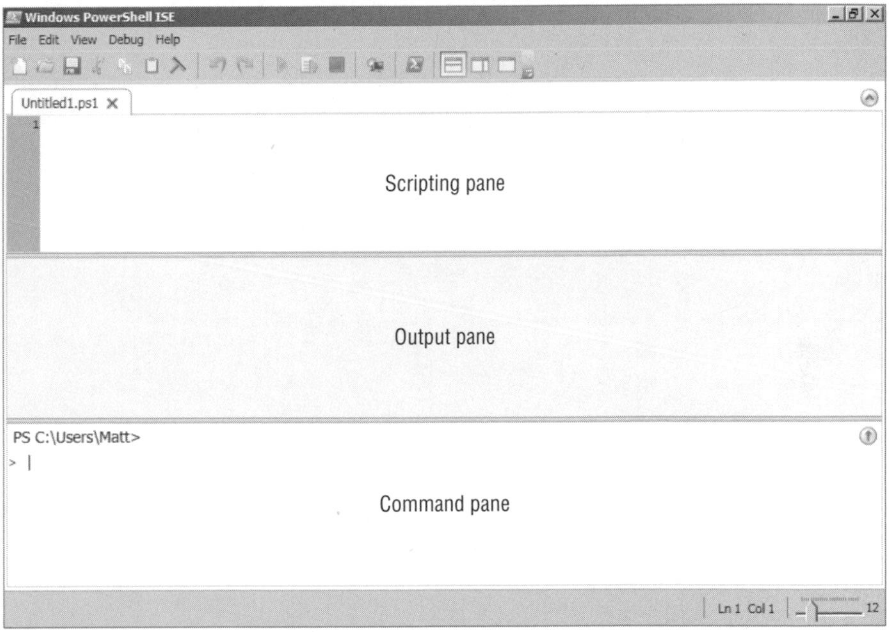

As you can see, the ISE provides a GUI that has three sections: the scripting pane, the output pane, and the command pane. The command pane is similar to the PowerShell command prompt you are already familiar with. The only difference is that the output from commands entered in the command pane appear in the output pane.

The output pane not only displays the results of your PowerShell commands but also displays the results of your PowerShell scripts as you run them in the ISE. Another added benefit to the output pane is directly attributed to the GUI nature of the tool. You can easily copy and paste using your mouse or keyboard shortcuts. The output window is also scrollable, so you do not have to worry about having your output scroll off the screen.

A convenient feature of the ISE is that you can quickly clear the output screen without having to type in CLS. To clear the output pane, use the Clear Output Pane button (looks like a squeegee).

Creating Your Own Scripts

CHAPTER 5

The third pane, and the most useful in the ISE tool, is the scripting pane. This is where the true power of the ISE lies, and really this is what the ISE was built for. This is where the ISE provides a true PowerShell script editor for your scripts. Although Notepad is good in a pinch, you should consider using the ISE whenever possible.

Also unique to the ISE, you can have multiple (up to eight) independent PowerShell sessions running in the same ISE window. Each tab has its own environment, so you can work with several PowerShell sessions at the same time. Figure 5.17 shows the ISE with multiple tabs loaded.

FIGURE 5.17   Multiple sessions in the ISE

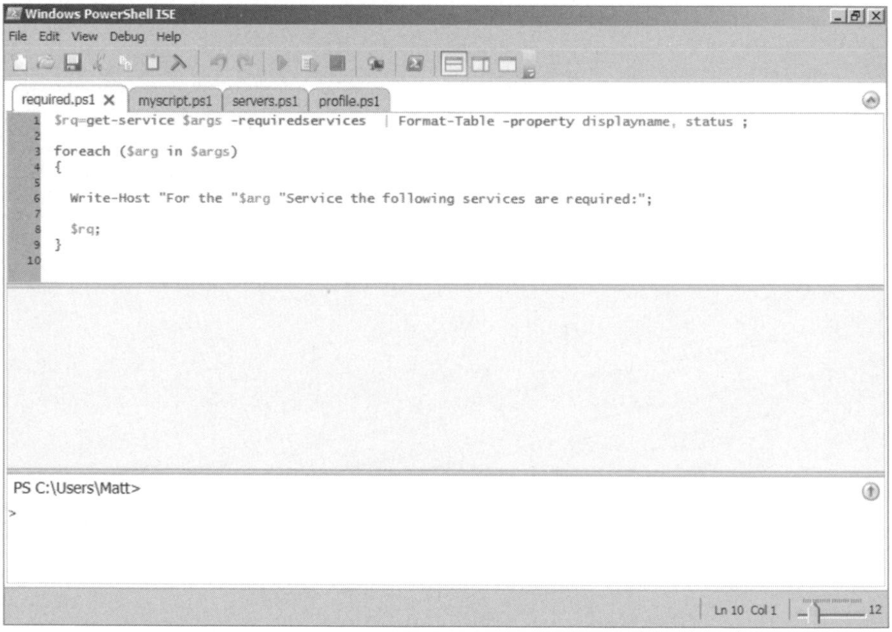

Another feature of the ISE is the context-sensitive help built into the tool. As you saw in Chapter 3, learning how to find answers and examples with the built-in help system is key to learning PowerShell. The ISE provides another way to access the help system. To see what this can do, perform the following steps:

1. Type the following in the command pane:

   ```
   Get-Service
   ```

2. Press the F1 key. You will see a screen similar to Figure 5.18.

FIGURE 5.18   ISE context-sensitive help

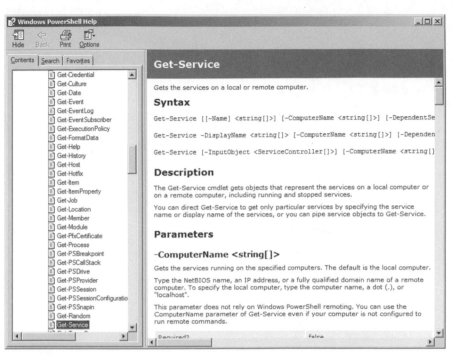

Use the ISE with Scripts

When you use the ISE to work with PowerShell scripts, you get some much-needed functionality not provided by Notepad such as some developer-like functions. Although the tool is not as robust as Microsoft Visual Studio, it does a great job with PowerShell scripts.

Although it does not include IntelliSense, the ISE shares the same keyboard short-cuts as Visual Studio. The keyboard shortcuts for running a program, working with breakpoints, and doing general debugging are the same commands as Visual Studio. So if you are a developer who thrives with keyboard shortcuts, this point of consistency should make you happy.

In the script pane, you can both write and edit your scripts. When you load a script into the ISE, you see color coding and line numbering, making the code much eas-ier to read and work with. The numbering alone is worth its weight in gold. If you have ever had to troubleshoot a long script in Notepad and all you had to go on was that there was an error in line 653 of your script, you know the pain. However, going

Creating Your Own Scripts

CHAPTER 5

to line 653 is as simple as pressing Ctrl+G while in the script pane and entering the line number. This is an example of a Visual Studio keyboard shortcut in ISE.

To load a script into the ISE, select File ➤ Open; then browse to your script, and click OK. Figure 5.19 shows the ISE with a script loaded.

FIGURE 5.19   ISE with a script

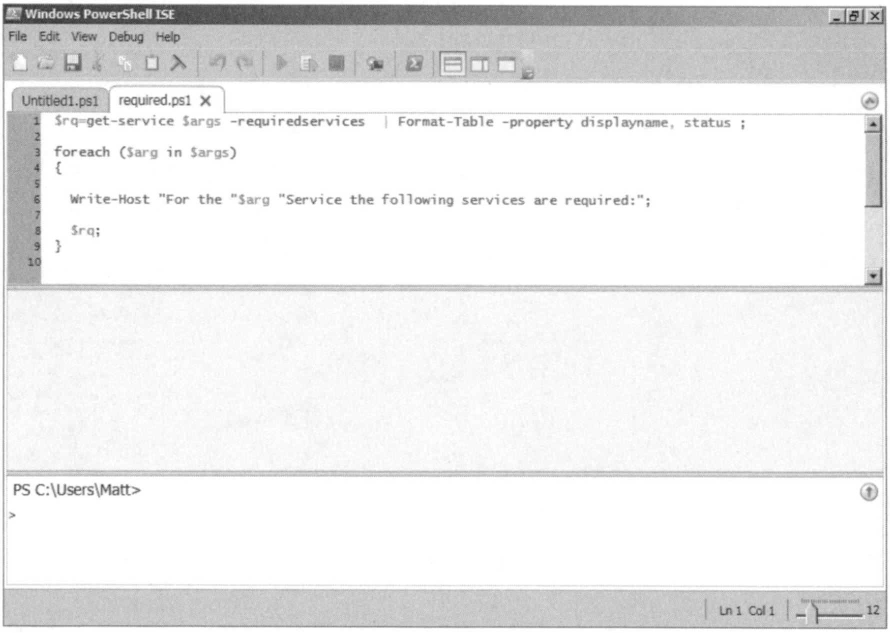

To run a script in the ISE, click the green Play button on the toolbar or press F5.

The ISE has a built-in debugger. This tool provides all the necessary basics, including breakpoints, for debugging commands, functions, and scripts for the PowerShell scripts you work with. Breakpoints allow you to not only step through your code but also check the values of variables as your script executes.

The key to debugging with breakpoints is knowing where you want your script to pause. Follow these steps to set and use a breakpoint in your script:

1. Place your cursor in the line you want to set the breakpoint on.

2. Select Debug ➢ Toggle Breakpoint, or press F9. This highlights the selected line, as shown in Figure 5.20.

FIGURE 5.20   Breakpoint in ISE

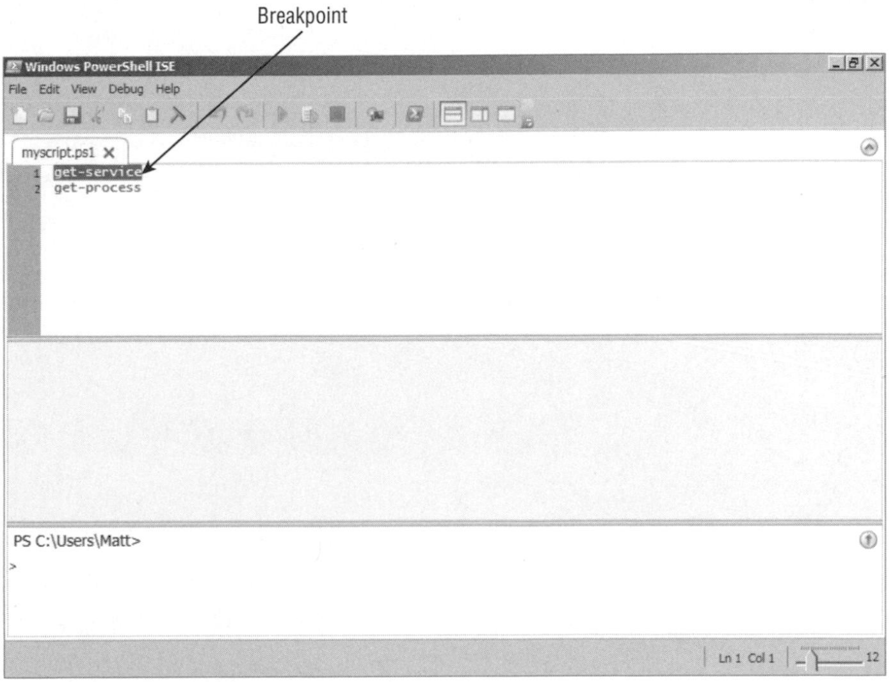

Breakpoint

[Screenshot of Windows PowerShell ISE]

File Edit View Debug Help

myscript.ps1 X

```
1  get-service
2  get-process
```

PS C:\Users\Matt>
>

Ln 1 Col 1   12

3. After you set your breakpoint, run your script by either pressing F5 or clicking the green Play button on your toolbar.

4. When the ISE hits your breakpoint, you see a screen similar to Figure 5.21. Notice also in your PowerShell output and command windows that the [DBG] indicator appears to notify you that the script is paused. Your script is marked as read-only while it is executing.

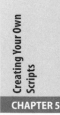

Creating Your Own
Scripts

CHAPTER 5

FIGURE 5.21   Breakpoint

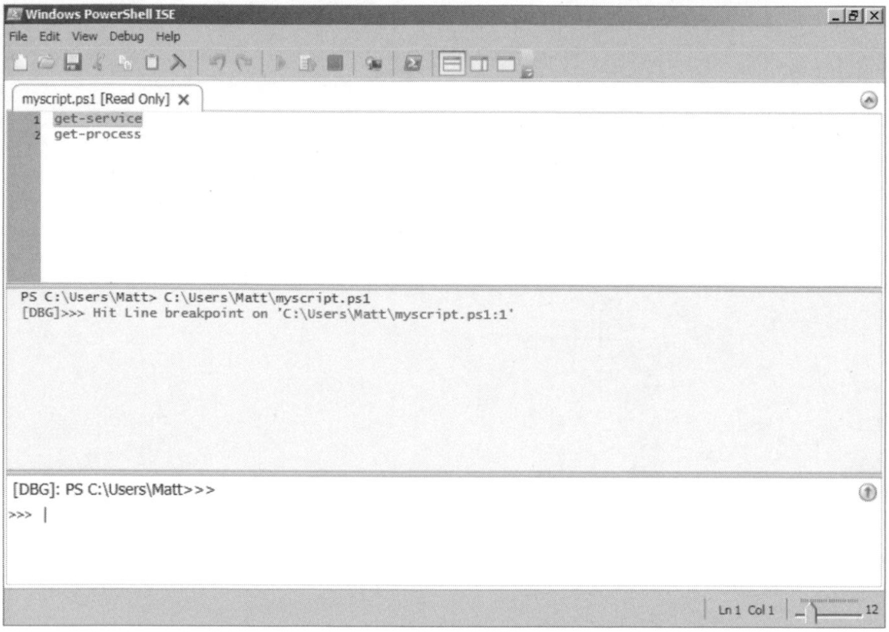

5. You have a few choices while your script is paused. You can do the following:

Step Into   When you select Step Into, you can walk your script, going line by line. If your script calls another procedure, you can step through the other procedure one line at a time.

Step Out   When you are stepping line by line through your script and you step into a secondary procedure called by your initial script, you can use Step Out to complete the procedure you are currently in and take you to the line after the one in your original script that called the second procedure.

Step Over   When you are stepping line by line through your script and you hit a line that runs another procedure in your script, you can select Step Over, which runs through the called procedure completely and returns you to the next line in your script paused.

Run/Continue   This runs your script up until completion or the next checkpoint.

Stop Debugger   This stops the execution of your script at the current point of execution. This does not complete your script.

Display Call Stack   This is an extremely valuable function that displays the value of your variables and arguments at that point in time in your script.

6. Once you are done debugging your script, you can stop your script or run it to completion.

Display the Call Stack with Scripts Requiring Parameters

When you are working with scripts requiring parameters to be entered into the script to execute properly, you have to run the script with the breakpoints slightly differently.

1. Set the breakpoints in your script.

2. Save the script.

3. Execute the script via the command pane in the ISE as if you are running the script normally. You see a screen similar to Figure 5.22 before running your script.

FIGURE 5.22   ISE script with parameters

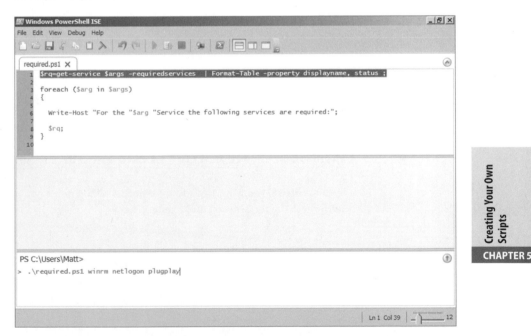

4. If you want to see the values of your arguments for the script, then select Debug ➢ Display Call Stack. Your screen looks similar to Figure 5.23.

FIGURE 5.23   ISE display call stack

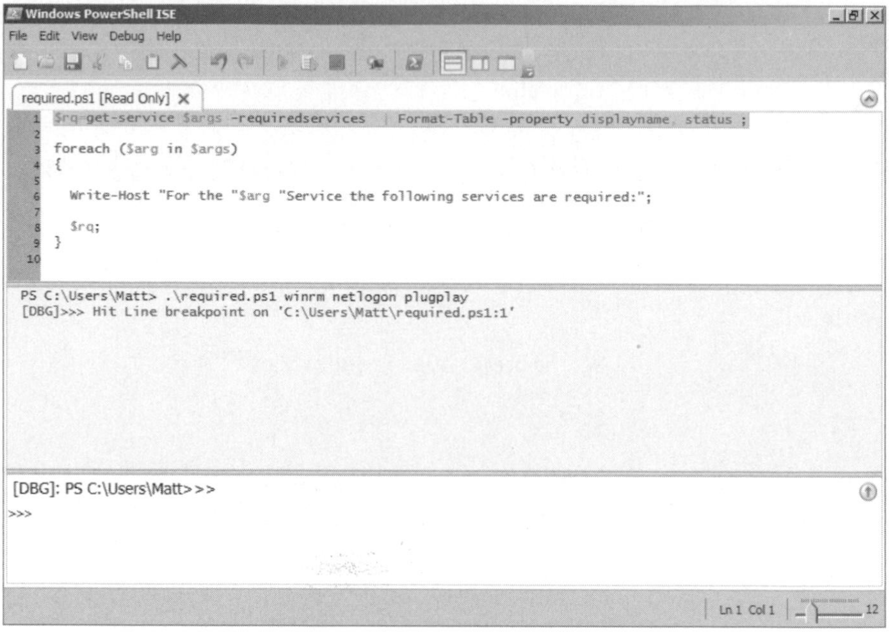

5. Finish running or stepping through your script.

As you have seen in this section, the ISE provides a powerful and useful tool for your PowerShell tool belt, especially when you are working with scripts. Learn to use the tool, and you will soon have your scripts running smoothly.

EXERCISE 5: CREATE A SCRIPT TO FIND STARTUP PROGRAMS

In this exercise, you will write a script that lists all the processes that run on startup. Hint: check the registry `Run` and `RunOnce` keys.

Remoting with PowerShell 2.0

IN THIS CHAPTER, YOU WILL LEARN TO:

owerShell 2.0 lets you run PowerShell commands on remote Windows Server 2008 R2 servers and other systems that have PowerShell 2.0 installed. PowerShell remoting expands the horizons of PowerShell; with it, you can manage your entire Microsoft environment.

Prior to PowerShell 2.0, you may have run remote commands on other systems by using Remote Desktop Connection, Terminal Services, or some other remote control. Although you can still use these tools, they are not the most efficient. Using the built-in remoting capabilities provides a faster and more efficient way to work with PowerShell on remote systems.

PowerShell provides the ability not only to bring up a remote PowerShell session but also to run commands on your local server to gain access on remote servers. For example, you can run a PowerShell command that would give you the running services or processes, you can walk the registry, and you can run any other PowerShell commands you want on your current servers and also any other server you want to know about.

In this chapter, you will learn how to enable PowerShell remoting on your PowerShell 2.0 systems, as well as become familiar with the internal components that are required to allow remoting. You will also see how to run PowerShell commands on remote servers, via either a remote session or remote commands.

Configure PowerShell Remoting

Remoting is disabled by default. This is by design to ensure the security of your environment. You need to enable remoting not only on the systems you want to manage but also on the systems from which you will run the PowerShell commands.

By enabling PowerShell remoting, you are configuring the system and firewall to handle the remote PowerShell requests. In this section, you will take a look at the components that work on your infrastructure.

Learn the Requirements

Before you enable PowerShell remoting in your infrastructure, you should understand the components you need for your environment. Specifically, you need two components in addition to PowerShell 2.0 to enable remoting on your systems:

► .NET Framework 2.0 or later

► Windows Remote Management (WinRM) 2.0

WinRM is the main component used by PowerShell remoting for your PowerShell 2.0 systems. WinRM 2.0 is part of Windows 7 and Windows Server 2008 R2. However, you need to download this if you are working with other operating systems. This is available via the integrated installation package in the Windows Management Framework, as mentioned in Chapter 2. WinRM is installed as a service. Although the service is installed, it is not enabled by default.

WinRM is a remote management service and is Microsoft's implementation of the WS-Management protocol. The WS-Management protocol allows remote systems to communicate; it's designed to help heterogeneous systems—both hardware and software—perform commands remotely in your infrastructure.

This type of communication used to be handled by protocols like Remote Procedure Call (RPC). WinRM is an easy-to-configure, standards-based protocol that works seamlessly with your firewalls and your infrastructure's security.

In addition to having WinRM on the systems you want to manage with PowerShell, you also need to make sure you have the proper permissions to run the remote commands. You need to be a member of the local administrators group on the remote computer to establish a connection and be able to run the commands remotely on other systems. You can also provide the administrative credentials if you are not currently logged on as an administrative account.

A WORD ON NETWORK LOCATION

In operating systems such as Windows Server 2008 R2 and Windows 7, you have the choice of three network locations: domain, private, or public. The network location primarily helps determine the proper security level for your systems on your network. It also determines how the firewall is configured. You can change your network location in the Network and Sharing Center.

For remoting to be configured on your system, the current network location has to be domain or private. If you are on a public network location, you will not be able to configure PowerShell remoting, because when you are in a public location, the `Enable-PSRemoting` function (see the "Enable Remoting for PowerShell 2.0" section in this chapter) is unable to create the firewall exception for WinRM. You will get an error similar to Figure 6.1.

Remoting with PowerShell 2.0

CHAPTER 6

FIGURE 6.1   Network location error

Enable PowerShell Remoting

Enabling PowerShell remoting is as simple as using one command, regardless of the operating system. To enable PowerShell remoting, run the following function from an administrative PowerShell session:

```
Enable-PSRemoting
```

The function actually runs the Set-WSManQuickConfig cmdlet; it takes care of all the automated processes to run WinRM and PowerShell remote commands. If you try running this command from a regular, nonadministrative PowerShell session, you will see an error similar to Figure 6.2.

FIGURE 6.2   Access denied for **Enable-PSRemoting**

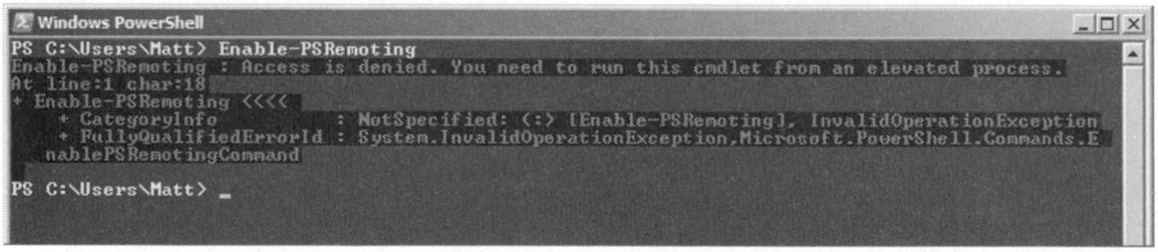

If you see this error, execute an administrative PowerShell session. After you load a PowerShell session as an administrator, you can then enable PowerShell remoting with the Enable-PSRemoting command. After you run Enable-PSRemoting, you will see a screen similar to Figure 6.3.

FIGURE 6.3 Enable-PSRemoting

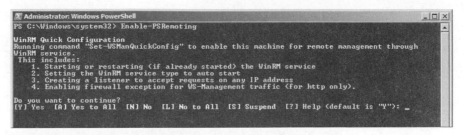

Type **Y** to continue the PowerShell remoting configuration of the WinRM service. You see a screen similar to Figure 6.4.

FIGURE 6.4 Confirmation of PowerShell remoting

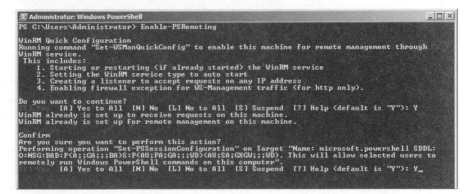

Type **Y** to confirm the configuration of PowerShell remoting, and you are returned to your PowerShell command prompt.

Instead of typing **Y** to verify the configuration of your systems, you can also type **A** (yes to all), after which the Enable-PSRemoting function runs to completion. Alternatively, if you do not want to see the prompts for confirmation in the PowerShell session, you can run the following command:

```
Enable-PSRemoting -Force
```

By running Enable-PSRemoting with the -Force switch, you suppress the confirmations during PowerShell remoting configuration.

Remoting with PowerShell 2.0

CHAPTER 6

XP Mode

As you saw in Chapter 2, you can install PowerShell on the XP mode virtual machine on a Windows 7 machine. You can also enable remoting on the XP mode system with the Enable-PSRemoting function. However, when you first run the function, you will see a screen and error similar to Figure 6.5.

FIGURE 6.5   XP mode Enable-PSRemoting error

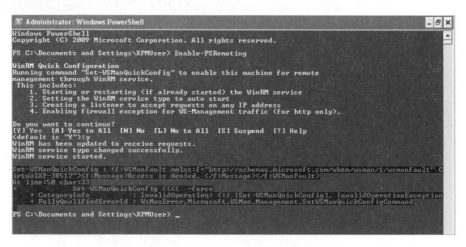

The error indicates the default security parameter in XP mode and how it handles authentication for network logons when the system is using a local account. The default setting maps all the users to a local guest account, and it does not have enough permissions to change the setting. You can change the setting so the account used for network logons is not mapped to the guest account but mapped to the actual authenticated account. To change the setting in XP Mode, modify the local computer policy setting by using the following procedure:

1. On the XP mode virtual machine, select Start ➢ Run.

2. Type **gpedit.msc**, and press Enter. This loads the Group Policy Editor for the local XP mode system.

3. Click the Computer Configuration container, and expand the tree.

4. Navigate to Windows Settings ➢ Security Settings ➢ Local Policies ➢ Security Options.

5. Find Network Access: Sharing And Security Model For Local Accounts. Double-click the setting to modify the current value.

6. Change the value to Classic – Local Users Authenticate As Themselves. Your screen will look similar to Figure 6.6.

FIGURE 6.6   XP mode Group Policy setting

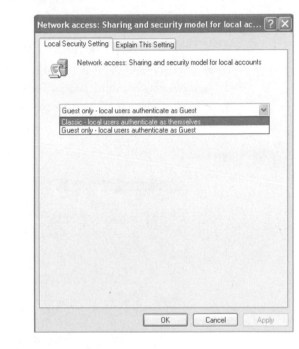

7. Click OK.

8. Close the Group Policy Editor.

After you have modified the setting, you can return to the PowerShell session in XP mode and run the Enable-PSRemoting function, which should now run without error.

Getting to Know Enable-PSRemoting

When you run the Enable-PSRemoting function, you may notice that it tells you it is going to do four main things:

► Start or restart (if already started) the WinRM service

► Set the WinRM service type to autostart

Remoting with
PowerShell 2.0

CHAPTER 6

- ▶ Create a listener to accept requests on any IP address

- ▶ Enable firewall exception for WS-Management traffic (for HTTP only)

`Enable-PSRemoting` performs several tasks. For example, the `Enable-PSRemoting` function runs the `Set-WSManQuickConfig` cmdlet. The `Set-WSManQuickConfig` cmdlet performs several vital configurations on your system:

- ▶ Starts up the WinRM service and sets the service startup type to Automatic.

- ▶ Creates a listener to listen for and accept requests on an IP address.

- ▶ Enables a firewall exception for Windows Remote Management via WS-Management communications. The default port is TCP 5985, and you can see an example of the firewall rule from a Windows Server 2008 R2 in Figure 6.7.

FIGURE 6.7   WinRM firewall port

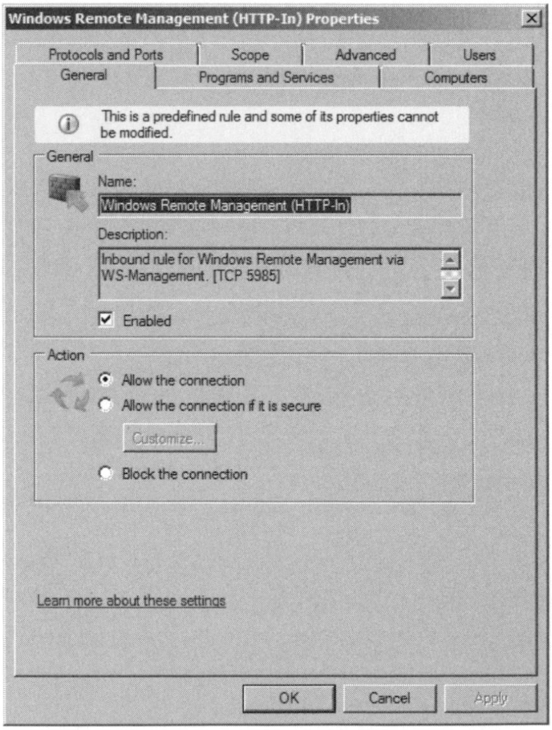

- ▶ Enables all the registered PowerShell session configurations to receive instructions from remote computers.

► Registers the `Microsoft.PowerShell` session configuration (unless it has already been registered).

► Registers the `Microsoft.PowerShell32` session configuration on 64-bit systems (unless it has already been registered).

► Removes the Deny Everyone setting from the security descriptor for all registered session configurations.

► Restarts the WinRM service to finalize the configurations and settings.

Disable PowerShell Remoting

If you no longer want to have PowerShell remoting enabled on your systems, you can run another function to disable remoting:

```
Disable-PSRemoting
```

However, when you run the command, you will see a screen similar to Figure 6.8.

FIGURE 6.8 `Disable-PSRemoting`

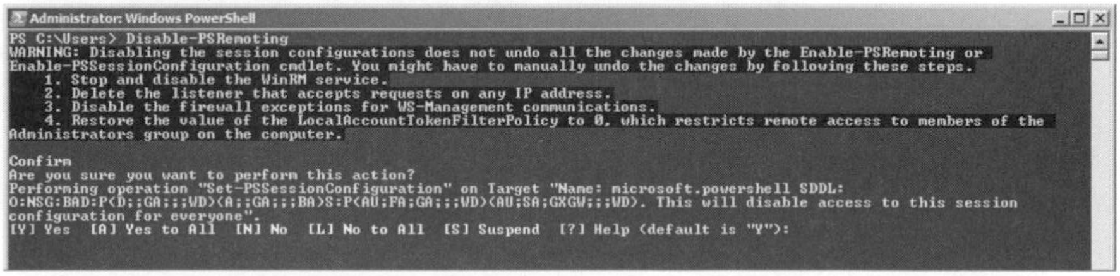

Although this function effectively disables remoting for the server, it does not undo all the changes that `Enable-PSRemoting` makes. As the warning note states, you may still have to do the following:

► Delete the WinRM listener

► Stop and disable the Windows Remote Management service

► Remove the firewall exception for WinRM

► Restore the value of the `LocalAccountTokenFilterPolicy` to 0 in the registry

To finish undoing all the changes that were performed by `Enable-PSRemoting`, perform the following procedures, which will help you complete the process.

However, before you complete them, make sure you do not have other applications running on your system that require the settings you will be disabling.

Delete the WinRM Listener

1. Open a command prompt window by selecting Start ➤ Command Prompt.

2. You need the address of the listener to delete. To see all the listeners, use the following command to get the address:

   ```
   winrm enumerate winrm/config/listener
   ```

You will see a screen similar to Figure 6.9.

FIGURE 6.9   WinRM listeners

3. Write down the address for the listener that has `Port=5985` and `Transport=HTTP`. In Figure 6.10, the address is an `*`.

4. To delete the listener, enter the following command, placing your address in the italicized address parameter:

   ```
   winrm delete winrm/config/Listener?Address= ↵
   Address+Transport=HTTP
   ```

5. Press Enter to delete the listener and close your session.

Stop and Disable the Windows Remote Management Service

1. On the system, open the Services control panel by selecting Start ➢ All Programs ➢ Administrative Tools ➢ Services.

2. In the Services control panel, scroll down to the Windows Remote Management (WS-Management) service.

3. Right-click the service and select Properties, or double-click the service. You will see a screen similar to Figure 6.10.

FIGURE 6.10   WinRM service

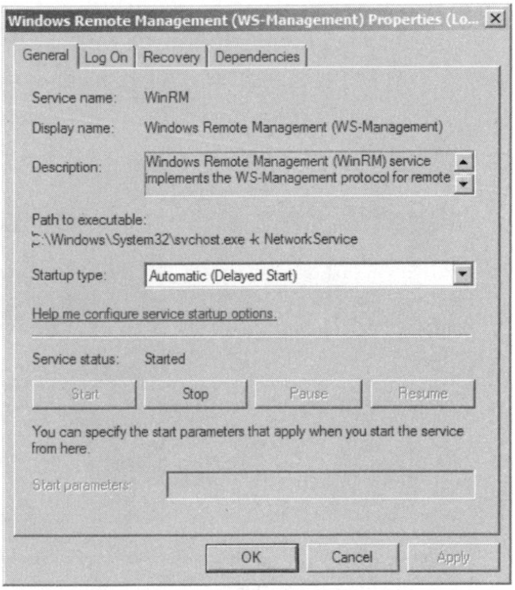

4. Click Stop to stop the service.

5. Click the Startup Type drop-down list, and select Disabled.

6. Click OK.

7. Close the Services control panel.

As an alternative, you can also use PowerShell to stop and disable the service with the following cmdlets:

```
Stop-Service WinRM
Set-Service WinRM -StartupType Disabled
```

Disable the Firewall Exception for WinRM

1. Open the Windows Firewall with Advanced Security program by selecting Start ➢ All Programs ➢ Administrative Tools ➢ Windows Firewall With Advanced Security.

2. Click Inbound Rules.

3. Scroll down the list of the rules to the Windows Remote Management (HTTP-In) rule, and select it. Your screen will look like Figure 6.11.

FIGURE 6.11   Disabling the WinRM firewall exception

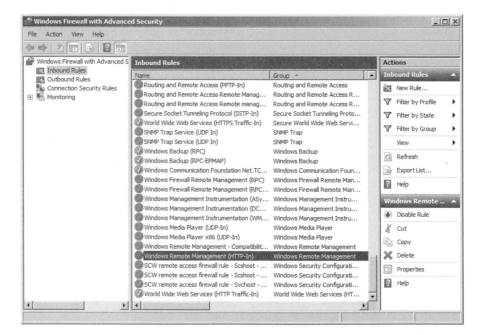

4. With the rule highlighted, click Disable Rule in the action pane on the right, or right-click the rule and select Disable Rule.

5. Close the Windows Firewall with Advanced Security program.

Restore the Value of the LocalAccountTokenFilterPolicy to 0

You may find this setting in client operating systems like Windows 7. You may not see this registry key when you look in your local registry.

> **WARNING**   Be very careful whenever you are modifying the registry; if you modify the registry incorrectly, with unwanted results, you may have to reinstall your system.

1. Select Start ➢ Run. Type **regedit.exe**, and press Enter to start the Registry Editor.

2. If prompted with a User Account Control dialog box, click Yes to continue.

3. Navigate to the following location in the registry: HKEY_LOCAL_MACHINE\ SOFTWARE\Microsoft\Windows\CurrentVersion\Policies\System.

4. Find the LocalAccountTokenFilterPolicy key. If you do not see the registry key, close the Registry Editor.

5. Double-click the LocalAccountTokenFilterPolicy key, and change the value to **0**. Your screen will look like Figure 6.12.

FIGURE 6.12   LocalAccountTokenFilterPolicy

legalnoticecaption	REG_SZ	
legalnoticetext	REG_SZ	
LocalAccountTokenFilterPolicy	REG_DWORD	0x00000001 (1)
PromptOnSecureDesktop	REG_DWORD	0x00000001 (1)
scforceoption	REG_DWORD	0x00000000 (0)
shutdownwithoutlogon	REG_DWORD	0x00000001 (1)
undockwithoutlogon	REG_DWORD	0x00000001 (1)
ValidateAdminCodeSignatures	REG_DWORD	0x00000000 (0)

Edit DWORD (32-bit) Value

Value name:

LocalAccountTokenFilterPolicy

Value data: Base

0   ◉ Hexadecimal
                            ○ Decimal

OK   Cancel

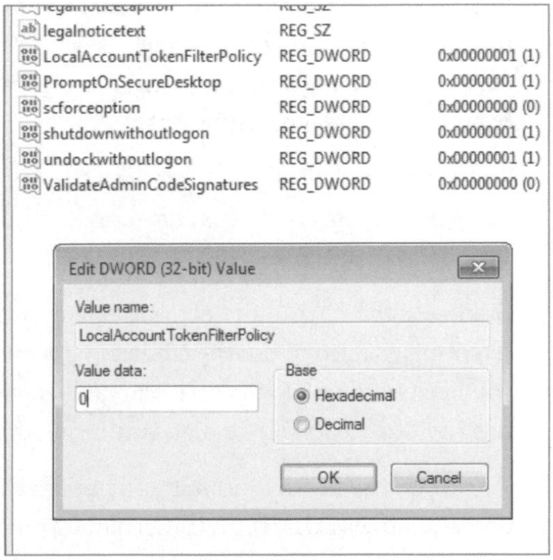

6. Click OK.

7. Close the Registry Editor.

Remoting with
PowerShell 2.0

CHAPTER 6

Again, since this is a PowerShell book, you can also run the following command to change the value of the `LocalAccountTokenFilterPolicy` key:

```
Set-ItemProperty -path ↵
HKLM:\SOFTWARE\Microsoft\Windows\CurrentVersion ↵
\Policies\System -Name "LocalAccountTokenFilterPolicy" ↵
-Value "0"
```

Run Commands on Remote Systems

After you enable remoting on your Windows Server 2008 R2 and other PowerShell 2.0 systems, you can use this administrative tool. With PowerShell 2.0 remoting, you can begin to work with remote servers in two ways. First, you can run commands on your local server that pull data from the remote servers you place in the PowerShell command by using the `invoke-command` cmdlet. Second, you can start a PowerShell session on your local administrative system. The session allows you to have an interactive PowerShell session on the remote system.

In addition to enabling the remote capabilities of PowerShell, several cmdlets do not require remoting to be enabled to be effective. Some cmdlets have the `ComputerName` parameter. If a cmdlet has this parameter, you may not need to have PowerShell remoting enabled for it to work. Some of the more common administrative cmdlets, such as `Get-Service`, `Get-Process`, and `Get-Eventlog`, support the `ComputerName` parameter and therefore work without having PowerShell remoting enabled.

To find a list of all the cmdlets with the `ComputerName` parameter, you can run `Get-Help * -parameter ComputerName`. The results will be similar to Figure 6.13.

Even with the `ComputerName` parameter in a cmdlet, you still may need to have remoting enabled to use the cmdlet in a remote fashion. If you are not sure whether you need remoting for a particular cmdlet, you can use the `Get-Help` cmdlet. For the `Invoke-Command` cmdlet, your results will look similar to Figure 6.14.

When you use the `ComputerName` parameter, you can use either the fully qualified domain name (FQDN), NetBIOS name, or IP address of the system or systems you are going to be working with.

FIGURE 6.13 Cmdlets with the `ComputerName` parameter

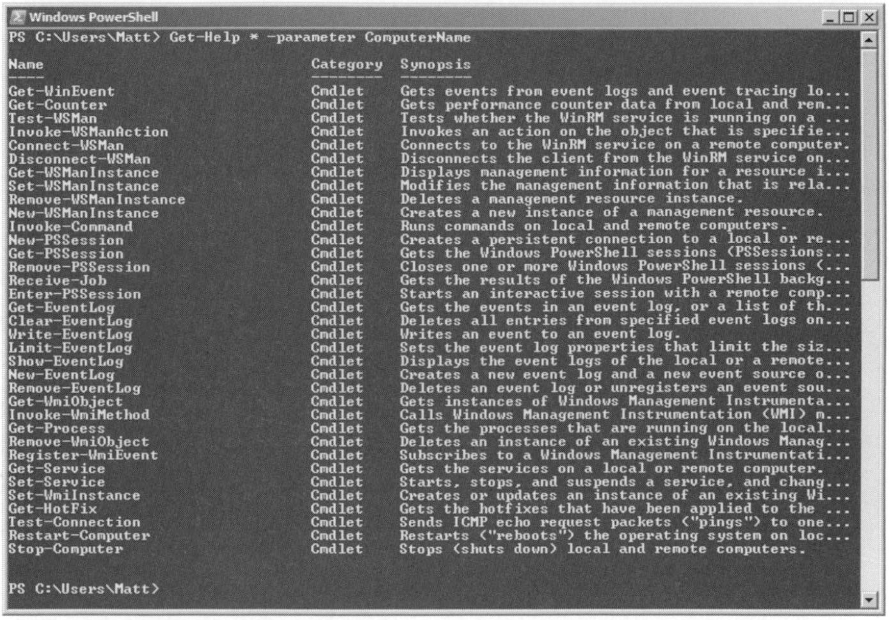

```
PS C:\Users\Matt> Get-Help * -parameter ComputerName

Name                      Category  Synopsis
----                      --------  --------
Get-WinEvent              Cmdlet    Gets events from event logs and event tracing lo...
Get-Counter               Cmdlet    Gets performance counter data from local and rem...
Test-WSMan                Cmdlet    Tests whether the WinRM service is running on a ...
Invoke-WSManAction        Cmdlet    Invokes an action on the object that is specifie...
Connect-WSMan             Cmdlet    Connects to the WinRM service on a remote computer.
Disconnect-WSMan          Cmdlet    Disconnects the client from the WinRM service on...
Get-WSManInstance         Cmdlet    Displays management information for a resource i...
Set-WSManInstance         Cmdlet    Modifies the management information that is rela...
Remove-WSManInstance      Cmdlet    Deletes a management resource instance.
New-WSManInstance         Cmdlet    Creates a new instance of a management resource.
Invoke-Command            Cmdlet    Runs commands on local and remote computers.
New-PSSession             Cmdlet    Creates a persistent connection to a local or re...
Get-PSSession             Cmdlet    Gets the Windows PowerShell sessions (PSSessions...
Remove-PSSession          Cmdlet    Closes one or more Windows PowerShell sessions (...
Receive-Job               Cmdlet    Gets the results of the Windows PowerShell backg...
Enter-PSSession           Cmdlet    Starts an interactive session with a remote comp...
Get-EventLog              Cmdlet    Gets the events in an event log, or a list of th...
Clear-EventLog            Cmdlet    Deletes all entries from specified event logs on...
Write-EventLog            Cmdlet    Writes an event to an event log.
Limit-EventLog            Cmdlet    Sets the event log properties that limit the siz...
Show-EventLog             Cmdlet    Displays the event logs of the local or a remote...
New-EventLog              Cmdlet    Creates a new event log and a new event source o...
Remove-EventLog           Cmdlet    Deletes an event log or unregisters an event sou...
Get-WmiObject             Cmdlet    Gets instances of Windows Management Instrumenta...
Invoke-WmiMethod          Cmdlet    Calls Windows Management Instrumentation (WMI) m...
Get-Process               Cmdlet    Gets the processes that are running on the local...
Remove-WmiObject          Cmdlet    Deletes an instance of an existing Windows Manag...
Register-WmiEvent         Cmdlet    Subscribes to a Windows Management Instrumentati...
Get-Service               Cmdlet    Gets the services on a local or remote computer.
Set-Service               Cmdlet    Starts, stops, and suspends a service, and chang...
Set-WmiInstance           Cmdlet    Creates or updates an instance of an existing Wi...
Get-HotFix                Cmdlet    Gets the hotfixes that have been applied to the ...
Test-Connection           Cmdlet    Sends ICMP echo request packets ("pings") to one...
Restart-Computer          Cmdlet    Restarts ("reboots") the operating system on loc...
Stop-Computer             Cmdlet    Stops (shuts down) local and remote computers.

PS C:\Users\Matt>
```

FIGURE 6.14 `ComputerName` requiring remoting

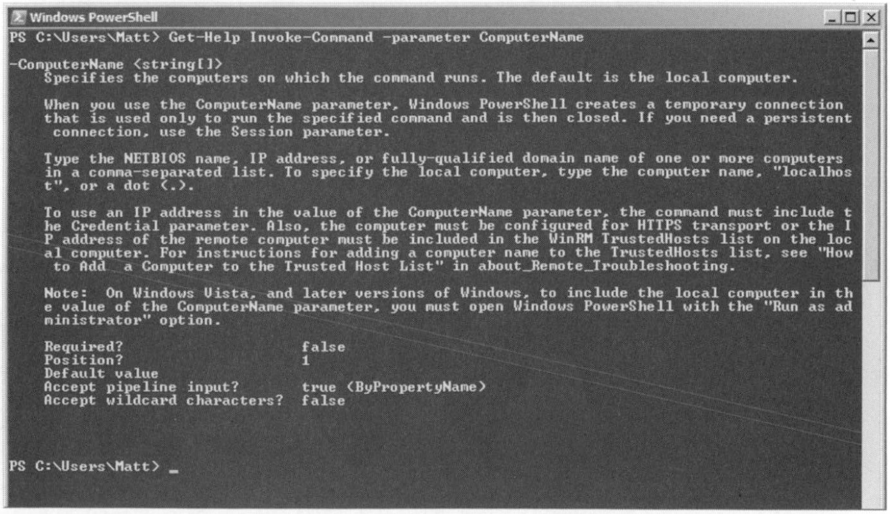

```
PS C:\Users\Matt> Get-Help Invoke-Command -parameter ComputerName

-ComputerName <string[]>
    Specifies the computers on which the command runs. The default is the local computer.

    When you use the ComputerName parameter, Windows PowerShell creates a temporary connection
    that is used only to run the specified command and is then closed. If you need a persistent
     connection, use the Session parameter.

    Type the NETBIOS name, IP address, or fully-qualified domain name of one or more computers
    in a comma-separated list. To specify the local computer, type the computer name, "localhos
    t", or a dot (.).

    To use an IP address in the value of the ComputerName parameter, the command must include t
    he Credential parameter. Also, the computer must be configured for HTTPS transport or the I
    P address of the remote computer must be included in the WinRM TrustedHosts list on the loc
    al computer. For instructions for adding a computer name to the TrustedHosts list, see "How
     to Add  a Computer to the Trusted Host List" in about_Remote_Troubleshooting.

    Note:  On Windows Vista, and later versions of Windows, to include the local computer in th
    e value of the ComputerName parameter, you must open Windows PowerShell with the "Run as ad
    ministrator" option.

    Required?                    false
    Position?                    1
    Default value
    Accept pipeline input?       true (ByPropertyName)
    Accept wildcard characters?  false


PS C:\Users\Matt> _
```

Use Invoke-Command

You can use the `Invoke-Command` cmdlet to run cmdlets on a remote server. This allows you to run a script block of PowerShell commands on the servers you specify. With `Invoke-Command`, PowerShell connects temporarily to the server you want to manage and runs the commands you specify. The basic syntax of the `Invoke-Command` cmdlet is `Invoke-Command -ComputerName {Scriptblock}`.

So if you had the following command, it would restart the Windows Update service on the following servers: Server4, Server8, and Server15:

```
Invoke-Command -ComputerName Server4, Server8, Server15 ↵
   {Restart-Service -name wuauserv}
```

Once the commands are sent to the remote computer, they will run until completion. If you want to stop the command running on the remote computer, you can send an interruption request by pressing **Ctrl+C**.

Use PowerShell Remote Sessions

You can run PowerShell commands in an interactive session remotely via the `Enter-PSSession` cmdlet. This lets you have a temporary interactive session directly on the server you are remoting to. When you run the cmdlet, will have a direct connection to the remote server until you exit the remote session. Once you are connected to the remote session, you have access to built-in cmdlets on the remote server. For example, if you wanted to have a PowerShell session on a server named Server3, your cmdlet would be `Enter-PSSession Server3`, as shown in Figure 6.15.

FIGURE 6.15   Example of a remote PowerShell session

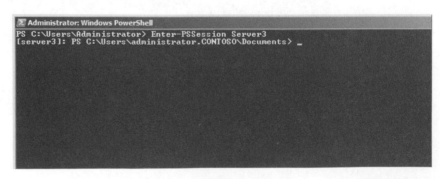

When you are in the remote session, the system you are connected to is referenced in the prompt with brackets ([ ]). When you are done with managing the remote servers and want to return to your local PowerShell session, type the following cmdlet:

```
Exit-PSSession
```

This takes you out of your current remoting session.

You can have multiple persistent sessions. Use the New-PSSession cmdlet to create these persistent connections. If you want to create a session for a server named Server2, type the following:

```
New-PSSession Server2
```

If you use New-PSSession without specifying a computer name, the cmdlet creates a new session for the local system. When you create a new session with the New-PSSession cmdlet, the session is given an ID. The ID can also be used to enter the remote session. You can see an example of the output of three sessions created with the New-PSSession cmdlet in Figure 6.16.

FIGURE 6.16   New sessions

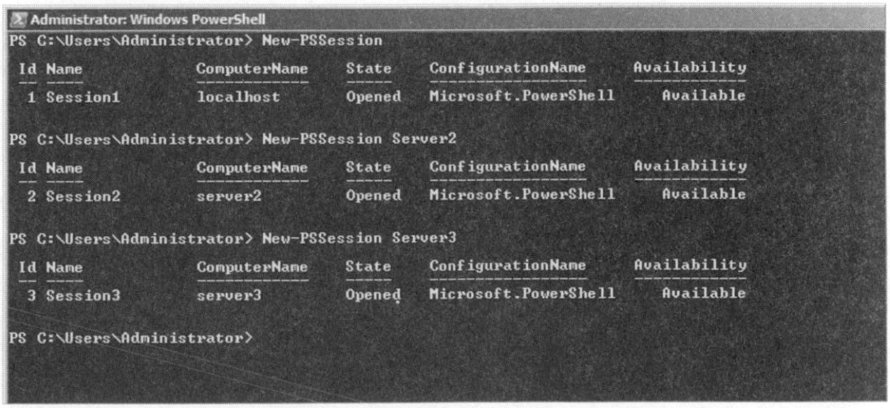

You can also create multiple remote PowerShell sessions by using the ComputerName parameter with the New-PSSession cmdlet. For example, the following cmdlet would create three remote PowerShell sessions for the computers named Server3, Server5, and Server6:

```
New-PSSession -ComputerName Server3, Server5, Server6.
```

One of the advantages of using the New-PSSession cmdlet is that it creates a persistent connection during your local PowerShell session so you can easily switch

Remoting with
PowerShell 2.0

CHAPTER 6

between the sessions on your systems. To see what sessions you currently have started on your system, type the following cmdlet:

```
Get-PSSession
```

Figure 6.17 shows an example of the output of the Get-PSSession cmdlet.

FIGURE 6.17   Get-PSSession

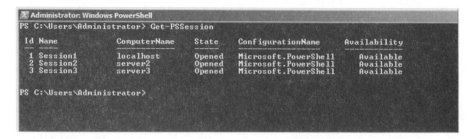

After you have created the sessions, you can run commands by either the Invoke-Command or Enter-PSSession cmdlet using the session ID, instead of the computer names for the systems you want to remotely manage. You can also assign variables for any or all of the sessions you want to use. For example, the following cmdlet would assign the variable $psr to all the remote sessions currently started on the server:

```
$psr=Get-PSSession
```

You can then use this variable in your commands to simultaneously communicate with remote servers. For example:

```
Invoke-Command -Session $psr {Get-Service}
```

Figure 6.18 shows the output of another command using this variable.

To enter one of the existing sessions, you can use the Enter-PSSession mentioned earlier in this section in combination with the session ID to access the session. So if you wanted to access PowerShell session with ID 2, you would type the following:

```
Enter-PSSession -ID 2
```

When you enter the remote PowerShell session, you will have an interactive session with the remote server. However, since you have created a persistent connection with the New-PSSession cmdlet, the remote session remains open when you use the Exit-PSSession cmdlet. The PowerShell sessions remain open as long as your local PowerShell session is open. If you do not want the PowerShell session to be open, you can run the `Remove-PSSession` cmdlet followed by the ID number to close the remote PowerShell session. For example, to close the session with ID 3, you would type this command:

```
Remove-PSSession -ID 3
```

FIGURE 6.18   Variable for `Invoke-Command`

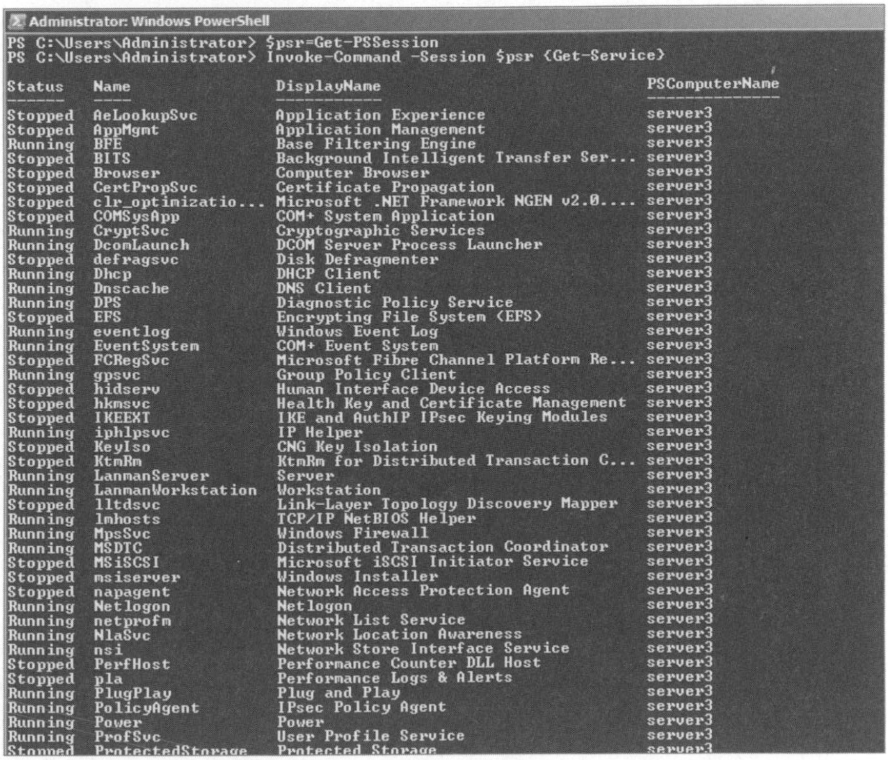

Use Remoting in the ISE

You can also leverage PowerShell remoting in the Integrated Scripting Environment (ISE) to host your remote sessions. Within the ISE, you can create tabs, as you saw in Chapter 5, to host remote sessions. To start a remote session in the ISE, do the following:

1. With the ISE open, click File ➤ New PowerShell Remote Tab. You will see a screen similar to Figure 6.19.

Remoting with
PowerShell 2.0

CHAPTER 6

FIGURE 6.19   New PowerShell Remote tab in the ISE

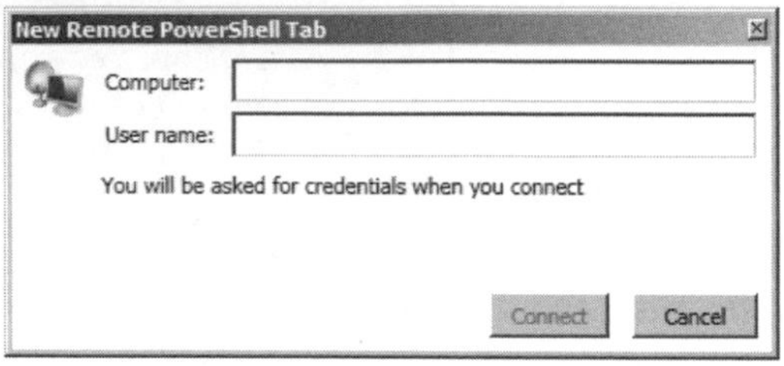

2. In the New Remote PowerShell Tab dialog box, enter the computer name, and if you want to use a different user credential than you are currently logged on with, you can enter it here as well.

3. After you have finished filling out the form, click Connect. You will see a screen similar to Figure 6.20, with the new tab in the ISE.

FIGURE 6.20   ISE with PowerShell remote tab

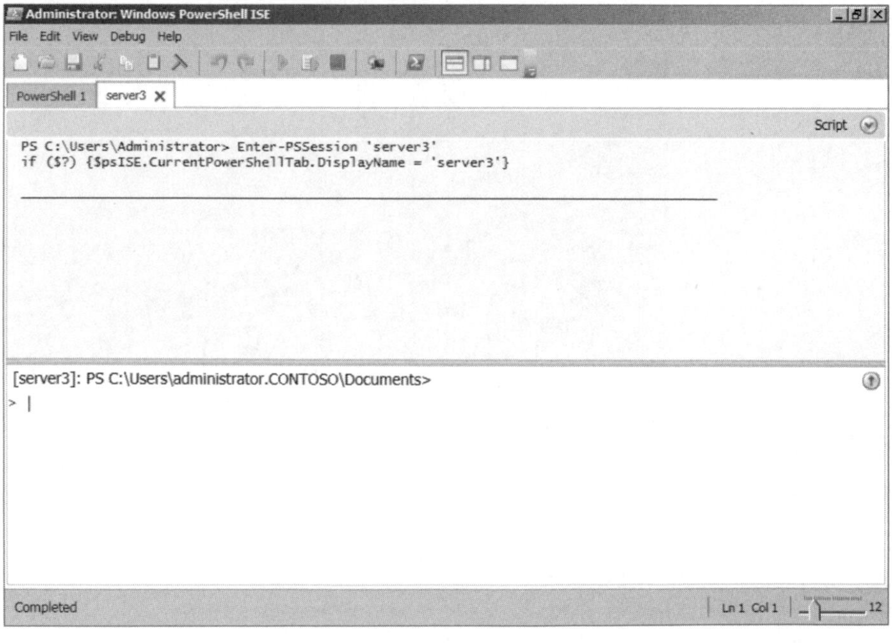

You may have noticed after you loaded the session that the ISE used the Enter-PSSession cmdlet to start the session. This session ends when the tab is closed in the ISE.

You also saw when you brought up the new PowerShell remote tab that it asked for alternate credentials. Using the ISE is not the only way to start a remote PowerShell session. You can use the cmdlets `Invoke-Command`, `Enter-PSSession`, and `New-PSSession` to provide alternate credentials for the remote session. All three of the cmdlets provide support for the `-credential` parameter, as well as an authentication method to allow you to use the proper user accounts with permissions to perform the tasks you may need in the remote PowerShell session.

EXERCISE 6: SET UP A REMOTE POWERSHELL SESSION

Create a PowerShell management environment that has remote PowerShell sessions ready at your fingertips.

Remoting with
PowerShell 2.0

CHAPTER 6

Server Essentials in PowerShell

IN THIS CHAPTER, YOU WILL LEARN TO:

aving PowerShell built into Windows Server 2008 R2 gives you flexibility in managing your server. Several PowerShell cmdlets let you perform many of the key administrative jobs you may need to do on a daily basis, including installing features for your Windows Server 2008 R2 server, backing up your server, analyzing the server, and many others. PowerShell lets you perform many of these tasks consistently on a batch basis.

This chapter outlines key modules for managing day-to-day server administration, including using Server Manager, using Best Practices Analyzer, doing backup and recovery, performing network load balancing, and troubleshooting.

Work with Your Server in PowerShell

One of the fundamental tasks you will perform on your servers is adding new roles and services, which provide your infrastructure with added functionality. Although you can use the Server Manager GUI to perform tasks, you can easily install new features on your server with PowerShell.

In this section, you will work with the Server Manager module for PowerShell, which provides the ability to install and remove features on your Windows Server 2008 R2 servers. The Server Manager module can be imported on Server Core installations as well. This allows you to use the same commands to install the features on both the full and Server Core installations of Windows Server 2008 R2.

Once you have installed PowerShell on a Server Core installation, you can use the Server Manager cmdlets to install features. This provides an alternative to the DISM installation tool on your Server Core installations.

Work with Server Manager Cmdlets

Before you can install new features with PowerShell on your Windows Server 2008 R2 server, you have to import the Server Manager module into your PowerShell session. Run this command to import the Server Manager module into your PowerShell session:

```
Import-Module ServerManager
```

FINDING OTHER POWERSHELL MODULES

Several PowerShell modules may be available to you on your Windows Server 2008 R2 server. As you may recall from Chapter 3, you can run the `Get-Module -ListAvailable` cmdlet to see what modules are available to you and verify the correct spelling of the module names.

After you have imported the Server Manager module, you need to know how to use three main cmdlets for working with your server features:

```
Get-WindowsFeature

Add-WindowsFeature

Remove-WindowsFeature
```

With `Get-WindowsFeature`, you can see all the features available to install on your Windows Server 2008 R2 server. When you run `Get-WindowsFeature`, you will see a screen similar to Figure 7.1.

FIGURE 7.1   `Get-WindowsFeature`

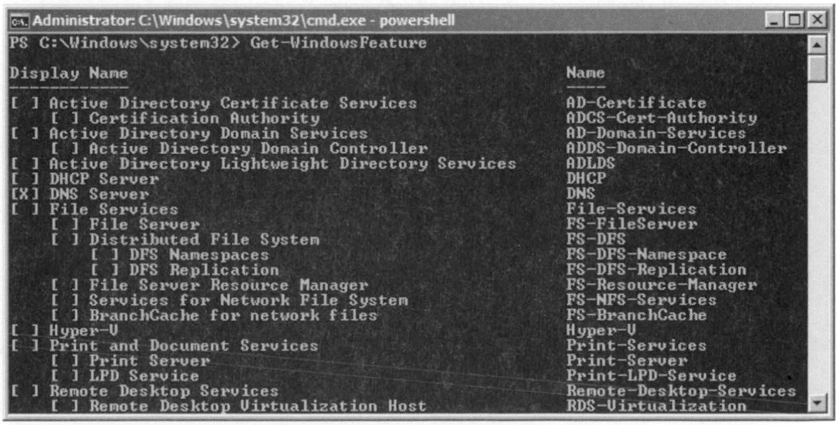

Take note of a couple of things in the output of the cmdlet. First, you can identify which features are available to install by the empty brackets: `[]`. (Already installed features are noted by `[X]`.) Second, the `Name` column tells you all the names of the features you can install on your server. Those names are also used in the `Add-WindowsFeature` and `Remove-WindowsFeature` cmdlets.

For example, if you want to install DNS on your server, use the following command:

```
Add-WindowsFeature DNS
```

Likewise, if you want to remove the DNS role from your server, you run this command:

```
Remove-WindowsFeature DNS
```

Although some features are easily installed, other features may require additional planning and configuration after you install the feature with PowerShell. For example, with Active Directory, you have to run `DCPROMO.exe` after you have installed the Active Directory role.

You can also add or remove multiple roles at a time by separating the names of the roles or features with commas. When you install or remove the features, you may also be required to restart your server. You can restart the server manually, or you can add the `-restart` parameter in your PowerShell commands. For example, the following command installs the Branch Cache and Windows Backup tools on your server:

```
Add-WindowsFeature BranchCache, Backup-Features
```

Analyze Your Server

The Best Practices Analyzer (BPA) is now built into Windows Server 2008 R2 servers. It provides instant analysis for many of the roles installed on your server, giving guidance for improvements. Although you can run the BPA tool in Server Manager, you can also run the tool from a PowerShell session. In this section, you will see how to use PowerShell with the BPA tool.

The BPA tool scans your system with a series of criteria and rules, comparing your server configuration against known best practices from Microsoft as well as Microsoft's early adopters. This allows you to discover room for improvement or fix errors on your Windows Server 2008 R2 server.

Loading the BPA Module

With the BPA providing PowerShell support, you can run just a handful of commands to analyze all the roles on your server. Additionally, the PowerShell tools provide the ability to run BPA scans of multiple roles at one time with one cmdlet.

To run the BPA PowerShell commands, you need to load both the Best Practices Analyzer and Server Manager modules into your PowerShell session. Although you can run scans without the Server Manager module, its additional capabilities enable a better experience with the BPA tool. In an administrative PowerShell session, enter the following at the prompt:

```
Import-Module ServerManager
Import-Module BestPractices
```

After you have the BPA module loaded, you can then analyze your system and see how it compares to the best practices. There are four cmdlets you need to know in order to effectively use PowerShell with the BPA, as described in Table 7.1.

TABLE 7.1   BPA PowerShell commands

Command	Usage
Get-BPAModel	Allows you to view the roles installed on the server where you run BPA scans. This tool also shows you when the last scan on a particular role was run.
Get-BPAResult	Allows you to view the results for any given BPA scan you have performed.
Invoke-BPAModel	Allows you to run a BPA scan on your server for a particular role.
Set-BPAResult	Allows you to filter the BPA report from the Get-BPAResult command.

Using the BPA with PowerShell

Before you can scan the system with the BPA tool, you need to know the ID name for the role you want to scan. To determine which roles currently installed on the server can be scanned with BPA, use the following command, resulting in a screen similar to Figure 7.2:

```
Get-BPAModel
```

As you may have noticed, not only can you see the role ID name, but you can also see whether a scan has been done on the role before. However, you need to take note of the ID names. The role IDs are used in the other BPA commands to perform designated tasks.

When Windows Server 2008 R2 initially shipped, there were only five roles you could scan with the BPA tool:

► Active Directory Certification Services (AD CS)

► Active Directory Domain Services (AD DS)

► DNS

► Remote Desktop Services (RDS)

► Internet Information Services (IIS)

As Windows Server 2008 R2 has matured in the technology market, Microsoft has added several updates to the BPA tool via Windows Update. Even though you may have updated your servers and installed the BPA updates, you can use the BPA scan only if the role has been installed on the server. You may not see all the possible IDs for your own Windows Server 2008 R2 server.

Table 7.2 describes some of the current role ID names that can be used with the BPA tool.

TABLE 7.2   BPA role IDS

BPA role ID	Role
Microsoft/Windows/CertificateServices	Active Directory Certification Services (AD CS)
Microsoft/Windows/DirectoryServices	Active Directory Domain Services (AD DS)
Microsoft/Windows/DNSServer	DNS
Microsoft/Windows/TerminalServices	Remote Desktop Services (RDS)

BPA role ID	Role
Microsoft/Windows/WebServer	Internet Information Services (IIS)
Microsoft/Windows/Hyper-V	Hyper-V
Microsoft/Windows/ApplicationServer	Application Server
Microsoft/Windows/WSUS	Windows Software Update Services
Microsoft/Windows/NPAS	Network Policy and Access Services
Microsoft/Windows/FileServices	File Services
Microsoft/Windows /DHCP	DHCP

For example, to scan the Active Directory Domain Services on your server, run the following command:

```
Invoke-BPAModel -id Microsoft/Windows/DirectoryServices
```

Although you can scan each role individually, you may want to scan all the roles on your Windows Server 2008 R2 server. To scan all of the roles, run the following command, with results similar to Figure 7.3:

```
Get-BPAModel | Invoke-BPAModel.
```

FIGURE 7.3   Multiple BPA scans on a server

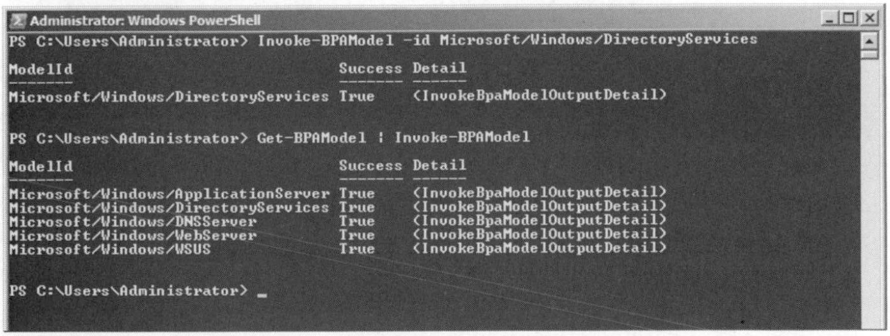

After you have run the scans, you will want to look at the results. You can use the Get-BPAResult cmdlet to see the results of your scan. If you see an error message similar to Figure 7.4, this indicates a scan has not yet been run for the role you indicated.

FIGURE 7.4 Role not scanned by BPA

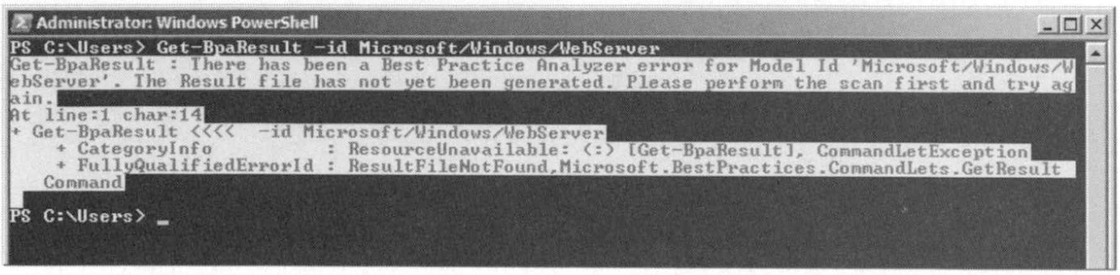

To see the report for your Hyper-V role, run the following command, with results similar to Figure 7.5:

```
Get-BPAResult -id Microsoft/Windows/Hyper-V
```

FIGURE 7.5 **Get-BPAResult** for Hyper-V

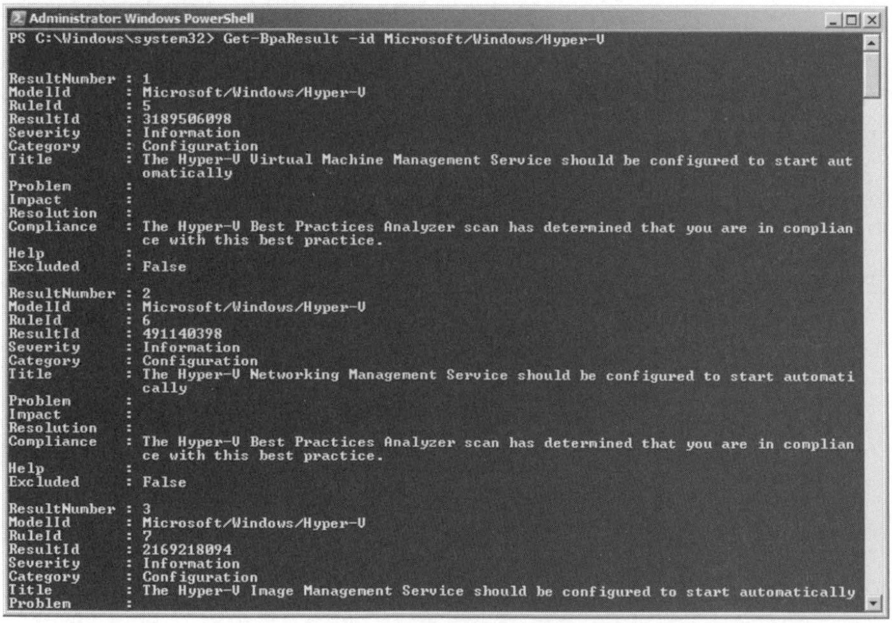

You can filter results in PowerShell with the Get-BPAResult cmdlet and a Where clause. If you want to view a BPA report for Hyper-V for only errors, run the following command, with results similar to Figure 7.6:

```
Get-BPAResult -id Microsoft/Windows/Hyper-V|↵
  Where { $_.Severity -eq "Error" }
```

FIGURE 7.6   Hyper-V errors only

```
Administrator: Windows PowerShell                                      _ □ ×
PS C:\Windows> Get-BpaResult -id Microsoft/Windows/Hyper-V | Where { $_.Severity -eq "Error")

ResultNumber : 9
ModelId      : Microsoft/Windows/Hyper-V
RuleId       : 13
ResultId     : 1193784167
Severity     : Error
Category     : Configuration
Title        : More than one network adapter should be available
Problem      : This server is configured with one network adapter, which must be shared by the
               management operating system and all virtual machines that require access to a ph
               ysical network.
Impact       : Networking performance may be degraded in the management operating system.
Resolution   : Add more network adapters to this computer. To reserve one network adapter for e
               xclusive use by the management operating system, do not configure it for use wit
               h an external virtual network.
Compliance   :
Help         : http://go.microsoft.com/fwlink/?LinkId=154016
Excluded     : False

ResultNumber : 13
ModelId      : Microsoft/Windows/Hyper-V
RuleId       : 17
ResultId     : 2417974980
Severity     : Error
Category     : Policy
Title        : Use RAM that provides error correction
Problem      : The RAM in use on this computer is not error-correcting (ECC) RAM.
Impact       : Microsoft does not support Windows Server 2008 R2 on computers without error-cor
               recting RAM.
Resolution   : Verify the server is listed in the Windows Server catalog and qualified for Hype
               r-V.
Compliance   :
Help         : http://go.microsoft.com/fwlink/?LinkId=154020
Excluded     : False


PS C:\Windows> _
```

Although you can view the results in the PowerShell window, you can see there is
a lot of data in the scan. You can also use the `|more` command or even the`|Out`
command to help organize your output. PowerShell provides great ways to work
with this data, but remember you can always view the results in the Server Manager
interface even if you ran the scan from PowerShell. So if you want to view the full
report, I recommend using the Server Manager interface. You can find the BPA
reports in the role summary screens under each individual role. You can see an
example of the Hyper-V BPA report in Figure 7.7.

FIGURE 7.7   Hyper-V BPA in Server Manager

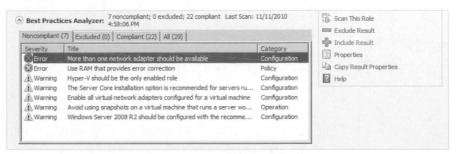

Add Reliability to Your Server

One of the most common daily tasks you should perform on your servers is a backup. With Windows Server 2008 R2 and PowerShell, you have a powerful tool to help you automate this process. This helps ensure that your backups occur frequently and consistently on your servers.

Install the Backup Tools

The backup tools are not installed by default in Windows Server 2008 R2. You can quickly install the tools on your server in an administrative PowerShell session, though. Use Add-WindowsFeature, mentioned earlier in this chapter, to install backup features on a server. Whether this is a full Windows Server 2008 R2 server installation or a Server Core installation, the procedure in PowerShell is the same:

```
Import-Module ServerManager
Add-WindowsFeature Backup-Tools
```

This not only installs the core components for Windows Backup but also installs the necessary components to perform a backup from PowerShell or a command line. After the command is run, your screen will look similar to Figure 7.8.

FIGURE 7.8   Installing the backup tools

If you are prompted to restart the server, restart it before working with the backup tools.

Perform a Backup with PowerShell

After you install the PowerShell backup tools, you can use the PowerShell cmdlets on Windows Server 2008 R2 to perform backups and recoveries. Before you can run these tools, though, you have to verify the PowerShell snap-in for backup has been loaded. Snap-ins are like modules in that they contain a collection of

PowerShell cmdlets; however, they do have differences. In Appendix E you can see the differences between the two.

To verify the tools have been loaded in a PowerShell session, run the following command to verify `Windows.ServerBackup` was loaded:

```
Get-PSSnapin
```

If you do not see `Windows.ServerBackup` in your loaded snap-ins, run the following commands:

```
Add-PSSnapin windows.serverbackup
Get-PSSnapin
```

The result should look similar to Figure 7.9.

FIGURE 7.9   `Windows.ServerBackup` snap-in loaded

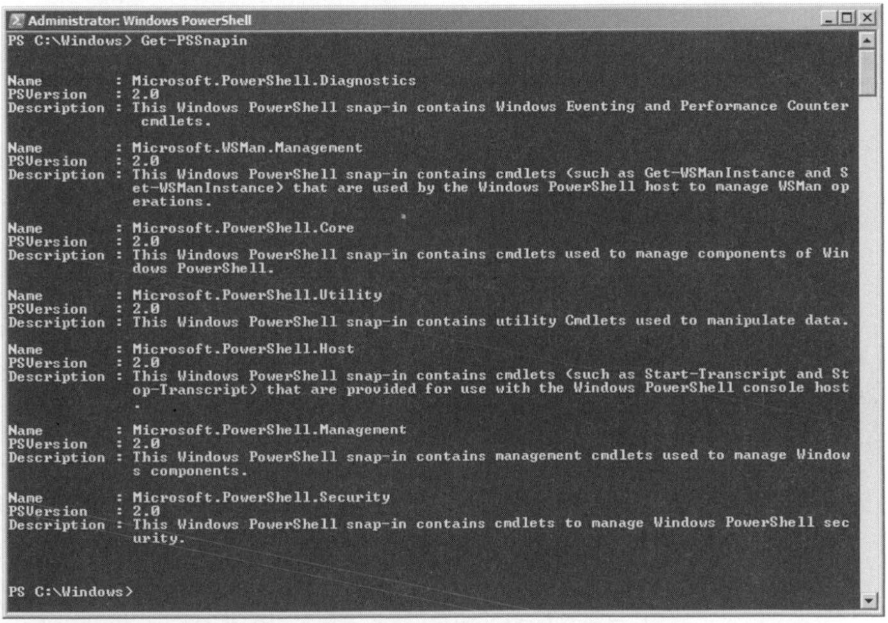

After you load the backup snap-in, you will have access to a tool allowing some flexibility for performing backups. To perform backups in PowerShell, you have to define the backup policy for your server. The backup policy for PowerShell is stored in an object called `WBPolicy`. The `WBPolicy` object contains all the settings for the backup, including the schedule, backup types, backup targets, and so on.

You need to set the values for the `WBPolicy` object when working with PowerShell and backup. Table 7.3 lists some of the common PowerShell commands used for backup and recovery and for setting the parameters for `WBPolicy`. For a full listing of the PowerShell backup cmdlets, run the following cmdlet:

```
Get-Command *wb* -commandtype cmdlet
```

TABLE 7.3   PowerShell backup cmdlets

Cmdlet	Explanation
Get-WBPolicy	Displays the current settings for the WBPolicy object on the server
Set-WBPolicy	Sets the parameters for the WBPolicy
Add-WBVolume	Adds a volume to the WBPolicy object to be backed up
Add-WBSystemState	Adds the system state to the WBPolicy object to be backed up
Set-WBSchedule	Sets the time for your daily backup schedule
Start-WBBackup	Starts a one-time backup
Get-WBJob	Shows the current status of a running backup job

As you can see in Table 7.3, there are only a few cmdlets to work with the `WBPolicy`. Here a couple of examples to allow you to get used to using PowerShell with backup policies.

The following two lines back up your system with your current backup policy settings:

```
$policy = Get-WBPolicy
Start-WBBackup -Policy $policy
```

This first line sets the `$policy` variable to the current settings in `WBPolicy`. The second line starts the backup process with settings currently in `$policy`.

The following script backs up the `c:` drive, `d:` drive, and system state on your system to your `z:` drive. The script uses a variety of the `add` cmdlets to modify the value of the variable `$policy`, as well as variables for target and paths:

```
$policy = New-WBPolicy
$volume = get-WBVolume -VolumePath c:
Add-WBVolume -Policy $policy -volume $volume
$volume1 = get-WBVolume -VolumePath d:
Add-WBVolume -Policy $policy -volume $volume1
Add-WBSystemState -Policy $policy
$target = New-WBBackupTarget -VolumePath Z:
```

```
Add-WBBackupTarget -Policy $policy -target $target
Start-WBBackup -Policy $policy
```

Load-Balance Your Network

One of the core features built into Windows Server 2008 R2 servers is network load balancing (NLB). NLB enables your server to even out traffic across TCP/IP clusters on your network and offers easy scalability to your web-based servers and applications in your infrastructure.

As with many of the Windows features mentioned in this chapter, you can use PowerShell to install NLB. In an administrative PowerShell session, enter the following at the prompt:

```
Import-Module ServerManager
Add-WindowsFeature NLB
```

After NLB is installed, almost all the configuration of NLB can be done in PowerShell. You can create NLB clusters, manage port rules, or work with your nodes, all in PowerShell. Before you can access the cmdlets, you need to load the `NetworkLoadBalancingClusters` module with the following command:

```
Import-Module NetworkLoadBalancingClusters
```

After you have loaded the module, you can view all NLB cmdlets by running the following command:

```
Get-Command -Module NetworkLoadBalancingClusters
```

The result should look similar to Figure 7.10.

After installing the feature, a cluster needs to be set up. You can create a new cluster with the `New-NLBCluster` cmdlet. Table 7.4 lists the parameters that are used by this cmdlet.

The following command will create a new NLB cluster tied to the network interface named `web1` with the IP address for the cluster set to `10.0.0.156`.

```
New-NLBCluster -InterfaceName web1 ↵
-ClusterNamePrimaryIP 10.0.0.156
```

After you have configured an NLB cluster, you can quickly get basic information on the properties of the cluster with this cmdlet:

```
Get-NLBClusterDriverInfo
```

The result should look similar to Figure 7.11.

FIGURE 7.10   NLB cmdlets

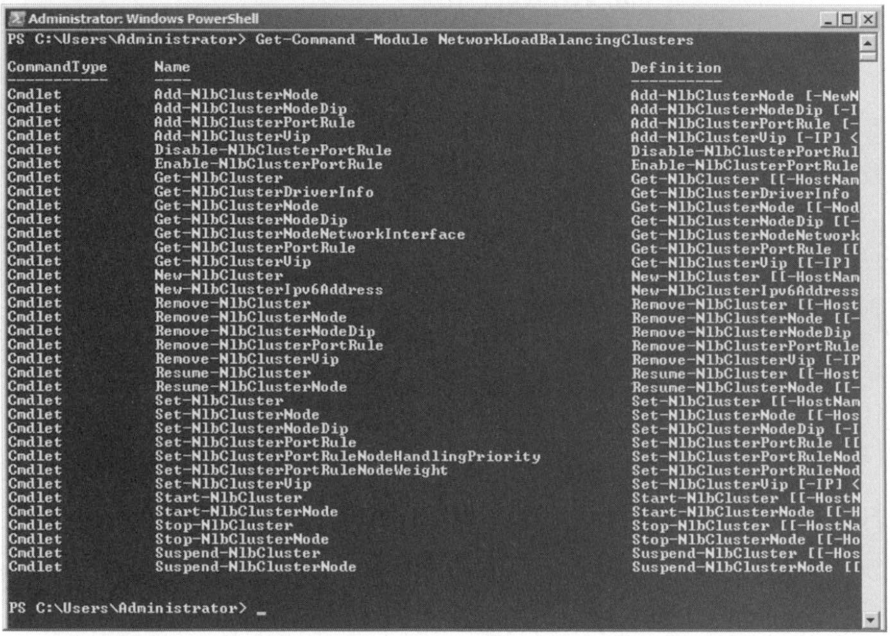

TABLE 7.4   **New-NLBCluster parameters**

Parameter name	Description
InterfaceName	Name of the network interface for NLB to use. You can get a list of the names available on your local machine from the following command: gwmi win32_NetworkAdapter | FL NetConnectionID, AdapterType, NetworkAddresses. The NetConnectionID is what is used for the InterfaceName parameter.
ClusterName	Name of the cluster.
ClusterPrimaryIP	The primary IP address for this cluster. A cluster has one primary IP address and can have other IP addresses associated with it as virtual IP addresses (VIPs).
HostName	Used for clustering on a remote machine. If this parameter is not specified, then the local machine is the target node.
DedicatedIP	The dedicated IP address for the targeted node. If this parameter is not specified, the default value is the existing static IP address on the targeted node.
DedicatedIPSubnet	The subnet mask for the dedicated IP address. If this parameter is not specified, the default value is the existing static IP address subnet mask on the targeted node.
OperationMode	The operation mode for the cluster. There are three types of operation modes: unicast, multicast, and igmpmulticast. If this parameter is not specified, the default value is unicast.

FIGURE 7.11 `Get-NLBClusterDriverInfo`

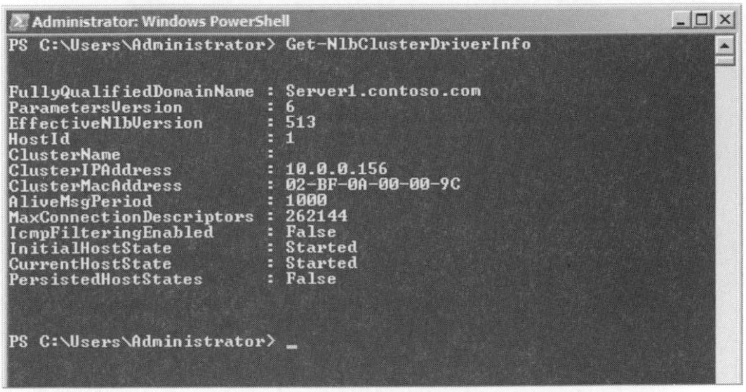

There are several cmdlets used to work with NLB clusters. Table 7.5 lists some of the common cmdlets.

TABLE 7.5 Common NLB cmdlets

Cmdlet	Description	Example
`Get-NLBCluster`	Displays the cluster name and IP address; can be piped into other cmdlets	To list information about the cluster, run `Get-NLBCluster`.

`Add-NLBClusterNode`	Lets you add nodes to an existing cluster	To add server5 to an existing NLB cluster (with the NLB primary server1) using the network interface nlb5 on node5, you would use the following:
		`Get-NLBCluster server1 |`
		`Add-NLBClusterNode`
		`-NewNodeName server5`
		`-NewNodeInterface nlb5`

`Remove-NLBClusterNode`	Removes an existing node from the cluster	To remove server4 from the NLB cluster, use this: `Remove-NLBClusterNode -HostName server4`. This cmdlet prompts you for confirmation. If you do not want to be prompted, you can use the `-force` parameter to bypass confirmation.
`Suspend-NLBCluster`	Pauses all the nodes in the NLB cluster; commonly used when performing maintenance on the cluster; also stops any tasks running remotely on the cluster	`Suspend-NLBCluster` suspends the cluster on the local machine; you can use the `-HostName` parameter to specify the host to suspend.

(continues)

TABLE 7.5 *(continued)*

Cmdlet	Description	Example
Resume-NLBCluster	Restarts all the nodes in the NLB cluster if it is currently suspended	Resume-NLBCluster resumes a suspended cluster on the local machine; you can use the -HostName parameter to specify the host to resume.
Stop-NLBClusterNode	Drains the connections on the node and then stops clustering on this node	You may need to stop clustering on a node for maintenance. Use the -Drain parameter to drain any existing connections on the node before stopping. Use the -Timeout parameter to set the maximum wait time before stopping the node. Suppose you wanted to stop the current node, having it drain connections and force the stop to happen in 15 minutes even if connections are not fully drained. Use the following command: Stop-NLBClusterNode -Drain -Timeout 15.
Start-NLBClusterNode	Puts a stopped cluster node back into the cluster	After maintenance on the current node, you would run the following command to put it back in the cluster: Start-NLBClusterNode.
Get-NLBClusterNode	Gets nodes of a cluster	This can be piped to other commands to be run on multiple nodes.
Set-NLBClusterNode	Sets the node properties	Properties include HostPriority and InitialHostState. HostPriority is the ID for the cluster node and should be between 1 and 32. InitialHostState can be started, stopped, or suspended. To set the current node to HostID 4, use the following command: Set-NLBClusterNode -HostPriority 4. To set all nodes in this cluster to the initial state of started, use Get-NLBClusterNode | Set-NLBClusterNode -InitialHostState started.
Get-NLBClusterVip	Displays the virtual IP addresses of the cluster	Get-NLBClusterVIP displays the IP address being used by the cluster.
Set-NLBClusterVip	Changes the VIP for the cluster; both IPv4 and IPv6 are supported	To change the IP address of the cluster to 10.0.0.225, use Get-NLBClusterVIP| Set-NLBClusterVip -NewIP 10.0.0.225. By using the | to pass the current VIP, you will not need to interact with the cmdlet.

Although Table 7.5 lists most of the cmdlets, there is one other set of cmdlets to know when it comes to managing NLB clusters—Get-NLBClusterPortRule,

`Set-NLBClusterPortRule`, `Add-NLBClusterPortRule`, and `Remove-NLBClusterPortRule`. These are used to manage port rules for the cluster.

For example, suppose you have to support ASP.NET code that relies on session states in a clustered web environment. Suppose your cluster is currently set up with the affinity set to None to take advantage of the load balancing among all nodes in the cluster. That means a website visitor may hit one node the first time they load a page and then another node of the cluster another time they load the page. This can cause problems for some ASP.NET applications. You can adjust the NLB cluster's affinity so that once a visitor hits a node, they stay on that node for the length of their current session. To do this, you would need to adjust the web port's affinity from None to Single. The following code could be used:

```
Set-NlbClusterPortRule -NewStartPort 80 ↵
-NewEndPort 80 -Port 80 -NewAffinity Single
```

Although these are just a few things you can do manage with NLB clusters, you can always get more examples from running `Get-Help` with any of the NLB cmdlets using the `-examples` parameter.

Use Other PowerShell Utilities for the Server

Many tools and PowerShell modules can help you perform routine server maintenance functions. In this section, you will see how PowerShell can be used to work with the registry on your systems and how to use the troubleshooting module.

Use the Registry with PowerShell

As you briefly saw in Chapter 6, you can use PowerShell to work directly with the registry. When you work with the registry in PowerShell, you are using a built-in structure called a *provider*. Providers give PowerShell the ability to navigate a data store on your system. You can find more about providers in Appendix C.

WARNING   Make sure you back up your registry and your system prior to modifying the registry. Modifying the registry can cause unwanted errors, including system errors, that may require reinstallation.

Many types of drives are available in PowerShell. Some of the PowerShell drives include your hard drives, like `c:` or `d:`. Other drives include the registry, certificates, and environment variables. You will find a full listing in Appendix C. To see the list of PowerShell drives available in your current PowerShell session, run the following command, which should look similar to Figure 7.12:

    Get-PSDrive

FIGURE 7.12   `Get-PSDrive`

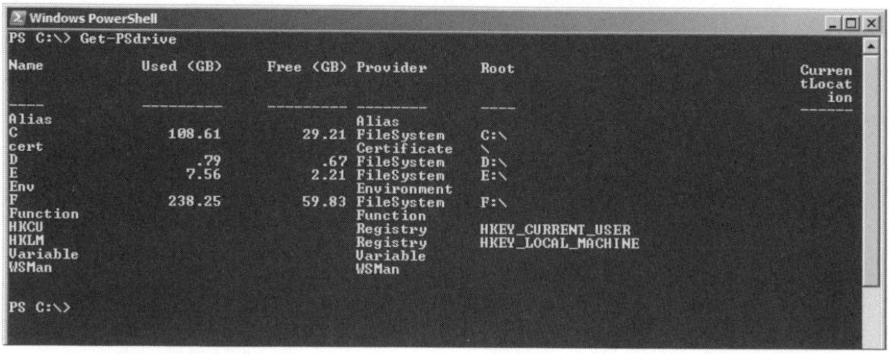

You will see the two main hives of the registry listed with the `Get-PSDrive` cmdlet:

▶ `HKEY_CURRENT_USER` (HKCU) is the hive key for the current user.

▶ `HKEY_LOCAL_MACHINE` (HKLM) is the hive key for the local machine.

With PowerShell drives, you can navigate the registry just like you would any other drive on the system. You can use the commands, such as `cd`, `dir`, or `ls`, to move through the keys. For example, if you wanted to switch to `HKCU`, you can use this command:

    cd HKCU:

Then you can work through the registry structure just like working through a file structure. In Figure 7.13, you see the results of running `dir` in the `HKCU` root.

FIGURE 7.13   `dir` for HKCU

```
Windows PowerShell                                                            _ □ ×
PS HKCU:\> dir


    Hive: HKEY_CURRENT_USER


SKC  VC Name                          Property
---  -- ----                          --------
  2   0 AppEvents                     {}
  0  38 Console                       {ColorTable00, ColorTable01, ColorTable02, ColorTable...
 10   0 Control Panel                 {}
  0   3 Environment                   {TEMP, TMP, path}
  4   0 EUDC                          {}
  3   0 Keyboard Layout               {}
  0   0 Network                       {}
  4   0 Printers                      {}
 18   0 Software                      {}
  1   0 System                        {}
  1   8 Volatile Environment          {LOGONSERVER, USERDOMAIN, USERNAME, USERPROFILE...}

PS HKCU:\> _
```

As you begin navigating through the registry, you may notice you cannot see
registry values with the `dir` commands. There are some unique aspects of navigating the registry. After you navigate to the desired registry location, you can use the
`Get-ItemProperty` cmdlet to see the values in the local directory. You will also
have to add the . (period) to reference the local directory in the registry. This is
shown in Figure 7.14. The results are from the Desktop Windows Manager location
in the registry.

```
Get-ItemProperty .
```

FIGURE 7.14   `Get-ItemProperty`

```
Windows PowerShell                                                            _ □ ×
PS HKCU:\software\microsoft\windows\dwm> Get-ItemProperty .

PSPath                             : Microsoft.PowerShell.Core\Registry::HKEY_CURRENT_USER\so
                                     ftware\microsoft\windows\dwm
PSParentPath                       : Microsoft.PowerShell.Core\Registry::HKEY_CURRENT_USER\so
                                     ftware\microsoft\windows
PSChildName                        : dwm
PSDrive                            : HKCU
PSProvider                         : Microsoft.PowerShell.Core\Registry
Composition                        : 1
ColorizationColor                  : 977313534
ColorizationColorBalance           : 16
ColorizationAfterglow              : 977313534
ColorizationAfterglowBalance       : 10
ColorizationBlurBalance            : 74
ColorizationGlassReflectionIntensity : 0
ColorizationOpaqueBlend            : 1
EnableAeroPeek                     : 0
AlwaysHibernateThumbnails          : 0


PS HKCU:\software\microsoft\windows\dwm>
```

Alternatively, you can specify the path in the Get-ItemProperty cmdlet so you do not have to fully navigate to the location:

```
Get-ItemProperty -path HKCU:\software\microsoft\windows\dwm
```

If you know the name of the key you explicitly want to look at, you can specify it using the -name parameter. If you just wanted to see the EnableAeroPeek value, you would run the following:

```
Get-ItemProperty . -name EnableAeroPeek
```

When you want to set or change the values in the registry, use the Set-ItemProperty cmdlet. You saw the following example of this cmdlet in Chapter 5:

```
Set-ItemProperty -path ↵
HKLM:\SOFTWARE\Microsoft\PowerShell\1\ShellIds↵
\Microsoft.PowerShell -Name "ExecutionPolicy" ↵
-Value "RemoteSigned"
```

The -path and -name parameters work the same way as they do in the Get-ItemProperty cmdlet. The unique parameter for Set-ItemProperty is the -value parameter. When you work with the registry in PowerShell, you may have to do some research to make sure you put in the proper value and proper type of data. This will avoid any errors or misconfigurations.

Use PowerShell Troubleshooting Packs

PowerShell 2.0 includes a module called TroubleshootingPack. This module and its cmdlets can help you run system diagnostics on various aspects of your Windows Server 2008 R2 server. With the troubleshooting packs, you can check your network interface and program compatibility.

You already have two troubleshooting packs on your server, for networking and program compatibility. To use them within PowerShell, load the TroubleshootingPack module with this command:

```
Import-Module TroubleShootingPack
```

This module gives you two cmdlets:

```
Get-TroubleShootingPack
```

```
Invoke-TroubleShootingPack
```

These cmdlets let you identify and work with the troubleshooting packs. To be able to run to troubleshooting cmdlets, you need know their location on your system. They are located by default in the %windir%\diagnostics\system directory on your system. Once you locate the directory on your Windows Server 2008 R2 server, you should see the two directories for Networking and PCW, as shown in Figure 7.15.

FIGURE 7.15   Diagnostics directories

Starting the TroubleshootingPack module launches an interactive session. Run the PowerShell session as an administrator to allow troubleshooting to perform actions to diagnose and fix your system. After you have launched an administrative PowerShell session, run the following command. This will launch the networking diagnostics troubleshooter:

```
Get-TroubleShootingPack -path ↵
C:\Windows\Diagnostics\System\Networking |↵
Invoke-TroubleShootingPack
```

After you launch the command, you will be asked to specify an instance ID. Press the Enter key, and you will see a screen similar to Figure 7.16.

FIGURE 7.16   Network troubleshooting

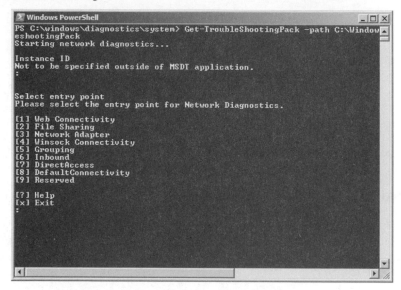

As you can see, you are able to check various aspects of your network connectivity on your server by stepping through the menus. To work with the troubleshooter, just specify the option you want to work with using the corresponding number. In Figure 7.17, you can see how the troubleshooter discovered the problem with a network adapter and suggested a resolution.

FIGURE 7.17   Network resolution

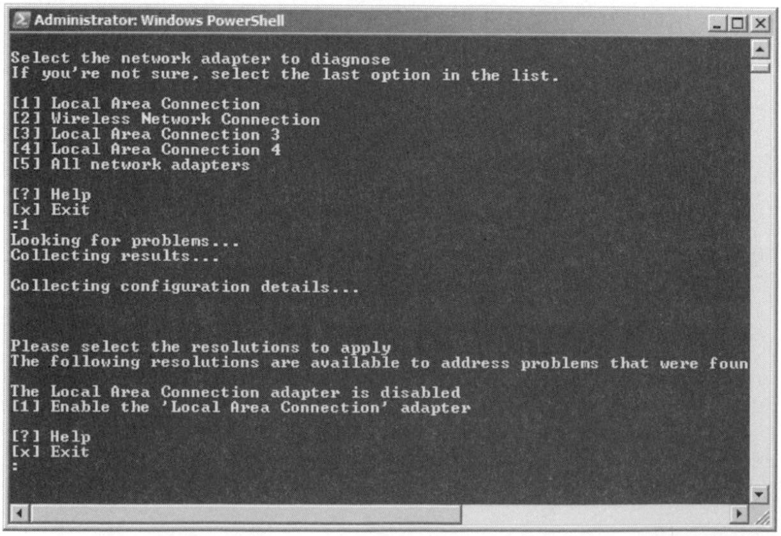

TROUBLESHOOTING PACKS ON WINDOWS 7

With Windows Server 2008 R2 servers, you have two packs you can leverage. With Windows 7, there are several more troubleshooting packs you can use:

- ► Aero
- ► Audio
- ► Device
- ► DeviceCenter
- ► HomeGroup
- ► IEBrowseWeb
- ► IESecurity
- ► Networking
- ► PCW
- ► Performance
- ► Power
- ► Printer
- ► Search
- ► WindowsMediaPlayerConfiguration
- ► WindowsMediaPlayerMedialLibrary
- ► WindowsMediaPlayerPlayDVD
- ► WindowsUpdate

You can use PowerShell remoting to take advantage of these extended troubleshooting packages on Windows 7 systems.

Schedule PowerShell Scripts

As you work with PowerShell, you might run into a situation where you want to run a PowerShell script on a schedule. Scheduling a PowerShell task is straightforward, using three tools to make it happen:

- ► `powershell.exe`

► Command prompt

► Task Scheduler

The command prompt may appear to be the odd one in the list, but you can start a PowerShell session from the command prompt by simply typing **powershell.exe**. If you have a PowerShell script you want to run, you can put the path of the script and script name at the end of the command prompt line. For example, the following will run a script called myscript.ps1 stored in the scripts directory:

```
powershell c:\scripts\myscript.ps1
```

You can include the -noninteractive parameter for powershell.exe to allow your script to run without interaction from the user on the system. For example, the command to run myscript.ps1 without an interactive prompt is as follows:

```
powershell -NonInteractive c:\scripts\myscript.ps1
```

Since you can run PowerShell and add a script to the session, you then need to use the Task Scheduler to run your command on a schedule. You can find the Task Scheduler in your Administrative Tools. On Windows Server 2008 R2 server, click Start ➢ All Programs ➢ Administrative Tools ➢ Task Scheduler. You will see a screen similar to Figure 7.18.

FIGURE 7.18   The Task Scheduler

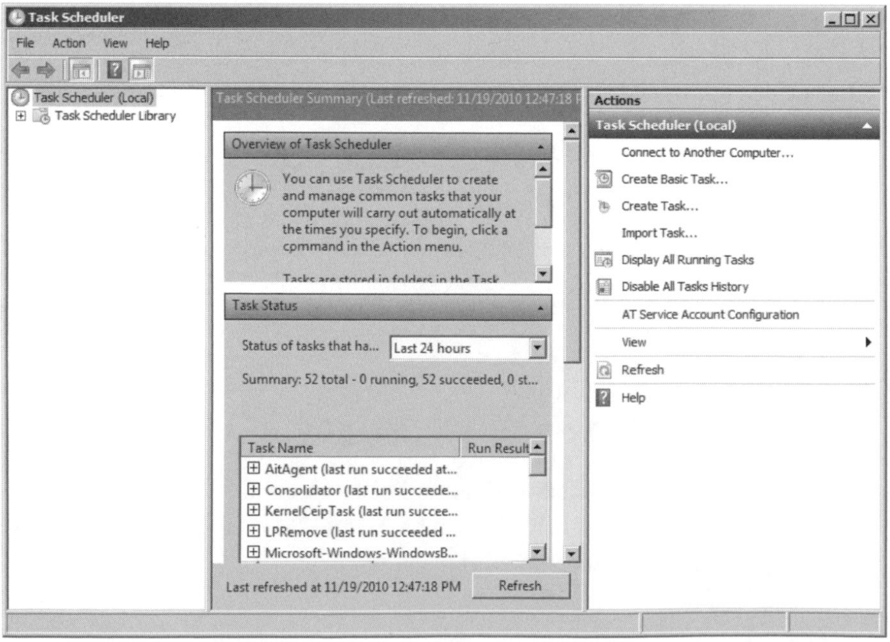

To create a task, you can choose either Create Task or Create Basic Task. For this example, you will use the Create Basic Task option:

1. Click Create Basic Task.

2. Enter the name and description of your task, and click Next.

3. Select how often you want to run the task, and click Next.

4. Based on your selection in step 3, you will be asked to set the parameters of when the script will run. For example, if you chose daily, you could have the script run at a specific time of day. After you have set the frequency, click Next.

5. On the Action screen, select Start A Program, and click Next.

6. In the Start A Program field, fill in the parameters as follows. When finished, click Next. Figure 7.19 shows an example task.

FIGURE 7.19   **Task created**

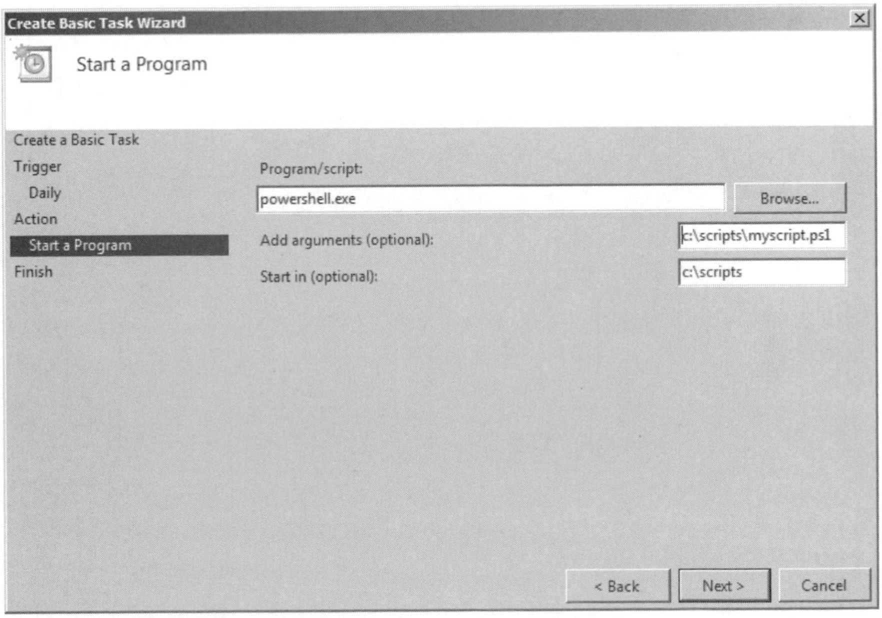

- ► Action: `powershell.exe`

- ► Add Arguments (Optional): The path and name of your script and any parameters, including `-noninteractive`

- ► Start in (Optional): The directory of your script

7. Review the summary screen, and click Finish.

Your scripts have to adhere to the script execution policy set on the server, as you saw in Chapter 5. Ensure you have the correct execution policy set, allowing your script to execute properly.

EXERCISE 7: CREATE A SCHEDULED BACKUP WITH POWERSHELL

In this exercise, create an automated process to back up the **c:** drive and system state on your Windows Server 2008 R2 server.

Managing Active Directory with PowerShell

IN THIS CHAPTER, YOU WILL LEARN TO:

PowerShell 2.0 has more than 90 cmdlets dedicated to Active Directory (AD). In PowerShell 1.0, you could work with AD objects, albeit not easily because doing so required a detailed knowledge of the Lightweight Directory Access Protocol (LDAP). Although you still need to know about LDAP in PowerShell 2.0, you do not have to delve as deep as you did in PowerShell 1.0.

PowerShell 2.0 and its built-in AD cmdlets make it easier for you to work with users, groups, organizational units (OUs), and many other objects in AD. This chapter outlines some of these new cmdlets and how PowerShell can directly interact with AD. The cmdlets are in the AD module that comes with the Active Directory server role; this chapter will show you how to access the cmdlets.

You can use PowerShell 2.0 not only to work with core AD objects but also to work with several other domain functions.

In addition to the AD cmdlets in PowerShell 2.0, Windows Server 2008 R2 offers several new services for AD. Windows Server 2008 R2 has two new powerful features for AD—managed service accounts and the AD recycle bin.

Work with Active Directory

PowerShell lets you automate users and groups in your AD environment. In Windows Server 2008, you could use PowerShell to manage objects, but it was cumbersome. Windows Server 2008 R2 includes several improvements and additions for easy management with Windows PowerShell. Newly created PowerShell cmdlets and the new AD recycle bin provide easier access to working with AD at a PowerShell level. You will see both of these in this section.

Load the AD PowerShell Module

Before you can begin using the new cmdlets, you need to load the AD PowerShell module. The AD PowerShell modules are installed by default on your Windows Server 2008 R2 server after you install Active Directory Domain Services. There are two ways you can load the AD module:

► Open the Active Directory module for PowerShell by selecting Start ➤ Administrative Tools ➤ Active Directory Module For PowerShell.

► Load a Windows PowerShell session (preferably an administrative session since many cmdlets will require administrative privileges), and import the

Active Directory module manually, using the command `Import-Module ActiveDirectory`.

You may prefer to load the Active Directory module for PowerShell instead of starting a PowerShell session. The main benefit of loading the AD module this way is that the Active Directory module for PowerShell automatically loads an administrative PowerShell session. A majority of the AD commands require administrative privileges.

Verify the module was loaded by running `Get-Module`.

Managing Active Directory with PowerShell

CHAPTER 8

MANAGING ACTIVE DIRECTORY WITH POWERSHELL ON A WINDOWS 7 CLIENT

You may want to manage your AD environment from a Windows 7 client workstation. Microsoft provides a free downloadable tool set called the Remote Server Administration Tools (RSAT) for Windows 7.

These tools can be installed only on computers running Windows 7 Enterprise, Windows 7 Professional, or Windows 7 Ultimate. RSAT contains three PowerShell modules you can use for managing your servers:

▶ **Active Directory**

▶ **Failover Cluster**

▶ **Network Load Balancing**

Having the AD module on your system allows for quick access to working with the AD environment from your management console.

You can download the tools here:

```
www.microsoft.com/downloads/en/details
.aspx?FamilyID=7d2f6ad7-656b-4313-a005-4e344e43997d
```

You should see the Active Directory module loaded. You can see a list of all the AD cmdlets by running the command `Get-Command *-ad*` or the command `Get-Command -Module ActiveDirectory`, resulting in a screen similar to Figure 8.1.

All the nouns in the Active Directory cmdlets begin with AD. This will help you learn the new cmdlets and explore their functionality.

PowerShell provides access to the AD data structure in a way that is similar to accessing the registry (see Chapter 7). So, you can use the same directory-style commands (such as `cd` or `dir`) to move around the AD structure; the command `cd AD:` lets you access the AD structure.

When you run the `cd AD:` command, the command prompt changes to `PS AD:\>`. This prompt reflects your current location in the Active Directory hierarchy. From there you can run `dir` to see the objects at the root and navigate to the domain. Before you can navigate, you need to know some of the basic LDAP naming conventions. You also need to know the basic navigation terminology and how Microsoft uses the terms in AD. Table 8.1 describes some of the basic terms.

TABLE 8.1   Basic LDAP navigation terminology

Terms	Description
dc	Domain component. The *components* of a domain name are separated by dots. The sequence of components in AD goes from the lowest level to the top level. For example, if your domain is called `deploy.com`, then you would refer to it in LDAP terminology as `dc=deploy, dc=com`.
ou	Organizational unit. Use this to move into OUs. The finance OU in the `deploy.com` domain would be `ou=finance, dc=deploy, dc=com`. If you have nested OUs, list the deeper OUs first. For example, the Cleveland OU inside the Finance OU in the `deploy.com` domain would be `ou=cleveland, ou=finance, dc=deploy, dc=com`.
cn	Container. In AD, this lets you navigate into special containers, such as Users. The Users container in the `deploy.com` domain would be `cn=Users, dc=deploy, dc=com`.

You will see this terminology used throughout this chapter with many of the AD cmdlets. Whether you are creating, navigating, or restoring users, understanding the basics will allow you to navigate inside AD quickly and easily. If you do not use the correct naming conventions as you are working with AD, you may see the error shown in Figure 8.2.

FIGURE 8.2 Navigation error

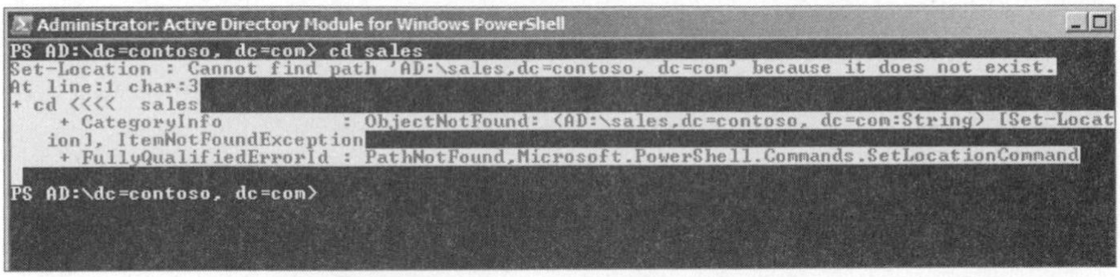

Using the basic naming conventions, you can navigate through your domain with cd. To change to the root of your domain, you would run a command similar to cd "dc=yourdomainname, dc=com" (or your FQDN ending). Additionally, you can also use tab completion here; this will help you avoid typing in the wrong domain path.

After you have navigated to the root of your domain, you then can navigate to the OU or container with cd. To change to your container after you have navigated to your domain structure, run this command:

    cd cn=*containername*

If you want to switch to an OU, the command is slightly different:

    cd ou=*Organizational Unit*

Once you have navigated to the desired location in AD, you can run the dir command to see the contents in that particular location. Figure 8.3 shows an example of the dir command in an OU.

FIGURE 8.3 dir in Active Directory

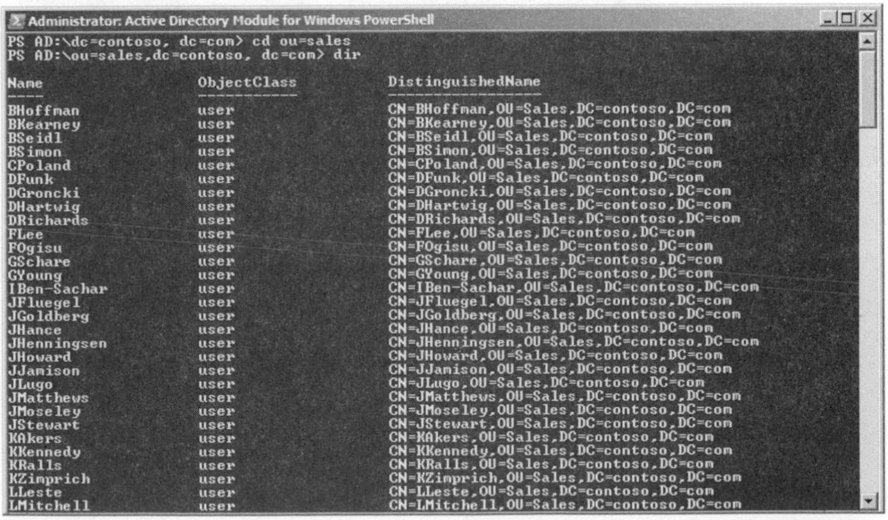

Understand PowerShell Active Directory Basics

This section covers some of the basics of working with domains, domain controllers, and forests (collections of namespaces, each of which may be a tree containing multiple domains). Forests provide a security boundary for your organization in AD, and you can manage them with PowerShell.

To display directory service–specific entries (DSEs) for your domain and configuration, run `Get-ADRootDSE`. This cmdlet displays the directory information tree for the domain, as shown in Figure 8.4.

FIGURE 8.4 `Get-ADRootDSE`

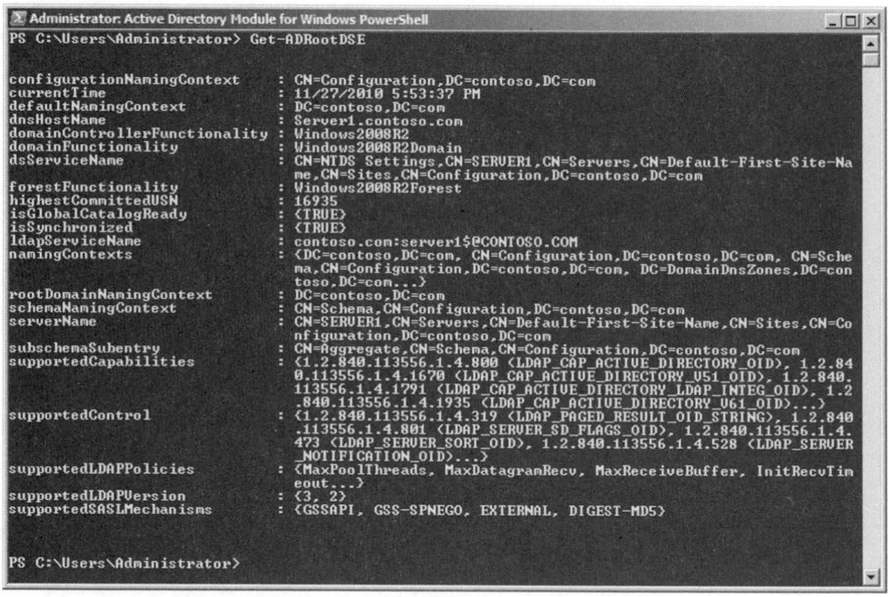

This shows the basic information about your domain and naming conventions. You can then use that information for many other commands. If you want to see all the domain controllers, use `Get-ADDomainController -Discover`. Then add the domain you are looking at, and you can find all the DCs in your environment. The following cmdlet will find the DCs in the `contoso.com` domain:

```
Get-ADDomainController -Discover -DomainName contoso.com
```

Your results may look like Figure 8.5.

FIGURE 8.5   `Get-ADDomainController`

You can also work with your global catalog (GC) servers via several cmdlets. GCs contain a subset of the data stored in AD. They are used to process all queries in the domain. If you are looking for users, groups, or printers, GC will process the requests across your entire forest. This functionality is not only used by AD but is also used by Microsoft Exchange for address book requests. Because GCs span multiple domains, they assist in user authentication and universal group membership processing. Knowing where your GCs are helps keep your AD environment running smoothly. To see what GCs are loaded in your forest, run this command:

```
Get-ADForest deploy.com | FL GlobalCatalogs
```

You can also enable or disable the GC status for a server with the following PowerShell command. For the options parameter, 1 enables a GC and 0 disables the GC. The following example disables the GC for Server1 in the `deploy.com` domain:

```
Set-ADObject "CN=NTDS Settings,CN=Server1,CN=Servers,↵
CN=Default-First-Site-Name,CN=Sites,CN=Configuration,↵
DC=deploy,DC=COM" -Replace @{options='0'}
```

To verify that the GC has been enabled or disabled on a server with the `Get-ADRootDSE` cmdlet, look for the value next to `IsGlobalCatalogReady`. If it is `true`, then the GC has been enabled. Enabling a GC on a server can take several minutes depending on your AD environment. You can also filter just the value for the global catalog with the `Get-ADRootDSE` cmdlet. This cmdlet looks at the global catalog value from the directory services information tree for Server1:

```
Get-ADRootDSE -Server Fabrikam-DC1 | FT GlobalCatalogReady
```

Figure 8.6 shows an example of the results.

FIGURE 8.6   Global catalog status

Working with the FSMO Roles

One of the other administrative tasks you may have done in the past is working with flexible single master operation (FSMO) roles. Typically you may have wanted to view the roles or transfer the roles to another server. With the new AD cmdlets, you can work with these roles on your server.

In PowerShell, you need to know the role names and how they are referred to in the cmdlets. There are five roles, listed in Table 8.2 with their PowerShell counterparts.

TABLE 8.2   FSMO roles in PowerShell

Role name	PowerShell name	Description
Schema Master	`SchemaMaster`	Holds the schema, or definition, for all the AD objects in your forest. There can be only one for the entire forest.
Domain Naming Master	`DomainNamingMaster`	Controls the addition and removal of domains in your forest. There can be only one for the entire forest.
PDC Emulator	`PDCEmulator`	Processes all the password change requests from your users. It will also replicate the change across the entire domain. There is one per domain in your forest.
RID Master	`RIDMaster`	Sequences the relative IDs (RIDs) for the entire domain when you create new objects. The relative ID is combined with the domain SID to ensure that a unique identifier is created for every new object in the domain. There is one per domain in your forest.
Infrastructure Master	`InfrastructureMaster`	Helps keep information about objects in the domain the Infrastructure Master role resides in consistent by comparing it to a GC for the domain. The primary purpose is to ensure the groups that users belong to from other domains are properly maintained and correct. There is one per domain in your forest, and generally it is not placed on the same server as a GC.

If you are looking for the Schema Master or Domain Naming Master role, use the `Get-ADForest` cmdlet. For example:

```
Get-ADForest deploy.com | FT SchemaMaster,DomainNamingMaster
```

If you are looking for the PDC Emulator, RID Master, or Infrastructure Master, use the `Get-ADDomain` cmdlet. This command shows all three of those FSMO roles for the `deploy.com` domain:

```
Get-ADDomain contoso.com | FT PDCEmulator,RIDMaster, ↵
InfrastructureMaster
```

Figure 8.7 shows an example of both commands being run. For either command, add or remove FSMO names for the particular roles you are interested in.

FIGURE 8.7   Discovering FSMO roles

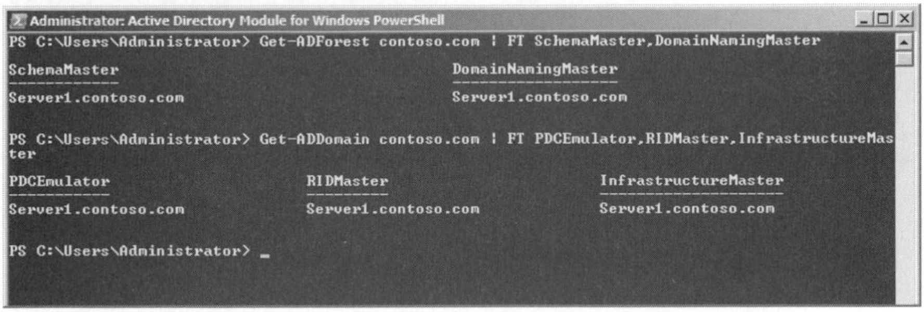

To transfer the FSMO roles to another server, run the following command. As with viewing the FSMO roles, add or remove the role names based on what roles you want to work with. This moves the Infrastructure Master role to Server2:

```
Move-ADDirectoryServerOperationMasterRole ↵
-Identity Server2 -InfrastructureMaster
```

To seize control over an FSMO role, add the `-force` parameter to the previous command, as shown here:

```
Move-ADDirectoryServerOperationMasterRole ↵
-Identity Server2 -InfrastructureMaster -force
```

You may have converted or upgraded your domain from previous versions of Windows Server to Windows Server 2008 R2. The version of operating system on your domain controllers determines your forest functional level. The forest functional level ensures proper functionality and communication in your domain. It can also determine what features are available in your domain. For example, you can use the AD recycle bin in Windows Server 2008 R2 only if your forest functional level is `Windows2008R2Forest`.

In PowerShell, you can view what your forest mode is by running `Get-ADForest`, as shown in Figure 8.8.

FIGURE 8.8 Forest mode

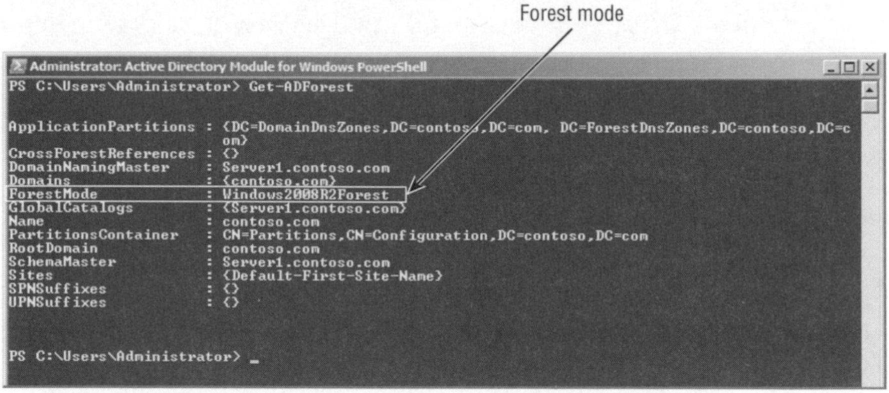

Forest mode

To change your forest mode, use the `Set-ADForestMode` cmdlet. You can use one of the four following parameters to raise your forest functional level:

▶ `Windows2003InterimForest`

▶ `Windows2003Forest`

▶ `Windows2008Forest`

▶ `Windows2008R2Forest`

This PowerShell command raises the forest functional level to `Windows2008R2Forest` for the `deploy.com` domain:

```
Set-ADForestMode -Identity deploy.com ↵
  -ForestMode Windows2008R2Forest
```

WARNING When you raise the forest functional level, this is a one-way trip. Once you raise the level of your forest, you cannot go backward.

Work with Users, Groups, and OUs

Table 8.3 lists some of the common tasks for using PowerShell with your users and groups. When you run the commands listed in the table, they run from the directory you are currently located in.

You can quickly find out which domain you are currently managing by running the `Get-ADRootDSE` cmdlet mentioned earlier in this chapter. You can also change to the AD provider with `cd AD:` and run `dir` to see which domain you are currently working in. Figure 8.9 shows an example.

FIGURE 8.9   `dir` on the root of the AD provider

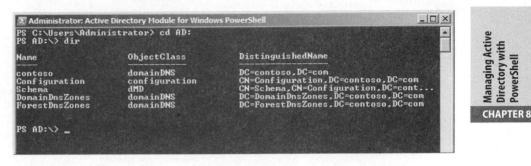

```
PS C:\Users\Administrator> cd AD:
PS AD:\> dir

Name                   ObjectClass           DistinguishedName
----                   -----------           -----------------
contoso                domainDNS             DC=contoso,DC=com
Configuration          configuration         CN=Configuration,DC=contoso,DC=com
Schema                 dMD                   CN=Schema,CN=Configuration,DC=cont...
DomainDnsZones         domainDNS             DC=DomainDnsZones,DC=contoso,DC=com
ForestDnsZones         domainDNS             DC=ForestDnsZones,DC=contoso,DC=com

PS AD:\> _
```

You can also use the LDAP terminology to navigate to the path of the object you want to modify. You can use `Get-Help` with any of the commands in Table 8.3 to learn more.

TABLE 8.3   Common PowerShell AD object commands

Cmdlet	Description	Example
Get-ADobject	Lists multiple AD objects, including users and groups. Works similarly to other Get cmdlets. Uses filter, ldapfilter, and searchbase to query the information. Use this with format and out switches to work with the command's output.	This command lists all the objects in AD: `Get-ADObject -Filter {name -like "*"}`
Get-ADuser	Lists the AD users in the domain. Uses filter, ldapfilter, and searchbase to query the information. Use this with format and out switches to work with the commands output.	This command lists all the users at your current level of the AD hierarchy: `Get-ADUser -Filter {name -like "*"}`

(continues)

TABLE 8.3   *(continued)*

Cmdlet	Description	Example
New-ADuser	Creates a new user in your AD environment. You can also control most of the properties for this cmdlet. You need to set a password and enable the account for use.	This command creates a user John Smith in the Marketing OU in the `admin.com` domain, with the display name and given name filled out: `New-ADuser johnsmith -GivenName "John" - Surname "Smith" -Displayname "John Smith" -Path 'OU=Marketing,DC=admin,DC=com'`
Set-ADaccountpassword	Sets the password for an AD account. Depending on how you use this command, you may be presented with a series of prompts to set the password. When you run this command, you do not need to specify the OU or domain name if you are located in the OU that contains the user.	This command resets the password of John Smith with a new password of `pa55w3rd`: `Set-adaccountpassword -identity johnsmith -reset -newpassword (Convert To-SecureString -AsPlainText "pa55w3rd" -force)`
Remove-ADuser	Removes a user from AD. When you run this command, you do not need to specify the OU or domain name if you are located in the OU that contains the user.	This command deletes the johnsmith user: `Remove-aduser johnsmith`
New-ADgroup	Creates a new group. You can also specify group type, scope, and other properties of the group.	This command will create a new global security group called Accounting: `New-adgroup Accounting -group-scope global`
Add-ADGroupMember	Allows you to modify the membership of an AD group. Use the `get-ADgroup` command to select a group.	This command adds John Smith to the Marketing group in the admin.com domain: `Get-ADGroup -SearchBase "DC=admin,DC=com" -SearchScope Subtree -Filter {Name -Like "*Marketing*"}	Add-ADGroupMember -Member John Smith`
New-ADorganizationalunit	Creates a new AD organizational unit.	This command creates a new OU called Finance in the `admin.com` domain: `New-ADOrganizationalUnit -Name "Finance" -Path "DC=admin,DC=com"`

When you are creating one of the many AD objects, you also have to become familiar with many of the parameters associated with the object type you are trying to create. For example, the `New-ADUser` cmdlet has many optional parameters you can use. Like all PowerShell cmdlets, you can ask for help. With the AD cmdlets, the `-full` switch for `Get-Help` displays a wealth of information and examples.

With any of the AD objects, you need to also learn the many properties associated with the objects. Knowing the properties allows you to manage your AD environment in scale. One of the tricks to working with the AD properties is knowing the names of the properties. To get the property names and to work with your AD objects, you can use the `Export-CSV` cmdlet. For example, the following command will export all the user objects in AD to a CSV file; you can then import the output into a spreadsheet to see all the property names:

```
Get-ADUser -filter * -properties * | Export-CSV alladdusers.csv
```

Understand Managed Service Accounts

Installing an application such as Exchange Server or IIS on your server typically requires a dedicated account to run it securely. This account is called a *service account*.

Typically, these accounts are associated with the services running behind the scenes. These accounts also govern the security privileges your applications have as they interact with your system. These accounts are like typical AD accounts; they have passwords that need to be maintained. If the passwords were to expire or change for these accounts, the applications they are associated with would normally stop working. As you can imagine, fixing this problem can be an administrative headache.

In the past, you may have set their passwords to never expire after creating a secure password, thus creating a stale password and leaving a security vulnerability in your environment. Some administrators may have used the same account or built-in accounts for multiple services. This would not provide service isolation; if the account became unusable, multiple applications on the server would have been affected.

Understand Managed Service Accounts

Managed service accounts are special accounts you create on your server to help with the management of your applications. These accounts are tied to your server's applications, but they avoid the pitfalls of the past. These accounts also provide a built-in capability to isolate your services for the different applications on your server. This helps avoid a single point of failure for your infrastructure and creates an easier troubleshooting path.

Even more effective at saving your time and effort is the automatic password management with managed service accounts. This helps you avoid manual password resets, stale passwords, and other possible issues in your infrastructure.

You create a service account tied to a specific server; you cannot have a service account shared by multiple servers. One of the key benefits is that service accounts allow server renaming under Windows Server 2008 R2 domain functional mode.

Create Managed Service Accounts

Creating a service account in your domain environment requires at least one Windows Server 2008 R2 domain controller. Several cmdlets allow you to work with managed service accounts. You need to be a domain administrator to be able to create managed service accounts. If your domain is in native Windows Server 2008 R2 mode, you are ready to begin working with managed service accounts. However, if your environment is in Windows Server 2008, Windows Server 2003, or another mixed-mode domain environment, you need to prepare your forest and domain. To prepare your environment, run these two commands on your Windows Server 2008 R2 domain controller:

- ► `adprep /forestprep`
- ► `adprep /domainprep` in every domain where you want to create and use managed service accounts

After your domain is prepared, you can create managed service accounts. Load the administrative PowerShell session with the AD module loaded. You can do this by clicking Start ➣ Administrative Tools ➣ Active Directory Module For PowerShell.

To create a managed service account, use the `New-ADServiceAccount` cmdlet. By default, managed service accounts are created in the Managed Service Accounts container. You can specify a different location if you want. The account will also be enabled after you create it. The following command creates a managed service account called Exchange2010 in the default Managed Service Accounts container:

```
New-ADServiceAccount Exchange2010
```

This command creates a managed service account called `WebServer` in the `web` organizational unit in the `contoso.com` domain:

```
New-ADServiceAccount WebServer -path "ou=web,dc=contoso,dc=com"
```

After you have created your managed service accounts or if you want to know what managed service accounts are on your server, you can run the following command:

```
Get-ADServiceAccount -filter *
```

Your results will look similar to Figure 8.10.

FIGURE 8.10   Managed service accounts

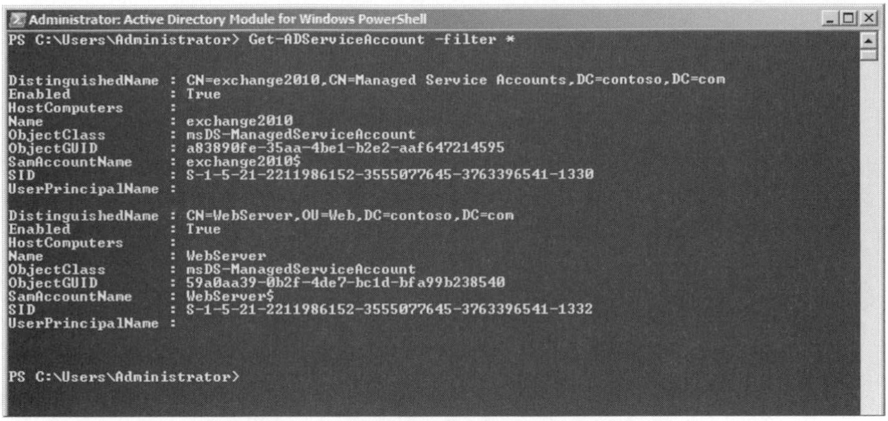

You may have noticed that when the managed service account is created, you do not need to specify a password. You can specify a password if you want; however, you should let Windows Server 2008 R2 handle the password. If you do not specify a password, the system generates a random password of 240 cryptographically random characters.

Not having to manage the passwords for the managed service accounts is a key benefit for you as an administrator. This formerly time-consuming process is now taken care of by the system. Managed service accounts are also subject to the domain's password policy, and their passwords will be changed automatically to comply with the policy.

If you no longer want to use a managed service account, you can remove the account with the Remove-ADServiceAccount cmdlet. To avoid downtime, make sure the managed service account is no longer in use before you remove the account. The following command removes the WebServer managed service account from the server:

```
Remove-ADServiceAccount  WebServer
```

When you run the command, you are asked to confirm deleting the account, as shown in Figure 8.11. Enter **Y**, and the account will be deleted.

FIGURE 8.11   Removing a managed service account

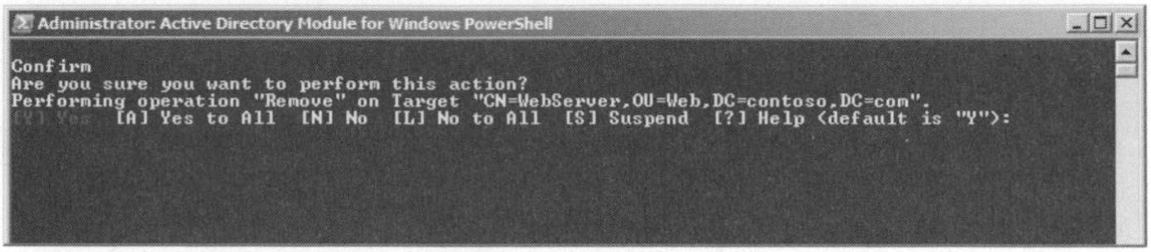

Install and Use Managed Service Accounts

After creating the managed service account, you then need to install the service account on the server or system on which you want to use the service account. After you install the account, you then need to configure the service with the managed service account.

Install the managed service account on the system via the `Install-ADServiceAccount` cmdlet. For example, to install a managed service account called `WebServer` on your system, run the following command:

```
Install-ADServiceAccount WebServer
```

After you install the managed service account on the server, it gets marked in AD to prevent it from being used on another server. A managed service account can be used by only one server.

After installing the account, configure the service to use the managed service account:

1. Start the Services console by selecting Start ➢ Administrative Tools ➢ Services.

2. Right-click the service you want to configure, and select Properties.

3. Click the Log On tab.

4. Click the This Account radio button.

5. You can type the name of the account in the format of **domainname\ accountname,** or you can click Browse to search for the account. After you have put the account name in the Services console, type a dollar sign ($) at the end of the account name to ensure proper configuration.

6. Ensure that the password field is blank. Your screen will look similar to Figure 8.12.

FIGURE 8.12   Configured managed service account

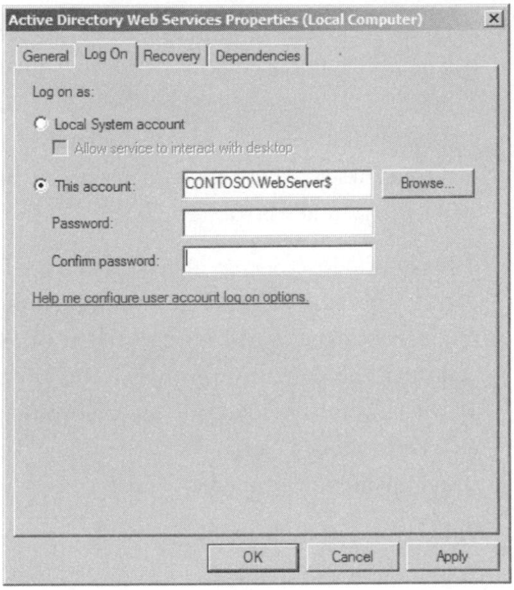

7. Click OK.

8. Before you close the Services console, you can click Start or restart to verify the service was properly configured.

You can also use managed service accounts with your Internet Information Services application pools. Chapter 10 shows how to configure IIS application pools with a managed service account.

If you are done with a managed service account on the system, you can uninstall the account with the `Uninstall-ADServiceAccount` cmdlet. For example, this cmdlet uninstalls the `WebServer` managed service account:

```
Uninstall-ADServiceAccount WebServer
```

Work with the Active Directory Recycle Bin

You may have at one time deleted a user by accident. In previous versions of Windows, you had to implement AD disaster/recovery scenarios for recovering the deleted object when an accidental deletion occurred. This method was complicated. Although using the recycle bin can be part of your overall backup and recovery strategy, you still need to perform your regular backups in your environment.

Understand How the Recycle Bin Works

Windows Server 2008 R2 includes the AD recycle bin. This is an addition to AD and an optional tool you can enable on your Windows Server 2008 R2 domain controllers. The recycle bin provides a tool for you to recover deleted users, groups, OUs, and other AD objects. All attributes of the object are automatically restored, including description, password, group membership, managed by, and formerly problematic linked attributes.

Prior to Windows Server 2008 R2 and the AD recycle bin, when you deleted an object, it became a tombstone object. By default, the tombstone object was still on the server and available for recovery for 180 days. During that time, you could restore the object with an authoritative restoration of your Active Directory. After 180 days, a garbage collection process would permanently remove the object from AD. Performing an authoritative restore of your AD was time-consuming and could involve downtime for your server.

After you enable the AD recycle bin, the process changes for deleted objects. When an object is deleted, it is placed in a container called Deleted Objects. By default, the object is in the Deleted Objects container for 180 days. During that time, you can use PowerShell to recover the object. After 180 days, the object becomes a recycled object. The object is in a tombstone state for another 180 days until the garbage collection process removes the object from AD.

You can change the default time for the recycle bin and tombstone by modifying their attribute values. To change the recycle bin, modify the msDS-DeletedObjectLifetime attribute. You can use the Set-ADobject cmdlet to change the object. The following command would set the recycle bin lifetime to 60 days for the deploy.com domain:

```
Set-ADObject -Identity "CN=Directory Service,CN=Windows NT ↵
,CN=Services,CN=Configuration,DC=deploy,DC=com" ↵
-Partition "CN=Configuration,DC=deploy,DC=com" ↵
 -Replace:@{ "msDS-DeletedObjectLifetime" = 60}
```

To change the tombstone lifetime, modify the tombstoneLifetime attribute. You can use the Set-ADobject cmdlet to change the object. The following command would set the tombstone lifetime to 60 days for the deploy.com domain:

```
Set-ADObject -Identity "CN=Directory Service,CN=Windows NT, ↵
CN=Services,CN=Configuration,DC=deploy,DC=com" -Partition ↵
```

```
"CN=Configuration,DC=deploy,DC=com" ↵
-Replace:@{ "tombstoneLifetime" = 60}
```

The new timeframe applies only to newly deleted objects. Any object deleted before you enable the recycle bin follows normal deletion processes.

Enable the AD Recycle Bin

By default, the recycle bin is not enabled on your server. There are several things you need to know about the recycle bin before you enable it. The first thing is that once it has been enabled, you cannot disable it. The only way to work around the recycle bin is to reduce the lifetime of the recycle bin by modifying the msDS-DeletedObjectLifetime attribute.

Before you enable the AD Recycle Bin, make sure your forest functional level is set to Windows Server 2008 R2. This is required to ensure that all domain controllers preserve attributes necessary to complete a successful object recovery. To raise the forest functional level to Windows Server 2008 R2, you need to have all of your domain controllers running Windows Server 2008 R2 as their operating system.

OTHER DOMAIN FUNCTIONAL MODES

Before enabling the recycle bin, you may need to perform some additional tasks on your domain. If your environment was in Windows Server 2008, Windows Server 2003, or other mixed-mode domain environments, you need to prepare the schema with the attributes necessary to support the recycle bin. You need to prepare the forest and the domain after you upgraded your domain controllers to Windows Server 2008 R2.

To prepare the forest, run the following command on the server that is the schema master operations master:

```
adprep /forestprep
```

Run the following command on the server that is the infrastructure operations master role:

```
adprep /domainprep /gpprep
```

If your domain has read-only domain controllers (RDOCs), you also need to run the following command:

```
adprep /rodcprep
```

Raising the functional level really has no effect other than allowing optional features, such as the recycle bin, to be enabled. You can raise the functional level with confidence and avoid any unnecessary side effects. Enabling the recycle bin can lead to a growth of the Active Directory database file of around 5–10 percent when installed on a new DC. The growth of the database depends on the size and frequency of object deletions in your domain.

To see whether the recycle bin has already been enabled on your server, run the following command:

```
Get-ADOptionalFeature 'Recycle Bin Feature'
```

Your results should look similar to Figure 8.13.

FIGURE 8.13   Recycle bin feature disabled

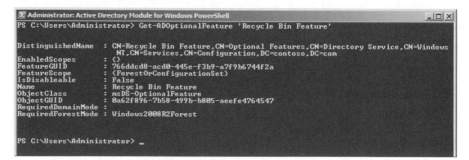

If you do not see anything in the EnabledScopes parameter, the recycle bin is currently disabled. To work with the recycle bin, you need to enable the optional feature with the AD modules for PowerShell. To enable the recycle bin, perform the following procedure:

1. Load the Active Directory module in PowerShell in administrator mode. You can do this with Import-Module ActiveDirectory.

2. Type the following command to enable the recycle bin. You will see a screen similar to Figure 8.14.

```
Enable-ADOptionalFeature "Recycle Bin Feature" -Scope↵
    ForestorConfigurationSet -Target 'your domain name'
```

FIGURE 8.14   Enabling the recycle bin

3. Type **Y** to enable the feature.

4. Verify the recycle bin has been enabled by running the following command. Your screen will look similar to Figure 8.15.

```
Get-ADOptionalFeature 'Recycle Bin Feature'
```

FIGURE 8.15   Enabled recycle bin

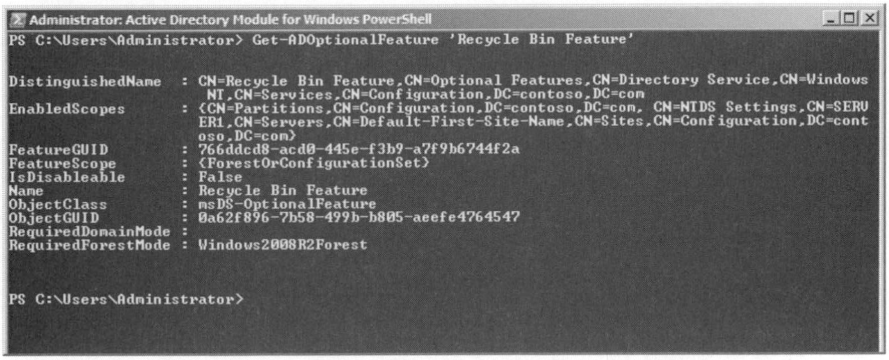

Notice now the enabled scope has your domain referenced in the parameter.

Use the AD Recycle Bin

After enabling the recycle bin, you can access the container by using PowerShell. If you have deleted a user and need to bring that AD object back, you can recover the object from the recycle bin with the AD module for PowerShell.

Before restoring an Active Directory object, you need to know the ObjectGUID for the object you want to restore. To recover an object from the recycle bin, perform the following procedure:

1. With the AD module loaded, use the following command to view the objects in the recycle bin:

```
Get-ADObject -SearchBase "CN=Deleted Objects, ↵
DC=your domain name,DC=Com" -ldapFilter "(objectClass=*)" ↵
  -includeDeletedObjects | format-list
```

Another useful cmdlet you can leverage here is Out-GridView. This makes it easier to see the objects, and with the built-in sorting capabilities, you can find the necessary ObjectGUID quickly. Figure 8.16 is an example of the previous command, using Out-GridView.

FIGURE 8.16   Recycle bin in GridView

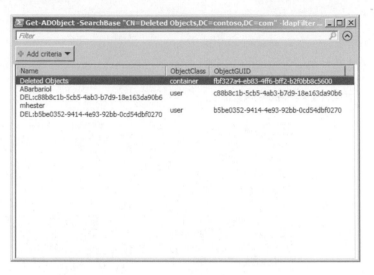

To filter the results even more, you can modify the `objectClass` parameter from the previous command. To recover user objects, change the `object-Class` parameter to `user`. To see just the user objects in your recycle bin, change your command to look like the following:

```
Get-ADObject -SearchBase "CN=Deleted Objects, ↵
DC=your domain name,DC=Com" -ldapFilter "(objectClass=user)" ↵
 -includeDeletedObjects | format-list
```

2. Write down or copy the `ObjectGUID` for the object you want to recover; this is the identity of the object you have deleted. You can use PowerShell to help copy the text. This procedure is similar to previous command prompt knowledge you may have. To copy text from a command prompt, right-click and then select Mark. Highlight the text to copy, and then press Enter. To paste, right-click and then click Paste.

3. Recover the object with the following command:

```
Restore-ADObject -Identity ObjectGUID from step 2
```

4. To verify the object has been recovered, you can check your AD or run the following command:

```
Get-ADObject -Filter {displayName -eq "users display name"} ↵
 -IncludeDeletedObjects
```

Figure 8.17 shows an example of the command. Notice the `deleted` parameter is no longer marked as true.

FIGURE 8.17   Recovered AD object

Recovering Multiple Users

Although knowing how to recover an individual user can be extremely useful, the process can be time-consuming. What if you deleted an entire OU by accident, with 100 users or more? Do you need to find each `ObjectGUID` and recover each user individually? The answer is no. You can use the power of the pipe symbol to tie together the `Get-ADObject` and `Restore-ADObject` cmdlets.

You can run this with one PowerShell command. To make your job easier, you need to know the name of the deleted OU. The following command is an example to recover all the deleted users from the `Marketing` OU in the `deploy.com` domain:

```
Get-ADObject –SearchBase "CN=Deleted Objects, ↵
DC=your domain name,DC=Com" -Filter {lastKnownParent ↵
-eq "OU=marketing,DC=deploy,dc=com"} -includeDeletedObjects ↵
| Restore-ADObject
```

Depending how many users you want to recover, this command may take several minutes to run in your AD environment.

EXERCISE 8: POPULATE AN ACTIVE DIRECTORY TEST ENVIRONMENT

Create a PowerShell procedure that creates 10 users. Create an OU called test, and put the 10 users in the OU. Delete all 10 users after you create them. Using the recycle bin, recover the users.

Managing Desktops with PowerShell

IN THIS CHAPTER, YOU WILL LEARN TO:

When you have installed Active Directory into your infrastructure, one of your goals should be centralization. In other words, you want to be able to control security, management, and resource access from one central location. You also want to be able to manage and control your desktops.

Active Directory has a tool, called Group Policy, for centrally managing your desktops. With Group Policy you can manage virtually everything on the systems in your infrastructure — from the color of the wallpaper to what applications can run to how security works. This includes not only your client desktops but also your servers.

This chapter provides an overview of Group Policy and how it functions. You will also see how you can use PowerShell to help manage the Group Policy environment, working with not only the settings themselves but also the administrative maintenance of Group Policy objects. The chapter closes with a look at a new feature for Windows 7 and Windows Server 2008 R2 called AppLocker.

Access Group Policy

In managing the systems in your network, one goal to strive for is consistency across all of the systems. To do this, Active Directory provides a tool called Group Policy.

Group Policy allows you to provide daily control and maintenance of your users' desktops from a centralized location. Group Policy can help configure either the computers or the users in your Active Directory. By targeting a computer with Group Policy, you can maintain the desktop and ensure that every user who uses the desktop has a default configuration you mandate for your systems. When you target users with Group Policy, the users' settings based on the group policies travel with the users within your AD environment.

Group Policy also allows you to define your corporate desktop configuration. There are thousands of settings you can configure, including settings for security, startup scripts, mapped printers, application standardization, quality of service (QoS), and Internet Explorer maintenance. This is not only for maintaining and configuring your infrastructure but also for protecting your infrastructure by managing these settings in a centralized location and allowing you to prevent users from changing these settings. Being effective with Group Policy can save you time and energy when working with the desktops and users in your environment.

Although Group Policy gives you centralized control over your users' environment, you also have to balance control with workability. In other words, do not be so restrictive with Group Policy that it negatively affects your users' needs to accomplish their jobs.

Understand Group Policy

Group Policy allows you to enforce your IT policies, implement any necessary security settings, and implement a standard computing environment across your Active Directory environment.

Having a standard environment provides a consistent base and helps alleviate support desk calls. Group Policy helps simplify your day-to-day administrative tasks and leverage your existing knowledge of the AD environment. Before you begin working with Group Policy, you need to be aware of some basic terms. You need to understand the scope of policy management as well how Group Policy is processed by the client systems. Table 9.1 describes some of the terms used with this tool.

TABLE 9.1   Group Policy terminology

Term	Description
Group Policy Management Console (GPMC)	The main interface where you can create Group Policy objects (GPOs). GPMC creates the links defining what objects the GPO will target. There are three main scopes managed in GPMC: sites, domains, and organizational units (OUs).
Group Policy object (GPO)	Objects that contain all of the settings you want to apply to your users or computers. GPOs are linked to organizational units.
Group Policy link	Links a GPO to the portion of your AD environment where you want the GPO to be applied. This is referred to as the scope. There are three main levels you apply GPOs to: site, domain, and OU.
Administrative template file (ADMX file)	Defines the location of the settings and configuration on the local systems and creates the interface you use to modify the settings in the Group Policy Editor, which is the GUI for managing Group Policy.
Group Policy preferences	Provide alternatives to working with companywide images to manage settings previously not easily configured in Group Policy. The settings, initially set by the administrator, reflect a default state of the operating system and are not enforced.
Resultant Set of Policy (RSOP)	RSOP is the set of policy settings applied after all the Group Policy processing is complete. This could be a combination of many levels of Group Policy.

Managing Desktops with PowerShell

CHAPTER 9

Understand How Group Policy Works

Effective AD design provides the basis of management of Group Policy. Group Policy can be applied to the site, domain, or organizational unit level. Table 9.2 shows the impact and recommendations for using the different levels with Group Policy.

TABLE 9.2　Scopes of Group Policy management

Scope	Objects affected	Recommendation
Site	All of the domains and the objects in the AD site. This is the largest scope of impact.	Sites are useful when you are setting network security settings, such as proxy server or IPSec policies. You also need to be an enterprise administrator to create GPOs at this level.
Domain	All of the objects in the chosen domain.	The domain scope is used for your password policies (length, complexity, expiration, and so on) and other security settings where you want consistent application.
Organizational unit	All of the objects in the chosen OU, as well as any nested OUs and their objects.	This is the recommended scope for Group Policy application. OUs provide the easiest-to-manage location for all of your Group Policy needs.

As stated in Table 9.2, organizational units are the recommended scope for group policies. One of the benefits of having an effective OU design is that the design can assist you in applying group policies. Using OUs can help you control the application of Group Policy by allowing you to target the unique needs for the users and computers in each OU.

When Group Policy is enforced on your systems, it modifies the registry of those systems. The policies may persist in the registry or may be refreshed as the policy is updated. If a user has the ability to make changes to settings you have modified with Group Policy, background processing refreshes them. Policies are updated in the background at various intervals, which are also configurable via Group Policy settings. If the system is a domain controller, the policy is refreshed every five minutes by default. On all other systems, the refresh interval is 90 minutes plus a random interval of up to 30 minutes by default; so, a policy could take up to 2 hours before the changes you made to the GPO are reflected on the target system. However, if the system can be rebooted, this shortens that wait period, because group policies targeting computers are always updated when a system starts. The refresh interval is the same length for group policies targeting users; user policy updates are also run at login, so logging out and back in can refresh a user's group policies that target the user. You can also manually update the Group Policy settings by running `gpupdate /force` in a PowerShell session or in a command prompt.

GROUP POLICY REFRESH INTERVALS

As previously noted, group policies are refreshed at certain intervals that are configured within their own policies. You can set these refresh intervals from 0 minutes to 45 days. If you set the interval to 0 minutes, the system tries to update every seven seconds. However, this causes a spike in network traffic and is typically not recommended.

Since this is set within a policy, this policy can be disabled. If the policy is disabled, the group policies update at their normal interval — 5 minutes for domain controllers and 90 minutes for other systems. If you want to stop the refreshing of group policies, look into the group policy called "Disable background refresh of Group Policy."

Also note that the group policies for users, computers, and domain controllers can be updated at different intervals. There are three policies for managing these refresh intervals: "Group Policy refresh interval for users," "Group Policy refresh interval for computers," and "Group Policy refresh interval for domain controllers."

Managing Desktops with PowerShell

CHAPTER 9

Manage Group Policy

Group Policy, like many other tools, has a dedicated module for storing all the cmdlets you can use to manage Group Policy. However, the Group Policy module is not available on all the systems that have PowerShell installed.

You can get the Group Policy module only if your system is one of the following:

- ► Domain controller
- ► A member server of the domain member with the Group Policy Management Console (GPMC) installed
- ► Windows 7 with the Remote Server Administration Tools (RSAT) installed

To import the Group Policy module, run the following command:

```
Import-Module grouppolicy
```

If you try to import the Group Policy module on a system not meeting one of the previous criteria, you will see a screen similar to Figure 9.1.

FIGURE 9.1　Group Policy module error

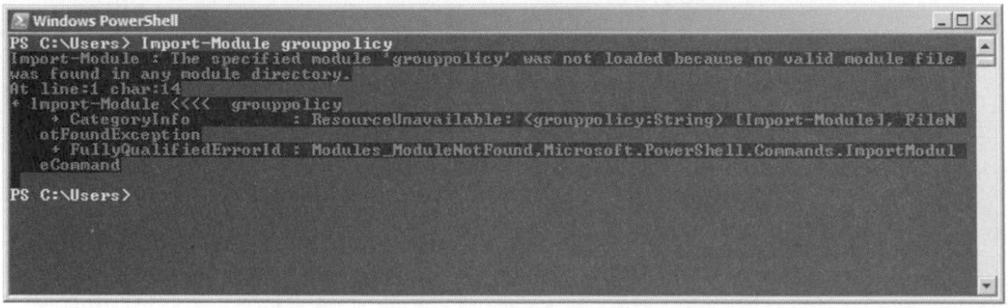

After you have successfully imported the Group Policy module, you can see a list of the cmdlets available by running this:

```
Get-Command -module grouppolicy
```

Your results will look similar to Figure 9.2.

FIGURE 9.2　Group Policy cmdlets

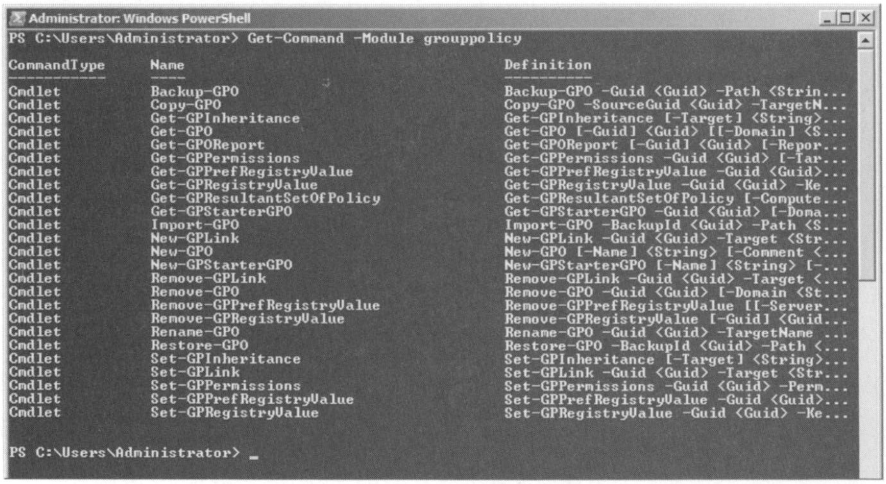

When you work with Group Policy, you should perform common administrative tasks, such as backup and recovery, on a regular basis. These tasks can be performed through the GPMC, as well as in PowerShell. The most common administrative task you will do with Group Policy is configure settings or preferences. Table 9.3 describes common cmdlets for working with Group Policy settings.

The Get-GPO cmdlet allows you to see the Group Policy objects (GPOs) in your domain. To see all of the GPOs, run the following command. This command lists the basic information (settings, status, name, and GUID) for the GPOs in your domain:

```
Get-GPO -All
```

TABLE 9.3   Policy and preferences cmdlets

Cmdlet	Description
Get-GPO	Lists all the GPOs in the domain; you can list a specific GPO, or you can list all of the GPOs for the domain.
New-GPO	Creates a new Group Policy object in your domain.
New-GPLink	Creates a new Group Policy link for an existing GPO in your domain.
Set-GPRegistryValue	Sets a policy setting. For your Group Policy object to be effective with this cmdlet, you need to know the location in the registry of the GPO you want to modify.
Set-GPPrefRegistryValue	Sets a preference setting. For your Group Policy object to be effective with this cmdlet, you need to know the location in the registry of the GPO you want to modify.

Your results will look similar to Figure 9.3.

FIGURE 9.3   Get-GPO -All

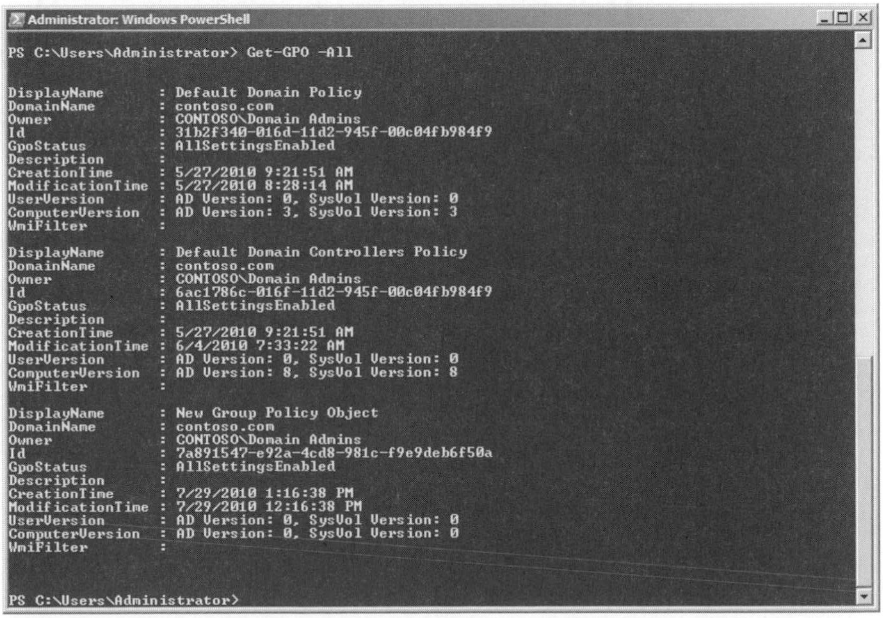

When you are working with GPOs in PowerShell, you can use either the display name or the ID parameter. The ID is also used to help keep track of the GPOs when they are replicated to other domain controllers. The Group Policy objects are stored in %windir%\SYSVOL\domain\Policies. When you browse to the directory, you will see each GPO ID has its own folder. The SYSVOL directory maintains a central location for the GPO files. Figure 9.4 shows an example of browsing to the Policies directory.

FIGURE 9.4   GPO listing in SYSVOL

If you want to see just the settings of a particular GPO, you can use one of the following commands:

► If you use the ID, use `Get-GPO -ID <GUID of GPO>`.

► If you use the display name, use `Get-GPO -DisplayName <Display name of GPO>`. Or, since display name is positional, use `Get-GPO - <Display name of GPO>`. If the display name has spaces, place quotation marks (`""`) around the name.

Create Group Policy Objects

Creating a new GPO you will do two things, first you will create a GPO to store all of your settings and then you will create a GPO link to associate it with a level of management. See the "Understand Group Policy Order of Precedence" section later in this chapter to understand the effect of placing a link.)

Creating a GPO in PowerShell involves combining the two cmdlets: New-GPO and New-GPLink. For example, the following command would create a GPO called RemoveRun linked to the marketing OU in the deploy.com domain:

```
New-GPO -Name RemoveRun | New-GPLink ↵
-target "ou=marketing,dc=deploy, dc=com"
```

Although you can create GPOs and not link them, you will normally create both GPOs and Group Policy links at the same time so they take effect right away.

When you create and link a GPO, the default security is also set. The default security is set to allow all the domain users group to apply GPO for the systems. Using the Get-GPPermissions cmdlet, you can see the permissions for a given GPO. This command lists permissions for a GPO called test:

```
Get-GPPermissions test -all
```

Your results will look similar to Figure 9.5.

FIGURE 9.5 **Get-GPPermissions**

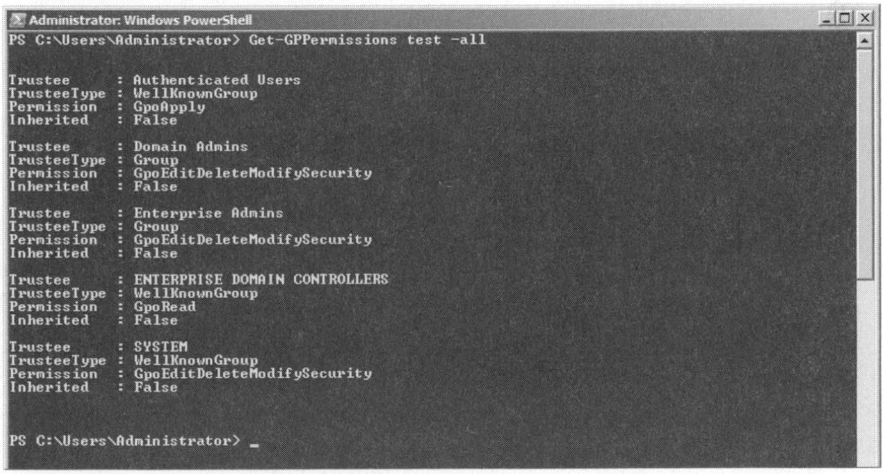

You may also need to set security on the files so they can be used by users. There are five levels of security you can set on a GPO using the Set-GPPermissions cmdlet. Table 9.4 describes the five permission levels.

This command sets the permissions to GPOEdit level on the GPO called test for the group called Test Administrators:

```
Set-GPPermissions -Name Test -TargetName ↵
 "Test Administrators" -TargetType Group ↵
-PermissionLevel GpoEdit
```

TABLE 9.4   Group Policy permission levels

Permission level	PowerShell value	Description
Read	GpoRead	Basic permission allowing the read of the GPO; mandatory to be able to apply the GPO
Apply	GpoApply	Allows the GPO to be applied to the targeted user or computer and includes the read permission
Edit	GpoEdit	Allows editing of the GPO settings
GPO Administrator	GpoEditDeleteModifySecurity	Allows editing of the GPO settings and all other administrative tasks, from deleting link to delegating administrative permissions
None	None	Removes permissions from the GPO

When you use the Set-GPPermissions cmdlet, by default it does not replace the permissions on the GPO if they are currently higher than what you are trying to set. If you want your permissions change to replace the existing level, you need to use the -Replace switch. This command forces your security setting:

```
Set-GPPermissions -Name Test -TargetName ↵
  "Test Administrators" -TargetType Group ↵
-PermissionLevel GpoEdit -Replace
```

Use Starter GPOs

In Group Policy there are several template files with preconfigured settings. There are eight system starter GPOs that were introduced with Windows Server 2008 R2 and Windows 7 with Remote Server Administration Tools. The GPOs are for Enterprise Client (EC) and Specialized Security Limited Functionality (SSLF) systems. The standards and settings for EC and SSLF are defined in the security guides for Windows Vista and Windows XP.

- ► Windows Vista EC Computer Starter GPO
- ► Windows Vista EC User Starter GPO
- ► Windows Vista SSLF Computer Starter GPO
- ► Windows Vista SSLF User Starter GPO
- ► Windows XP SP2 EC Computer Starter GPO
- ► Windows XP SP2 EC User Starter GPO
- ► Windows XP SP2 SSLF Computer Starter GPO
- ► Windows XP SP2 SSLF User Starter GPO

When you first work on your Windows Server 2008 R2 server, the starter GPOs are not installed. The `Get-GPStarterGPO -all` command is used to show the starter GPOs on the system. If you run the cmdlet and see the error in Figure 9.6, you need to load the starter GPOs.

FIGURE 9.6   No starter GPOs

To load the GPOs on the system, you can use the Group Policy Management Console, or you can use `New-GPStarterGPO`. When you run the `New-StarterGPO` cmdlet, you have to specify a name for the new starter GPO. If you have not yet installed the system starter GPOs on the system when you run the `New-GPStarterGPO` cmdlet, it creates the starter GPOs for you. Figure 9.7 shows the results of `Get-GPStarterGPO -all` after you have the starter GPOs installed.

FIGURE 9.7   Starter GPOs

```
Administrator: Windows PowerShell                                          _ |□| x|
PS C:\Users\Administrator> New-GPStarterGPO

cmdlet New-GPStarterGPO at command pipeline position 1
Supply values for the following parameters:
Name: test

DisplayName       : test
Id                : 13df98a2-895e-41be-b016-6b213b44bd80
Owner             : BUILTIN\Administrators
CreationTime      : 12/15/2010 12:59:54 PM
ModificationTime  : 12/15/2010 12:59:54 PM
UserVersion       : 0
ComputerVersion   : 0
StarterGpoVersion :
StarterGpoType    : Custom
Author            :
Description       :


PS C:\Users\Administrator> Get-GPStarterGPO -all

DisplayName       : Windows XP SP2 SSLF User
Id                : 0874086b-4ad8-4b4d-9321-dcba3aa69c8c
Owner             : BUILTIN\Administrators
CreationTime      : 12/15/2010 12:59:52 PM
ModificationTime  : 6/10/2009 12:44:02 PM
UserVersion       :
ComputerVersion   :
StarterGpoVersion : 0
StarterGpoType    : System
Author            : Microsoft
Description       : This Starter GPO contains the user Group Policy settings recommended for th
                    e Specialized Security Limited Functionality (SSLF) client environment desc
                    ribed in the Windows XP security guide.

                    For more information about each of these settings, see the Windows XP Secur
                    ity Guide <http://go.microsoft.com/fwlink/?LinkID=121854>.

DisplayName       : test
Id                : 13df98a2-895e-41be-b016-6b213b44bd80
Owner             : BUILTIN\Administrators
```

When you create a GPO, you can specify a starter GPO using the previous names and the New-GPO cmdlet. For example, the following command will create a new GPO called XpSP2sslfUser using the Windows XP SP2 SSLF User Starter GPO linked to the XPDesktops organizational unit in deploy.com.

```
New-GPO -Name XpSP2sslfUser -StarterGPOName↵
 "Windows XP SP2 SSLF User Starter GPO" ↵
| New-GPLink -target "ou=XPDesktops,dc=deploy, dc=com"
```

Work with Settings

You can also work with individual settings for GPOs in PowerShell. This can be useful for modifying multiple GPOs at once. However, for one-off changes to GPOs, although PowerShell can be used, you may prefer to use the Group Policy Editor. The main reason why you would want to use the Group Policy Editor is you need to know the registry locations as well the values needed in the registry, and the Group Policy Editor provides a nice interface for seeing these locations. To use the following PowerShell cmdlets, you may need to do some investigative work in the Group Policy Editor prior to making changes in PowerShell.

To make changes in PowerShell to the settings in a GPO, you can use two cmdlets — one for policies and the other for preferences:

```
Set-GPRegistryValue
```

```
Set-GPPrefRegistryValue
```

Both of these cmdlets can be used to modify the registry once you know the registry locations and values. For example, this command enables the Run menu on the Start menu of a Windows 7 client for the RunUsersRun GPO:

```
Set-GPRegistryValue -Name "RunUsersRun" -key↵
 "HKCU\Software\Microsoft\Windows\CurrentVersion\Policies↵
\Explorer" -ValueName ForceRunOnStartMenu ↵
-Type DWORD -value 1
```

The cmdlets work similarly; however, there is a difference between the two that you need to understand. See "Understand the Difference Between Policies and Preferences" later in this chapter.

You can also quickly look at the settings for any GPO with the Get-GPOReport cmdlet, which creates an XML or HTML output file of all the settings in a particular GPO. This cmdlet generates a report for the RunUsersRun GPO in HTML format:

```
Get-GPOReport -Name RunusersRun -ReportType ↵
HTML -path c:\users\matt\desktop\runusersrun.html
```

Figure 9.8 shows an example of the HTML report.

FIGURE 9.8   HTML report

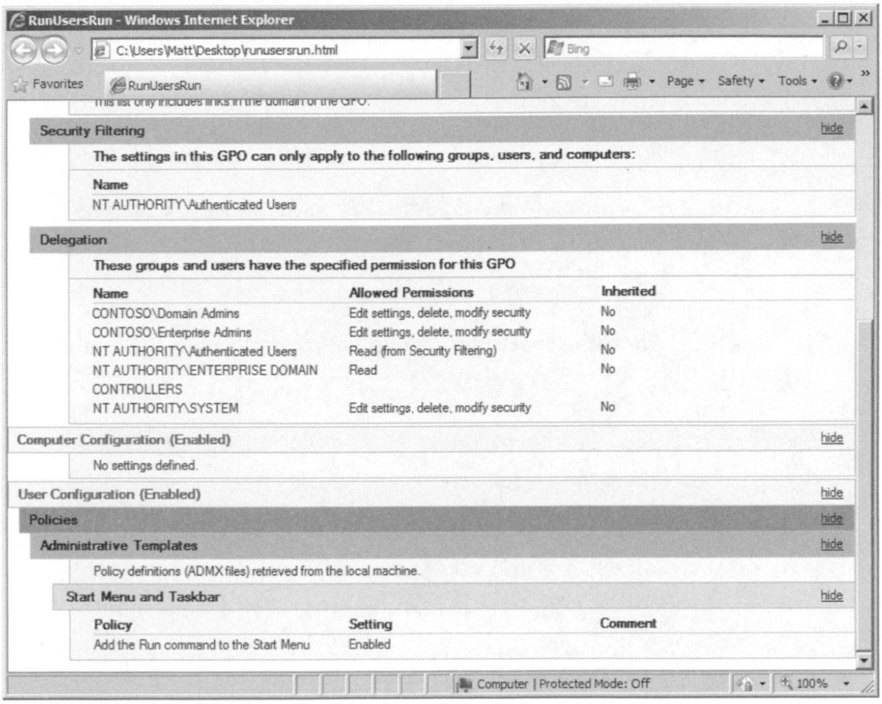

Depending on your browser, you may be prompted to enable ActiveX controls before viewing the report. These allow for tab expansion to browse through the file quickly. You can also use the -All parameter instead of a name of a specific GPO to get a report for all the GPOs for your domain.

Understand the Difference Between Policies and Preferences

Table 9.3 lists cmdlets to work with two different groups of settings in Group Policy:

► Polices

► Preferences

As you work with Group Policy settings, you need to know the difference between them. Both policies and preferences can modify both user and computer objects; however, they serve two different purposes. The main difference is enforcement; policies are enforced, while preferences are not strictly enforced.

Policies

When you are working with policies, the settings and interface are based on administrative templates. Policies make changes to the registry as directed by the administrative template. There are special sections in the registry hives that are controlled by Group Policy. The Group Policy settings stored in these locations are known as true policies.

Specifically, Group Policy works with these two locations for computer settings:

- ► HKEY_LOCAL_MACHINE \SOFTWARE\policies (preferred location)
- ► HKEY_LOCAL_MACHINE \SOFTWARE\Microsoft\Windows\ CurrentVersion\policies

For the user settings, Group Policy works with the following two locations:

- ► HKEY_CURRENT_USER \SOFTWARE\policies (preferred location)
- ► HKEY_ CURRENT_USER \SOFTWARE\Microsoft\Windows\ CurrentVersion\policies

Every time a system processes Group Policy and gets the RSOP, these registry hives (all the keys and values) are erased and rewritten with the new RSOP. This occurs only as long as a valid Group Policy is still being applied to the computer or user.

Preferences

Introduced in Windows Server 2008, preferences provide an alternative to using scripts to perform common tasks. These tasks were traditionally not done easily, if at all, in Group Policy. Preferences allow you to modify local registry settings, local users and groups, files and folders, printers, local services, mapped drives, and many other local settings. Since preferences are not enforced on local systems, users have the ability to make changes. Additionally, preferences are useful for non-Group-Policy-aware applications and system settings. However, these changes rarely occur because of the nature of preferences requiring some kind of administrative credentials.

You can also target individual preference items through Group Policy filtering. This is very different from true policies, in that you cannot target individual settings inside Group Policy true policies.

Work with Domain Password Policies

Working with domain password policies allows you to control the settings for things such as password history, length, and complexity requirements for your domain. These policy settings help keep your domain secure and your users' passwords more secure. You can work with these policies in PowerShell; however, for these policies, you use cmdlets from the Active Directory module rather than the Group Policy module.

There are two main cmdlets you will use from the AD module to work directly with password policies:

```
Get-ADDefaultDomainPasswordPolicy

Set-ADDefaultDomainPasswordPolicy
```

To see the current password policy for the domain, run the following command:

```
Get-ADDefaultDomainPasswordPolicy -Identity contoso.com
```

Your results will look similar to Figure 9.9.

FIGURE 9.9   Default password policy

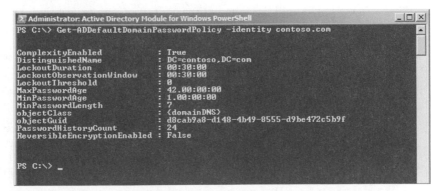

When setting the password policy, you need to know what parameters to change. The main parameters are as follows:

- `ComplexityEnabled`: Can be `$true` or `$false` and is used to enforce complex passwords

- `MaxPasswordAge`: Defines how old a password can be before a user has to change it

- `MinPasswordAge`: Defines how old a password has to be before a user can change it

- `MinPasswordLength`: Defines the minimum length of characters for a password

- `PasswordHistoryCount`: Defines how many passwords AD will remember until a user can reuse a former password

To set the password policy for the contoso.com domain to have passwords that need to be changed every 50 days with a length of 15 characters, you would use the following command:

```
Set-ADDefaultDomainPasswordPolicy -Identity contoso.com↵
-MaxPasswordAge 50.00:00:00 -MinPasswordLength 15
```

There also three other parameters you can use with the Set-ADDefaultDomainPasswordPolicy cmdlet that control the account lockout policy. The account lockout policy determines how tolerant AD is with failed logon attempts.

► LockoutDuration: Defines how long an account will be locked out for when the LockoutThreshold is reached.

► LockoutObservationWindow: Defines how long before the LockoutThreshold counter is reset.

► LockoutThreshold: Defines how many failed logon attempts AD will allow until the account becomes locked out. By default this value is set to 0, which means the accounts will never be locked out.

If your domain is contoso.com and you want three failed logon attempts before the account is locked out, with an account locked out for 45 minutes, run the following command:

```
Set-ADDefaultDomainPasswordPolicy -Identity contoso.com↵
 -LockoutDuration 00:45:00 -LockoutThreshold 3
```

Understand Order of Precedence

When you create group policies, you are not limited to just one GPO or one scope of management. By default, the RSOP is the culmination of all the scopes and all the GPOs. In other words, the RSOP could be the combination of multiple GPOs from multiple scopes. You could have an RSOP containing settings from the site, domain, and OU scopes. Typically, there is little conflict when working with policies, and all the settings apply as you go through the levels.

However, it is important you understand the default order of precedence. This becomes important when you have two or more group policies having conflicting settings. The rule of thumb when working with multiple GPOs is that the GPO closest to the object (user or computer) wins.

The default order of precedence is as follows:

1. Local policies (while local policies are not GPOs, they live on the local system and are applied first; the GPOs are applied after this and override the local settings, including multiple local policies on Windows Vista systems or newer)

2. Site

3. Domain

4. Parent OU

5. Child OU (if you have nested OUs, these are called child OUs, and they can have separate settings as well)

For example, if you have a setting to remove the Run command at the domain scope and a setting to enable the Run command at the OU level, the setting at the OU level will "win," and the Run command will be enabled by default.

Control Group Policy Order of Precedence

With Group Policy, you also can have multiple GPOs per site, domain, or OU. When this happens, you need to understand link order. Link order determines the order in which policies are applied. The link with the highest order, with 1 being the highest order, is applied last and therefore has the highest precedence for a given site, domain, or organizational unit.

You can view the link order for a particular OU using the Get- GPInheritance cmdlet. For example, the following command displays the GPO links for the sales OU in contoso.com:

```
Get-GPInheritance -target "ou=sales, dc=constoso, dc=com"
```

Your results will look similar to Figure 9.10.

FIGURE 9.10   Displaying link order

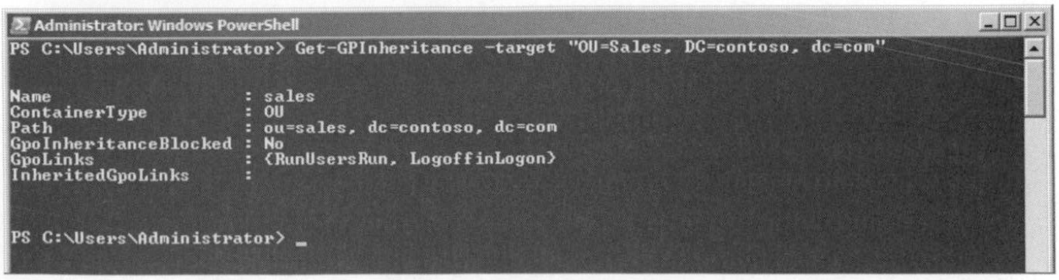

Managing Desktops with PowerShell

CHAPTER 9

As shown in Figure 9.10, `RunUsersRun` is listed first in `GpoLinks`, and `LogoffinLogon` is second. Therefore, `RunUsersRun` will be applied last. To change the link order, use the `Set-GPLink` cmdlet. This command sets the Group Policy link order for `LogoffinLogon` to link order position 1 for the sales OU in `contoso.com`.

```
Set-GPLink -name LogoffinLogon -target ↵
"ou=sales, dc=constoso, dc=com" -order 1
```

Your results will look similar to Figure 9.11.

FIGURE 9.11   Setting link order

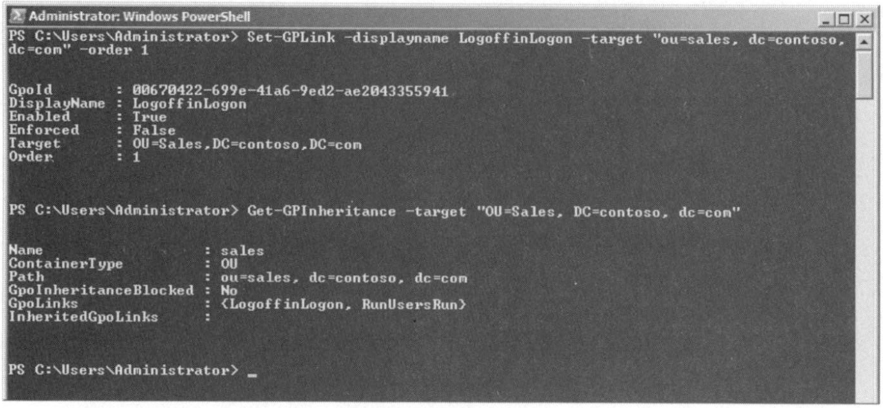

There are two other ways you can control how Group Policy is processed, and they are block inheritance and enforce (known as "no override" in previous operating systems).

Block inheritance prevents GPOs from higher scopes from being inherited, and thus applied, by the child scopes further down the chain. The only exception is if the GPO has been marked as enforced. Block inheritance is selected at either the domain or the OU level. For example, if you did not want domain-wide policies applying to the child OUs, you could block inheritance at the OU level, and the domain policies would not be inherited. To block inheritance in PowerShell, use the `Set-GPInheritance` cmdlet with the `IsBlocked` parameter, which can be Yes or No. The following command will block the inheritance for the marketing OU in `deploy.com`:

```
Set-GPinheritance -Target "ou=marketin,dc=deploy,dc=com" ↵
-IsBlocked Yes
```

Enforce is applied to the Group Policy link and marks the GPO to be processed last regardless of where the policy falls in the scope of management. In other words, an enforced policy will always win unless another enforced policy is further down the scope of management. To enforce a Group Policy link in PowerShell, use `Set-GPLink` with the `Enforced` parameter, which can be Yes or No. The following command will enforce the `RunUserRun` policy for the marketing OU in `deploy.com`:

```
Set-GPLink -Name RunUserRun -Target ↵
"dc=marketing, dc=deploy, dc=com"  -Enforced Yes
```

Work with RSOP

When you start to apply policies at many levels in a GPO, you need to know how to work with the Resultant Set of Policy (RSOP). RSOP shows the end result when you have multiple GPOs applied at multiple scopes of management. Essentially, with RSOP, you see which policies won and were applied.

To view the RSOP after a user or computer has applied the policy, use the `Get-GPResultantSetofPolicy` cmdlet. You can get the RSOP by specifying either the user or the computer you want to view. For example, this command will show you the RSOP policy for the user matt on the computer matt-pc.

```
Get-GPResultantSetofPolicy -user contoso\matt↵
-computer matt-pc -reporttype html -path c:\matt.html
```

You can see an example of an RSOP report in Figure 9.12.

FIGURE 9.12 RSOP report

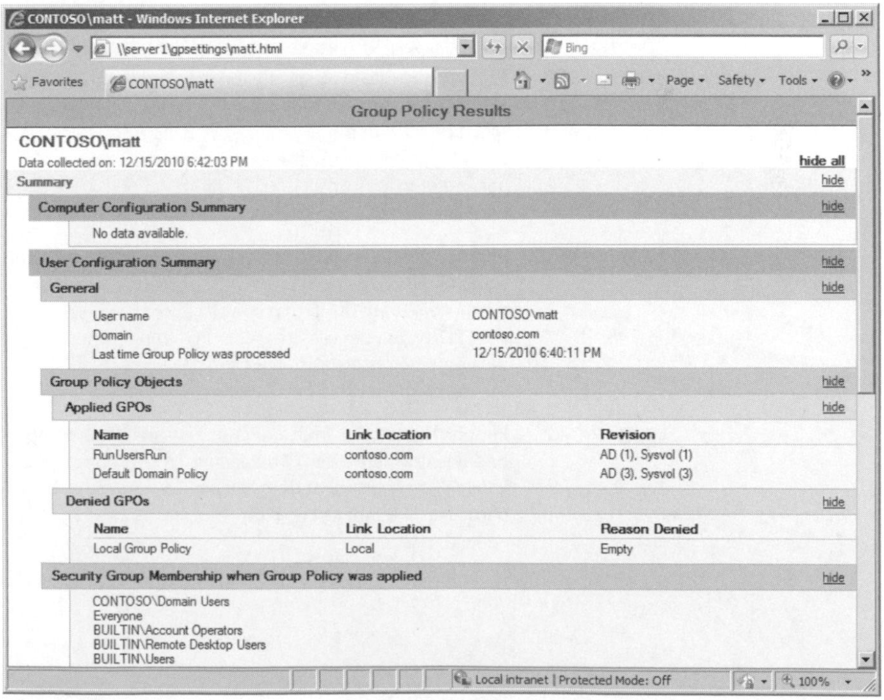

Managing Desktops with PowerShell

CHAPTER 9

When you remotely generate the RSOP report, you may receive an RCP server unavailable error message. This error may occur depending on how your security configuration is internally configured for the domain. You can change one Group Policy setting to fix this error. To enable the ability to get RSOP from remote systems, you need to enable the "Windows Firewall: Allow inbound remote administration exception" policy. This is located in the `Computer Configuration \` `Administrative Templates\Network \Network Connections\Windows Firewall\[Domain or Standard] Profile\` section of your GPO settings. You could also run this command:

```
Set-GPRegistryValue -Name "RunUsersRun" -key ↵
"HKLM\Software\Policies\Microsoft\WindowsFirewall\↵
DomainProfile\RemoteAdminSettings" -ValueName Enabled↵
 -Type DWORD -value 1
```

Back Up and Restore Group Policy Objects

You can back up and restore your GPOs in PowerShell. There are a few PowerShell cmdlets to help you with this daily maintenance. Table 9.5 shows the PowerShell cmdlets to work with the backup and restoration of GPOs.

TABLE 9.5 Backup and recovery cmdlets

Cmdlet	Description	Example
Backup-GPO	Backs up the GPOs you specify for your domain. You can back up a specific GPO with the ID or name of the GPO, or you can use the `-All` parameter to back up all the GPOs in the domain.	This example backs up all the group policies in the domain to \\server5\GPbackups: `Backup-GPO -all -path \\server5\GPbackups`
Restore-GPO	Restores the GPOs you specify for your domain. You can restore a specific GPO with the ID or name of the GPO, or you can use the `-All` parameter to restore all the GPOs in the backup directory.	This example restores all the group policies in the domain from \\server5\GPbackups: `Restore-GPO -all -path \\server5\GPbackups`
Import-GPO	Imports the settings from a GPO backup into a target GPO. This allows you to just import the settings for a particular GPO into a new GPO.	This example imports the settings from the `RunUsersRun` GPO located at \\server5\GPbackups to the `NewRunUsers` GPO: `Import-GPO -BackupGpoName RunusersRun -TargetName NewRunUsers -path \\server5\GPbackups`

Manage AppLocker

The ability to control what applications a user can run on their desktop has been in Group Policy via software restriction policies. These have been around for years, and they can be a bit challenging. With Windows 7 (Ultimate or Enterprise editions) and Windows Server 2008 R2, a new ability called AppLocker provides an easier way to control applications on a user's desktop. Before you apply AppLocker to your corporate environment, make sure you know the application needs of your users. This lets you design an effective policy that enables your users to maintain their effectiveness in their jobs.

AppLocker is important for tackling some of the security risks you face in desktop administration. Your users may be able to install nonstandard (to your business) applications. Even standard users can install some types of software on their desktops. These can cause security vulnerabilities or incompatibilities with your standard desktop applications.

AppLocker makes it easier for you to eliminate unwanted, unknown applications in your network and infrastructure. More importantly, AppLocker allows you as an administrator to enforce application standardization within your organization. AppLocker policies are easy to create and manage through Group Policy. More importantly, you can manage this in PowerShell.

This section gives a brief introduction to AppLocker and how to use PowerShell to manage AppLocker policies. If you want to know more about AppLocker, refer to the AppLocker Step-by-Step Guide located here:

```
http://technet.microsoft.com/en-us/library/dd723686(WS.10).aspx
```

Understand AppLocker

AppLocker is available only for Windows 7 and Windows Server 2008 R2 systems. To control applications on previous versions of Windows, use the software restriction policies. AppLocker helps reduce administrative overhead that was entailed in software restriction policies. AppLocker helps administrators control how users access and use files, including .exe files, scripts, Windows Installer files (.msi and .msp files), and DLLs.

AppLocker allows you to create rules for a specific product name, such as "Allow Adobe Acrobat version greater than 7.0 to run." With this type of rule, there is no need to change the software restriction hash rule. With the hash rules, you would have to change the policy with every application update or verify the path of the executable right or the access right of someone to write to that path. This type of rule can be general or specific, depending on the criteria that you select: publisher, product name, filename, or version. The information that the rule is based on is gathered from the digital signature of the application.

AppLocker can help organizations that want to limit the number and type of files that are allowed to run by preventing unlicensed or malicious software from running. It can reduce the total cost of ownership by ensuring that workstations are homogeneous across the enterprise and that users are running only the software and applications that are approved by the enterprise. It can also reduce the possibility of information leaks from unauthorized software.

Working with AppLocker is a two-step process:

1. Enable the Application Identity Service on the Windows 7 or Windows Server 2008 R2 systems you want to enforce your AppLocker policies on.

2. Configure the AppLocker policy.

The Application Identity Service helps determine and verify the identity of applications. By default, this service is stopped and is set to manual start. The identity of the applications is crucial to how AppLocker works on the clients.

You can use the `Start-Service` cmdlet from an administrative PowerShell session. This command will start the service:

```
Start-Service AppIDSvc
```

You will also want to set the service to automatic. This command will set the service to automatic startup:

```
Set-Service AppIDSvc -StartupType Automatic
```

After you have started the service, any AppLocker policy you configure will now be processed by the Application Identity Service.

Understand AppLocker Policy

An AppLocker policy works with collections. In creating a policy, the first decision to make is whether you are going to allow or deny applications to run. After you determine that, determine what type of executables or collections you want the rule to apply to. With AppLocker, you can allow or deny rules for these types of collections:

- ► Executable files: `.exe` and `.com`
- ► Windows Installer files: `.msi` and `.msp`
- ► Scripts: `.ps1`, `.bat`, `.cmd`, `.vbs`, and `.js`
- ► DLLs: `.dll` and `.ocx`

After you determine the rules, then determine the conditions in which AppLocker will be applied. The conditions help determine the scope of the policy. There are three main conditions:

- ► Publisher
- ► Path
- ► File hash

The publisher condition leverages digital signatures from applications' manufacturers. This rule condition works only if the applications have a digital signature from the publisher. You can work with the entire scope of the publisher, allowing all applications published by a specific publisher to run. You can also specify all applications with a minimum file version number or greater to run. You can even specify the product name or the actual filename (`word.exe`) to run.

The path condition allows you to specify the file path location for the programs you want to manage. This also includes the subdirectories by default. You can also choose to explicitly exclude the directories. For example, you can specify all applications in the `%windir%\system32` directory except the Games directory.

The file hash condition allows you to use the unique file hash assigned to each file. This condition uses the hash to work with the application. If the application is updated, you also need to update the rule.

Configure AppLocker

Working with AppLocker in PowerShell simply requires loading the AppLocker module with the following command:

```
Import-Module AppLocker
```

After you have loaded the AppLocker module, you can view the cmdlets by running the following command:

```
Get-Command -module AppLocker
```

Your results will look similar to Figure 9.13.

FIGURE 9.13 Get AppLocker commands

The PowerShell cmdlets provide a lot of control of AppLocker, even though there are only a few of them. Table 9.6 lists the AppLocker cmdlets.

TABLE 9.6 AppLocker cmdlets

Cmdlet	Description
Get-AppLockerFileInformation	Shows you the file hash, publisher information, and version for a specified directory. This cmdlet, when piped into other cmdlets, is key to working quickly in PowerShell with AppLocker policies.
Get-AppLockerPolicy	Shows the AppLocker policy. Depending on the context, this may be the local, domain, or effective AppLocker policy for the system you ran it on.
New-AppLockerPolicy	Creates an AppLocker policy. You will typically use this cmdlet to create an XML file that you import with the Set-AppLockerPolicy cmdlet.
Set-AppLockerPolicy	Applies the AppLocker policy to a specified GPO.
Test-AppLockerPolicy	Tests an AppLocker policy to verify it has the desired effects. This allows you to tune your policy before you place it into production.

One of the keys to using AppLocker is knowing the publisher information, file hash, or even directory the applications are located in. Although knowing the file directory is straightforward, the publisher and file hash may not be as evident. With the Get-AppLockerFileInformation cmdlet, you can quickly parse through a directory. This command gets the information for all the .exe files in the Microsoft Games directory:

```
Get-AppLockerFileInformation -directory↵
  "c:\Program Files\Microsoft Games" -recurse ↵
-filetype exe
```

Although the results in a PowerShell session may not be easy to read, using the Out-Gridview cmdlet makes the results easier to work with. So if you pipe the previous command to Out-Gridview, your results will look similar to Figure 9.14.

As you can see, there is a lot of information that you can leverage in AppLocker with the Get-AppLockerFileInformation cmdlet. This is the information you need to use in the New-AppLockerPolicy cmdlet, and you can combine the cmdlets to create an AppLocker policy. This command makes a publisher rule for the .exe files in the c:\program files\microsoft games directory. It will also create an XML file of the policy. One good switch is the optimize switch to automatically reduce the number of AppLocker policies by grouping similar AppLocker policies together if possible.

FIGURE 9.14   Get-AppLockerFileInformation

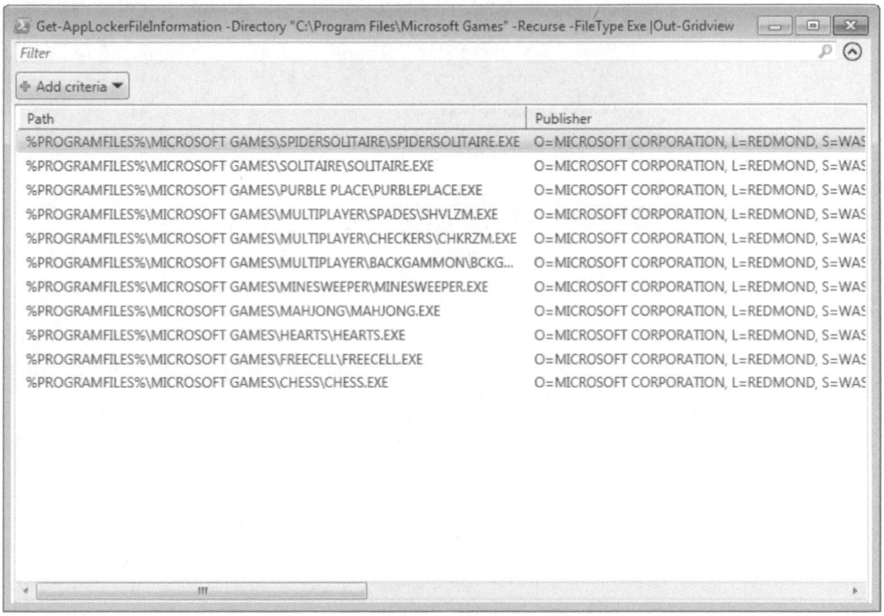

```
Get-AppLockerFileInformation -directory ↵
"c:\program files\microsoft games" -recurse ↵
-Filetype exe | New-AppLockerPolicy -RuleType Publisher↵
 -user everyone -RuleNamePrefix Games ↵
-Optimize -XML > c:\applocker\games.xml
```

One last function you can work with on AppLocker policies is to test to make sure your policy has the desired outcome. With the Test-AppLockerPolicy cmdlet, you can take a look at the results of a AppLocker policy. This command checks to see the effects of the AppLocker policy from the games.xml file for solitaire.exe:

```
Test-AppLockerPolicy c:\applocker\games.xml↵
-path "c:\program files\microsoft games\↵
solitaire\solitaire.exe" -user everyone
```

Your results will look similar to Figure 9.15.

FIGURE 9.15   `Test-AppLockerPolicy`

EXERCISE 9: TURN OFF THE DISPLAY CONTROL PANEL IN GROUP POLICY WITH POWERSHELL

Use PowerShell to create a new Group Policy object linked to an OU that turns off the display control panel for the users in the Executive OU.

Managing IIS Web Server with PowerShell

IN THIS CHAPTER, YOU WILL LEARN TO:

Managing your web servers and web farms is an ideal scenario for PowerShell. With PowerShell you can configure IIS as well as manage applications, sites, application pools, and many other aspects of IIS.

Managing the core server configuration of IIS is one key aspect of working with IIS. Another scenario is working with the websites themselves, including the sites, directories, and web applications on the server. From working with your server configuration to deploying your applications, PowerShell can help you accomplish this in a scalable, automated, and consistent fashion.

This chapter highlights working with PowerShell and the many aspects of IIS.

Use PowerShell and IIS

You need to load the `WebAdministration` module from an administrative PowerShell session or with an account that has administrative rights to manage Internet Information Services (IIS). If you do not have administrative access and try to import the `WebAdministration` module, you will see an error similar to Figure 10.1.

FIGURE 10.1   Importing **WebAdministration**: access denied

From an administrative PowerShell session, run the following command:

```
Import-Module WebAdministration
```

To see the list of commands for the `WebAdministration` module, run the following command:

```
Get-Command -module WebAdministration
```

Your results will look similar to Figure 10.2.

FIGURE 10.2   IIS cmdlets

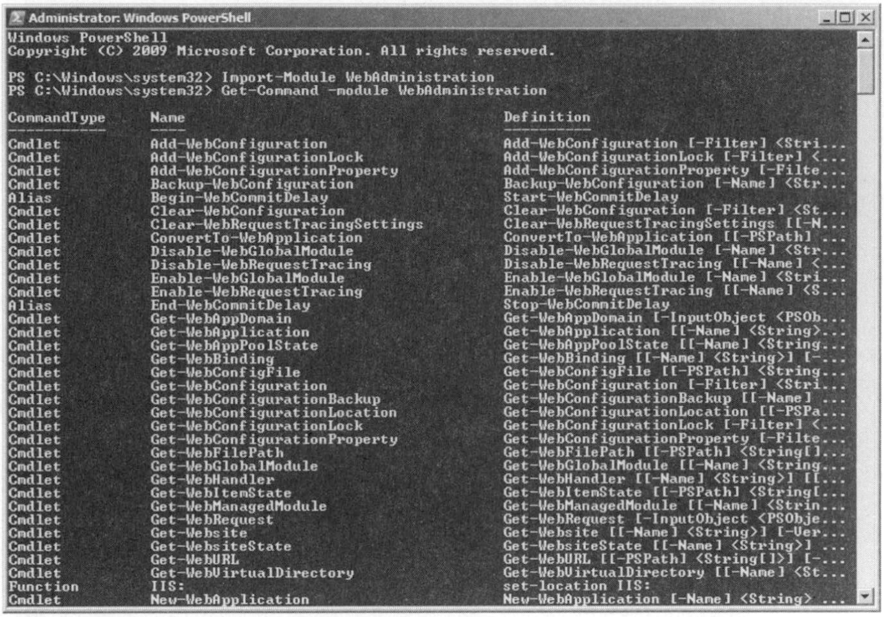

Work with Configuration Files

In IIS 7.0 and IIS 7.5, configuration is stored in XML files. (In prior versions, the configurations were stored in a location called the *metabase*.) These XML files can be stored in a centralized location and are much easier to work with compared to the metabase. This enables a shared configuration for all your web servers.

Three main files make up the IIS manager configuration. The files are by default located in your Windows directory in the System32\Inetsrv\Config folder:

administration.config   This configuration file contains all the management settings for your IIS server and your management console.

applicationhost.config   This stores all the settings for the websites located on your web server.

redirection.config   This file allows you to have centralized settings. You can use the redirection.config file to redirect the IIS server's configuration to a central server location.

These files set the main default settings for your web server. To learn more about the shared configuration files, see `http://learn.iis.net/page.aspx/264/shared-configuration/`.

You can use PowerShell to work with these configuration files as well. Several cmdlets allow you to work with the configuration files, as described in Table 10.1.

TABLE 10.1   IIS configuration cmdlets

Cmdlet	Description
`Get-WebConfigFile`	Displays the location of the web configuration file on your server (`applicationhost.config`). You need to know this location to be able to view or modify settings.
`Add-WebConfiguration`	Allows you to add a section to the web configuration file.
`Get-WebConfiguration`	Allows you to locate the various values of the web configuration to take a look at the sections of the web configuration.
`Clear-WebConfiguration`	Clears a section out of the configuration file. With the configuration file being shared centrally and inherited, this lets you clear certain sections for specific websites.
`Get-WebConfigurationProperty`	Displays the property value from a specific section in the configuration file. This lets you see how the website is configured.
`Set-WebConfigurationProperty`	Lets you configure a specific property in a web configuration section.
`Remove-WebconfigurationProperty`	Clears a property of a specific section in the web configuration files.
`Backup-WebConfiguration`	Backs up the web configuration files on your IIS server. This backs up all three web configuration files.

You can use the `Get-WebConfigFile` cmdlet to look at the configuration files of an IIS server. With this cmdlet, you can also look at the configuration of a specific website. This command gets the configuration file for a website called `MyCompanySite`:

```
Get-WebConfigFile 'IIS:\sites\MyCompanySite
```

Your results will look similar to Figure 10.3.

You can view what sections are in the web configuration file by running the following command:

```
Get-WebConfiguration system.webserver
```

FIGURE 10.3 `Get-WebConfigFile`

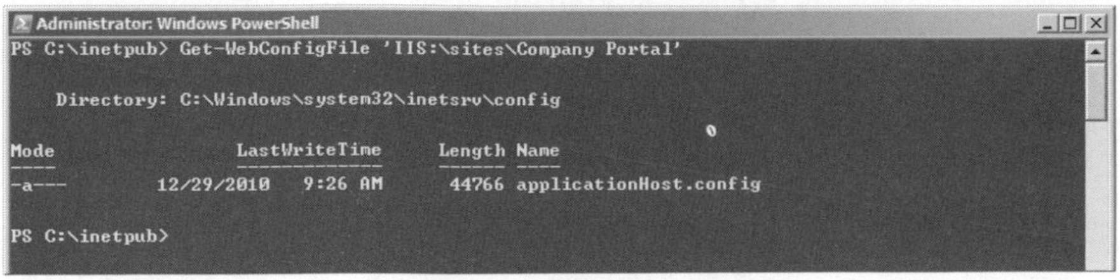

Although the previous command shows you the available sections for the central configuration, you can also target specific sites. For example, if you want to see all the sections of the configuration file for the site `MyCompanySite`, use the following command:

```
Get-WebConfiguration system.webserver/* ↵
iis:\sites\MyCompanySite |Format-Table ↵
-property sectionpath
```

Your results will look similar to Figure 10.4.

FIGURE 10.4 Web configuration sections

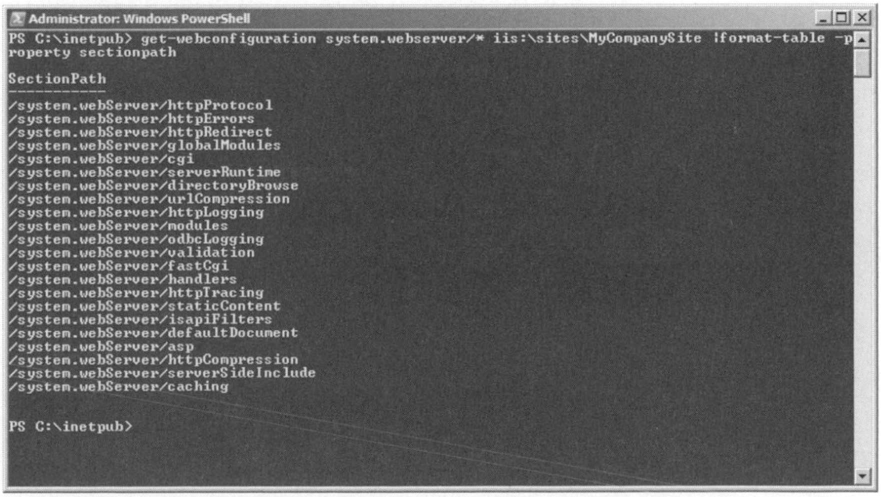

Once you know what sections are available, you can change or view the specific properties with the `Get-WebConfigurationProperty` or `Set-WebConfigurationProperty` cmdlet.

For example, to see the ASP section of the configuration file for the website MyCompanySite, run the following command:

```
Get-WebConfiguration system.webserver/asp/* ↵
iis:/sites/mycompanysite
```

Your results will look similar to Figure 10.5.

FIGURE 10.5   ASP configuration

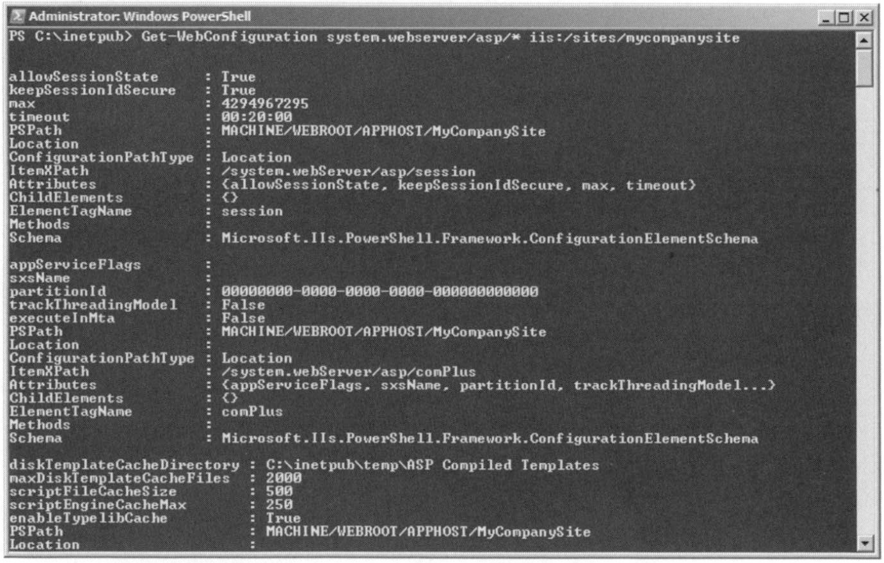

To see just a specific property, you need to know its name. Then you can reference it to either view it or change it. For example, if you wanted to look at the scriptFileCacheSize property for the site MyCompanySite, you would run the following command:

```
Get-WebConfigurationProperty system.webserver/asp/*↵
iis:/sites/mycompanysite -name scriptfilecachesize
```

Your results will look similar to Figure 10.6.

FIGURE 10.6   Script file cache size

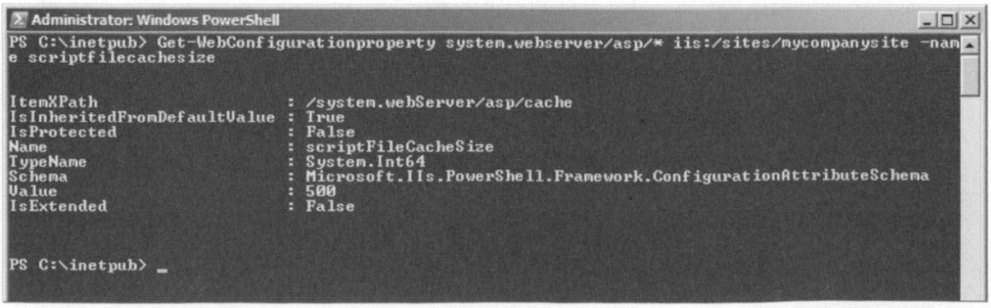

You can set the value of the `scriptFileCacheSize` property with the following command:

```
Set-WebConfigurationproperty system.webserver/asp/cache↵
  iis:/sites/mycompanysite -name ↵
scriptfilecachesize -value 600
```

When you are working with the configuration files, you may run into sections that are locked, as shown in Figure 10.7.

FIGURE 10.7   Locked configuration section

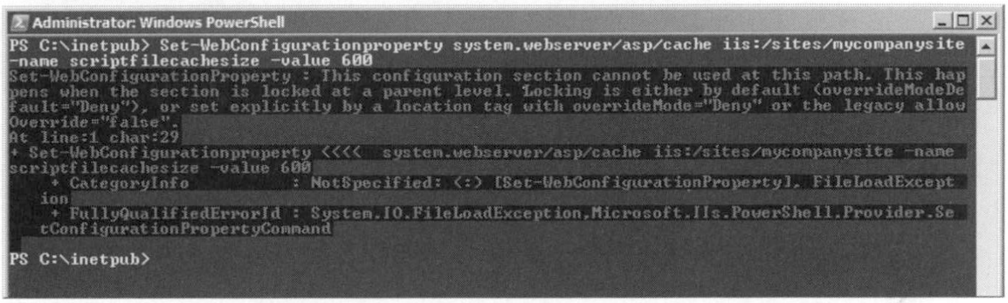

This can occur when you are working with a section that is inherited from a central configuration file. You can work around this by using the `PSPath` and `Location` parameters:

```
Set-WebConfigurationproperty system.webserver/asp/cache↵
  -name scriptfilecachesize -value 600 ↵
-pspath iis:\ -location mycompanysite
```

Working with the configuration files can take some time and investigative work at first, but PowerShell can ease the process of managing these configuration files for your entire web farm.

Back Up and Recover IIS Configuration

Making sure your IIS configuration is properly backed up is an essential part of administering a web server. Fortunately, with IIS you get some help from the Application Host Helper Service (`AppHostSvc`). By default, `AppHostSvc` checks for changes in the `ApplicationHost.config` file every two minutes. If the service detects a change, it will create a backup automatically. This feature, introduced with IIS 7.0, is called IIS Configuration History.

The backup is stored in the `%system drive%\inetpub\history` directory. The file has a default name beginning with `CFGHISTORY_` and a 10-digit serial number. To view the current backups of your IIS configuration, run the following command:

```
Get-WebConfigurationBackup
```

Managing IIS Web
Server with PowerShell

CHAPTER 10

Your results will look similar to Figure 10.8.

FIGURE 10.8   Current web backups

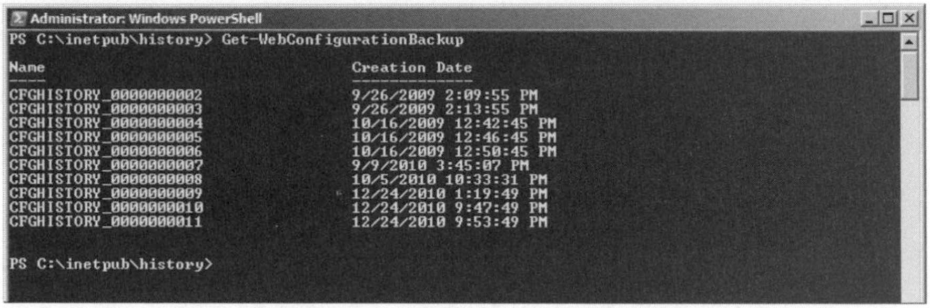

You can also create your own manual backups using PowerShell. To create a backup called WebConfigBackup, run the following command:

```
Backup-WebConfiguration -name WebConfigBackup
```

Your results will look similar to Figure 10.9.

FIGURE 10.9   Backed-up web configuration

APPSVCHOST BACKUPS

The AppSvcHost backups are a bit different from the Backup-WebConfiguration backups. The directory for Backup-WebConfiguration is different for the AppSvcHost backup folder. AppSvcHost stores its backup information in %windir%\System32\ inetsrv\backup. In addition to being stored in different locations, they back up different files. For example, AppSvcHost backs up ftp_schema and DAV_schema, whereas Backup-WebConfiguration does not. However, Backup-WebConfiguration backs up more than just the application config files. It also includes the metabase files and redirection.config file. So, AppSvcHost does a little more than just IIS, and Backup-WebConfiguration is purely IIS. These differences explain issues you may see when trying to restore from the AppSvcHost backups.

If you need to recover your web configuration files, you can do so with the `Restore-WebConfiguration` cmdlet. You need to know the name of the backup you want to restore, which you can obtain with the `Get-WebConfigurationBackup` cmdlet. To restore a web configuration backup called `WebConfigBackup`, run the following command:

```
Restore-WebConfiguration -name WebConfigBackup
```

One special note for the `Restore-WebConfiguration` cmdlet: it cannot be used to restore the backups created by `AppSvcHost`; those backups need to be restored manually. You can do so by copying the configuration files from the backup directory to the configuration directory.

Deploy Websites, Application Pools, and Virtual Directories with PowerShell

As you begin to manage websites in IIS, you need to understand how three components work together for a website. The three components are as follows:

- ► Websites
- ► Web applications
- ► Virtual directories

Websites are the location where you store your web documents. These contain at least one web application. Websites are the core building block to the web infrastructure. Web applications are the second building block, and the nature of web applications can vary dramatically — from web applications accomplishing collaboration to expense reporting, marketing products, and services to customer relationship management. The possibilities for applications in IIS are endless, and they fill a variety of business needs. Virtual directories map to a physical directory on a local or remote server. Web applications use virtual directories to reference data for the application. Virtual directories, although helpful, are not mandatory for a website unless your infrastructure requires it. All three components can work together for a website. In this section, you will see how to work with all three components in PowerShell.

Manage Sites with PowerShell

You can create new websites or manage existing ones via PowerShell. With the `New-Website` cmdlet, you can create a new website with any settings.

To create a new website called Company Portal on port 8080 with the website stored on the f:\cp drive location, you would run the following PowerShell command:

```
new-website "Company Portal" -port 8080 -physicalpath "f:\cp"
```

Your results will look similar to Figure 10.10.

FIGURE 10.10   New website created

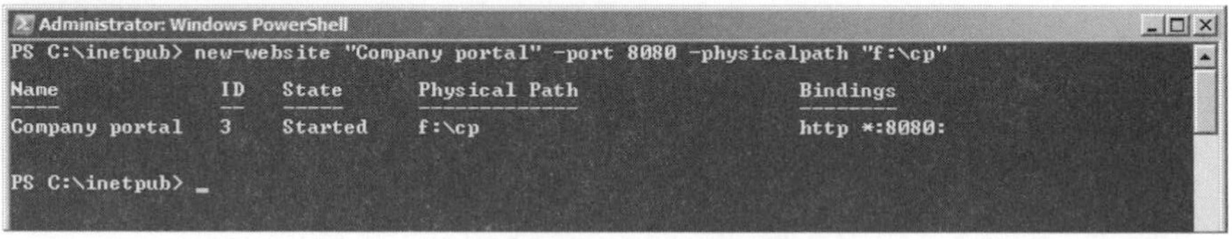

When you create a new website with a specific path, make sure the directory exists; otherwise, you will see an error similar to Figure 10.11.

FIGURE 10.11   New website error

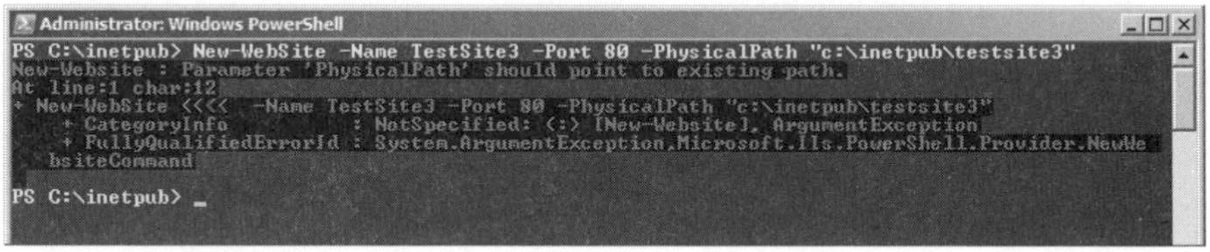

Depending on your current server and how the website was created, it may not be started by default. You can start the website after you have created the site with the Start-Website cmdlet. For example, this command would start the website called Company Portal:

```
Start-Website 'Company Portal'
```

You could also pipe the New-Website cmdlet into the Start-Website cmdlet to create a new website and start it:

```
new-website "Company Portal" -port 8080 ↵
-physicalpath "F:\CP" |Start-Website
```

If you do not want have the website started or you want to stop the website, you can use the Stop-Website cmdlet.

Working with Bindings

When setting up websites, you need to understand how to work with web bindings. Bindings for your websites control how your server responds to requests for websites from users. Bindings also allow you to provide security to your websites with SSL.

Although site visitors will use something like www.companyportal.com, behind the scenes that is being sent to a server binding. A server binding consists of three components: IP address, port, and host header. Host headers are useful because they allow multiple websites with the same port to share the same IP address. The binding for a particular site has to be unique for your website or the website will not start. Figure 10.12 shows an example of a website failing to start because of a port conflict.

FIGURE 10.12   Port conflict error

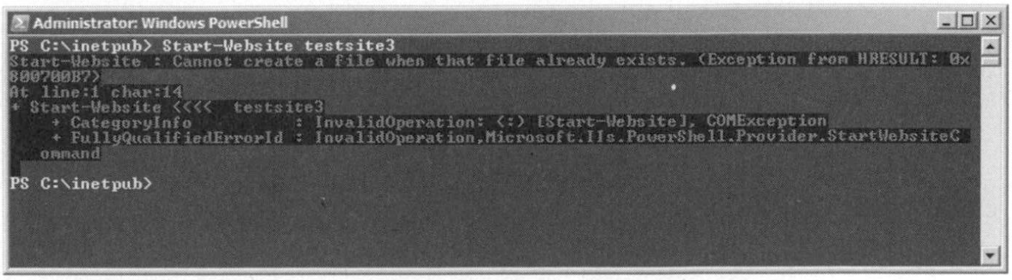

When you work with websites in PowerShell, you can control the bindings to avoid conflicts and add security. The default website binding in IIS is set to *:80:*. This sends all web requests to the default site.

To see what bindings are currently used on your server, run the following command:

```
Get-WebBinding
```

Your results will look similar to Figure 10.13.

FIGURE 10.13   IIS server web bindings

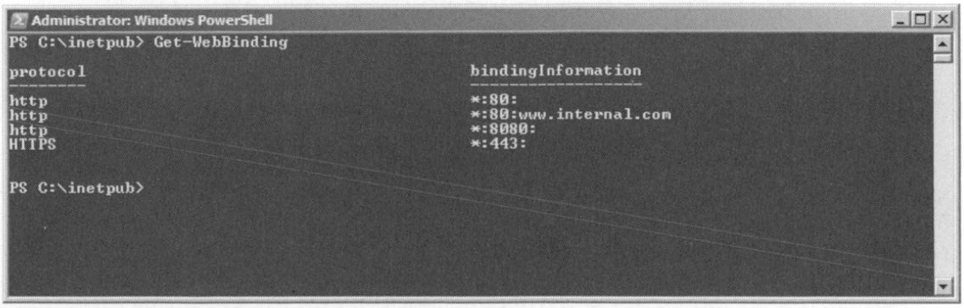

When you want to add a binding to a website, use the New-WebBinding cmdlet. The following command adds the HTTPS protocol for all IP addresses over port 443 for the MyCompanySite website:

```
New-WebBinding -Name "MyCompanySite" -IP "*" -Port 443 -Protocol https
```

Managing IIS Web
Server with PowerShell

CHAPTER 10

In the previous example, the HTTPS protocol was assigned for the Company Portal site. Although this enables the port for secure communication, it does not secure the communication for the website. To finish configuring the SSL binding for the site, you will need to work with the IIS provider.

Working with the IIS Provider

In addition to using the WebAdministration cmdlets, you can use the IIS provider to access the web server configuration. To access the IIS configuration, you can use the built-in function IIS:. This takes you directly to the IIS configuration and website locations.

When using the IIS provider, you can navigate to three locations. You can navigate to application pools, sites, and SSL bindings. Figure 10.14 shows the IIS provider.

FIGURE 10.14   IIS configuration

You can view any of those areas by using directory navigation commands such as cd and dir to view the information. With the simple dir command, you can see the following:

► Website name

► Website path for the physical files for the website

► Status, if the website is started or stopped

► Bindings for ports and protocols of the different sites on the server

Figure 10.15 shows an example of the sites on an IIS server.

FIGURE 10.15   Sites on an IIS server

You can also get the same results in with the `Get-Website` cmdlet. When you run the `Get-Website` cmdlet, it displays the same information you saw when you ran the `dir` command with the IIS provider.

You can also navigate to the `SslBindings` directory to work with security certificates on your server and add them with the HTTPS bindings on your server. If you have certificates already installed on your server, you can leverage them, or you can use a self-signed certificate for testing purposes.

To be able to add a certificate to a binding, you need to know the certificate hash. You can browse the certificate store to find the hash. Figure 10.16 shows listings for the self-signed certificate on the local machine.

FIGURE 10.16   Local machine certificate

After you know the hash, you can then use the following command to install the certificate and bind it for SSL to work properly. 0.0.0.0 is used to reference all IP addresses on the server. You can use specific addresses as well if you need to have SSL assigned to a particular IP.

```
Get-Item cert:\LocalMachine\my\↵
161F4EB304196D3C84FDA3CDC0A6C1DB3C6861E8 |↵
New-Item 0.0.0.0!443
```

Your results will look similar to Figure 10.17.

FIGURE 10.17   Certificate bound to all IP addresses on port 443

Managing IIS Web
Server with PowerShell

CHAPTER 10

You can run the `dir` command to be able to see all the existing certificate bindings on the server while you are in the SslBindings location of the IIS provider.

Work with Web Application Pools

Your websites may contain some type of dynamic content generated from an application on your web server. One of the areas you need to understand is how IIS works with web applications. Specifically, you need to understand the nature of application pools and how they work with websites.

Application pools allow you to separate running applications on your web server. If one application crashes on your server, it should not affect any other applications currently running on your web server. Working with application pools also lets you configure how applications are run on your server. However, working with application pools means you need to understand how the applications need to run on your server. You may need to speak to a website developer to make sure you provide the proper support for the application.

When you create an application pool, you need to know a couple of aspects about the application you are going to support. First, if the application is using managed code, it means the application requires the .NET Framework to properly run. Second, you need to know how the application pipe will be managed, either *integrated* or *classic*. *Classic* is provided for backward compatibility for application support and means IIS does not use the IIS integrated pipeline for managed code. Again, it is worth your time for a quick conversation to help provide adequate support to your web developers.

Application pools let you work with the access not only to your web server but potentially to databases and other servers on your network. An application pool has an identity associated with it. This identity is used to connect to a database with Security Support Provider Interface (SSPI) and is also used to access the file system. Application pools allow you to control and work with the identity for these applications.

To look at application pools currently on your server, use the IIS provider. When you access the IIS provider, you can access the `AppPools` directory. To see the application pools on your server, use `dir`. This command will show you the name of each application pool, its state, and the applications associated with the application pool. Figure 10.18 shows an example.

FIGURE 10.18   Web application pools

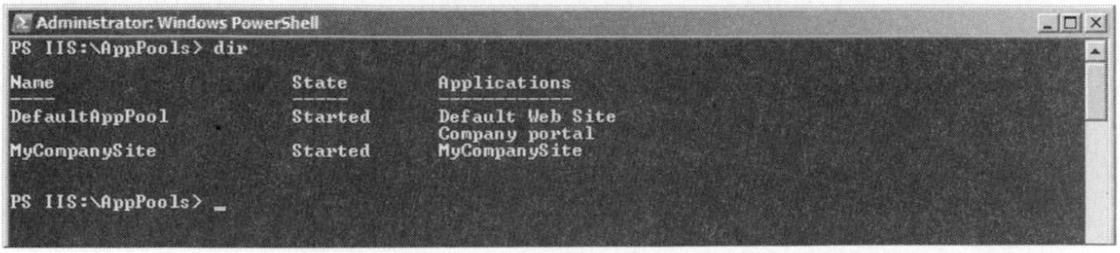

Working with application pools and web applications is a two-step process. Normally you create the application pool, and then you associate the web application to the pool. You also associate the web application with the website or websites that leverage the application. Both of these can be created in PowerShell. The following command creates and starts a new application pool called MyPool:

```
New-WebAppPool MyPool
```

After you have created the application pool, you can then assign a web application to the pool. When you first create a web application, you are just creating a directory that will hold all the files necessary to run the application. To create a new web application called MyApp for the MyCompanySite website stored on the f:\MyApp directory associated with the MyPool application pool, run the following command:

```
New-WebApplication -Name MyApp -Site 'MyCompanySite' ↵
  -PhysicalPath f:\MyApp -ApplicationPool MyPool
```

Your results will look similar to Figure 10.19.

FIGURE 10.19   New web application

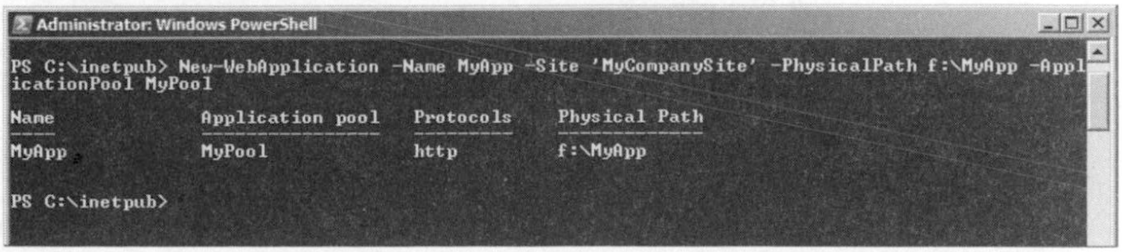

You can use the Get-WebConfiguration cmdlet to view the settings of an application pool. The following command will show you the settings for the MyPool pool:

```
get-webconfiguration "/system.applicationHost/↵
applicationPools/add[@name='MyPool']//." -PSPath iis:\↵
  | foreach { $_.attributes | select name,value }
```

Your results will look similar to Figure 10.20.

FIGURE 10.20 Application pool properties

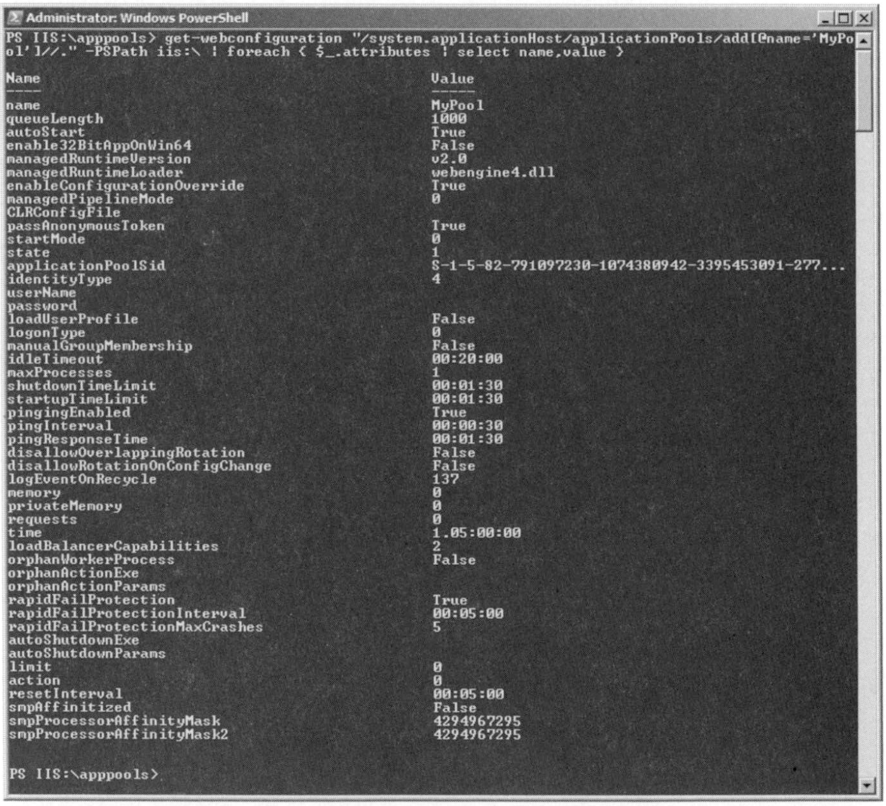

When you work with application pools, you may need to change the identity the application pool uses to access resources on the server as well as remote servers. You can configure the properties including the identity for the application pool by using the Set-ItemProperty cmdlet. The following command would change the identity for the `MyPool` application pool to `PoolUser` with the password of pass@word1:

```
Set-ItemProperty iis:\apppools\MyPool -name processModel↵
  -value @{userName="PoolUser";password="pass@word1";identitytype=3}
```

The last parameter `identitytype` specifies the type of account you are using; the values can be as follows:

- ► 0: Local system
- ► 1: Local service
- ► 2: Network service
- ► 3: Specific user

In Chapter 8, you saw how to use managed service accounts. Managed service accounts can be assigned to application pools. This offers the same benefits of security for service accounts with automatic password management. After you have installed the managed service account on your server, you then can assign the account to your application pool. When you assign the account, make sure you end the account name with a $, leave the password blank, and set `identitytype` to 3. The following command assigns the managed service account `Contoso\WebServer` to the web application pool `MyPool`:

```
Set-ItemProperty iis:\apppools\MyPool -name processModel↵
  -value @{userName="Contoso\WebServer$";identitytype=3}
```

After you assign the managed service account, use the `Stop-WebAppPool` and `Start-WebAppPool` cmdlets to stop and start the application pool you modified.

Although managed service accounts are useful, you may recall from Chapter 8 that managed service accounts are server-specific and are really good for a scenario where you have your websites on only one server. This may not work for your environment if you scale your web servers to multiple servers. In that case, you would need to use a common identity across the servers to make it easy to debug and develop, and you would normally create a separate dedicated user account for this.

One last task you may need to perform from time to time is recycling your application pool. This helps free up resources on your web server in case an application encounters an error. Recycling your application pools periodically lets you maintain your applications and keep them running smoothly. When you recycle an application pool, you essentially clear up system resources and system state information. This could negatively impact users of your website, so you need to try to recycle the applications in off-hours. To recycle the web application pool called `MyPool`, you would run the following command:

```
Restart-WebAppPool MyPool
```

Work with Virtual Directories

Virtual directories can be an invaluable component to your websites. They allow you to keep files stored on separate directory locations so you do not have to move or use multiple copies of the same files. This lets you store files such as pictures on separate servers and distribute the workload.

Virtual directories can also add a small measure of security through obscurity. Because it is really not security, you will want to make sure you do have other security layers in place. Using virtual directory names that differ from the actual physical directories obscures the original directory location. Virtual directory names are displayed in the URL path of the web request.

To see the virtual directories for a particular site, you can run use the `Get-WebVirtualDirectory` cmdlet. The following command displays the virtual directories for the MyCompanySite website:

```
Get-WebVirtualDirectory -site MyCompanySite
```

Your results will look similar to Figure 10.21.

FIGURE 10.21   Virtual directories

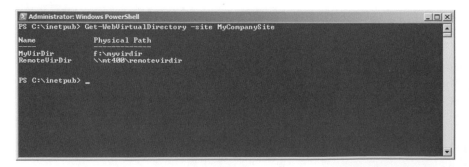

The following command creates a virtual directory called MyVirDir for the MyCompanySite website directory that is physically at f:\myvirdir. You can also use UNC path names for the PhysicalPath parameter as well.

```
New-WebVirtualDirectory -site "MyCompanySite" ↵
-name MyVirDir -PhysicalPath f:\myvirdir
```

If you wanted to map to a virtual directory to a share called rvdir on server5, the command would be the following:

```
New-WebVirtualDirectory -site "MyCompanySite" ↵
-name MySharedVirDir -PhysicalPath \\server5\rvdir
```

EXERCISE 10: CREATE A WEBSITE WITH POWERSHELL

Write a PowerShell script that creates a website called MySite. The site will have an application called App1 with the application pool called Pool1 assigned to MySite. Pool1 will have the user named WebApp. You will also need to create a virtual directory for pictures stored on a separate server. After you have created the site, create a backup of the configuration files.

PowerShell and Deployment Services

IN THIS CHAPTER, YOU WILL LEARN TO:

I f you have ever been asked to deploy an operating system, such as Windows 7, for your business, you have probably asked a few questions. You may have had some concerns about how to accomplish this task in the easiest fashion. You most likely looked at a centralized imaging solution (such as Symantec Ghost) to accomplish the deployment with the least amount of work to be done on the client.

Being able to deploy desktops in a centralized fashion can save you time and offer your users a consistent experience. Windows Server 2008 R2 servers, combined with some free tools, have the ability to deploy operating systems and applications in a standard image. This chapter focuses on two tools to create a centralized deployment environment using PowerShell: Windows Deployment Services (WDS) and Microsoft Deployment Toolkit (MDT).

WDS is a built-in role on your Windows Server 2008 R2 servers. WDS responds to Preboot Execution Environment (PXE) boots or booting across the network. With a PXE boot, WDS can forward the request to the centralized image store to deploy the desktop to the requesting system.

MDT is a free downloadable tool that provides similar capabilities. The toolkit allows you to automate the deployment of computers in your organization. It also lets you deploy custom drivers and set up a workflow. MDT directly supports PowerShell. The bottom line is that you can deploy faster and more easily with MDT 2010.

Although the tools by themselves are very useful, when combined, they become invaluable to working with your environment. Adding the ability to create PowerShell scripts to maintain the environment makes this a nice addition to your IT tool belt.

Work with Windows Deployment Services

One of the core roles you can install on your Windows Server 2008 R2 servers is Windows Deployment Services. Although this service does not have specific PowerShell cmdlets, you can work with WDS inside PowerShell either with a script or via the Windows Deployment Server COM.

To leverage WDS with PowerShell scripts, it is essential you understand this core service and how it works. This will help you understand the working relationship between WDS and MDT and how it provides a robust deployment environment.

Understand WDS

WDS is built on the former deployment tool set known as Remote Installation Services (RIS). WDS now replaces RIS and provides deployment services for your Windows Server 2008 R2 environment. WDS allows you to create a network installation and avoid going to each client system with a DVD or CD to deploy an operating system.

WDS leverages PXE boot systems as well as provides a location to store your installation files, with its centralized image repository. The repository contains boot images, install images, and files that you need specifically for network booting. In addition to the PXE environment over TFTP, there is a multicast component to help WDS scale.

WDS has two components that make up the server role:

► Deployment server

► Transport server

The deployment server is the main component that provides all the necessary services for a network boot environment. The PXE listener gives WDS and MDT the ability to handle network requests. The deployment server also provides a WDS image server, which supports booting and standard corporate images. When a PXE request is picked up by the WDS server, it gives the user the choice of images to use to continue the boot process. This role also supports both unicasting and multicasting, although using the transport server role for multicasting is recommended.

UNICAST VS. MULTICAST

The main difference between unicast and multicast is the number of connections and streams of data the server sends to the clients. In unicast, the server sends a single dedicated stream of data to each client requesting the data. The server has a one-to-one relationship with each of the requesting clients.

With multicasting, the server sends a single stream of data to a multicast address. The clients subscribe or connect to this address, and they all share and receive the stream of data. The server has a one-to-many relationship with the clients being provisioned by the server.

In general, if you are a large organization with bandwidth restrictions and large amount of deployments, you should consider multicasting. This can really help reduce network load since the deployment image is sent out just once. If you just have a few clients and no bandwidth restrictions, unicast is the way to go.

The main role the transport server provides for WDS is multicasting support. Although the transport server does not need other servers in the environment, it is also used only in multicast scenarios. Basically this allows you to have a stand-alone server to support multicasting protocols without all the other WDS components.

WDS gets involved in the process when you have a PXE client. After the client gets an IP address from DHCP, the PXE listener on the server picks up the request and presents the client a boot menu. You can see an example of the boot menu in Figure 11.1.

FIGURE 11.1   WDS boot menu

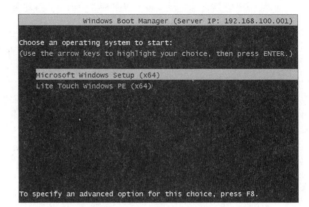

After the client makes their selection, WDS provides the necessary boot files from the image store, and the deployment to the client begins.

Install WDS

To install WDS, you have to be a member of the local administrators group and the domain users group for the domain. You also need to make sure your server and network meet the following prerequisites:

- ► Active Directory domain member or domain controller
- ► DHCP server to respond to PXE requests
- ► DNS
- ► NTFS volume for WDS image store

You can install WDS on your Windows Server 2008 R2 server using the Add-WindowsFeature cmdlet inside the ServerManager module. As you learned in Chapter 7, you can import the `ServerManager` module with the following command:

```
Import-Module ServerManager
```

After you have loaded the `ServerManager` module, install WDS by running the following command:

```
Add-WindowsFeature WDS
```

Your results will look similar to Figure 11.2.

FIGURE 11.2   Installing WDS

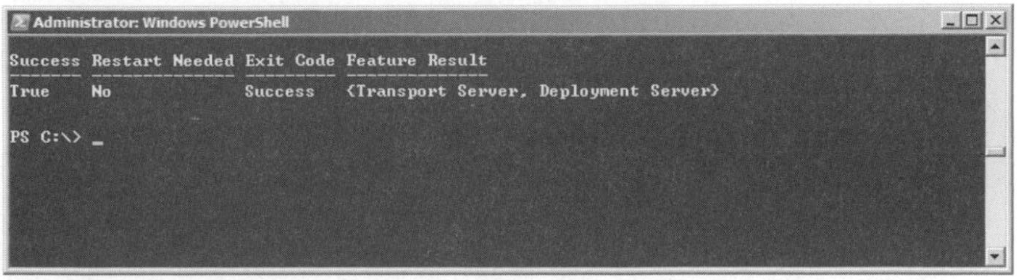

The WDS server installs the two service roles, the deployment server and the transport server, by default. You have two options when you install WDS: you can either install both services or install just the transport server. You can install the individual components.

If you just want to install one server role over the other, you can do so with the following commands.

To install just the deployment server, run this command:

```
Add-WindowsFeature WDS-Deployment
```

To install just the transport server, run this command:

```
Add-WindowsFeature WDS-Transport
```

Work with WDS in PowerShell

There are two ways to work directly with WDS in a PowerShell session. You can use the command prompt tool `WDSUTIL`, or you can load the WDS COM object. In this section, you will see how to work with both. However, the focus will be on `WDSUTIL`, because this tool provides an easier way to incorporate MDT into PowerShell scripts.

PowerShell and
Deployment Services

CHAPTER 11

Working with COM objects in PowerShell requires some exposure to the programmatic side of PowerShell. Having a developer background here will assist you in working with this area of PowerShell.

The COM object you need for WDS is `WdsMgmt.WdsManager`. You can access the COM object easily by setting a variable for the COM object with the following command:

```
$WDScom = New-Object -ComObject WdsMgmt.WdsManager
```

Use the `Get-Member` cmdlet to see what methods work with the COM Object. Using the previous variable, run this command:

```
$WDScom | Get-Member *
```

Your results will look similar to Figure 11.3.

FIGURE 11.3   **Get-Member** for WDS

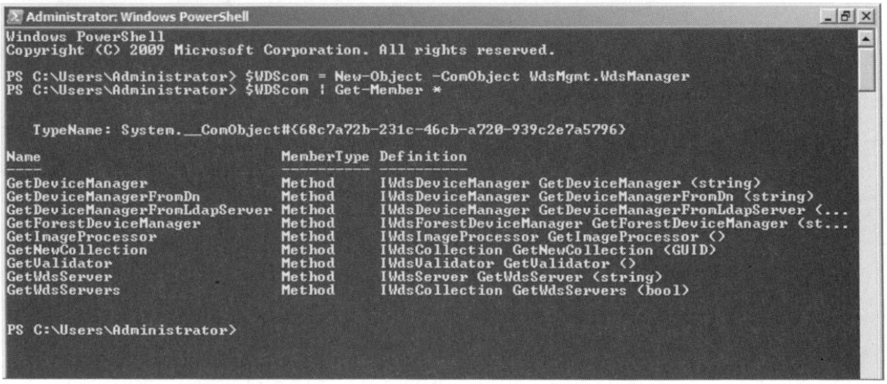

After you have loaded the WDS object, you can then access the different methods to work with the COM object. For more information on working with COM objects, see http://msdn.microsoft.com/en-us/library/ms680573(v=vs.85).aspx. Also, Ravikanth Chaganti discusses this on his blog at www.ravichaganti.com/blog/?p=1561.

Use WDSUTIL

Although working with the COM object provides access in PowerShell, leveraging WDSUTIL is a little more intuitive. This is installed when you install the WDS role on your Windows Server 2008 R2 server. More importantly, this tool is designed to specifically work with WDS on your server.

To see a list some of the switches available for `WDSUTIL`, run the following command:

    WDSUTIL /?

Running `/?` shows some of the switches for `WDSUTIL`. It mainly shows the prefixes for all the commands. One of the switches you may have noticed is the `/AllHelp` switch. When you run the following command, you will see some interesting switches:

    WDSUTIL /AllHelp

Your results will look similar to Figure 11.4.

FIGURE 11.4   Using `WDSUTIL`

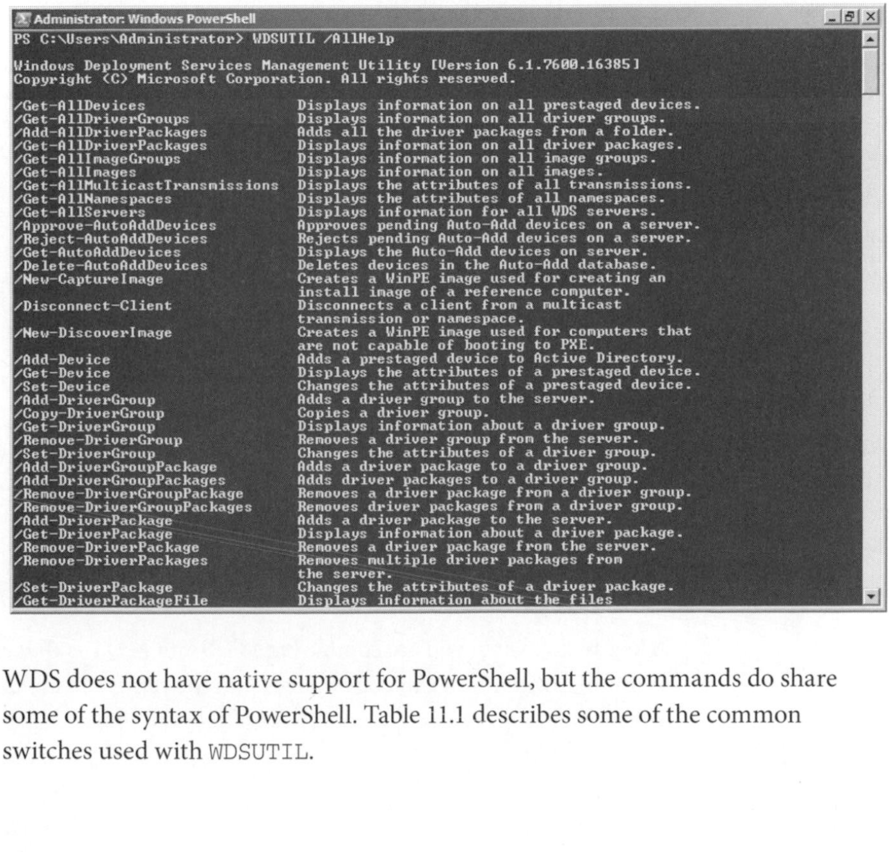

WDS does not have native support for PowerShell, but the commands do share some of the syntax of PowerShell. Table 11.1 describes some of the common switches used with `WDSUTIL`.

TABLE 11.1   WDSUTIL common switches

Switch	Description	Example
Initialize-Server	Used to perform the initial configuration of the server to enable the image share and the remote installation directories.	This example initializes WDS on Server1 and configures the remote installation directory to be located at d:\ RemoteInstall: /Server:Server1 / RemInst:"d:\RemoteInstall".
Add-Image	Allows you to add images to your WDS share for either boot systems or operating systems.	This example adds an install named corpimage.wim from the D:\MDT directory to the current server: WDSUTIL /ImageFile:"D:\MDT\corpimage .wim" /ImageType:Install.
Update-Serverfiles	Ensures the validity of your remote installation directory. Any time you make a change to your server's share or remote installation directory, you need to make sure the directory configuration is still valid.	This example updates the current server: WDSUTIL /Update-ServerFiles. You can also designate a specific server with the /server switch.
Set-Server	Used to configure the WDS server.	This example turns on the architecture autodiscovery method for the WDS; this specifically helps when X64 clients do not properly report their architecture: WDSUTIL /Set-Server / ArchitectureDiscovery:Yes.
Get-Server	Used in a variety of ways to learn the current configuration of the WDS server.	This example shows the current images configured on the current WDS server: WDSUTIL /Get-Server / Show:Images.

One of the switches mentioned in Table 11.1 was the Get-Server switch. With this switch you can view the configuration of the server. You can view just the information of the images or of the server or the information for both. For example, if you want to see the entire configuration for the current server, you run this command:

```
WDSUTIL /Get-Server /Show:All
```

Your results will look similar to Figure 11.5.

A key switch when you are combining WDS and MDT is the Add-Image switch. With this switch, you can copy images into the remote installation directory of your WDS server. In MDT, when you create your images and shares, files you create include boot images to direct you to the proper configuration on your MDT server. These boot images need to be copied into the WDS server so the PXE requests can be handled correctly. More importantly, once the boot image is loaded, then the server will access the MDT configurations.

FIGURE 11.5 WDS configuration

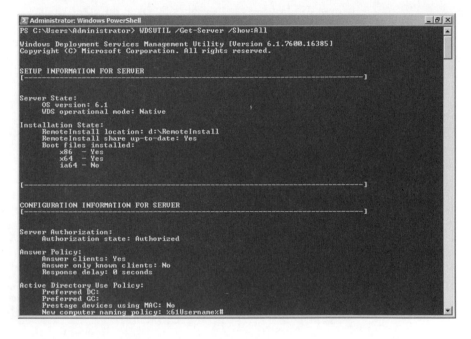

This command copies a boot image file named MDTboot.wim in the d:\mdt directory to your WDS server:

```
WDSUTIL /Add-Image /ImageFile:"D:\MDT\Boot.wim"↵
  /ImageType:Boot
```

While you are working with WDSUTIL, the tool's switches may not seem relevant for PowerShell. In the "Put It All Together" section of this chapter, you will see how it all comes together by combining WDSUTIL and your PowerShell scripts for deployment.

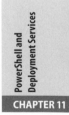

PowerShell and
Deployment Services

CHAPTER 11

A WORD ABOUT /VERBOSE AND /PROGRESS

Often when you are working with the WDS you are going to be working with a lot of output and large files. Image files can be several gigabytes in size, and sometimes the tasks you have WDSUTIL perform can take some time. The two switches /verbose and /progress can give you feedback on the commands you run with WDSUTIL.

These two switches can be used with any of the other WDSUTIL commands. These commands also have to be used directly after WDSUTIL. For example, this command shows the progress of copying the litetouchPE_x86.wim boot image file from d:\deploymentshare to the server:

```
WDSUTIL /verbose /progress /Add-Image ↵
/ImageFile:"D:\Deploymentshare\Boot\LiteTouchPE_x86.wim"↵
 /ImageType:Boot
```

Your results will look like this.

```
Administrator: Windows PowerShell                                    _ | 8 | X
PS C:\Users\Administrator> WDSUTIL /verbose /progress /Add-Image /ImageFile:"D:\Deploymentshare\
Boot\LiteTouchPE_x86.wim" /ImageType:Boot

Windows Deployment Services Management Utility [Version 6.1.7600.16385]
Copyright (C) Microsoft Corporation. All rights reserved.

Verifying the integrity of the data in image file "D:\Deploymentshare\Boot\LiteTouchPE_x86.wim".
..

Adding boot image "Lite Touch Windows PE (x86)" to the x86 the image store...

..............................................

Updating image metadata...

The command completed successfully.
PS C:\Users\Administrator> _
```

Without these two switches, you would not see an indicator that the command was running until the command completed. Using these two switches with your longer operations involving larger files is a good idea so that you can see the progress of your operations.

Work with the Microsoft Deployment Toolkit

The MDT allows you to create a custom image file for deployment in your infrastructure. The custom image not only contains a preconfigured operating system but can also contain custom drivers, update packages, language packages, and applications. This lets you fully deploy a desktop and all the components necessary for your users' desktops.

MDT 2010 supports the deployment of Windows 7 and Windows Server 2008 R2, in addition to the deployment of Windows Vista, Windows Server 2008, Windows Server 2003, and Windows XP. This section outlines how the MDT works, how to install it, and how to configure it to perform custom image deployments for your infrastructure.

Understand the MDT

Three terms for deploying software with Microsoft technologies indicate how much work you have to do on the client:

- ► High-touch
- ► Light-touch
- ► Zero-touch

High-touch installations usually involve doing a lot of work with the client system you are deploying to. There is no automation during the installation, and you have to perform the steps by hand. The most basic form of high-touch installations is placing a DVD or CD in the drive and stepping through the installation wizard.

Light-touch installations normally automate the majority of the installation process. You need to do some minimal work on the client systems you want to deploy to. This may involve starting a PXE boot on the client system (by pressing a function key like F12). You then need to make a selection from the MDT menu

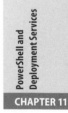

PowerShell and
Deployment Services

CHAPTER 11

to choose your deployment option. Figure 11.6 shows an example of the Windows Deployment Wizard for MDT.

FIGURE 11.6   Windows Deployment Wizard for MDT

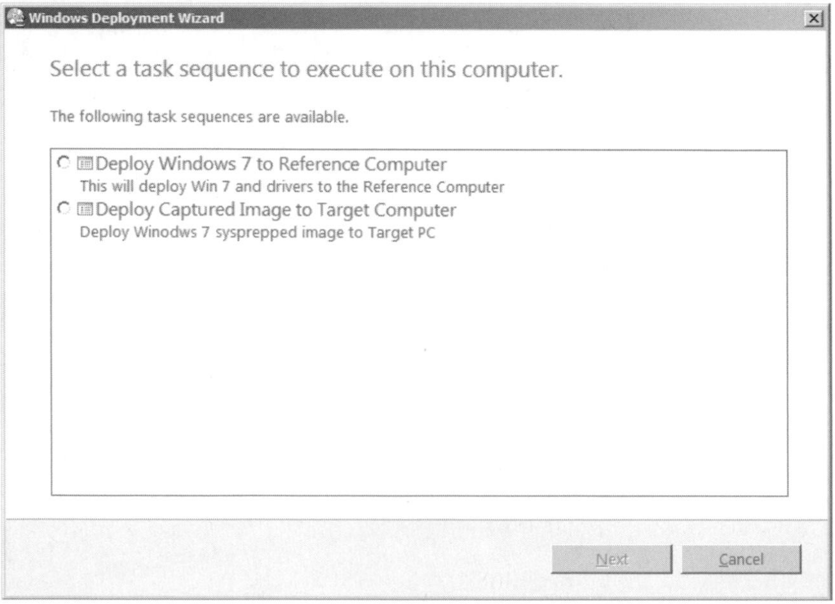

With light-touch installations, you have to do a little work to pull the installation down to the client system. After you make your selection, you can then step away from the system.

Zero-touch, as the name implies, allows you as the administrator to *push* the installation to the system, with no direct interaction on the client system. The MDT can be used to perform zero-touch installations; however, to accomplish zero-touch, you also need to have System Center Configuration Manager (SCCM) installed in your environment. This section focuses on light-touch installations involved in custom image deployment. To learn more about zero-touch, take a look at this article on zero-touch, high-volume deployment: `http://technet.microsoft.com/en-us/library/dd919178(WS.10).aspx`.

Deploy with Windows Imaging Format

Although MDT may seem similar to other imaging tools such as Symantec Ghost, it is quite different. Other imaging tools lay down a copy of a standard desktop to new systems, but MDT actually installs a new copy of the operating system and any other components you have in place for your standard desktops.

The key technology to the centralized deployment of Microsoft platforms is a file format for images called the Windows Imaging Format (WIM). The WIM format is also heavily utilized by the MDT tool. MDT creates both the boot WIM files for booting to the preinstallation environment and the custom desktop images.

WIM is a file-based image format that was introduced with the Systems Management Server (SMS) 2003 OSD feature pack. The WIM format lets you store multiple OS images in one file. With Windows 7, all the DVDs shipped are WIM files that have been prepared with Sysprep for a fresh installation of Windows 7. Windows 7 has two WIM files, `boot.wim` and `install.wim`, as shown in Figure 11.7.

FIGURE 11.7   Windows 7 WIM files

What happens when you install Windows 7 from a DVD in a high-touch fashion is that you are building the answer file as you go through the installation wizard. With MDT, when deploying the custom WIM file, you are also deploying an answer file (`Unattend.XML`), which creates the custom installation.

You could have one image for your marketing desktops and another image for your accounting desktops all stored in a single WIM file. This makes it easy to store and work with your images. The WIM file also supports compression and single instancing to help keep the size of the file at a minimum. Although the files can be 2GB–3GB in size on average, the WIM file is an efficient file format.

When a WIM file is applied to a system, it actually performs an installation, and this allows the WIM file to be hardware-agnostic. The WIM file relies on the driver detection of the installation process to make sure the system gets installed properly. This also has the added benefit that you can deploy WIM files to systems whose hard drives are of a different size than the WIM file being used. As long as the hard

PowerShell and Deployment Services

CHAPTER 11

drive is big enough to hold all the data in the WIM file, you will be able to use this added flexibility.

This is important because regardless of the hardware platform you are installing to, you can use one WIM file for them all. This is different from traditional imaging systems in that they normally would require a separate image for each hardware platform. The one exception is 32-bit vs. 64-bit architecture. Although there are some ways to combine the two architectures in the same file, it is not recommended.

Lastly, the WIM files can be serviced and maintained offline. This allows you to modify individual files in the WIM file or add additional files, such as DLL files, to make sure the WIM file is up-to-date with corporate standards. With other traditional imaging formats, if anything changed, even if it was a 1KB change, you would have to re-create the image.

Install MDT

To install MDT, you first need to download the tool, which is about 10MB. There are 32-bit and 64-bit versions of the tool. You can download MDT at www.microsoft .com/downloads/en/details.aspx?familyid=3bd8561f-77ac-4400- a0c1-fe871c461a89&displaylang=en&tm.

After you download MDT, step through the installation wizard. This installs the deployment workbench (GUI) and the PowerShell snap-in.

In addition to MDT, you also need to download and install the Windows Automated Installation Kit (WAIK). The WAIK is approximately 1.7GB in size, so you may need to plan for the download depending on the bandwidth of your network. You can download the WAIK at www.microsoft.com/ downloads/en/details.aspx?FamilyID=696dd665-9f76-4177-a811- 39c26d3b3b34&displaylang=en.

The file is in ISO format, so you have to burn a DVD, or you can use a free utility called Virtual CloneDrive (located at www.slysoft.com/en/virtual- clonedrive.html) with the WAIK files. When you load the DVD and insert it into your drive, you will see a screen similar to Figure 11.8.

To install the WAIK, make sure you select Windows AIK setup in the menu on the left. There are two main tools that are installed as part of the WAIK that you need to know about. First, the Windows System Image Manager is the component that provides the answer files for the customized image.

The second tool is ImageX, which is the utility that allows you to work directly with WIM files. ImageX allows you to capture, mount, and apply WIM files. MDT uses it under the covers to work with the WIM files, and it is the main component applying your custom images. ImageX primarily runs in the Windows PE, which is the primary installation environment used as a bootable tool that provides OS features for installation, troubleshooting, and recovery. Windows PE is a minimal operating system built from Windows components to help complete the installation. If you have ever installed Windows 7 from a boot DVD, you were working in Windows PE.

FIGURE 11.8   WAIK DVD autorun screen

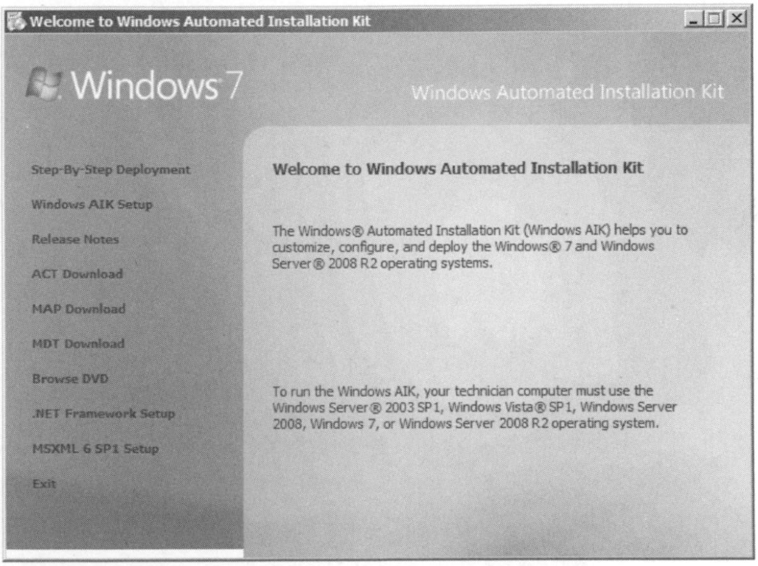

Work with MDT in PowerShell

Creating a light-touch installation point involves several steps. The MDT helps organize those steps to create your custom image. The overall steps for MDT are the following:

1. Create a deployment share.

2. Add your OS, applications, packages, and drivers to the share.

3. Create a task sequence to perform the installation.

4. Build the image.

5. Deploy the image.

PowerShell and Deployment Services

CHAPTER 11

This section shows how to use PowerShell to accomplish these steps.

To work with the MDT in PowerShell, you need to load the MDT snap-ins. For more information on the differences between snap-ins and modules, see Appendix E.

You can view which snap-ins are currently loaded in your PowerShell session by running the following command:

```
Get-PSSnapin
```

Your results will look similar to Figure 11.9.

FIGURE 11.9   Current PowerShell snap-ins

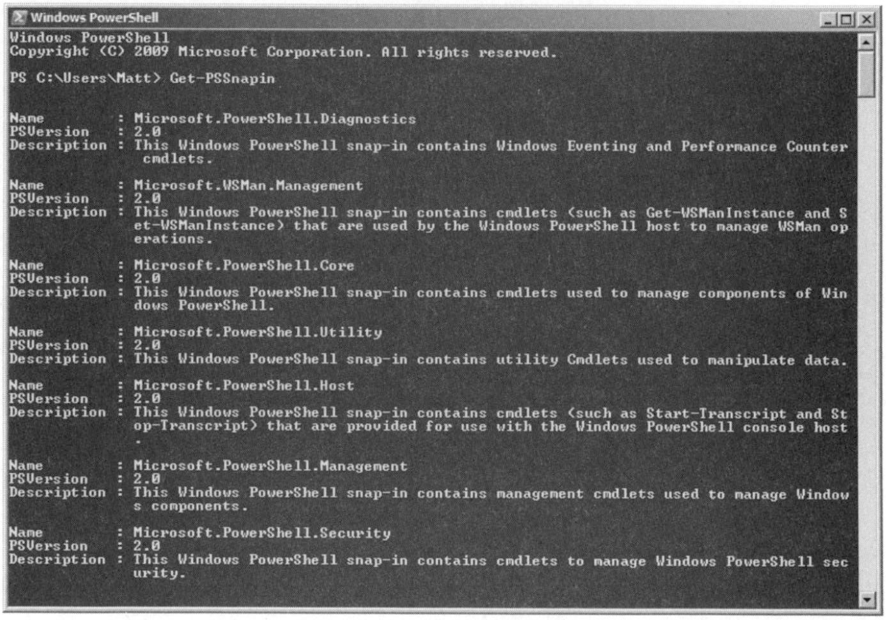

To load the MDT snap-in, run the following command:

```
Add-PSSnapin Microsoft.BDD.PSSnapin
```

To see a list of the MDT cmdlets, run the following command:

```
Get-Command -module Microsoft.BDD.PSSnapin
```

Your results will look similar to Figure 11.10.

One way to learn the cmdlets for MDT is to use the tool. Almost all the tasks you perform in MDT give you a chance to see the script that was created to perform the task. As you can see in Figure 11.11, which is the screen you get after adding an application to the deployment share, there is a button labeled View Script. Clicking this button shows you the underlying PowerShell script that performed the command. This provides another way to learn the PowerShell commands for MDT.

FIGURE 11.10   MDT cmdlets

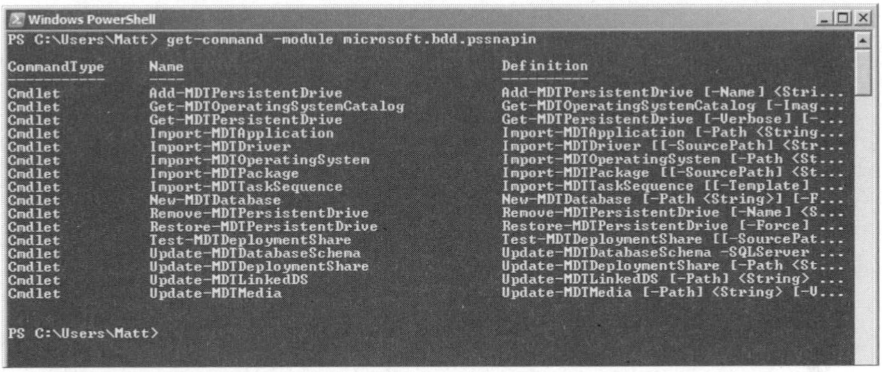

FIGURE 11.11   MDT view script

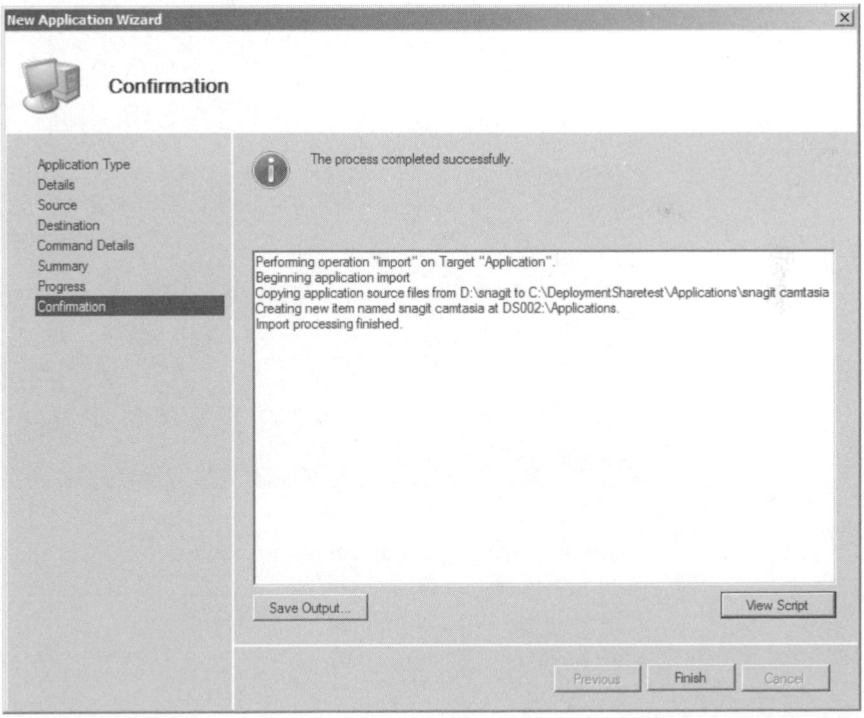

Along with cmdlets in the snap-in, you can work directly with the PowerShell provider for MDT. The provider for the MDT is named `MDTProvider`.

Working with a Deployment Share

The first task you need to do is create a deployment share. A deployment share is not created by default. After you have created the deployment share, you are then able to create all the necessary components to set up your centralized deployment.

The following command creates a deployment share with a name of `MDT01`and a description of `My MDT Share`; it's located at `d:\MyMDTShare` with the share UNC name `\\2008R2DEP\MyMDTShare$`. The `$` makes the share hidden. `Add-MDTPersistentDrive` allows you to make the drive available and persistent so it can be reused.

```
New-PSDrive -Name "MDT01" -PSProvider "MDTProvider" ↵
-Root "d:\MyMDTShare" -Description "My MDT Share"↵
 -NetworkPath "\\2008R2DEP\MyMDTShare$" -Verbose ↵
| add-MDTPersistentDrive -Verbose
```

Your results will look similar to Figure 11.12.

FIGURE 11.12   Creating a deployment share

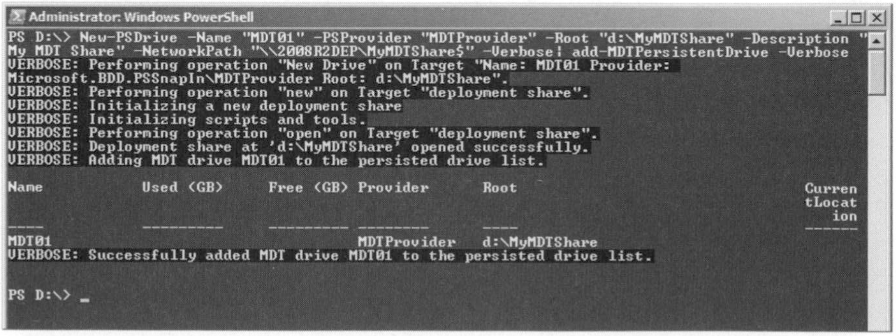

As you work with MDT and create multiple deployment shares, you can access them in PowerShell. Before you can access them in a PowerShell session, you need to run the following command:

```
Restore-MDTPersistentDrive
```

To see what persistent drives are available to you in your PowerShell session, run the following command:

```
Get-MDTPersistentDrive
```

Your results will look similar to Figure 11.13.

FIGURE 11.13   Deployment shares

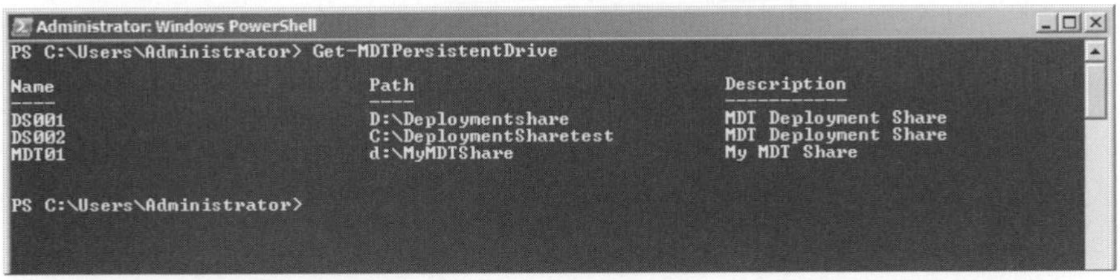

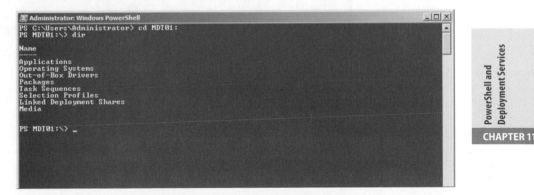

With the MDT provider you can access the shares directly in PowerShell by typing in the name of the deployment share. For example, if you wanted to see the contents of the deployment share called MDT01, you would type in the following:

```
cd MDT01:
```

You can then work with the provider like any other providers. You will be able to use dir, cd, and many other commands to access the deployment share. Figure 11.14 shows the dir command run in the MDT01 share.

FIGURE 11.14   Deployment share contents

After you create the deployment share, you then can add all the components from operating systems, applications, drivers, and packages. The PowerShell commands to add these different components to your deployment share all follow a similar pattern. Before you begin managing your deployment share directory, you need to make sure your MDT persistent drives have been loaded. You can load the drives directly via the provider with a command similar to this one:

```
New-PSDrive -Name "MDT01" -PSProvider "MDTProvider" ↵
-Root "d:\MyMDTShare"
```

Alternatively, you can load all the drives with the `Restore-MDTPersistentDrive` mentioned earlier.

The following command copies the Windows 7 operating system from `D:\source\Windows7` to the operating systems folder on the `MDT01` share:

```
Import-MDTOperatingSystem -path "MDT01:\Operating Systems" ↵
 -SourcePath "D:\Source\Windows7" -DestinationFolder "Windows 7" ↵
 -Verbose
```

Your results will look similar to Figure 11.15.

FIGURE 11.15   Importing the OS

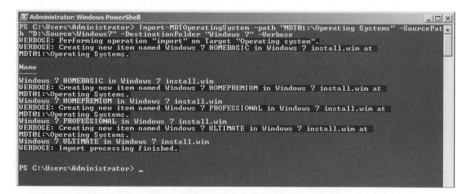

In Figure 11.15, you see a list of four different operating systems — Home Basic, Home Premium, Professional, and Ultimate — stored in a Windows 7 WIM file.

The `CommandLine` switch configures the installation of the application. To make the installation as silent as possible, you will have to research how to install each application silently. For example, this command silently installs Adobe Reader:

```
AdbeRdr930_en_US.exe /sAll /rs /l /msi"/qb-! ↵
/norestart ALLUSERS=1 EULA_ACCEPT=YES DISABLE_AIR↵
_SHARE=1 SUPPRESS_APP_LAUNCH=YES"
```

This command imports the application SnagIt from `D:\source\snagit` to the `applications` folder on the `MDT01` share and installs it, despite not having the silent switch:

```
Import-MDTApplication -path "MDT01:\Applications"↵
 -enable "True" -Name "Camtasia Snagit" -ShortName↵
 "snagit" -Version "" -Publisher "camtasia" ↵
-Language "" -CommandLine "snagit.exe" ↵
-WorkingDirectory ".\Applications\snagit" ↵
-ApplicationSourcePath "D:\source\snagit" ↵
-DestinationFolder "snagit" -Verbose
```

The following command imports the drivers from `D:\source\drivers` to the `Out-of-Box` drivers folder on the `MDT01` share. The `ImportDuplicates` switch allows your driver to be used over the Windows driver if one exists.

```
Import-MDTDriver -path "MDT01:\Out-of-Box Drivers" ↵
-SourcePath "D:\source\drivers\" -ImportDuplicates ↵
-Verbose
```

This imports the Dutch language pack from `d:\source\dutch` to the `packages` folder on the `MDT01` share:

```
Import-MDTPackage -path "MDT01:\packages" ↵
-SourcePath "D:\source\dutch\" -Verbose
```

Creating a Task Sequence

After importing all the files necessary for your standard desktop, you can create a task sequence. The task sequence controls the order and process of your custom image deployment. In MDT, you have six XML templates you can use to create a task sequence and a custom XML template for your installation. The templates are located in the `%SystemDrive%\Program Files\Microsoft Deployment Toolkit\Templates` directory. Table 11.2 describes the templates and the filenames you would use in the MDT script.

TABLE 11.2   Task sequence templates

Task sequence	Description	File name
Sysprep and Capture	Prepares a client machine by using a utility called Sysprep. When sysprep is run on a client machine it removes the unique properties of the system. After sysprep is run then this task sequence will capture the desktop in a WIM file and places it on the MDT deployment share.	CaptureOnly.xml
Standard Client Task Sequence	Standard desktop deployment including OS, applications, and drivers. This sequence could include user state migration and replacement.	Client.xml
Standard Client Replace Task Sequence	Captures the state of the client system and then cleans the client system for replacement.	ClientReplace.xml
Litetouch OEM Task Sequence	Deployment option for OEM computer providers.	LTIOEM
Standard Server Task Sequence	Allows you to also deploy server roles as part of your deployment process. MDT can also deploy servers in your environment.	Server
Post OS Installation Task Sequence	Allows you to perform tasks that occur after the OS is already deployed. This sequence could help cover anything you could not deploy as part of the standard deployment process.	StateRestore
Custom Task Sequence	Sequence to utilize the custom tasks. MDT allows you to create custom tasks.	Custom.xml

The following command creates a task sequence using the standard client template and deploying Windows 7 Professional with a username of Desktop User and the IE home page of www.bing.com.

```
Import-MDTTaskSequence -path "MDT01:\Task Sequences"↵
 -Name "Deploy Windows 7" -Template "Client.xml" ↵
-Comments "Select this task Sequence to deploy the ↵
standard Windows 7 desktop" -ID "DepWin7" -Version ↵
"1.0" -OperatingSystemPath "MDT01:\Operating Systems↵
\Windows 7 PROFESSIONAL in Windows 7 x64 install.wim"↵
```

```
-FullName "Desktop User" -OrgName "deploy.com"↵
-HomePage "www.bing.com" -Verbose
```

Your results will look similar to Figure 11.16.

FIGURE 11.16   Importing a task sequence

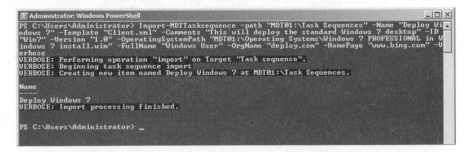

With the task sequence, you also control what the menu item looks like on the client system you are deploying to. Whatever text you place in the `-comments` parameter will be displayed on the client side. This is your opportunity to provide guidance to the user or administrator performing the installation to make sure they make a proper choice. So, make sure you provide descriptive documentation to help ensure a successful deployment.

Put It All Together

After you have created the task sequence, the last step is to update the deployment share. Updating the deployment share ties together all of your work. This updates the configuration and generates custom versions of the Windows PE environment. Specifically, the update process creates the `LiteTouchPE_x86.iso` and `LiteTouchPE_x86.wim` files for 32-bit target computers or `LiteTouchPE_x64.iso` and `LiteTouchPE_x64.wim` files for 64-bit target computers in the `Boot` folder of your deployment share.

Updating the deployment share can take several minutes depending on your server configuration. To update a deployment share named `MDT01`, run the following command:

```
Update-MDTDeploymentShare -path "MDT01: " -Verbose
```

PowerShell and
Deployment Services

CHAPTER 11

Your results will look similar to Figure 11.17.

FIGURE 11.17   Updated deployment share

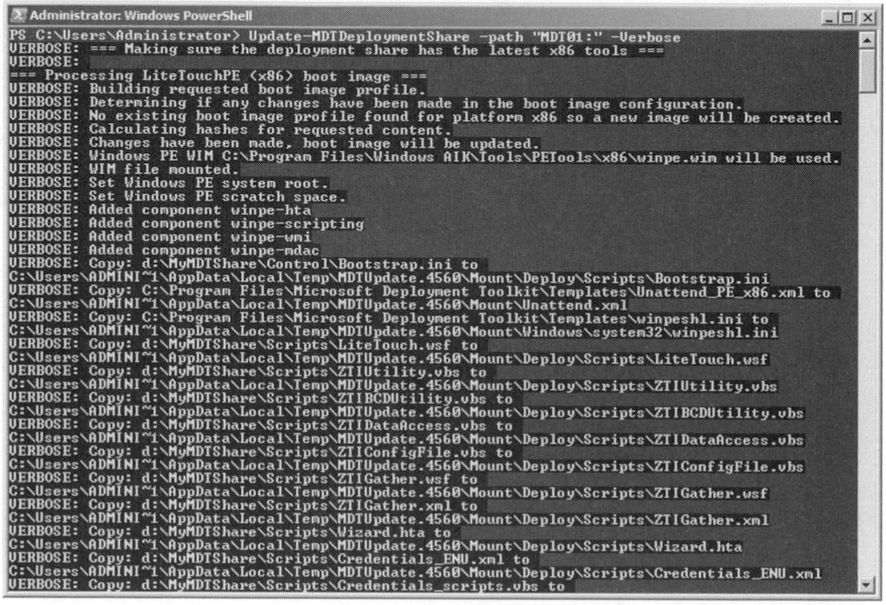

The boot directory on the MDT share includes WIM files and ISO files. You can take the ISO files and burn them to DVDs, and if you boot the client system to the DVD, this is the same as if they made a selection from a PXE boot.

To tie together MDT and WDS, add the light-touch WIM boot file to the WDS boot images. This creates the choice in the PXE boot menu of the client for the light-touch image you added. After the MDT option is selected from the PXE menu, the request will then be handled by the MDT process. The architecture of the client, 32-bit or 64-bit, determines which file to copy — LiteTouchPE_x86.wim or LiteTouchPE_x64.wim, respectively.

The following command adds the 64-bit light-touch file to the WDS boot images:

```
WDSUTIL /verbose /progress /Add-Image ↵
/ImageFile:"D:\Deploymentshare\Boot\LiteTouchPE_x64.wim" ↵
 /ImageType:Boot
```

EXERCISE 11: CREATE A DEPLOYMENT SHARE

Create a deployment share called Win7 that will deploy Windows 7 Ultimate.

Optionally, if you have WDS, you can add the 32-bit boot image to the WDS boot images.

PowerShell and Virtualization

IN THIS CHAPTER, YOU WILL LEARN TO:

irtualization technologies are common in today's IT environments. Being able to effectively work with and configure your virtual servers is key to successfully maintaining a proper virtual environment. Microsoft's Hyper-V platform lets you virtualize a wide variety of environments. In fact, a majority of the examples and samples used in this book were done in a Hyper-V environment.

You can use PowerShell with Hyper-V to configure, provision, and maintain your virtualization environment. PowerShell provides the necessary tool set to quickly work with your virtual infrastructure.

This chapter shows how to install Hyper-V with PowerShell for Windows Server 2008 R2 servers. The main focus of the chapter is how to work with virtual servers, from creating the virtual networks to connecting your servers to maintaining the virtual servers.

The chapter touches briefly on Windows Management Instrumentation (WMI). You may be familiar with using WMI to manage virtual servers. However, you will also see a new tool set used to manage the virtual environment from PowerShell cmdlets.

Install and Access Hyper-V

Hyper-V is Microsoft's virtualization technology for Windows Server 2008 R2 servers. Hyper-V allows you to run virtual guest operating systems on your host server. This provides an environment to help you consolidate and fully utilize your existing hardware. Hyper-V also provides a platform for testing and developing future applications for the business.

Currently in its second version, Hyper-V provides support for virtualization of many operating systems, including Windows Server 2003 through the current version of Windows servers and some versions of Linux distributions including SUSE and Red Hat. With such a wide variety of client support, you can build production and test environments off a single server. This helps you avoid server sprawl and improve your IT infrastructure.

The systems you create with Hyper-V are fully functional systems in your infrastructure; the only difference is they are virtual and do not have their own hardware. This means you need to install, configure, back up, and maintain these servers like full-fledged members of your network. Before you can begin working with Hyper-V, you need to install it.

Install Hyper-V

Hyper-V is an installable role on Windows Server 2008 R2 servers. Hyper-V can be installed on the Standard, Enterprise, or Datacenter versions of Windows Server 2008 R2. You can also install Hyper-V on Windows Server 2008 R2 Server Core installations.

Hyper-V has specific hardware requirements:

► The system needs to be 64-bit. The system must support hardware-assisted virtualization. Specifically, the processors need to support Intel VT or AMD-V technology.

► Hardware-assisted virtualization also needs to be enabled in the BIOS. Normally this is not enabled by default.

► The processors also must have hardware-enforced data execution prevention (DEP), which is enabled in BIOS as well. This is normally enabled by default.

To install Hyper-V with PowerShell, import the Server Manager module. After you have imported the Server Manager module, you can then run the following command to install Hyper-V on either full or core versions of Windows Server 2008 R2:

```
Import-Module ServerManager
Add-WindowsFeature Hyper-V
```

Your results will look similar to Figure 12.1.

FIGURE 12.1   Installing Hyper-V

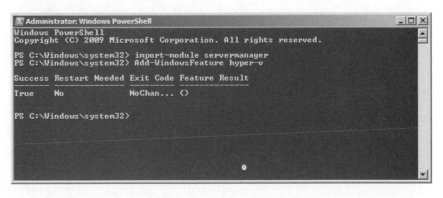

When you run the Add-WindowsFeature cmdlet, you may see a screen similar to Figure 12.2.

PowerShell and Virtualization

CHAPTER 12

FIGURE 12.2 Wrong processor

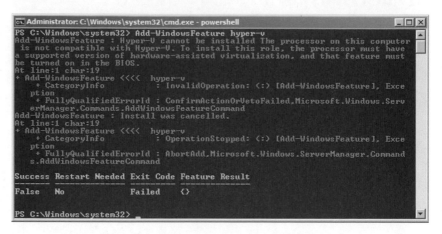

This indicates the processor you currently have installed on your Windows Server 2008 R2 server does not have hardware-assisted virtualization. An error similar to this could also indicate you have not enabled the hardware-assisted virtualization in the BIOS of your system. You need to install Hyper-V on another server.

Access Hyper-V in PowerShell

After you install Hyper-V, you can begin working with virtual servers. There are two methods you can use in working with PowerShell and Hyper-V. The first leverages the ability of PowerShell to work directly with the Windows Management Instrumentation (WMI) provider. The second method uses a free, downloadable Hyper-V module built after Windows Server 2008 R2 was launched.

Take a Quick Look at WMI

WMI is a key management technology for Windows systems. WMI essentially provides a logical data structure of information describing the various aspects of your server. This data structure contains all aspects of the server you want to manage and maintain. This data structure is referred to as a *namespace*. Namespaces are made up of classes and instances. Classes and instances help define the various aspects of the system you can manage. Classes can also be organized into subclasses. When you are working with WMI, you will do a majority of your configuration in the classes.

WMI is one of the first tools scripters used to manipulate and manage systems with scripts prior to PowerShell. WMI allows you to manage local settings and remote computers. Before you can start to dig into the various classes you can mange with WMI via PowerShell, you will want to know what namespaces you can work with on your system. To view the namespaces on your server, you can run the following command:

```
Get-WmiObject  -namespace "root" -class "__Namespace" | Select Name
```

Your results will look similar to Figure 12.3.

FIGURE 12.3   Namespaces

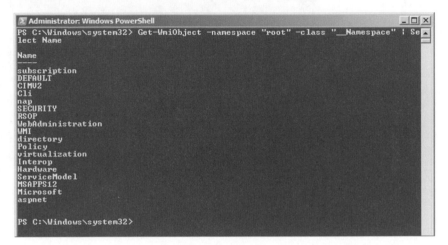

These namespaces all have the prefix of root, and when you want to reference them in your PowerShell commands, you need to use root\ before each WMI namespace you want to access. For example, if you wanted to use the virtualization namespace, you would use root\virtualization. Likewise, if you wanted to see the WebAdministration namespace, you would use root\webadministration.

Each namespace contains all the classes and instances under the hood, allowing you to manage and maintain the various aspects of your system. The default and most common namespace is root\cimv2. This contains the main classes for your server, from hardware to BIOS settings.

Access the different WMI classes in PowerShell with the Get-WmiObject cmdlet. To see a list of the available aspects in the default namespace (root\cimv2) you can access in WMI, use the following command:

```
Get-WmiObject -List
```

If you want to see just the classes used for Hyper-V, run the following command:

```
Get-WmiObject -Namespace root\virtualization -List
```

Your results will look similar to Figure 12.4.

PowerShell and
Virtualization

CHAPTER 12

FIGURE 12.4   Hyper-V classes in WMI

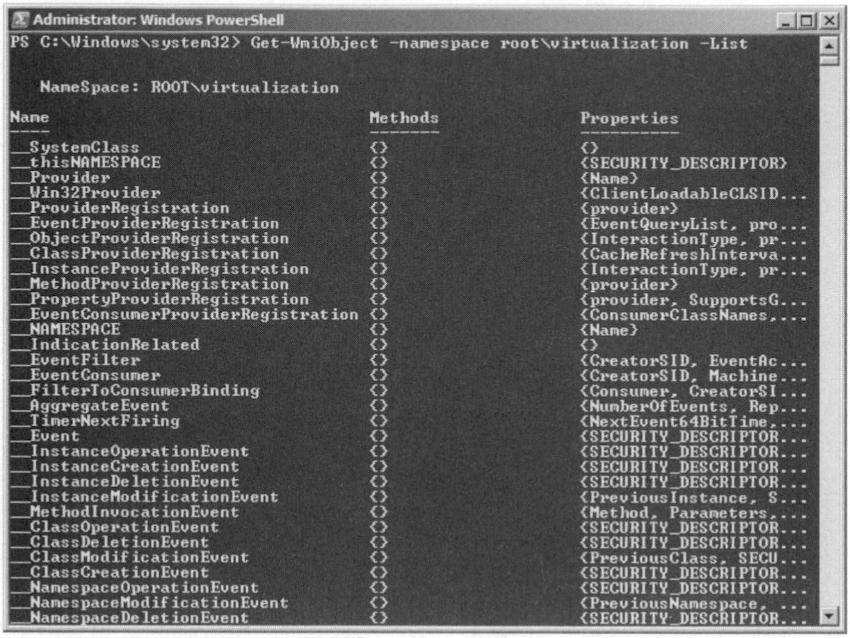

To access any of the aspects of Hyper-V with WMI, you have to know the name of the class and instance you want to modify. Although this can be extremely powerful and detailed, digging into WMI can take some time.

Appendix F touches on some of the Win32 classes in WMI. You can also find a more detailed look at all the classes available for Hyper-V. Check out the Hyper-V provider reference here:

```
http://msdn.microsoft.com/en-us/library/cc136992(v=VS.85).aspx
```

Use the Hyper-V Module

WMI is a tool you can use in PowerShell to access components with no built-in cmdlets, but working with the WMI provider can sometimes be daunting. Fortunately, for managing Hyper-V, the IT pros at Microsoft made a Hyper-V module. This provides access to your Hyper-V environment using PowerShell cmdlets without having to dig deep into WMI. The rest of this chapter focuses on using these cmdlets to manage your Hyper-V environment.

The Hyper-V module is located in the PowerShell Management Library for Hyper-V located on CodePlex and is free. You can download the management library from `http://pshyperv.codeplex.com/`.

The file is in ZIP format. You may need to unblock the file so it can install properly. Before you extract the ZIP file, go to the properties of the file and click Unblock, as shown in Figure 12.5.

FIGURE 12.5 Unblocking the download

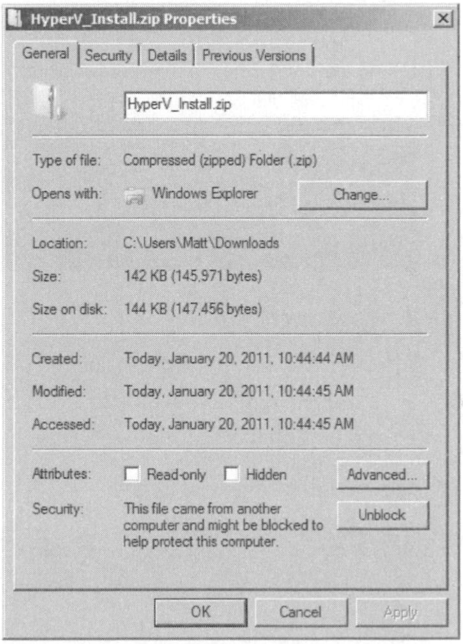

If you do not unblock the file, you will see an error message similar to Figure 12.6.

FIGURE 12.6 Security error

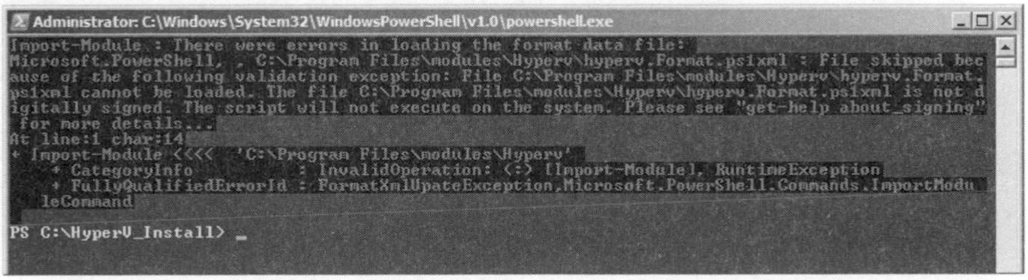

Even though the error message indicates the certificate-signing issue, you will still see the error regardless of your remote execution policy level.

After you have unblocked and extracted the files, you can then install the module. The developers created an install.cmd to step through the configuration of the tool set. From an administrative PowerShell session, navigate to the extracted directory, and perform the following procedure:

1. Run `.\install.cmd` from the directory. Remember that when you run a command from PowerShell, you have to include the `.\` to represent the directory you are currently located in. After you run the command, you will see a screen similar to Figure 12.7.

FIGURE 12.7   Installing the PowerShell Management Library for Hyper-V

2. Press any key to continue the installation process.

3. After the installation verifies the prerequisites, review the results, and then press any key to continue to extract the modules and support files. Your screen will look similar to Figure 12.8.

FIGURE 12.8   Extracting the management library

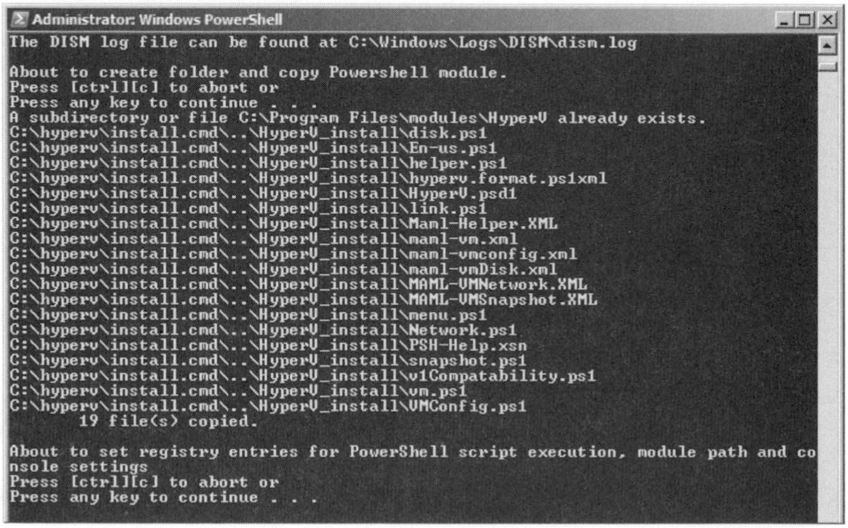

4. Press any key to continue. The installation process makes changes to the registry. You will see a warning similar to Figure 12.9. Click Yes to continue.

FIGURE 12.9   Registry warning

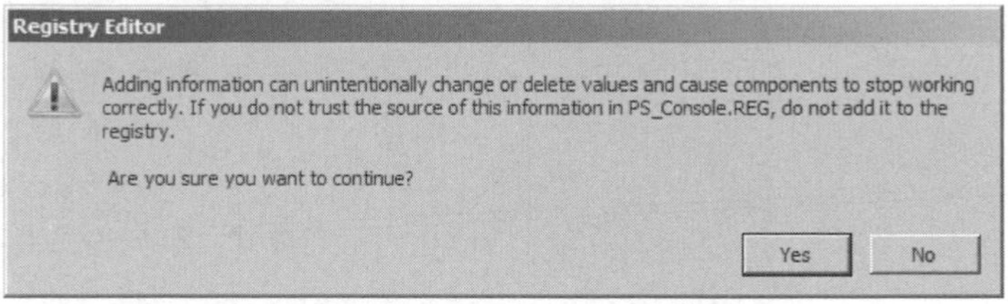

5. After the changes have been made, click OK, and return to the PowerShell session you started the installation from. Press any key. This launches a PowerShell session with the Hyper-V module loaded.

After you have successfully installed the PowerShell Management Library for Hyper-V, you can work with the Hyper-V cmdlets. If you close the PowerShell session and you want to use the cmdlets again, you can always import them with the following command:

```
Import-Module HyperV
```

After you have loaded the module, you can then see all the cmdlets in this module by running the following command:

```
Get-Command -module hyperv
```

Your results will look similar to Figure 12.10.

As you can see from the extensive list of cmdlets, the developers of the PowerShell Management Library for Hyper-V did a thorough job to include the necessary cmdlets to manage Hyper-V. Make sure you check back regularly at http://pshyperv.codeplex.com/ to see whether they have made any additions to the library.

PowerShell and Virtualization

CHAPTER 12

FIGURE 12.10   Hyper-V cmdlets

```
 Administrator: Windows PowerShell                                        _ □ ×
PS C:\Windows\system32> import-module hyperv
PS C:\Windows\system32> get-command -module hyperv

CommandType        Name                            Definition
-----------        ----                            ----------
Alias              Add-NewVMHardDisk               Add-VMNewHardDisk
Function           Add-VMDisk                      # .ExternalHelp  MAML-VMDisk...
Function           Add-VMDrive                     # .ExternalHelp  MAML-VMDisk...
Function           Add-VMFloppyDisk                # .ExternalHelp  MAML-VMDisk...
Function           Add-VMKVP                       # .ExternalHelp  MAML-VMConf...
Function           Add-VMNewHardDisk               # .ExternalHelp  MAML-VMDisk...
Function           Add-VMNIC                       # .ExternalHelp  MAML-VMNetw...
Function           Add-VMPassThrough               # .ExternalHelp  MAML-VMDisk...
Function           Add-VMRASD                      # .ExternalHelp  MAML-VMConf...
Function           Add-VMSCSIController            # .ExternalHelp  MAML-VMDisk...
Function           Add-ZIPContent                  <#...
Alias              Apply-Snapshot                  Restore-VMsnapshot
Alias              Choose-List                     Select-List
Alias              Choose-Tree                     Select-Tree
Alias              Choose-VM                       Select-VM
Alias              Choose-VMExternalEthernet       Select-VMExternalEthernet
Alias              Choose-VMNIC                    Select-VMNIC
Alias              Choose-VMPhysicalDisk           Select-VMPhysicalDisk
Alias              Choose-VMSnapshot               Select-VMSnapshot
Alias              Choose-VMSwitch                 Select-VMSwitch
Alias              compact-VHD                     Compress-VHD
Function           Compress-VHD                    # .ExternalHelp  MAML-VMDisk...
Function           Connect-VHDParent               # .ExternalHelp  MAML-VMDisk...
Function           Convert-DiskIDtoDrive           # .ExternalHelp  Maml-Helpe...
Function           ConvertTo-Enum                  ...
Function           Convert-VHD                     # .ExternalHelp  MAML-VMDisk...
Function           Convert-VMState                 ...
Function           Copy-ZipContent                 <#...
Function           Dismount-VHD                    # .ExternalHelp  MAML-VMDisk...
Function           Expand-VHD                      # .ExternalHelp  MAML-VMDisk...
Function           Export-VM                       # .ExternalHelp  MAML-VM.XML...
Function           Get-FirstAvailableDriveLetter   # .ExternalHelp  Maml-Helpe...
Function           Get-VHD                         # .ExternalHelp  MAML-VMDisk...
Function           Get-VhdDefaultPath              # .ExternalHelp  MAML-VMDisk...
Function           Get-VHDInfo                     # .ExternalHelp  MAML-VMDisk...
Function           Get-VHDMountPoint               # .ExternalHelp  MAML-VMDisk...
Function           Get-VM                          # .ExternalHelp  MAML-VM.XML...
Function           Get-VMBuildScript               # .ExternalHelp  MAML-VM.XML...
Function           Get-VMByMACAddress              # .ExternalHelp  MAML-VMNetw...
Function           Get-VMClusterGroup              ...
Function           Get-VMCPUCount                  # .ExternalHelp  MAML-VMConf...
Function           Get-VMDisk                      # .ExternalHelp  MAML-VMDisk...
Function           Get-VMDiskByDrive               # .ExternalHelp  MAML-VMDisk...
```

Work with Hyper-V

Once you have the PowerShell Management Library for Hyper-V, you can then directly manage your virtual environment using the Hyper-V cmdlets. From working with virtual networks to connecting to running virtual systems, this can all be done in PowerShell. This section focuses on the basic concepts of Hyper-V and how to access them in a PowerShell session.

Work with Virtual Networks

One of the first concepts in working with virtual systems is connecting them with other systems in your infrastructure. Normally, prior to creating virtual systems, you need to create virtual networks. This allows you to connect your virtual servers to keep them up-to-date and even isolate and sandbox your servers.

In Hyper-V, you can create three types of virtual networks:

External   This type of virtual network binds the physical adapter on the host system so the virtual systems can access your physical network. This network allows your virtual systems to access your production infrastructure.

Internal   This type of virtual network allows only the virtual systems to communicate with other virtual systems on the local Hyper-V server. This network also allows communication with the local host.

Private   This type of virtual network allows only the virtual systems to communicate with the other virtual systems on the local Hyper-V server. This network does not allow communication with the local host. This network is ideal for sandboxing your virtual servers for testing to keep them from communicating with your production environment.

When you create virtual servers, it is not uncommon for a virtual server to have network adapters assigned to different virtual networks. There are three cmdlets to help you create these virtual networks: New-VMExternalSwitch, New-VMKInternalSwitch, and New-VMPrivateSwitch.

The following command creates an external virtual network called External Network bound to a physical adapter with a name beginning with Intel on the server MT400:

```
New-VMExternalSwitch -VirtualSwitchName "External Network"↵
  -ext "Intel" -Server MT400
```

You will be prompted for confirmation. Your results will look similar to Figure 12.11.

FIGURE 12.11   Hyper-V cmdlets

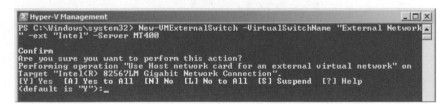

After you have created the virtual network, you can then assign the network adapter to a virtual server. The following command sets the virtual switch for the virtual server pshellR2 to the private1 virtual network:

```
Set-VMNICSwitch -NIC (Get-VMNIC pshellr2) -VirtualSwitch↵
  "Private1"
```

Your results will look similar to Figure 12.12.

PowerShell and
Virtualization

CHAPTER 12

FIGURE 12.12   Setting a virtual network

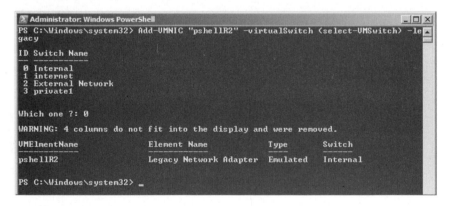

You can add one or multiple network adapters to either support cluster configurations or support other multiple NIC scenarios. You also have the choice to create a native network adapter or a legacy adapter. The legacy adapter is used mainly to perform PXE booting for network-based installations. The following command adds a legacy virtual network adapter to the virtual machine pshellR2 and lets you choose the virtual network to connect to the virtual NIC:

```
Add-VMNIC "pshellR2" -virtualSwitch (select-VMSwitch)↵
   -legacy
```

Your results will look similar to Figure 12.13.

FIGURE 12.13   Adding a virtual NIC

Configure Virtual Machines

Creating virtual machines and working with them involves a few steps. You first need to add the virtual machine to the Hyper-V server. The virtual machine you create consists of several components that are similar to a real server. You need to work with two main things when creating a virtual machine — the settings and the virtual hard drives. When you configure the virtual machine settings, you are basically configuring the BIOS settings for the server. The settings include the configuration for RAM, processors, hard drive controllers (Virtual SCSI and IDE are available), and network adapters. When you configure the virtual hard drives, you are configuring the storage location as well as the hard drives that will be present inside the virtual machine.

To create a new virtual machine called PShellVM on a server called MT400, type the following command:

```
New-VM -Name PShellVM -Server MT400
```

Your results will look similar to Figure 12.14.

FIGURE 12.14   Creating a VM

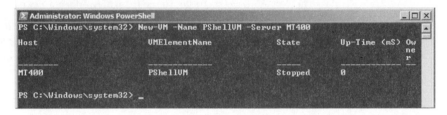

This creates a default virtual machine with 512MB of RAM, one processor, and two IDE controllers. This system does not have any hard drives attached to the system.

Understand Virtual Hard Drives

A virtual hard drive for your virtual server is a physical file with the .vhd file extension. This file is the storage location for your virtual machine and also the hard drive or drives appearing in your virtual server. You can create three main virtual hard drives in a virtual server:

Dynamically Expanding VHD   This is the default VHD file format. As the name suggests, it grows to meet the needs of your virtual machine. This file starts out small and increases as you use your virtual machine. Whenever you install new programs, add files, or work with the virtual machine, this file expands to meet the needs of the virtual machine until the limit of the VHD is met.

Fixed Size VHD   This is a VHD of a specific size. The VHD does not grow dynamically. No matter how much data or how many programs you add to the virtual machine, this file remains the same size you created it. This also means when you create a VHD of 300GB, you need that much free space on your host system to hold the file.

PowerShell and Virtualization

CHAPTER 12

Differencing VHD   This VHD allows you to create changes to a parent VHD drive without changing the parent VHD. All of the changes you make are stored in the differencing disk. The differencing disks help keep the need for storage space of the VHD to a minimum. The differencing VHDs are normally much smaller than the parent VHD from which they are created.

You can create a VHD as part of the creation of a new virtual machine. You can also connect an existing VHD file to a new or existing virtual machine. The following command creates a dynamically expanding VHD called `pshellvm.vhd` in the `F:\pshellvm` directory with a maximum size of 150GB. If you wanted to make a fixed size VHD, you would add the `-Fixed` switch to the command.

```
New-VHD F:\pshellvm\pshellvm.vhd -Size 150GB
```

Use the `Get-VHDInfo` cmdlet to see information for an existing VHD. When you use the `Get-VHDInfo` cmdlet on a dynamically expanding file, note the actual file size. It will be quite a bit less than the size presented in the virtual machine. The following command gets the information for the `pshellvm.vhd` file in the `F:\pshellvm` directory:

```
Get-VHDInfo f:\pshellvm\pshellvm.vhd
```

Your results will look similar to Figure 12.15.

Note that the actual file size is about 309KB.

FIGURE 12.15   VHD information

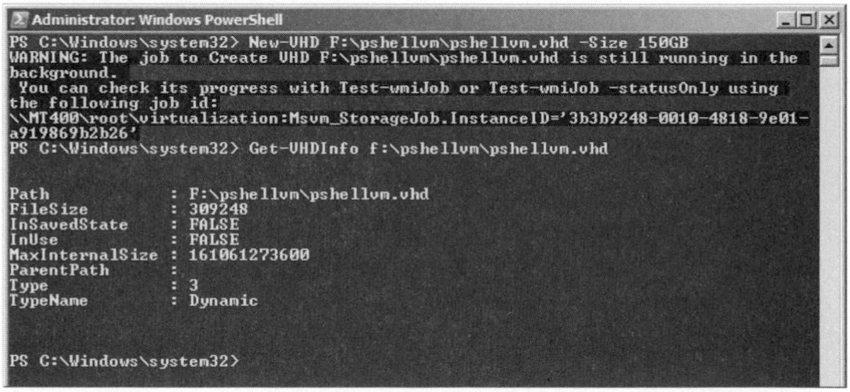

After you have created the VHD you want to use for an existing virtual machine, you can connect it to the virtual machine. The following command connects the

pshellvm.vhd file in the F:\pshellvm directory to PShellVM on the 0 hard
drive controller and the 0 drive:

```
Add-VmDisk -VM PShellVM 0 0 -path F:\pshellvm\pshellvm.vhd
```

The developers of the PowerShell Management Library for Hyper-V also included the
Add-NewVMHardDisk alias that combines the creation and connection of a VHD
to an existing virtual machine. This command creates a new virtual hard drive
called PShelldata.vhd in the F:\pshellvm directory. The drive is a dynamically
expanding drive of 100GB on the 0 controller and the 1 drive.

```
Add-NewVMHardDisk -VM PshellVM 0 1 -VHDPath ↵
f:\pshellvm\pshelldata.vhd -size 100GB
```

Your results will look similar to Figure 12.16.

FIGURE 12.16   VHD information

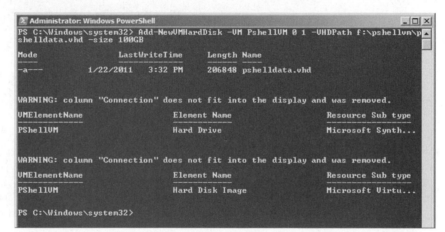

Work with the Virtual Machine Settings

After you have created the virtual machine, you can then configure all the
settings to meet the needs of your infrastructure. There are several cmdlets for
modifying the existing settings, including Set-VMMemory to configure the
RAM for the virtual machine and Set-VMCPUCount to add CPUs to an existing
VM. However, there is an easier way. There is a special function called
Show-VMMenu that provides a PowerShell console to make it easy to see and
configure the settings for a virtual server.

PowerShell and
Virtualization

CHAPTER 12

The following command displays the PowerShell console for the virtual machine PShellVM:

```
Show-VMMenu PShellVm
```

The menu will look similar to Figure 12.17.

FIGURE 12.17   Virtual machine menu

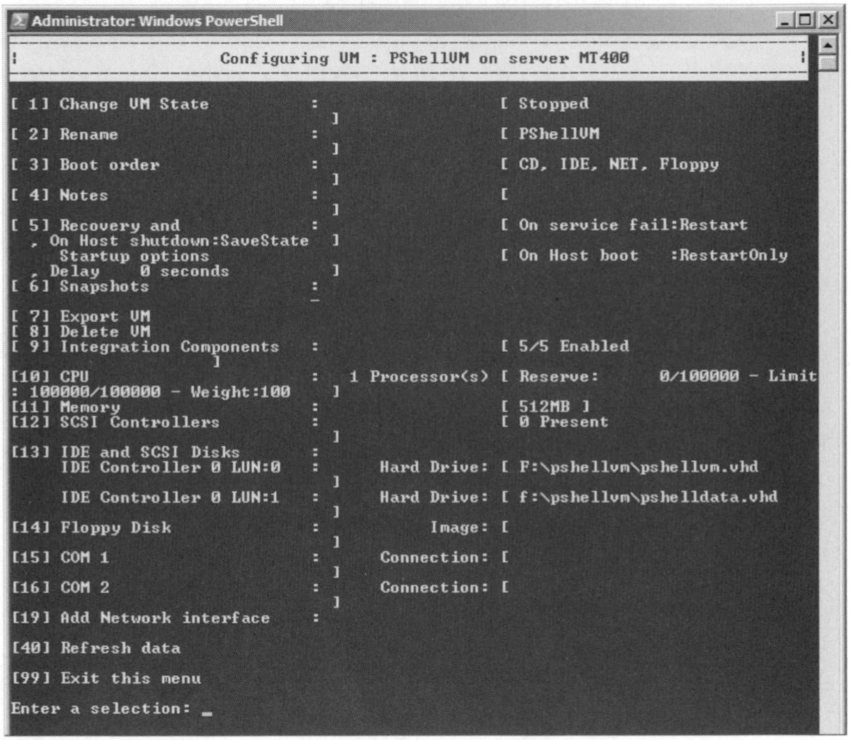

USING THE MENUS

Another way to manage the Hyper-V environment with the management library is a series of menus created in PowerShell. These PowerShell menus allow you to work directly with Hyper-V without having to use the cmdlets directly. These menus are intuitive and show the ability in PowerShell to make user-friendly interfaces. You can see how to create a GUI in PowerShell in Appendix F.

In the library, there are four functions to access the menus to manage Hyper-V:

Show-HyperVMenu   With Show-HyperVMenu, you can manage a local or remote Hyper-V server. From this menu, you can manage your virtual networks and create and import virtual machines. You also can access the virtual machines on the local Hyper-V server.

Show-VHDMenu   This allows you to manage the VHD files located on the current server. You can edit and inspect individual VHD files. By default, the menu is configured to work in the %system Drive%\users\public\documents\Hyper-V\ Virtual Hard Disks directory. This is the default directory where Hyper-V stores the VHD files. In the menu, you can change the directory to look at other directories.

Show-VMDiskMenu   This allows you to work with an individual virtual machine's hard drives.

Show-VMMenu   This menu allows you to work with a specific VM. This is the menu mentioned earlier in this chapter with which you can configure all the settings for a specific virtual machine.

Even though you can call the individual menus, the best menu option is Show-HyperVMenu. This is the master menu option that calls the other menus as you move through the various configurations.

```
Hyper-V Management                                         _ □ ×

¦──────────────────── Configuring MT400 ────────────────────¦

[ 1] Select a different Server
[ 2] Manage Server settings
                MAC address  range [          00155D016D00 - 00155D016D00
            ]
                Default   VM folder [ C:\ProgramData\Microsoft\Windows\Hyper-
V          ]
                Default VHD folder [ C:\Users\Public\Documents\Hyper-V\Virtu
al Hard Disks ]
[ 3] Manage Network settings
                    Virtual Network [ Internal
            ]
                    Virtual Network [ internet
            ]

[ 5] Manage Virtual Disk files

[ 6] Create Virtual Machine
[ 7] Import Virtual Machine

     Manage Virtual Machines ...
[10] DeployDC                          [ Suspended    ]
[11] pshellR2                          [ Stopped      ]
[12] pswin7                            [ Stopped      ]
[13] psxp                             [ Suspended    ]
[14] pxeboot                           [ Stopped      ]
[15] Server1                           [ Suspended    ]
[16] Server2                           [ Suspended    ]
[17] Server3                           [ Suspended    ]

[99] Exit this menu

Please enter a selection: _
```

Connect to Virtual Machines

After you create and configure virtual machines, you need to boot the systems to install an operating system and programs. To start a virtual machine, you can use the Start-VM cmdlet. The following cmdlet starts the PShellVm virtual machine:

```
Start-VM PShellVM
```

You can also connect to a virtual machine with the `New-VMConnectSession` cmdlet. This starts a GUI remote session into the specified VM. The following command opens a virtual machine connection to the DeployDC server:

```
New-VMConnectSession DeployDC
```

There are three cmdlets to turn off a virtual machine and have different results and impact on your virtual machine:

Stop-VM   This turns off the virtual machine in an unclean fashion. This is akin to hitting the power button on a system.

ShutDown-VM   This issues a shutdown command to the virtual machine so it performs a clean shutdown of the operating system loaded in the virtual server. Then the virtual machine will be turned off.

Save-VM   This suspends the VM in its current configuration. If you perform a `stop-VM` command to a virtual machine in a save state, the save state information is deleted. Essentially, the server is in a hibernated state waiting to be turned on to continue from the point where you turned it off.

To see the overall state of all the virtual machines on your Hyper-V server, you can run the following command:

```
Get-VMState |Format-List VMElementName, EnabledState
```

Your results will look similar to Figure 12.18.

FIGURE 12.18   Virtual machine state

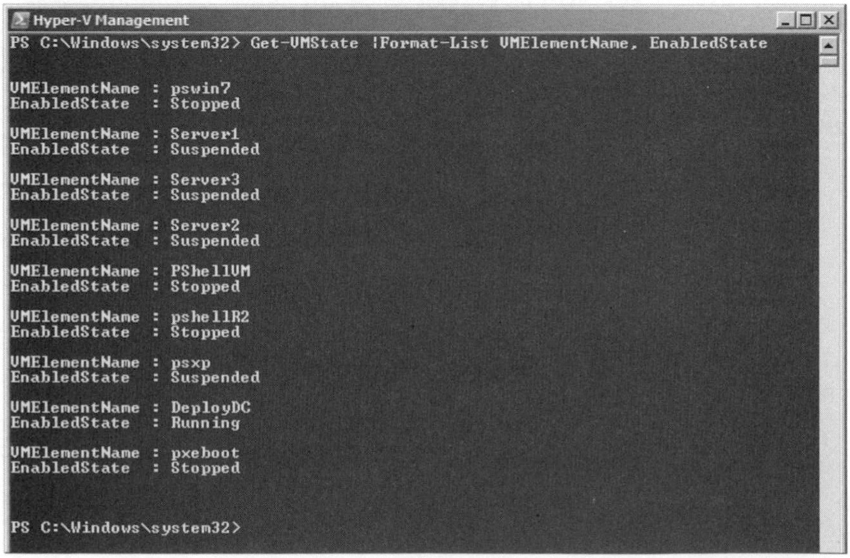

Work with Snapshots

A *snapshot* is a point-in-time picture of the server. Snapshots provide a way to set points of recovery in virtual machines. For example, you just finished building and properly configuring a new server. This is a perfect time to take a snapshot of the server. With a snapshot in hand, you can then begin to install the programs or modify other settings to allow this server to go into production. If the installation of the new applications causes issues in the server, you can revert to the previous build of the server stored in that snapshot.

Snapshots are stored in files with an .avhd file extension. You are allowed to have multiple snapshots of a virtual machine, essentially allowing you take the system back to any point in time you have saved. However, when you do revert to a snapshot, this takes a system completely back to the time of creation of the snapshot. This is important to note because any data created after the snapshot is created will be deleted when you revert to a previous snapshot. This includes all user data, security patches, and settings; it is just like stepping into a time machine for your server, taking it directly back to the day and time you created the snapshot. This also means snapshots are good for reverting an entire server to a point in time, but you still need to perform regular backups of your virtual machines if they are in production.

To take a snapshot of a virtual machine, use the New-VMSnapshot cmdlet. Taking a snapshot does not turn off a virtual machine if it is currently running. During the process, you should not perform any actions on the server. The following command will start the process to take a snapshot of the DeployDC and prompt the user for confirmation:

```
New-VMSnapshot DeployDc
```

Your results will look similar to Figure 12.19.

FIGURE 12.19   Taking a virtual machine snapshot

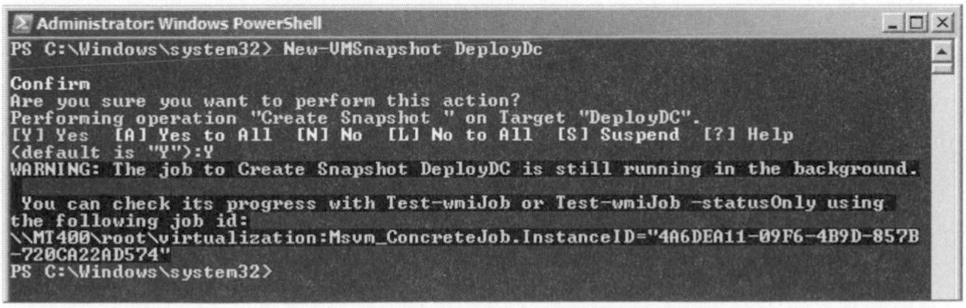

To list the snapshots of a current server, you can use either `Get-VMSnapshot` or `Get-VMSnapshotTree`. In Figure 12.20, you can see an example of both the cmdlets for the DeployDC virtual machine.

FIGURE 12.20   Virtual machine snapshots

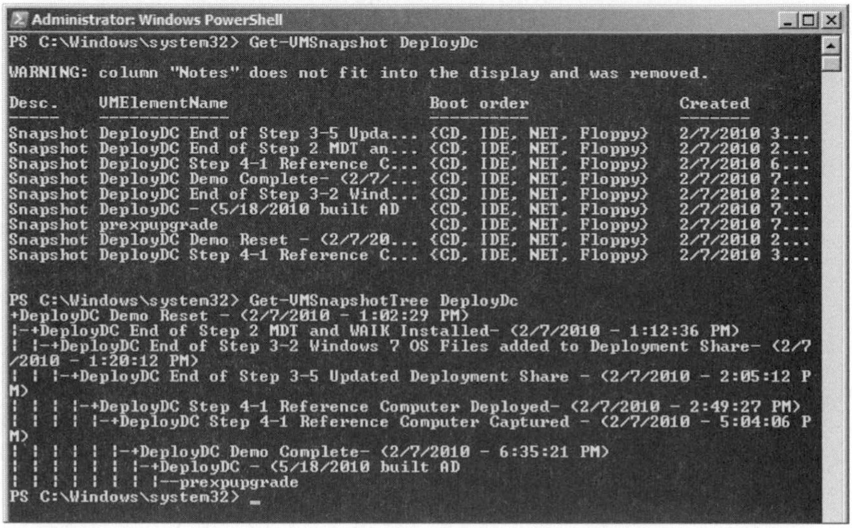

To revert to a snapshot, you need these two cmdlets: `Select-VMSnapshot` and `Restore-VMSnapshot`. The `Select-VMSnapshot` cmdlet allows you to choose the snapshot to be used if there is more than one for the virtual machine. If there is only one snapshot, it will be used. You can pipe the `Select-VMSnapshot` output into the `Restore-VMSnapshot` cmdlet to revert the virtual machine to a particular snapshot. The following command allows you to choose a snapshot to be restored on the DeployDC virtual machine:

```
Select-VMSnapshot DeployDC | Restore-VMSnapshot
```

Your results will look similar to Figure 12.21.

FIGURE 12.21 Restoring a snapshot

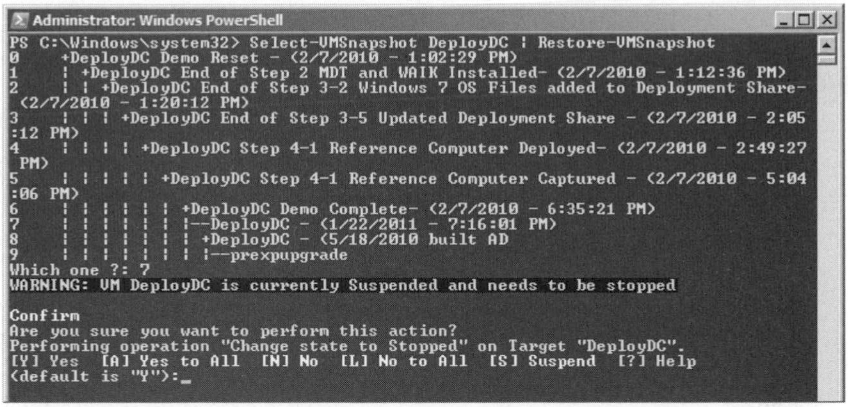

During the restoration of a snapshot, your virtual machine will be suspended or turned off if it is not turned off before starting the process.

EXERCISE 12: CREATE A VIRTUAL MACHINE AND TAKE A SNAPSHOT

Create a new virtual server with Internet connectivity and with a 200GB fixed size virtual hard drive. When you make the drive, make sure you have 200GB free space to perform the lab. If you do not have 200GB available, reduce the example size to 20GB. After you create the virtual machine, take a snapshot. For the purpose of the exercise, the virtual machine will be called VM2K8R2 and will leverage the PowerShell Management Library for Hyper-V.

Solutions to Exercises

IN THIS APPENDIX, YOU WILL LEARN TO:

Solution 1 : Inventory Your Scripts

This is one exercise for which you will not have a clear-cut solution. However, taking the time to look at your current scripts will allow you to gain a better understanding of your environment and where PowerShell is the best fit to help accomplish your tasks easier.

Solution 2: Install PowerShell

The great thing about XP mode is that it is a full 32-bit version of Windows XP running in your Windows 7 environment. Just like other operating systems, you can install PowerShell in XP mode by downloading and installing the necessary components.

1. On your Windows 7 system, start your XP mode virtual system.

2. Click Start ➢ All Programs ➢ Windows Virtual PC ➢ Select Virtual Windows XP.

3. Once your Virtual Windows XP loads, then you can install the components to make PowerShell work.

4. Download and install the 32-bit version .NET Framework version you want to install on XP.

5. Download and install the 32-bit version of the Windows Management Framework.

After you have completed this, you will have PowerShell installed on your XP mode system.

Solution 3: Create a PowerShell Profile

In this exercise, first you make a profile and then you add commands to the profile:

1. Create a profile:

   ```
   New-Item -Path $profile -ItemType File -force
   ```

2. Open the profile you just created:

   ```
   notepad $profile
   ```

3. Type the two following commands to load the proper modules for IIS and Active Directory on your server. If you do not have those roles installed, load another role of your choosing. If you are not sure which modules to load, use `Get-Module -ListAvailable` to show you a list of modules available to you.

```
Import-Module -Name ActiveDirectory
Import-Module -Name WebAdministration
```

4. Save the profile in Notepad: select File ➤ Save, and then close Notepad.

5. Exit your existing PowerShell session.

6. Start PowerShell, and run the following to verify the modules loaded correctly:

```
Get-Module
```

Ultimately when you are working with profiles, their effectiveness will be based on what tools and settings you want to use most frequently. Make profiles your own, and customize them to fit your needs.

Solution 4: Create Your Own Alias

This combines several techniques covered in Chapter 4 as well as Chapter 3.

The script can be done a number of ways.

You can pipe two `Where-Object` clauses together into one command line as follows:

```
Get-Service | Where-Object {$_.status -eq "running"} |↵
 Where-Object {$_.DependentServices} |↵
Format-Table -property status, servicename, dependentservices |↵
 Out-File c:\users\matt\depends.txt
```

You could also use the `-and` operator in the initial `Where-Object` cmdlet to combine the two, shortening the command line:

```
Get-Service | Where-Object {$_.status -eq "running" -and↵
 $_.DependentServices} |Format-Table -property ↵
status, servicename, dependentservices |↵
 Out-File c:\users\matt\depends.txt
```

If you wanted to make a function out of this command, simply place this script in the script block of the function command, as shown in the following code:

```
Function Get-Depend { Get-Service | Where-Object ↵
{$_.status -eq "running" -and$_.DependentServices} |↵
Format-Table -property status, servicename, dependentservices |↵
 Out-File c:\users\matt\depends.txt
```

If you wanted to make this an alias, you would to first need to create the function and then create an alias for the function. Using the previous function Get-Depend, the command would look like this:

```
New-Alias gds Get-Depend
```

Solution 5: Create a Script to Find Startup Programs

Here are the commands you would need to put into a PowerShell script file:

```
Write-Host {Here are the programs in the Run Registry}
Write-Host
Get-ItemProperty -path ↵
HKLM:\SOFTWARE\Microsoft\Windows\CurrentVersion\run
Write-Host {Here are the programs in the RunOnce Registry:}
Write-Host
Get-ItemProperty -path ↵
HKLM:\SOFTWARE\Microsoft\Windows\CurrentVersion\runOnce
```

Solution 6: Set Up a Remote PowerShell Session

This exercise is all about leveraging the power of profiles, which you learned about in Chapter 3. You can place the New-PSSession cmdlets for the servers inside the profile.

1. Open PowerShell, make sure you have created a local profile, and set your remote execution policy to RemoteSigned.

2. Enter **Notepad $profile**.

3. Use the New-PSSession cmdlet followed by the server names you want to manage. If you wanted to connect remotely to Server2 and Server3, for example, the cmdlet would look as follows:

```
New-PSSession Server2, Server3
```

4. Save the profile in Notepad.

5. Close the existing PowerShell session.

6. Reopen the PowerShell session, and verify the remote sessions are created. You can verify the sessions with the `Get-PSSession` cmdlet.

Solution 7: Create a Scheduled Backup with PowerShell

1. Create the following PowerShell script:

```
$policy = New-WBPolicy
$volume = get-WBVolume -VolumePath c:
Add-WBVolume -Policy $policy -volume $volume
Add-WBSystemState -Policy $policy
$target = New-WBBackupTarget -VolumePath Z:
Add-WBBackuptarget -Policy $policy -target $target
Start-WBBackup -Policy $policy
```

2. Give the script a name like `backup1.ps1`.

3. Create a Task Scheduler task to run `backup1.ps1`. The full command line would look like this if the script was stored in the scripts directory:

```
powershell -noninteractive c:\scripts\backup1.ps1
```

Solution 8: Populate an Active Directory Test Environment

Creating the users is straightforward, but you also have to remember the order of operations for this. Create the OU first, and then add the users. Also key to the success of this exercise is making sure you enable the recycle bin before deleting your users. Here is one example of the PowerShell commands you could run to perform the exercise. For this exercise, I used a Windows Server 2008 R2 native forest; you would replace the `deploy.com` with the domain you are working with:

1. Create the OU test:

```
New-ADOrganizationalUnit -Name "Test" -Path
"DC=deploy,DC=com"
```

2. Create the users:

```
New-ADuser chrissmith -GivenName "Smith" - Surname
 "Chris" -Displayname "Chris Smith" -Path
'OU=test,DC=deploy,DC=com'

New-ADuser sarahsmith -GivenName "Smith" - Surname
 "Sarah" -Displayname "Sarah Smith" -Path
'OU=test,DC=deploy,DC=com'

New-ADuser kevinsmith -GivenName "Smith" - Surname
 "Kevin" -Displayname "Kevin Smith" -Path
'OU=test,DC=deploy,DC=com'

New-ADuser debsmith -GivenName "Smith" - Surname
 "Deb" -Displayname "Deb Smith" -Path
'OU=test,DC=deploy,DC=com'

New-ADuser caitlinsmith -GivenName "Smith" - Surname
 "Caitlin" -Displayname "Caitlin Smith" -Path
'OU=test,DC=deploy,DC=com'

New-ADuser mitchellsmith -GivenName "Smith" - Surname
 "Mitchell" -Displayname "Mitchell Smith" -Path
'OU=test,DC=deploy,DC=com'

New-ADuser nicolesmith -GivenName "Smith" - Surname
 "Nicole" -Displayname "Nicole Smith" -Path
'OU=test,DC=deploy,DC=com'

New-ADuser mattsmith -GivenName "Smith" - Surname
 "Matt" -Displayname "Matt Smith" -Path
'OU=test,DC=deploy,DC=com'

New-ADuser billsmith -GivenName "Smith" - Surname
 "Bill" -Displayname "Bill Smith" -Path
'OU=test,DC=deploy,DC=com'
```

3. For the purpose of this exercise, you can choose to enable the accounts. When you first create the accounts, they are not enabled by default, and they do not have passwords set. When you enable each account, you also need to make sure the new passwords are set and they meet your domain's policy. To enable accounts, use a command similar to the following one for each of your user objects:

```
Enable-ADAccount -Identity kevinsmith
```

4. To set passwords, run a similar command for all your users:

```
Set-adaccountpassword --identity sarahsmith -reset ↵
-newpassword (ConvertTo-SecureString -AsPlainText↵
 "p@ssw0rd" -force)
```

5. Enable the recycle bin (depending on your environment you may need to prepare your domain):

```
Enable-ADOptionalFeature "Recycle Bin Feature" -Scope↵
 ForestorConfigurationSet -Target 'your domain name'
```

6. Delete the users in the Test OU:

```
Get-ADUser -Filter * -SearchBase "OU=test,DC=deploy,DC=com" ↵
| Remove-ADUser
```

7. After the users have been deleted, run the following:

```
Get-ADObject -SearchBase "CN=Deleted Objects,↵
DC=deploy,DC=Com" -Filter {lastKnownParent ↵
-eq "OU=test,DC=deploy,dc=com"} -includeDeletedObjects↵
| Restore-ADObject
```

Solution 9: Turn Off the Display Control Panel in Group Policy with PowerShell

This PowerShell command is a matter of piping three cmdlets together:

▶ New-GPO

▶ New-GPLink

▶ Set-GPRegistryValue

Order also matters. When you run the following command, you create the GPO first, set the values second, and then link it last. The following example will create a new GPO called `NoDisplay` with the Display Control Panel disabled and linked to the Executives OU in `sample.com`:

```
New-GPO NoDisplay | Set-GPRegistryValue  -key↵
"HKCU\Software\Microsoft\Windows\CurrentVersion\Policies↵
\System" -ValueName NoDispCPL -Type DWORD -value 1↵
| New-GPLink -target "ou=executive,dc=sample,dc=com"
```

Solution 10: Create a Website with PowerShell

This exercise combines all the techniques presented in this chapter to create the structure for a website:

```
New-WebSite -Name MySite -Port 80 -HostHeader MySite ↵
-PhysicalPath "c:\mysite"

New-WebAppPool Pool1
Set-ItemProperty iis:\apppools\Pool1 -name processModel↵
 -value @{userName="WebApp";password="pass@
word1";identitytype=3}

New-WebApplication -Name App1 -Site 'MySite ↵
-PhysicalPath c:\MyApp -ApplicationPool Pool1

New-WebVirtualDirectory -site "MySite" -name PictureVirDir↵
 -PhysicalPath \\server1\images

Backup-WebConfiguration -Name MySiteBackup
```

Solution 11: Create a Deployment Share

This exercise will require you to have the source file for Windows 7 on your server. You will also need to have downloaded and installed the MDT and WAIK tools. The exercise is then just applying what you saw in this chapter.

This creates the share:

```
New-PSDrive -Name "Win701" -PSProvider "MDTProvider" ↵
-Root "d:\win7" -Description "My Windows 7 Share" Share"↵
 -NetworkPath "\\<yourserver>\Win7$" -Verbose ↵
| add-MDTPersistentDrive -Verbose
```

This copies the Windows 7 files to your deployment share.

```
Import-MDTOperatingSystem -path "Win701:\Operating Systems"↵
 -SourcePath "<Source files for Win7>" -DestinationFolder
"Windows 7" ↵
-Verbose
```

This creates the task sequence:

```
Import-MDTTaskSequence -path "Win701:\Task Sequences"↵
 -Name "Deploy Windows 7" -Template "Client.xml" ↵
-Comments "Select this task Sequence to deploy the ↵
standard Windows 7 desktop" -ID "DepWin7" -Version ↵
"1.0" -OperatingSystemPath "Win701:\Operating Systems↵
\Windows 7 PROFESSIONAL in Windows 7 x64 install.wim"↵
 -FullName "Desktop User" -OrgName "deploy.com"↵
 -HomePage "www.bing.com" -Verbose
```

This updates the deployment share:

```
Update-MDTDeploymentShare -path "Win701:" -Verbose
```

To add the image to WDS if you have it installed, the command would be nearly identical (except the path for the light-to\uch file) to what you saw in this chapter:

```
WDSUTIL /verbose /progress /Add-Image ↵
/ImageFile:"D:\win7\Boot\LiteTouchPE_x64.wim"↵
 /ImageType:Boot
```

Solution 12: Create a Virtual Machine and Take a Snapshot

The first step is to create the virtual machine:

```
New-VM -Name VM2K8R2 -Server Hyperv1
```

Then you will create the external virtual machine switch and associate the new switch with the virtual machine. The first command creates the switch based on whether your NIC for your host starts with Intel on a server called Hyperv1.

```
New-VMExternalSwitch -VirtualSwitchName "External Network"↵
 -ext "Intel" -Server Hyperv1
```

Then you will add the virtual NIC to the virtual machine and associate it with the virtual machine:

```
Add-VMNIC " VM2K8R2" -virtualSwitch "External Network"
```

Then you will create the fixed size hard drive, if you store your hard drives on drive d:.

```
Add-NewVMHardDisk -VM PshellVM 0 1 -VHDPath ↵
d:\VM2K8R2\VM2K8R2.vhd -size 200GB -Fixed
```

Lastly, you will take a snapshot of the virtual machine:

```
New-VMSnapshot VM2K8R2
```

Developing at a Command Prompt

IN THIS APPENDIX, YOU WILL LEARN TO:

lthough the chapters in this book cover the fundamentals of PowerShell from an IT perspective, you may want a guide for scripting some processes to make the IT team's job a lot easier. The first part of this appendix is for any developer who is not familiar with or comfortable developing at a command prompt or with such simple tools.

Understanding objects and how to write scripts for objects can be a little intimidating because some developers struggle with understanding the concepts of objects and object-oriented programming. In the second part of this appendix, you will look at objects and how properties are tied to these objects, learning about object-oriented concepts with PowerShell.

Choose Between the ISE and the Command Prompt

As a developer, you may be used to working in Visual Studio, WebMatrix, LightSwitch, or another integrated development environment (IDE), rather than working at a command prompt. In fact, some developers may panic and get writer's block when they see a command prompt. However, as intimidating as it may seem to write code without a GUI and without IntelliSense, PowerShell is fairly easy to work with and can be a good experience even for the most timid developer at the command prompt.

You may see the Integrated Scripting Environment (ISE) and find comfort in that environment. Although you may prefer to do all of your work in the GUI, there will be times when you should load just the command prompt. For example, if you have to scramble at work to resolve an emergency and need to use PowerShell to solve it, it is quicker to just type the code at the command prompt, rather than loading all of the goodies that come with the ISE. This section covers these two environments and explains when you would want to work in each particular environment.

STARTING POWERSHELL FROM THE TASKBAR

Although you can start PowerShell from the menu, you may find it tedious to go through Start ➢ All Programs ➢ Accessories ➢ Windows PowerShell every time you want to start it. Save yourself time and take advantage of one of the operating system's features: pin it to the taskbar. By doing this, you only have to click the shortcut on the taskbar to start PowerShell. In addition, the Run As Administrator, Import system modules, ISE, and help file shortcuts appear on the context menu of the taskbar icon. This will be especially helpful when you need to open PowerShell quickly in order to deal with an emergency.

Write Code at a Command Prompt

As noted in Chapter 2, starting PowerShell is simple. You can find it on your menu under Start ➢ All Programs ➢ Accessories ➢ Windows PowerShell. To work strictly with a command prompt, choose one of the options without *ISE* in their name.

When you open PowerShell, you start at its command prompt. Rather than panicking at seeing the command prompt, remember the problem you are trying to solve. Think about the problem in English first, and then use PowerShell's commands to resolve your issue.

Although there isn't any IntelliSense to help you remember syntax, you do have the following tools to help you:

▶ Get-Help

▶ Get-Command

▶ Tab completion

Suppose you notice that a print spooler on a particular server has been problematic and needs to be restarted, and this just happens to be broken when the CEO needs to print handouts for a meeting that started a few minutes ago. Although you could go through the windows in the operating system to start and stop the print spooler, you could get the job done quicker with a script. Try the following command:

```
Restart-Service Spooler
```

If this spooler were on a remote machine and if remoting and security allowed it, you could restart the spooler remotely with the following command:

```
Invoke-Command -ComputerName Server1 -ScriptBlock {Restart-
Service Spooler}
```

With a script that short and without having to connect to the server and navigate through various screens to restart the service, you could quickly get the print spooler back up and running.

When you can solve your problem in a few lines of code, go with the command prompt. If you happen to find yourself writing more than a few lines of code in the command prompt, then it's time to move to the ISE. You can launch the ISE from the command prompt by running the following alias:

```
ise
```

Write Scripts in the ISE

The command prompt is great for quick solutions. But what if you need to write more than one line of code? What if you wanted to add some logic, putting to use what was covered in Chapter 5? Sure, you could use the command prompt. However, the interface for working with logic can be a bit clunky.

Suppose your company hosts websites, and you need to allocate IP addresses to machines in two environments — one for developers to work on proofs of concept and one for production. Rather than set up the websites manually, you should find it helpful to script the website setup. The following code sample is a snippet of what you might use in your script:

```
$ComputerName = Get-Content Env:\COMPUTERNAME
if ($ComputerName -contains "Developer"){
    $WebsiteIPAddress = "172.16.42.1"
} else {
    $WebsiteIPAddress = "10.10.42.1"
}
$WebsiteIPAddress
```

It's already more than a few lines of code, and this is just the beginning of the script. Although you could write this at the command prompt, it is a bit awkward to read. Take a look at Figure B.1 to see what this looks like.

FIGURE B.1 Script block at the command prompt

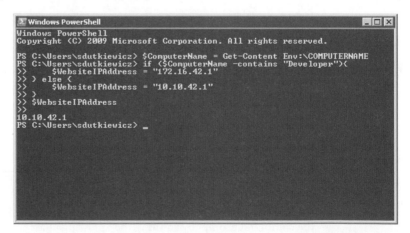

Although the tabs help keep some of the code in line, it is hard to read when the start of the code doesn't line up with the rest of the code. This is one of those cases where the command line isn't ideal. So, in this case, you should start the ISE. Figure B.2 shows how readable the code is when displayed in the script pane of the ISE.

FIGURE B.2   Script block in the ISE

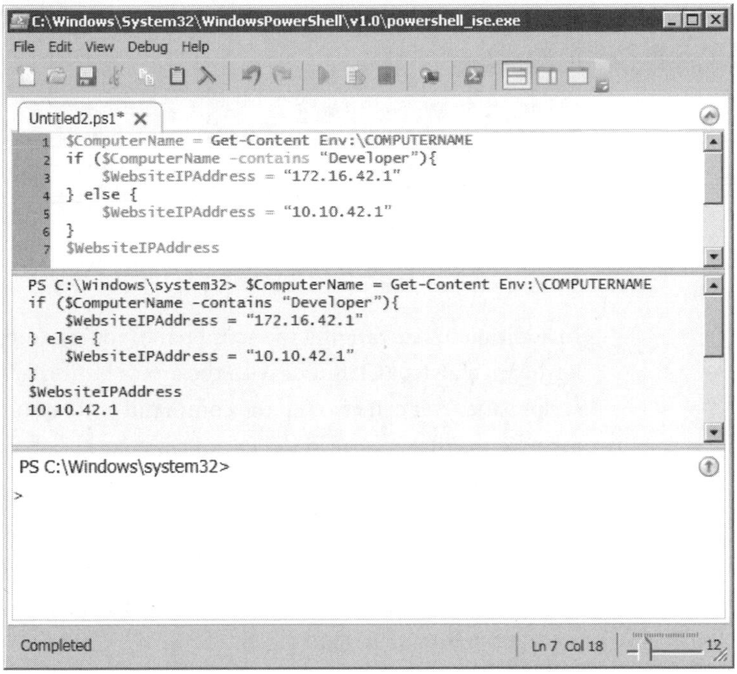

In addition to readability, the ISE lets developers who are familiar with Visual Studio adapt quickly thanks to the shared keyboard shortcuts between the two. These shared shortcuts help alleviate some of the pains that come with adjusting to a new development environment. Take a look at some of these shared developer-specific keyboard shortcuts in Table B.1.

TABLE B.1   Shared developer-specific keyboard shortcuts

Command	Keyboard shortcut
Run/Continue	F5
Stop Debugging	Shift+F5
Toggle Breakpoint	F9
Remove All Breakpoints	Ctrl+Shift+F9
Step Over	F10
Step Into	F11
Step Out	Shift+F11

Developing at a Command Prompt

APPENDIX B

Although the ISE comes with the script pane on top, the command pane in the middle, and the output pane on the bottom, you can reposition these default positions. Table B.2 lists other positions for the script pane, as well as the keyboard shortcuts to easily toggle through them.

TABLE B.2   Script pane positions

Position	Keyboard shortcut
Top	Ctrl+1
Right	Ctrl+2
Maximized	Ctrl+3

In addition to rearranging the script pane, you can toggle its visibility with the keyboard shortcut Ctrl+R or with the arrow button in the upper-right corner of the script pane. You can also flip the command and output panes, either using the green arrow icons that appear in the upper-right corner of the command pane or via the menu View ➢ Command Pane Up.

By combining these shortcuts and positions, you can find a setup that you are comfortable working with while using the ISE. Once you are comfortable in the ISE, you can use your developer understanding of logic plus the syntax of PowerShell to create some powerful scripts to help simplify your processes.

Work with Objects in PowerShell

Objects can be a tough concept to understand. However, I find that it's easier to understand them if you think of a problem first in English and then translate it to code.

Step away from the code for a minute, and think about the computer you're currently working with. Maybe you're working on a multiprocessor server with a lot of memory. It could be manufactured by Dell, IBM, Apple, or someone else. Perhaps it is part of a domain. If I were to ask you to describe your current machine to me, you probably could give me information like that.

In that exercise, your computer is considered an object. All of the other things I suggested — manufacturer, number of processors, amount of memory, whether it's on a domain — tell me more about your computer. These can be considered properties. Basically, objects have properties.

Understand Properties

Now that you have a basic understanding of what objects and properties are in English, let's look at them in terms of PowerShell. Start with the following command:

```
$MyComputer = Get-WmiObject win32_computersystem
```

Here you're storing the computer information in a variable to get a better understanding of objects. $MyComputer is a variable, specifically, an object representing the WmiObject that was returned by the Get-WmiObject cmdlet. Now what does win32_computersystem really tell you about your computer? You can find out that information — things that describe your computer, or its properties — just by typing the variable name at the PowerShell command prompt. When you do this, you should see something similar to Figure B.3.

FIGURE B.3 $MyComputer output

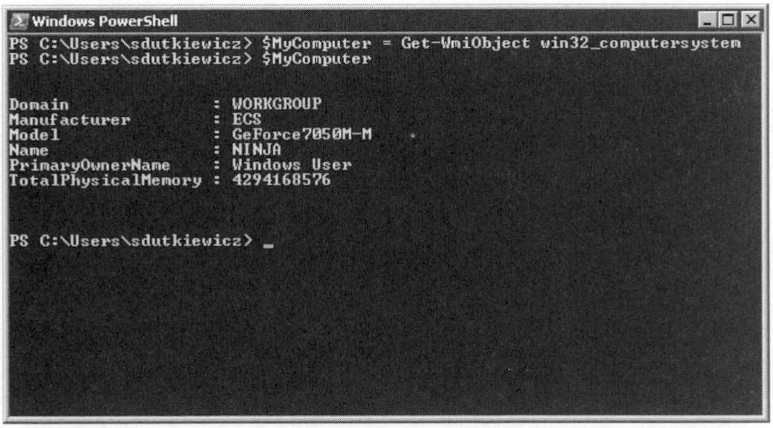

```
Windows PowerShell                                                      _ □ ×
PS C:\Users\sdutkiewicz> $MyComputer = Get-WmiObject win32_computersystem
PS C:\Users\sdutkiewicz> $MyComputer


Domain              : WORKGROUP
Manufacturer        : ECS
Model               : GeForce7050M-M
Name                : NINJA
PrimaryOwnerName    : Windows User
TotalPhysicalMemory : 4294168576


PS C:\Users\sdutkiewicz> _
```

By default, it shows only a few properties of your computer. WMI usually has a lot more information about the computer, and it is included in the $MyComputer object. So if WMI has more information and yet you're seeing only a few properties currently, how do you know what properties exist on your $MyComputer object?

As noted in Chapter 3, the Get-Member cmdlet can be useful when working with objects and wanting to learn more about a particular one. Get-Member shows you everything about an object, including the properties. Because WMI has a lot of information and because you are concerned only with properties at the moment, you need to run this command:

```
$MyComputer | Get-Member -type property
```

The output should look similar to Figure B.4. Here are some things to note:

▶ Every property has a name. Although some appear in PascalCase (or CamelCase) and others appear in ALL CAPS, these properties are not case sensitive.

▶ The definition of each property contains two pieces of information:

  ▶ The type of each property. In Figure B.4, these start with System. and are followed by the type name.

  ▶ What you can do with the property's value. If get; is present, then you are able to get the value of that property. If set; is present, then you are able to set the value of that property. More often than not, get; is present. However, read-only properties have only get;. They do not have set;.

FIGURE B.4   List of $MyComputer's properties

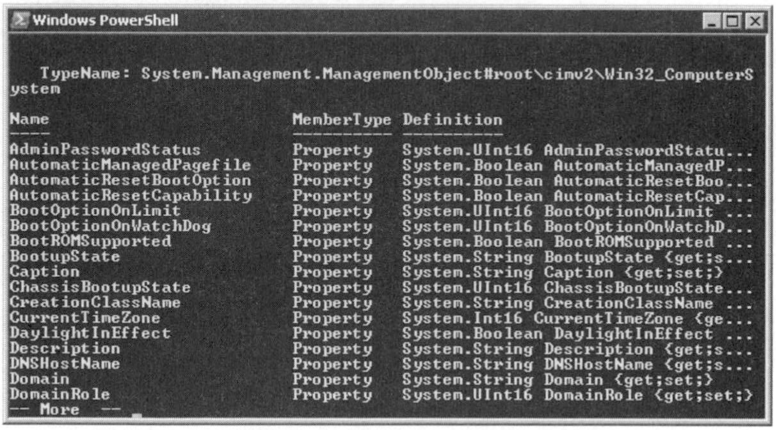

Now that you have used Get-Member to list the properties of your object, you can take this one step further and use these properties. Suppose you need to take inventory of the computers in your company. For this example, you need to keep track of the machine name, manufacturer, model, domain, and total physical memory. You may want to run something like this:

```
$MyComputer | Format-Table Name, Manufacturer, Model, Domain,
TotalPhysicalMemory
```

By looking at the list of properties provided while exploring $MyComputer with Get-Member, you can tailor this command to meet whatever details you may need to track if you did need to use this script. You could easily replace the list after Format-Table with any of the properties in the list.

Create Your Own Custom Object

Now that you understand objects and properties, you may be wondering how to create your own object so that you can use it with PowerShell's powerful pipelining. Although there are many ways to create custom objects, you will look at two ways to do this in PowerShell 2.0:

▶ Using New-Object with a hash table

▶ Compiling a class written in a .NET language with Add-Type

Using New-Object with a Hash Table

Although the New-Object cmdlet was the only way to create objects in PowerShell 1.01, it still works in PowerShell 2.0. In fact, they stepped it up a little bit to make it easier to create objects. You no longer have to pipe New-Object through Add-Member to append properties to the object. In PowerShell 2.0, you can now create a hash table with sample data to build your object. The following example would be helpful if you had multiple servers across multiple buildings and wanted to keep track of their location and wanted to create an object to track basic server location and identification information:

```
$TrackedServerProperties = @{
    SerialNumber = 'SN8675309';
    Building = 'Building 42';
    IsDomainController = $true;
    Floor = 3;
    Room = 311;
}
$TrackedServer = New-Object PSObject -property
$TrackedServerProperties
$TrackedServer
$TrackedServer.GetType().Name
```

You can see the output in Figure B.5. Note that the $TrackedServer object comes back as a PSCustomObject. When you want to create a custom object, rather than derive from an existing type, use PSObject with New-Object to return a PSCustomObject.

FIGURE B.5 Custom object from `New-Object`

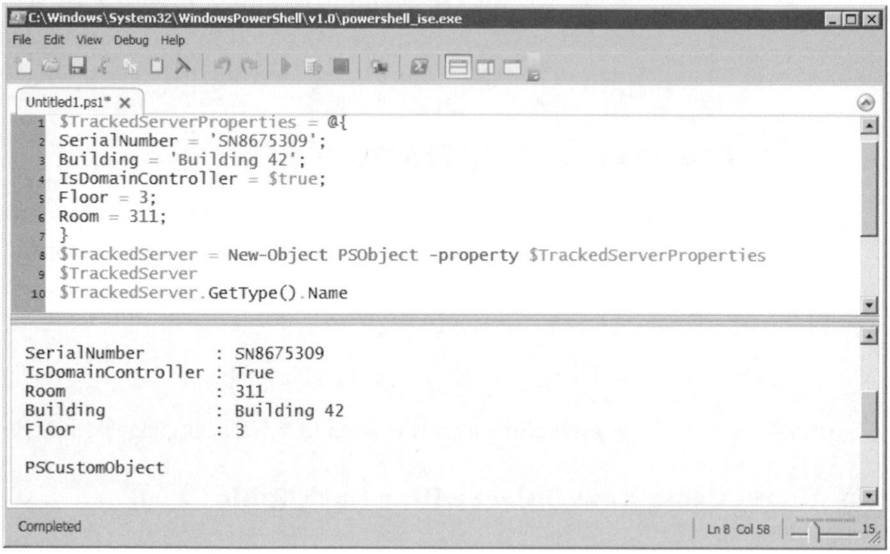

In PowerShell, you do not have to specify the type for each parameter. However, if you are curious as to how PowerShell handled those properties, pipe $TrackedServer through Get-Member to see more details. You should see something similar to Figure B.6.

FIGURE B.6 `Get-Member` results of `$TrackedServer`

```
PS C:\Windows\system32> $TrackedServer | Get-Member


    TypeName: System.Management.Automation.PSCustomObject

Name                MemberType    Definition
----                ----------    ----------
Equals              Method        bool Equals(System.Object obj)
GetHashCode         Method        int GetHashCode()
GetType             Method        type GetType()
ToString            Method        string ToString()
Building            NoteProperty  System.String Building=Building 42
Floor               NoteProperty  System.Int32 Floor=3
IsDomainController  NoteProperty  System.Boolean IsDomainController=True
Room                NoteProperty  System.Int32 Room=311
SerialNumber        NoteProperty  System.String SerialNumber=SN8675309
```

Something to note about those properties is that they were added as a NoteProperty property. Whenever you add a property to a PSObject that doesn't already exist, it gets added as `NoteProperty`. However, if you try adding a nonexistent property to any other type of object, PowerShell reports an error.

Creating objects with the `New-Object` cmdlet and a hash table of properties is fairly simple, which is great if you are just starting out with a scripting language or if you are in a hurry.

Compiling a Class with Add-Type

Although IT professionals with little developer experience may prefer using the `New-Object` cmdlet with a hash table to create their custom object, developers dabbling in PowerShell may feel more comfortable using the `Add-Type` cmdlet. Developers may think of objects more in terms of classes, and the `Add-Type` cmdlet is the way to bring the concept of classes to PowerShell 2.0. What's nice about this is that, as a .NET developer, you can use the .NET language of your choice to write the class. Using the same scenario as the previous example, here's what it would look like if you used a C# class:

```
Add-Type @'
public class TrackedServer{
    public string SerialNumber = "SN8675309";
    public string Building = "Building 42";
    public bool IsDomainController = true;
    public int Floor = 3;
    public int Room = 311;
}
'@

$TrackedServer = New-Object TrackedServer
$TrackedServer
$TrackedServer.GetType().Name
```

Notice in this case that `$TrackedServer` comes back as the `TrackedServer` class, rather than `PSCustomObject`. If you pipe `$TrackedServer` through `Get-Member`, as shown in Figure B.7, the properties are of the type `Property` rather than `NoteProperty`. You have better control over defining your property types when creating your own class.

If you want to create your own classes and work with your own data types, then use this `Add-Type` method before creating your object.

FIGURE B.7   Get-Member results from a custom type

```
PS C:\Windows\system32> $TrackedServer | Get-Member


   TypeName: TrackedServer

Name                 MemberType Definition
----                 ---------- ----------
Equals               Method     bool Equals(System.Object obj)
GetHashCode          Method     int GetHashCode()
GetType              Method     type GetType()
ToString             Method     string ToString()
Building             Property   System.String Building {get;set;}
Floor                Property   System.Int32 Floor {get;set;}
IsDomainController   Property   System.Boolean IsDomainController {get;set;}
Room                 Property   System.Int32 Room {get;set;}
SerialNumber         Property   System.String SerialNumber {get;set;}
```

At this point, you should be able to choose between the command prompt and the ISE. Should you need more help with the ISE, run the following:

```
help about_Windows_PowerShell_ISE
```

You should also be able to identify objects and properties in PowerShell or create your own. If you do find yourself in PowerShell and drawing a blank on how to work with objects or properties, the help system is there. You can always fall back on the following commands:

```
help objects
help properties
```

Providing for PowerShell

IN THIS APPENDIX, YOU WILL LEARN TO:

Whether you are working with the registry, using environment variables, or even working with the file system, providers are used for a variety of tasks. They make it easier to access data and objects that are typically hard to reach at a command line. Although the data is organized in a data store, there are few command-line utilities that make these easily accessible. In the first part of this appendix, you will work with the built-in providers. You will also look into some of the other providers that have been created to make administration easier.

Although the built-in providers and additional providers from custom modules are helpful, you may see a need to create your own provider. In the second part of this appendix, you will create a custom provider.

The beauty of PowerShell is that you can administer a large part of your server within PowerShell without having to open another administration tool. Providers are one of the tools that open up various avenues of administration. Working with certificate stores and managing parts of the registry are just a couple things that providers help with.

Work with Built-in Providers

As with many of the concepts in this book, there is a `Get-` cmdlet that shows all the providers in your session. That command is `Get-PSProvider`. Figure C.1 shows a list of the providers that come with the default installation of PowerShell.

FIGURE C.1   List of built-in providers

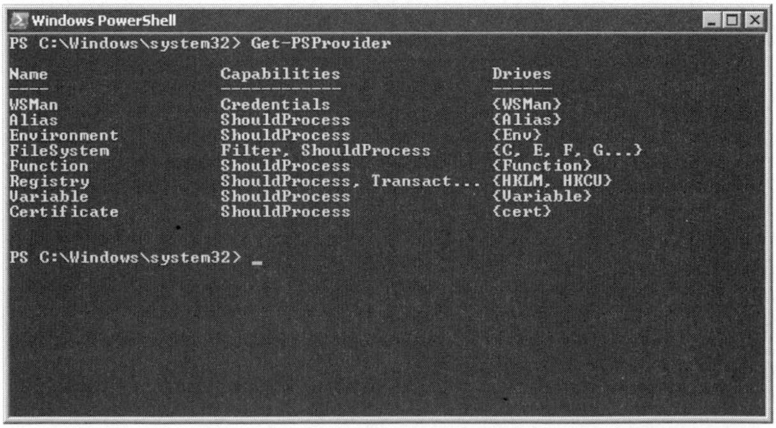

Some of these providers were created to make the PowerShell environment easier to work with, but others help with parts of everyday server administration. Before looking into the specific providers, there are a few concepts you need to understand.

Understand Provider Basics

Two columns in Figure C.1 need to be explained before going further. Capabilities and drives are a couple of the basics of providers you should understand. While you are looking at these, you will also learn about another unique feature called *dynamic parameters*.

Provider Capabilities

Provider capabilities note features that are supported by the provider. As shown in Figure C.1, a provider may have multiple capabilities. Table C.1 describes the supported capabilities.

TABLE C.1   Capabilities

Name	Description
None	Has no additional support other than what is provided in the base class
Include	Has the ability to include items via wildcards
Exclude	Has the ability to exclude items via wildcards
Credentials	Allows credentials to be included at the command line
Expand Wildcards	Supports wildcards within an internal path
Filter	Allows additional filtering via a string
ShouldProcess	Supports user confirmation before running its cmdlets and allows the -WhatIf parameter to be used
Transactions	Supports its cmdlets to be used within a transaction

Provider Drives

These are the tools that make it easier to access data stores. For example, the WebAdministration provider includes the IIS drive to access the IIS configuration. As another example, the Registry provider includes two drives that are set to the shortened versions of the long names of two popular Windows registry hives — HKEY_LOCAL_MACHINE and HKEY_CURRENT_USER.

Providing for PowerShell

APPENDIX C

These are listed as part of the default output of the Get-PSProvider cmdlet. Navigating provider drives is as simple as navigating disk drives at the command prompt. Thanks to the aliases provided by PowerShell, you can still use cd and dir to gain a better understanding of a drive's structure.

Dynamic Parameters

Dynamic parameters are parameters available only when a provider's cmdlet is being used with the provider's drive. For example, the Certificate provider has a CodeSigningCert parameter that can be used with the Get-Item and Get-ChildItem cmdlets when working with the cert: drive. Figure C.2 shows an example of how this parameter can be used and what happens when you try to use the CodeSigningCert parameter with a drive other than the cert: drive.

FIGURE C.2 CodeSigningCert dynamic parameter

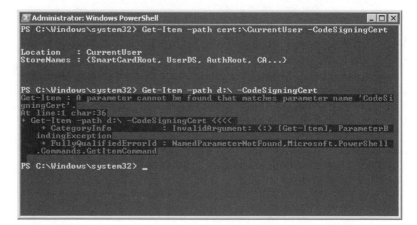

Use PowerShell-Specific Providers

The following providers are built around concepts within the PowerShell environment. Note that these providers do not support the Invoke-Item cmdlet.

Alias Provider

As noted in Chapter 4, you can create aliases to shorten commands in PowerShell. The Alias provider gives you a quick way of working directly with the aliases as objects. Although you can use Get-Alias to see a list of aliases currently available to you, you can also use `Get-Item -path alias:` to list these aliases. Another way you can see all aliases is via the following steps:

1. Run `cd alias:`.

2. Run `Get-Item -path *`.

TIP   If the path you are working with is in the current drive, you do not have to include the drive name as part of the path variable.

Although the `Alias` provider can provide access to the aliases as objects, you can still use the built-in cmdlets `Import-Alias`, `Export-Alias`, `New-Alias`, `Get-Alias`, and `Set-Alias` to work with aliases. If you prefer to work with the built-in cmdlets, you should not include the `alias:` drive.

Note that the built-in cmdlets do not include `Copy-Alias`, `Rename-Alias`, or `Remove-Alias`. However, the `Alias` provider supports working with the `Copy-Item`, `Rename-Item`, `Clear-Item`, and `Remove-Item` cmdlets. Thanks to this provider, you can create these commands.

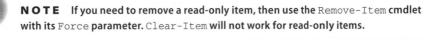

NOTE   If you need to remove a read-only item, then use the `Remove-Item` cmdlet with its `Force` parameter. `Clear-Item` will not work for read-only items.

As noted, the `Alias` provider has one dynamic parameter, the `Options` parameter, which can be used with the `New-Item` and `Set-Item` cmdlets. Table C.2 describes the values that can be used with the `Options` parameter.

TABLE C.2   Options values

Value	Description
None	Default value. No options.
AllScope	Alias is copied to any new scopes.
Private	Alias is in the current scope only.
Constant	Alias cannot be deleted and cannot be changed. This option is available only when creating an alias.
ReadOnly	The properties cannot be changed except by using the `Force` parameter. You need to use `Remove-Item -Force` to remove aliases that are marked `ReadOnly`.

Providing for PowerShell

APPENDIX C

Function Provider

Chapter 4 introduced the concept of functions. The `Function` provider allows you to work directly with the functions. As noted previously, `Get-Function` does not exist. However, thanks to the `Function` provider, you can create your own `Get-Function` command. `Remove-Function`, `Rename-Function`, and `Copy-Function` could also be created, similar to what was described for the `Alias` provider.

The `Function` provider gives you access to both functions and filters. The best way to see this is by doing the following:

1. If you do not have any filters in your PowerShell session, add a filter to your PowerShell session. For example, perhaps you want to list functions that do not refer to `Set-Location`. You may have a filter like this:

   ```
   filter NotSetLocation { $_.Definition ↵
   -notcontains "Set-Location" }
   ```

2. Run `dir Function:*`. This filter should appear in the output, with `Filter` as its `CommandType`.

Note that although the item is a type of filter, it still is listed under the `Function:` drive. There is no `Filter:` drive.

The `Function` provider has one dynamic parameter as well. Like the `Alias` provider, the `Function` provider's `Options` parameter can be used with the `New-Item` and `Set-Item` cmdlets. Its values are the same as those for the `Alias` provider; however, they apply to functions rather than aliases.

Variable Provider

Chapter 5 explains the concept of variables. The `Variable` provider allows you to work directly with variables as objects. Similarly to the `Alias` provider, there are built-in cmdlets to work with variables: `Get-Variable`, `New-Variable`, `Set-Variable`, `Remove-Variable`, and `Clear-Variable`. As with the `Alias` provider, you do not need to use the provider drive with the built-in `Variable` cmdlets. Also, if you are referencing a variable by name — such as `$ComputerName` — you do not need to include the drive name.

Use Other Built-in Providers

PowerShell also has built-in providers that bring administrative processes that normally occur outside of the PowerShell console to PowerShell. The following providers come in the default PowerShell installation and help make outside processes easier.

Certificate Provider

The `Certificate` provider makes it easy to work with X.509 certificates and their stores.

There are three levels when it comes to certificate stores:

► Store locations

► Certificate stores

► X.509 certificates

To gain a better understanding of how these work, follow these steps:

1. In your PowerShell session, run `cd cert:` to set your current location to the certificate provider's drive.

2. Run `dir` to see a list of the store locations. The output should be similar to Figure C.3.

FIGURE C.3   List of store locations

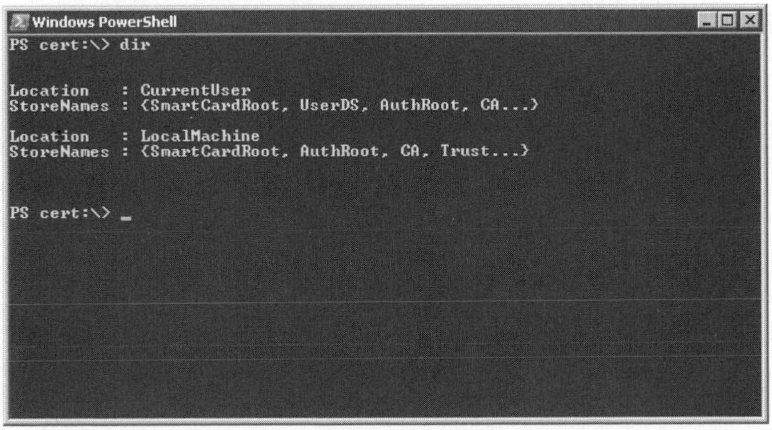

3. Let's look into the certificate stores that are in the `LocalMachine` store location. Change directories to `LocalMachine`.

4. Once the current location is set to `LocalMachine`, run `dir` to see the names of the certificate stores.

5. The X.509 certificates themselves are within those stores. Let's look into the `AuthRoot` certificate store. Change directories to `AuthRoot`.

6. Once in the `AuthRoot` certificate store, run `dir` to see a list of the X.509 certificates with the store. The output should be similar to Figure C.4.

FIGURE C.4 List of certificates

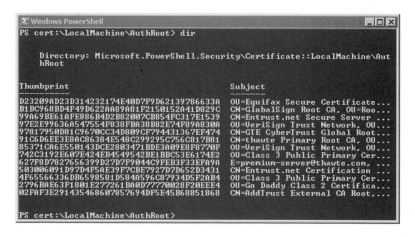

In addition to listing the data down to the certificates level, you can take it one step further with the `CodeSigningCert` dynamic parameter, which will allow you to find only the certificates that can be used for signing code. This can be extremely beneficial if you run many secure servers and have only a certain set of certificates that can be used to sign your developers' applications. This dynamic parameter can be used with the `Get-Item` and `Get-ChildItem` cmdlets.

One final thing to note with the `Certificate` provider is that, unlike the PowerShell-specific providers, it does support the `Invoke-Item` cmdlet. When you use the `Invoke-Item` cmdlet with the `Certificate` provider, you invoke the certificate manager. By running the following command, you should see something similar to Figure C.5.

```
Invoke-Item cert:\CurrentUser
```

FIGURE C.5   Certificate manager

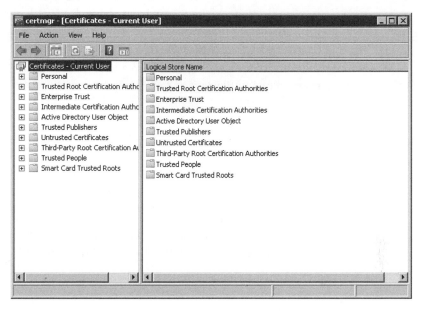

Environment Provider

The Environment provider makes it easy to work with environment variables. Listing environment variables' name and value pairs is as simple as dir env:*. The Environment provider supports adding, getting, setting, clearing, and removing environment variables. Like the PowerShell-specific providers, the Environment provider does not support the Invoke-Item cmdlet.

FileSystem Provider

The FileSystem provider makes it easy to work with the server's files and directories. Its provider drives map your local machine's drives — including those mapped to network shares — and allow you to access them from within PowerShell. This provider is what allows you to type dir c:\ and see the directory listing within your PowerShell environment.

The FileSystem has a few dynamic parameters: Encoding, Delimiter, and Wait. The Encoding dynamic parameter is used to note the file encoding, which is ASCII by default. It can be used with the Add-Content, Get-Content, and

Set-Content cmdlets. The Delimiter dynamic parameter is used to split a file into a collection of objects, based on a string. By default, it uses the new line escape (\n). This can be used with the Get-Content cmdlet. Finally, the Wait dynamic parameter waits for a file to change and then returns either the updated content or the entire file, depending on what change was made. Get-Content polls the file every second until you stop it with Ctrl+C.

Registry Provider

The Registry provider makes it easy to work with the registry. Although you can use regedit to invoke the Registry Editor to make changes to the registry, the Registry provider gives you the ability to maintain the registry via PowerShell.

For example, let's say you wanted to see what shell extensions were registered on a computer. You could run the following command, with output similar to Figure C.6:

```
Get-ItemProperty "hklm:software\microsoft\ ↵
windows\currentversion\shell extensions\approved"
```

FIGURE C.6 **Registry properties**

```
PSPath                                  : Microsoft.PowerShell.Core\Registry::HKEY_LOCAL_M
                                          ACHINE\software\microsoft\windows\currentversion
                                          \shell extensions\approved
PSParentPath                            : Microsoft.PowerShell.Core\Registry::HKEY_LOCAL_M
                                          ACHINE\software\microsoft\windows\currentversion
                                          \shell extensions
PSChildName                             : approved
PSDrive                                 : HKLM
PSProvider                              : Microsoft.PowerShell.Core\Registry
{80009818-f38f-4af1-87b5-eadab9433e58}  : MF ADTS Property Handler
{0907616E-F5E6-48D8-9D61-A91C3D28106D}  : Hyper-V Remote File Browsing
{B7056B8E-4F99-44f8-8CBD-282390FE5428}  : VirtualCloneDrive
{42042206-2D85-11D3-8CFF-005004838597}  : Microsoft Office HTML Icon Handler
{993BE281-6695-4BA5-8A2A-7AACBFAAB69E}  : Microsoft Office Metadata Handler
{C41662BB-1FA0-4CE0-8DC5-9B7F8279FF97}  : Microsoft Office Thumbnail Handler
```

The registry provider has one dynamic parameter — Type. You can use this dynamic parameter with the Set-Item and Set-ItemProperty cmdlets. Table C.3 shows the possible values.

Although the Certificate provider supports launching the certificate manager via the Invoke-Item cmdlet, the Registry provider does not launch the Registry Editor with Invoke-Item. This cmdlet is not supported by the Registry provider.

TABLE C.3   Registry types

Value	Registry equivalent	Description
String	REG_SZ	Null-terminated string
ExpandString	REG_EXPAND_SZ	Null-terminated string that contains unexpanded references to environment variables
MultiString	REG_MULTI_SZ	An array of null-terminated strings, terminated by two null characters
Binary	REG_BINARY	Binary
DWord	REG_DWORD	32-bit binary number
Qword	REG_QWORD	64-bit binary number
Unknown		Unsupported registry data type

WSMan Provider

The WSMan provider makes it easy to work with Web Services for Management (WS-Management, or WSMan for short) configuration information. WS-Management is discussed in Chapter 6. The WSMan provider supports adding, changing, clearing, and deleting WSMan configuration data. Of all the providers covered here, the WSMan provider has the most dynamic parameters — more than 50 dynamic parameters. Table C.4 shows some of its dynamic parameters.

TABLE C.4   Some WSMan dynamic parameters

Name	Supported cmdlets	Description
Address	Get-Item	Specifies an address for the selected listener. This value can be bound to * (all IP addresses), IP: (followed by a specific IPv4 or IPv6 address), or MAC: (followed by a specific MAC address).
AllowRemoteShellAccess	Get-Item, Set-Item	Enables access to remote shells. The default value is true.
AllowUnEncrypted	Get-Item, Set-Item	Allows the client to request unencrypted traffic. As the name suggests, the client defaults to requiring encrypted data.
Certificate	Get-Item, Set-Item	Allows certificates to be used for authentication purposes.
Port	Get-Item, Set-Item	Defines the listener's TCP port, within a range of 1 - 65535.

For a detailed list of the `WSMan` dynamic parameters, see the following site:

`http://technet.microsoft.com/en-us/library/dd819476.aspx`

Work with Additional Providers

Other Microsoft teams and other vendors are creating their own providers to further help automate administration. As mentioned in Chapter 10, the `WebAdministration` module makes it easy to manage IIS at the command line. Other providers that may be of interest to you as an administrator include providers for Remote Desktop Services, BizTalk, Exchange Server, and Windows Mobile. Some of these providers may be installed with the software package, as is the case with Exchange Server. Others may be available when a server role is enabled, as is the case with Remote Desktop Services. Finally, you can find others via a search engine online and install them once downloaded, as is the case with BizTalk and Windows Mobile.

 NOTE   Although this book covers Windows Server 2008 R2, the `WebAdministration` provider is also available for IIS 7. However, in order to install the `WebAdministration` provider for IIS 7, you have to add it using the `Add-PSSnapIn` cmdlet. You can download the IIS 7 PowerShell snap-in from `www.iis.net/download/PowerShell`.

Install and Remove Providers

Providers can be loaded via two methods — modules and snap-ins. Appendix E explains how to create your own custom modules and snap-ins. When you import a custom module, such as the `WebAdministration` module, you automatically get everything in the module, including providers. So when you run `Import-Module WebAdministration`, you get the beauty of navigating the IIS setup through the `IIS:` drive. Snap-ins are just as easy to work with. Use the `Add-PsSnapin` cmdlet to add the snap-in to your session.

Removing providers is as easy as installing them. If you imported the provider via a module, you can remove the provider when you remove the module via the `Remove-Module` cmdlet. If you added the provider via a snap-in, you can remove the provider via `Remove-PSSnapIn` cmdlet. If you want to remove only a drive created by a provider, you can use the `Remove-PSDrive` cmdlet.

One thing to note about modules vs. snap-ins is that modules are the more modern way of deploying providers, cmdlets, and functions. Appendix E discusses further differences between modules and snap-ins.

Create Your Own Provider

Despite all the providers for management tasks, you may have an idea for creating your own provider. Programming your own provider requires some developer experience, because the tools to write them purely in PowerShell are still being developed. You need to reference `System.Management.Automation.Provider` in your Visual Studio Class Library project. Many of the objects discussed in this section come from this library.

Understand Basic Provider Concepts

In addition to the provider basics discussed earlier, you need to understand a few more concepts before creating your own provider. You will look at the functionality, paths, supported cmdlets, and help file structure before you build your own custom provider.

Provider Functionality

When programming your provider, you need to state the functionality it supports by inheriting from a base class or interface. Table C.5 explains the base classes and interfaces that can be derived from.

TABLE C.5   Functionality

Type	Base Class/Interface	Description
Container-Enabled	ContainerCmdletProvider	Allows users to manage containers
Content-Enabled	IContentCmdletProvider	Allows users to manage items' content; allows getting, setting, and clearing content
Drive-Enabled	DriveCmdletProvider	Defines what drives are available to the user and whether drives can be added or removed
Item-Enabled	ItemCmdletProvider	Allows users to manage the items in the data store; allows getting, setting, and clearing items
Navigation-Enabled	NavigationCmdletProvider	Allows users to move items in the data store
Property-Enabled	IPropertyCmdletProvider, IDynamicPropertyCmdletProvider	Allows users to manage items' properties; allows getting, setting, clearing, removing, moving, and renaming

Provider Paths

Because your provider will be accessing a data store at some time, it needs to support paths. Table C.6 explains the types of paths that a provider can support.

TABLE C.6   Provider paths

Type	Description
`Drive-Qualified`	Combines the Windows PowerShell drive, the container and any subcontainers, and the object name. For example: `D:\Projects\PowerShell`.
`Provider-Qualified`	Allows PowerShell to initialize and uninitialize your object. These start with the provider name. For example: `FileSystem::\\netserver\shared\folder`.
`Provider-Direct`	Allows remote access to your provider. For example, the `Registry` provider supports `\\remoteserver\registrypath`.
`Provider-Internal`	Allows accessing data via non-PowerShell APIs. This is the part after `::` in the provider-qualified path. So, in line with the provider-qualified example, the provider-internal path would be `\\netserver\shared\folder`.

Provider Cmdlet and Cmdlet Parameters

In addition to functionality and paths, there are certain cmdlets that can be used in providers. Many of these cmdlets are described throughout the book. Table C.7 breaks them down into different categories and includes some notes on their implementations.

TABLE C.7   Provider cmdlets

Category	Cmdlet name	Notes
PSDrive (`DriveCmdletProvider`)	`Get-PSDrive`	Does not need any overrides
	`New-PSDrive`	Overrides `NewDrive` and `NewDriveDynamicParameters`
	`Remove-PSDrive`	Overrides `RemoveDrive`
Item (`ItemCmdletProvider`)	`Clear-Item`	Overrides `ClearItem` and `ClearItemDynamicParameters`
	`Copy-Item`	Overrides `CopyItem` and `CopyItemDynamicParameters`
	`Get-Item`	Overrides `GetItem` and `GetItemDynamicParameters`

Category	Cmdlet name	Notes
	Get-ChildItem	**Overrides** `GetChildItems,` `GetChildItemsDynamicParameters,` `GetChildNames,` `GetChildNamesDynamicParameters`
	Invoke-Item	**Overrides** `InvokeDefaultAction`
	Move-Item	**Overrides** `MoveItem` **and** `MoveItemDynamicParameters`
	New-Item	**Does not need any overrides**
	Remove-Item	**Overrides** `RemoveItem` **and** `RemoveItemDynamicParameters`
	Rename-Item	**Overrides** `RenameItem` **and** `RenameItemDynamicParameters`
	Set-Item	**Overrides** `SetItem` **and** `SetItemDynamicParameters`
Item content (`IContentCmdletProvider`)	Add-Content	**Does not need any overrides**
	Clear-Content	**Overrides** `ClearContent` **and** `ClearContentDynamicParameters`
	Get-Content	**Overrides** `GetContentReader` **and** `GetContentReaderDynamicParameters`
	Set-Content	**Overrides** `GetContentWriter` **and** `GetContentWriterDynamicParameters`
Item property	Clear-ItemProperty	**Overrides** `IPropertyCmdletProvider` `.ClearProperty` **and** `IPropertyCmdletProvider` `.ClearPropertyDynamicParameters`
	Copy-ItemProperty	**Overrides** `IDynamicPropertyCmdletProvider` `.CopyProperty` **and** `IDynamicPropertyCmdletProvider` `.CopyPropertyDynamicParameters`
	Get-ItemProperty	**Overrides** `IPropertyCmdletProvider` `.GetProperty` **and** `IPropertyCmdletProvider` `.GetPropertyDynamicParameters`
	Move-ItemProperty	**Overrides** `IDynamicPropertyCmdletProvider` `.MoveProperty` **and** `IDynamicPropertyCmdletProvider` `.MovePropertyDynamicParameters`

(continues)

TABLE C.7 *(continued)*

Category	Cmdlet name	Notes
	New-ItemProperty	Overrides IDynamicPropertyCmdletProvider.NewProperty and IDynamicPropertyCmdletProvider.NewPropertyDynamicParameters
	Remove-ItemProperty	Overrides IDynamicPropertyCmdletProvider.RemoveProperty and IDynamicPropertyCmdletProvider.RemovePropertyDynamicParameters
	Rename-ItemProperty	Overrides IDynamicPropertyCmdletProvider.RenameProperty and IDynamicPropertyCmdletProvider.RenamePropertyDynamicParameters
	Set-ItemProperty	Overrides IPropertyCmdletProvider.SetProperty and IPropertyCmdletProvider.SetPropertyDynamicParameters
Location	Get-Location	Does not need any overrides
	Set-Location	Does not need any overrides
	Push-Location	Does not need any overrides
	Pop-Location	Does not need any overrides
Path	Join-Path	Overrides NavigationCmdletProvider.MakePath
	Split-Path	Does not need any overrides
	Convert-Path	Does not need any overrides
	Resolve-Path	Does not need any overrides
	Test-Path	Overrides ItemCmdletProvider.ItemExistsDynamicParameters

Provider Cmdlet Help

PowerShell has a great internal help system for figuring out the language. Adding Get-Help support to provider cmdlets is easy to do once you understand the format. For more information on writing help files, see Appendix E.

Build a Custom Provider

It's time to bring all the previous knowledge together and write a provider! As noted earlier, there are tools that are being developed to write your providers in PowerShell, but they are not stable as of this writing. Since these tools are still in beta, you will create your custom provider in Visual Studio 2010 using C#. For this example, you are taking the module approach of working with providers, as opposed to working with a snap-in.

Before you get started writing code, let's take a look at what the goals are for this provider. For this appendix, you will look at the basics of implementing a provider with the premise of being able to work with Windows 7 Libraries, including Documents, Pictures, and Music. The sample code in this book allows you to change directories to a special drive for these libraries and list what is in the Libraries. Appendix D covers custom cmdlets related to these Windows 7 Libraries that would be included in a module. Appendix E walks through creating that module to distribute this Windows 7 Library provider and the custom cmdlets.

To work with these Libraries, you need to get the Windows API code pack version 1.1 or higher for Microsoft .NET Framework:

```
http://code.msdn.microsoft.com/WindowsAPICodePack
```

Once you have the code pack downloaded and unpacked, you are ready to get into the code. To get started, create a new project within Visual Studio, complete with the necessary references, by following these steps:

1. Open Visual Studio.

2. Select File ➢ New Project.

3. Change the following settings:

   a. The target framework should be .NET Framework 3.5. Note: .NET Framework 4.0 will not work, as PowerShell 2.0 console and ISE run on the .NET 2.0 core rather than the .NET 4.0 core.

   b. The type of project should be Class Library.

   Your screen should look similar to Figure C.7.

4. Click OK.

Providing for PowerShell

APPENDIX C

FIGURE C.7　New Project window

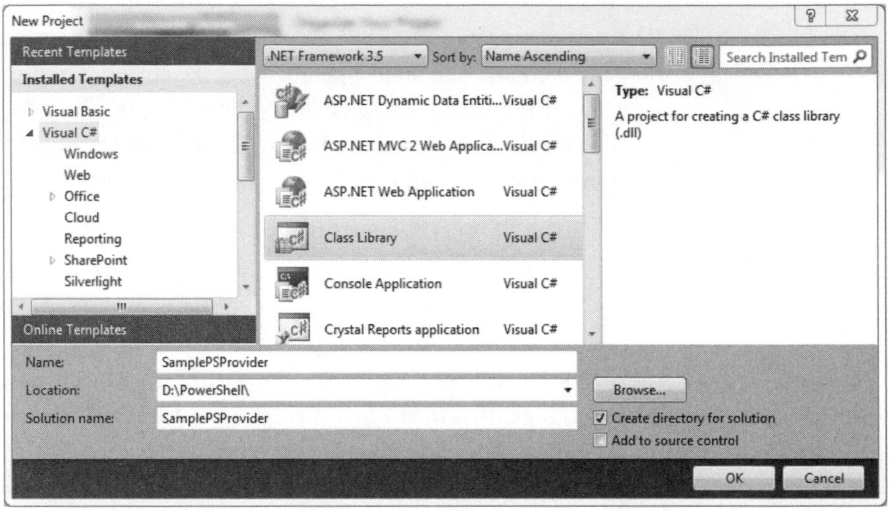

At this point, you should be in the application. To access the PowerShell libraries, you need to add a couple references. To do so, follow these steps:

1. Open the Solution Explorer. You can access it via the View ➤ Solution Explorer menu.

2. Right-click the References folder, and select Add Reference. A window similar to Figure C.8 should appear.

FIGURE C.8　Add Reference window

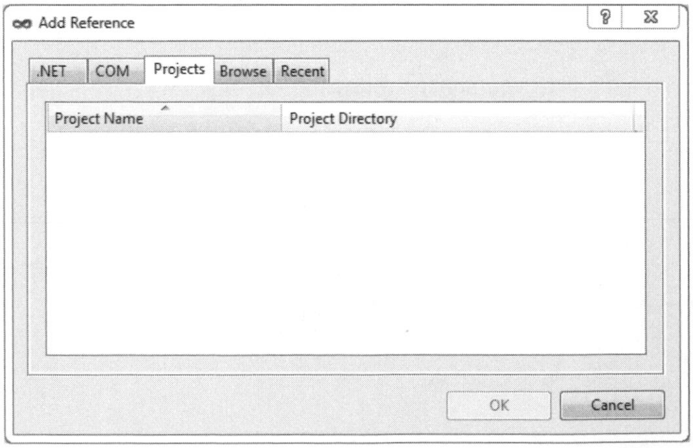

3. Click the .NET tab. Select System.Management, and then click OK.

4. Repeat step 2. This time, click the Browse tab.

5. Navigate to the following path: C:\Program Files\Reference Assemblies\Microsoft\Windows PowerShell\v1.0. Note that if you are working on a 64-bit machine, you may need to check in the Program Files (x86) folder rather than the Program Files folder.

6. Select System.Management.Automation.dll, and then click OK.

   At this point, System.Management and System.Management.Automation should appear in your references list, as shown in Figure C.9.

FIGURE C.9   References list in the Solution Explorer

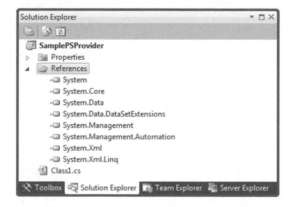

7. Using steps 5 and 6 as a guide, add references to Microsoft .WindowsAPICodePack.dll, Microsoft.WindowsAPICodePack .Shell.dll, and Microsoft.WindowsAPICodePack .ShellExtensions.dll, which should be in the folder where you have unpacked the Windows API code pack for Microsoft .NET Framework.

At this point, all the references should be set up at the project level. Now let's look at the code. First, set up the using statements, specifying which namespaces to refer to. Because this example uses the file system (specifically files and directories), include a reference to System.IO. Also, because this example references collections, include a reference to System.Collections.ObjectModel. The other namespaces listed here should look familiar:

```
using System.Collections.ObjectModel;
using System.IO;
using System.Management.Automation;
```

```
using System.Management.Automation.Provider;
using Microsoft.WindowsAPICodePack;
using Microsoft.WindowsAPICodePack.Shell;
```

Once the namespaces are set up, you need to write the code to name your provider and declare the provider type. In this example, you will call the provider `Win7LibraryProvider`. The namespace declaration will be used in Appendix D as well. Here is what the provider's namespace and naming code should look like:

```
namespace Win7LibraryProvider
{
    [CmdletProvider("Win7LibraryProvider",↵
ProviderCapabilities.None)]
    public class Win7LibraryProvider :↵
NavigationCmdletProvider
    {
```

The `CmdletProvider` attribute tells the compiler that this `Win7LibraryProvider` class is going to be a provider for PowerShell. The `ProviderCapabilities` option allows you to specify which capabilities, as noted in Table C.1, are supported. For this example, you will leave it at `None`. However, this book's companion web page includes examples of how to implement these provider capabilities.

This is an example of a `NavigationCmdletProvider`, which is also included in that declaration. Table C.5 notes other types of providers that you can implement.

You need to set up some variables that will be used throughout this example. Set up the following variables:

```
private string _defaultlibraryLocation = ↵
ShellLibrary.LibrariesKnownFolder.Path;
private string _libraryExtension = ".library-ms";
private const string _pathSeparator = @"\";
```

These variables set up important default variables — the default library location, the file extension for library files, and the path separator.

Ideally, the path structure you are going for is as follows:

```
lib:\LibraryName\
```

Since you know which drive you want to use (`lib:`), create the drive. To do this, override the `InitializeDefaultDrives()` method and have it create the `lib` drive. Here is the code for that:

```
protected override Collection<PSDriveInfo>
InitializeDefaultDrives()
{
   Collection<PSDriveInfo> driveInfoCollection = ↵
new Collection<PSDriveInfo>();
   PSDriveInfo info = new PSDriveInfo("lib", ↵
this.ProviderInfo, _defaultlibraryLocation, ↵
"Libraries", PSCredential.Empty);
   driveInfoCollection.Add(NewDrive(info));
   return driveInfoCollection;
}
```

The PSDrive line is configuring the lib: drive, and the line after it is adding it to the collection of drives. Finally, InitializeDefaultDrives returns the collection of drives that the provider is using.

Now that the drive is created, you need to work with its path and items. For this example, the drive level (lib:) is considered the Root, the library level of the path will be the Library, and everything else will not be a concern, so you will call it Invalid. First, set up the path segment types:

```
private enum PathType
{
   Root,
   Library,
   Invalid
}
```

Next, create a method to determine the path and type of segment you may be working with:

```
private PathType GetTypeFromPath(string path)
{
   bool bPathTest = ↵
(path == (_defaultlibraryLocation + "\\"));
   path = GetLibraryFromPath(path);
   string[] pathSegments = ↵
path.Split(_pathSeparator.ToCharArray());
   PathType pathType;
   if (path.Trim() == string.Empty || bPathTest)
      pathType = PathType.Root;
```

```
      else if (pathSegments.Length == 1)
         pathType = PathType.Library;
      else
         pathType = PathType.Invalid;
      return pathType;
   }
```

The previous code mentions a method called `GetLibraryFromPath(string)`. This method will get the library name based on a path. The code for this is as follows:

```
   protected string GetLibraryFromPath(string path)
   {
      return path.Replace(_defaultlibraryLocation + "\\",↵
   "");
   }
```

To add PowerShell support to this `NavigationCmdletProvider` parameter, override `IsValidPath(string)`. This code determines whether a path is valid. The following code states that paths that are null or empty, as well as paths specified as `Invalid`, are invalid:

```
   protected override bool IsValidPath(string path)
   {
      bool IsValid = true;
      if (string.IsNullOrEmpty(path))
         IsValid = false;
      else
      {
         PathType pathType = GetTypeFromPath(path);
         if (pathType == PathType.Invalid)
            IsValid = false;
      }
      return IsValid;
   }
```

Although this is what you are using for the definition of valid in this example, you can include the logic for any particular pattern and define a path's validity based on your own business requirements.

The following code determines whether an item is a container:

```
   protected override bool IsItemContainer(string path)
   {
```

```
    bool IsContainer = true;
    PathType ContainerPathType = GetTypeFromPath(path);
    if (ContainerPathType == PathType.Invalid)
        IsContainer = false;
    return IsContainer;
}
```

Code needs to be in place to determine whether an item exists. This code is run at various points, including whenever you try to use tab completion and when you run a directory listing on the current folder. In this case, based on the path type, you are checking to see whether the library exists:

```
protected override bool ItemExists(string path)
{
    PathType pathType = GetTypeFromPath(path);
    bool TestPath = false;
    if (pathType == PathType.Invalid)
        TestPath = false;
    else
    {
        switch (pathType)
        {
            case PathType.Root:
                TestPath = true;
                break;
            case PathType.Library:
                try
                {
                    ShellLibrary lib = ↵
ShellLibrary.Load(path, false);
                    TestPath = true;
                }
                catch
                {
                    TestPath = false;
                }
                break;
            default:
                TestPath = false;
                break;
        }
```

```
        }
        return TestPath;
    }
```

Executing `dir` on a path runs the `Get-ChildItem` cmdlet. Use the following code to support `Get-ChildItem` in your provider:

```
protected override void GetChildItems↵
(string path, bool recurse)
{
    if (HasChildItems(path))
    {
        PathType pathType = GetTypeFromPath(path);
        switch (pathType)
        {
            case PathType.Root:
                string[] Files =↵
Directory.GetFiles(↵
Path.Combine(_defaultlibraryLocation, path), ↵
"*" + _libraryExtension);
                foreach (string FileName in Files)
                {
                    FileInfo FileDetails = new ↵
FileInfo(FileName);
                    PSDriveInfo thisDriveInfo = new ↵
PSDriveInfo(FileDetails.Name.Replace(_libraryExtension,↵
""), this.ProviderInfo, FileName, ↵
FileDetails.Name.Replace(_libraryExtension, "") +↵
 " Library", PSCredential.Empty);
                    WriteItemObject(thisDriveInfo, ↵
Path.Combine(path, FileName), true);
                }
                break;
            case PathType.Library:
                string LibraryName = ↵
GetLibraryFromPath(path);
                ShellLibrary lib = ShellLibrary.Load(path, ↵
 _defaultlibraryLocation, false);
                WriteItemObject(lib, path, true);
```

```
            break;
        case PathType.Invalid:
        default:
            WriteWarning("This has not been implemented.");
            break;
        }
    }
}
```

If the path has child items, then the child items will be listed. Otherwise, nothing is done. The HasChildItems code is as follows:

```
protected override bool HasChildItems(string path)
{
    bool HasChildren = false;
    PathType pathType = GetTypeFromPath(path);
    switch (pathType)
    {
        case PathType.Root:
            string[] Files = Directory.GetFiles(↵
Path.Combine(_defaultlibraryLocation, path),↵
"*" + _libraryExtension);
            if (Files.Length > 0)
                HasChildren = true;
            break;
        case PathType.Library:
            ShellLibrary lib = ShellLibrary.Load(path,↵
 false);
            if (lib.Count > 0)
                HasChildren = true;
            break;
        case PathType.Invalid:
        default:
            WriteWarning("Cannot determine child items.↵
Not implemented.");
            break;
    }
    return HasChildren;
}
```

The `GetChildItems` code is displaying the `Library` names if the path is `Root`. If you are running `dir` on a `Library`, it should output the list of items. Otherwise, it will display the warning that the feature hasn't been implemented. This is done to add some simplicity to this example. `WriteItemObject(object item, string path, bool isContainer)` is the way to write objects to the PowerShell session when dealing with `GetChildItems`.

USING WARNING MESSAGES

When writing a provider, it might help to see when these methods are called. Try using the following command in your methods to tell when a method is getting called:

```
WriteWarning("MethodName");
```

An example of this is shown here.

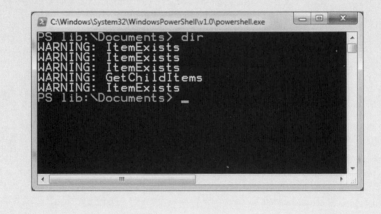

Finally, for those piecing these snippets together in Visual Studio while reading this, make sure to include the closing brackets for the class and the namespace declarations, as follows:

```
    }
}
```

 NOTE   This example simply shows the general layout of a provider. This book's companion web page offers a more complete version of this code.

With the little work you have done so far, you have a provider to navigate the Libraries. If you want to create, delete, and work further with libraries, continue to Appendix D. If you are eager to deploy your provider, look at Appendix E, where you can learn about snap-ins and modules.

If you are more comfortable in PowerShell than in C#, you may want to check out the PowerShell Script Provider at `http://psprovider.codeplex.com/`.

Now that you have built a sample provider, use this as a guide for when you are ready to create your own provider.

Providing for PowerShell

APPENDIX C

APPENDIX D

Custom Cmdlets and Advanced Functions

IN THIS APPENDIX, YOU WILL LEARN TO:

lthough you can do plenty of things with existing commands, you may find a need that is not fulfilled by any existing commands. This is when you need to look into advanced functions and custom cmdlets. The first thing you will look at in this appendix is how to decide which to use.

After comparing and contrasting cmdlets and functions, I will show how you can create advanced functions to fill some of the gaps you saw earlier. Specifically, you will improve on the Get-Function example used in Chapter 4.

In Appendix C, I covered writing a custom provider for the libraries feature in Windows 7. In this appendix, you will create some custom cmdlets to work with those libraries. Finally, in Appendix E, you will deploy your cmdlets and provider from the previous appendixes.

Choose Between an Advanced Function and a Cmdlet

Functions and cmdlets may seem similar in functionality, but they are created differently. Functions are scripts written in PowerShell, whereas cmdlets are typically written in a .NET language and then compiled. Although you have to use the verb-noun naming convention for cmdlets, it is not mandatory to follow that convention for functions. Cmdlets and advanced functions are also similar in many ways, including attributes, parameters, output, and runtime life cycle.

Parameters and Attributes

Both custom functions and custom cmdlets use attributes to identify important parts of their code. The CmdletBinding attribute of functions — introduced in PowerShell 2.0 — is similar to the Cmdlet attribute of cmdlets. If you use the CmdletBinding attribute on a function and create an advanced function, you unlock a lot of the Cmdlet capabilities and features. Both cmdlets and advanced functions use the Parameter attribute to mark their parameters, specifying more details via attribute keywords. Although these attribute keywords are optional, they are beneficial to use. Table D.1 shows the shared attribute keywords for the Parameter attribute.

TABLE D.1 Parameter attribute keywords

Keyword	Description
Mandatory	Notes whether a parameter is required when the command is run. If this is omitted, the parameter is optional.
Position	Specifies the order of the parameter in the command. If this is omitted, the parameter is considered a named parameter and must be referenced by name in commands. If the position is stated, the parameter is considered a positional parameter and does not need its name specified.
HelpMessage	Provides a message to be displayed within context. For example, if you run a cmdlet that has parameters without its parameters, you may get prompted for the parameter values. This message is displayed then. Note that this is not the message that is displayed when you run Get-Help.
ParameterSetName	Specifies the parameter set for a parameter. For more information, see the note on parameter sets later in this appendix.
ValueFromPipeline	Specifies whether the value can come from an incoming pipeline object.
ValueFromPipelineByPropertyName	Specifies whether the value can come from a property of an incoming pipeline object.
ValueFromRemainingArguments	Specifies whether the parameter accepts all remaining arguments for this parameter.
HelpMessageBaseName	Specifies the name of a resource assembly that has help messages for international support. If this is used, the HelpMessageResourceID attribute keyword must also be used. Note that this message is displayed only when the command is run and does not appear when you run Get-Help.
HelpMessageResourceID	Specifies the resource identifier for the help message.

When creating parameters, be it for a cmdlet or an advanced function, you cannot use certain parameter names because they belong to common parameters,

parameters added to all cmdlets, and `CmdletBinding` functions at runtime by default. Those names include the following:

- ► `Confirm`

- ► `Debug`

- ► `ErrorAction`

- ► `ErrorVariable`

- ► `OutVariable`

- ► `OutBuffer`

- ► `UseTransaction`

- ► `Verbose`

- ► `WarningAction`

- ► `WarningVariable`

- ► `WhatIf`

There are a couple other things to be aware of when creating parameters. The parameter needs to be marked as `public` in cmdlets to be seen by PowerShell. If a parameter is not marked `public`, it is recognized as `internal` and cannot be seen by PowerShell. Also, type selection makes a huge difference in terms of validation. Use .NET types rather than assigning all of your parameters to a string in order to get effective validation.

You can also use the `Alias` attribute to create aliases for a parameter. Suppose you have a parameter named `Overwrite`. You may want to use shorter versions in the command line, such as `OW` or `Ovrwrt`. Use the `Alias` attribute to specify these aliases in a comma-delimited string, as shown here:

```
[Alias("OW, Ovrwrt")]
[Parameter()]
public SwitchParameter Overwrite
{
    get { return _overwrite; }
    set { _overwrite = value; }
}
```

SWITCH PARAMETERS

The previous code sample shows a parameter of the type `SwitchParameter`. If this type of parameter is present in the command line, then the value is *true*. Otherwise, when omitted, the parameter is *false*. This is good for cases when something is either true or false. For cases where a value may be true, false, or unspecified, use a nullable Boolean (`Nullable<bool>`) parameter. This is a recommendation in Microsoft's "Strongly Encouraged Development Guidelines" documentation, which is available here:

```
http://msdn.microsoft.com/en-us/library/dd878270(VS.85).aspx
```

A unique feature of PowerShell is the ability to work with parameter sets. These parameter collections give the ability to return different results based on the supplied parameters. Although you can use multiple parameter sets, each set must have at least one unique parameter. It does not have to be specified for commands that can run without parameters, but it is preferred to use a mandatory parameter as the unique parameter. If multiple positional parameters are included in a parameter set, then their positions will have to be explicitly declared in the parameter set — one parameter per position. If a parameter is not marked as part of a specific parameter set, it will appear in all sets. Finally, with regard to taking values from the pipeline, multiple parameters can be marked with `ValueFromPipelineByPropertyName` set to true; however, only one parameter can be marked with `ValueFromPipeline` set to true.

When using multiple parameter sets, you can set a default parameter set using the `DefaultParameterSetName` cmdlet attribute. The cmdlet attributes, which come from `CmdletBindingAttribute` for advanced functions and `CmdletAttribute` for cmdlets, define the cmdlet name and some cmdlet capabilities. Table D.2 describes these attributes and which types support each one.

In addition to parameter and cmdlet attributes, cmdlets and advanced functions also share validation attributes. These help validate the parameters before attempting to use them. Table D.3 describes the validation attributes.

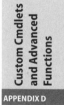

Custom Cmdlets and Advanced Functions

APPENDIX D

TABLE D.2   Cmdlet attributes

Name	Description	Supported by
VerbName	Name of the cmdlet verb. This is required for cmdlets.	CmdletAttribute
NounName	Name of the cmdlet noun. This is required for cmdlets.	CmdletAttribute
SupportsTransactions	Indicates whether the cmdlet can be used in transactions — a feature that allows you to group actions and then run them together and commit the actions only if all actions complete successfully. This is optional.	CmdletAttribute, CmdletBindingAttribute
SupportsShouldProcess	Indicates whether the cmdlet supports calls to the ShouldProcess method. This is optional. An example is provided in the "Create a Custom Cmdlet" section of this appendix.	CmdletAttribute, CmdletBindingAttribute
ConfirmImpact	Sets a threshold for calling to the ShouldProcess. This is optional. An example is provided in the "Create a Custom Cmdlet" section of this appendix.	CmdletAttribute, CmdletBindingAttribute
DefaultParameterSetName	Sets the default parameter set name. This is optional.	CmdletAttribute, CmdletBindingAttribute

TABLE D.3   Validation attributes

Name	Description
AllowNull	Allows a parameter to have a null value. This can be helpful if you want the parameter to have a null value and PowerShell's type conversion isn't treating the $null input as expected.
AllowEmptyString	Allows a parameter to be an empty string (" "), even if it is mandatory.
AllowEmptyCollection	Allows a parameter to be an empty collection, even if it is mandatory.
ValidateNotNull	Does not allow a parameter to have a null value. Empty values are allowed.
ValidateNotNullOrEmpty	Does not allow a parameter to have a null or empty value.

Name	Description
ValidateCount	Sets the minimum and maximum numbers of arguments for the parameter. For example, if a parameter should take two to four arguments, you would note it with the following attribute: `[ValidateCount(2,4)]`.
ValidateLength	Sets the minimum and maximum parameter length. For example, if you had a 128-bit IPv6 address written in hexadecimal with colons as a parameter, it should be no longer than 39 characters. This attribute would be noted as `[ValidateLength(0,39)]`.
ValidatePattern	Uses a regular expression to verify that the parameter matches a particular pattern. If the parameter is a collection, each item in the collection must match the pattern. For example, if you had to validate a parameter for a port number, you could use the attribute `[ValidatePattern("^\d*$")]` to verify the value is solely digits. If the parameter does not match the pattern, PowerShell will generate an error.
ValidateRange	Sets the minimum and maximum values acceptable for the parameter. For example, if you had a script checking individual octets of an IPv4 address, you would want a value between 0 and 255. The attribute would look like `[ValidateRange(0,255)]`.
ValidateSet	Sets a specific set of values that are acceptable for the parameter. For example, if you are writing a script to check a user's groups, you may want to specify that only administrators and power users can do a particular action. If you have a user group parameter, you could validate it like so: `[ValidateSet("Administrators", "Power Users")]`.
ValidateScript	Sets a script to handle the parameter validation. When regular expressions, ranges, lengths, and counts are not enough, you may need to use a script to validate the parameter. Using the IPv4 octets example, you could also use `[ValidateScript({$_ -le 255 - and $_ -ge 0})]`.

Something else to keep in mind with PowerShell parameters is the concept of dynamic parameters. These special parameters appear only when certain conditions are met. As mentioned in Appendix C, the CodeSigningCert parameter appears only when the Path parameter references the cert: path. You can create dynamic parameters based on your business requirements.

Output

Although parameters are helpful for getting user input, there is also the question of output. Cmdlets and advanced functions have similar ways for writing output. Table D.4 describes some of these writing cmdlets.

TABLE D.4   **Writing methods**

Name	Description
WriteCommandDetail	Writes a string to the execution log. To see this in the Windows PowerShell log, make sure that LogPipelineExecutionDetail is turned on. Once that is turned on, these entries will appear under "Pipeline execution detail."
WriteDebug	Writes a string to the host. This allows you to provide debugging information for their cmdlets.
WriteError	Writes an ErrorRecord of nonterminating errors to the error pipeline and continues processing. If you have an error that causes termination, look into using the ThrowTerminatingError method.
WriteWarning	Writes a warning string to the host. Although the output is normally discarded, it can be seen with -Verbose and -Debug command options or configured by the $WarningPreference shell variable.
WriteProgress	Writes a ProgressRecord of the command to the host.
WriteObject	Writes an object to the output pipeline. Note that this returns a single object, which can include an enumerable object.
WriteVerbose	Writes a user-level message to the host. This should not be used for error messages, but it can be used to let a user know what is going on while a command is processing.

The following example shows the different ways that some of these Write methods display their output (see Figure D.1):

```
[Cmdlet(VerbsCommunications.Write, "Sample")]
public class WriteExamples : Cmdlet
{
   protected override void ProcessRecord()
   {
      WriteDebug("This is debugging information");
      WriteWarning("This is a warning");
```

```
        WriteVerbose("This is verbose");
        WriteObject(this);
    }
  }
```

FIGURE D.1   Write-Sample example

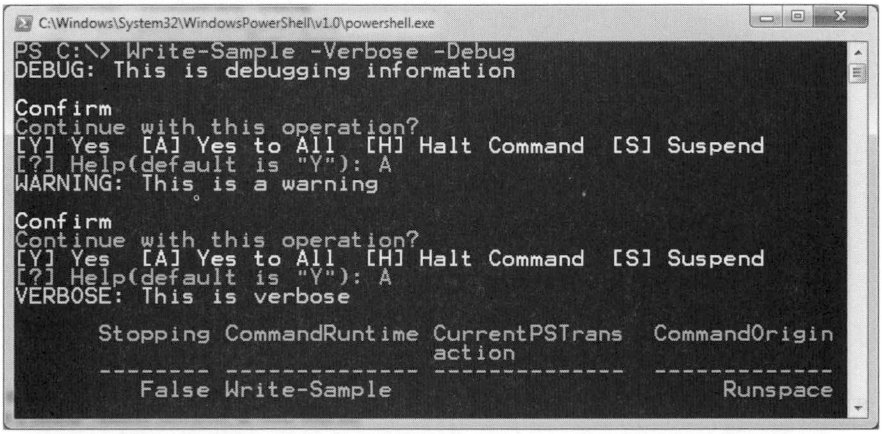

Runtime Life Cycle

In addition to attributes and parameter functionality, advanced functions and cmdlets also have a similar runtime life cycle, as seen with the input processing methods. When these commands are run, they execute code in the order shown in Table D.5.

TABLE D.5   Life cycle of input processing methods

Phase	Cmdlet method	Advanced function method
Starting	BeginProcessing	Begin
Processing	ProcessRecord	Process
Ending	EndProcessing	End
Stopping (when the cmdlet is stopped in the middle of running, for example, by pressing Ctrl+C)	StopProcessing	N/A (currently not supported in advanced functions)

You can write a simple function without referencing these methods, but it helps to tap into these methods to inject logic to handle parameters, for example, before processing the action. Another time this can be helpful is if you are trying to debug a function and want to see whether it is hitting each of these phases; you could insert write statements to write out something in each phase to indicate that the function made it through that phase. A simple example and its output of this is shown here (see Figure D.2):

```
function DoStuff{
    Begin{
        Write-Host "Beginning DoStuff"
    }
    Process{
        Write-Host "Processing DoStuff"
    }
    End{
        Write-Host "Ending DoStuff";
    }
}
```

FIGURE D.2 Life cycle in action

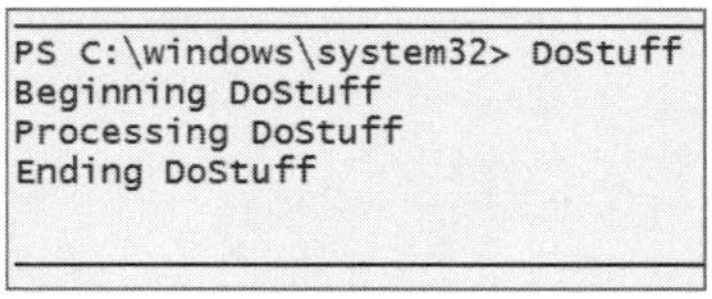

```
PS C:\windows\system32> DoStuff
Beginning DoStuff
Processing DoStuff
Ending DoStuff
```

How can you determine which to use when the `CmdletBinding` attribute makes functions complementary to cmdlets? If you want to unlock the power of .NET and work with .NET libraries that may not have been designed for PowerShell, you will need to use a cmdlet written in a .NET language that can be compiled.

As mentioned throughout this book, PowerShell comes with a wealth of help. If you want to learn more about functions vs. cmdlets, run `Get-Help about_Functions_Advanced` and `Get-Help about_Functions_CmdletBindingAttribute`.

Create an Advanced Function

In Chapter 4, I noted that there is no `Get-Function` cmdlet in PowerShell. However, I showed how to create a function to list all the functions with this code:

```
Function Get-Function { Get-ChildItem -path function: }
```

Although this function is helpful for listing functions in general, it does not support wildcards. If you tried running Get-Function m*, you would still get a list of all the functions, not functions whose names start with the letter m. This is because the code between the brackets does not take any user input into consideration. However, now that you have an understanding of parameters, you can create a function with a parameter to take in user input. Using the building blocks from this appendix and throughout this book, you can come up with something like this:

```
Function Get-Function{
    Param(
    [parameter(Mandatory=$true, ↵
ValueFromPipeline=$true)]
    [String[]]
    $FunctionName
    )
    Get-ChildItem -path function: | ↵
Where-Object {$_.Name -like $FunctionName}
}
```

Now, if you run Get-Function m*, you should get something similar to Figure D.3.

FIGURE D.3   Get-Function with wildcard support

```
PS C:\> Get-Function m*

CommandType     Name                        Definition
-----------     ----                        ----------
Function        M:                          Set-Location M:
Function        mkdir                       ...
Function        more                        $_
```

While writing your custom functions, you may want to find out more about what you are working with. Get-Help about_Functions_Advanced_Methods and Get-Help about_Functions_Advanced_Parameters cover more about these building blocks.

Create a Custom Cmdlet

The focus of this book is on Windows Server 2008 R2, but you may find yourself dealing with Windows 7 clients. In Appendix C, I showed how to create a provider to work with Windows 7's libraries feature. Now I'll show how to create some cmdlets to work with the Windows 7 libraries feature using the building blocks described in this appendix.

To work with these libraries, you need to include a reference to the Windows API Code Pack for Microsoft .NET Framework, which you can download here:

`http://code.msdn.microsoft.com/WindowsAPICodePack`

These examples are written in C# and are being stored in a `.cs` file. The frame of the `.cs` file looks like this:

```
using System.IO;
using System.Management.Automation;
using Microsoft.WindowsAPICodePack;
using Microsoft.WindowsAPICodePack.Shell;


namespace Win7LibraryProvider
{
// put cmdlet code here
}
```

What are some of the things you may want to do with these Windows 7 libraries from PowerShell? Creating a new library and removing a library are a couple of the common tasks that you may want to do. This first custom cmdlet will create a new library, which is why the cmdlet is named New-Library:

```
[Cmdlet(VerbsCommon.New, "Library")]
public class NewLibrary : Cmdlet
{
    private string _libraryname;
    private string _path;
    private bool _overwrite;

    [Parameter(Mandatory = true, ↵
HelpMessage = "Name of the library to create", ↵
Position = 0)]
    [ValidateNotNullOrEmpty]
    public string LibraryName
    {
        get { return _libraryname; }
        set { _libraryname = value; }
    }
```

```
    [Parameter(HelpMessage = "Folder path to create↵
the library (optional)")]
    public string FolderPath
    {
        get { return _path; }
        set { _path = value; }
    }


    [Parameter(HelpMessage = "Whether to overwrite↵
an existing library (optional)")]
    public SwitchParameter Overwrite
    {
        get { return _overwrite; }
        set { _overwrite = value; }
    }


    protected override void ProcessRecord()
    {
        ShellLibrary library;
        if (string.IsNullOrEmpty(FolderPath))
            library = new ShellLibrary(LibraryName,↵
Overwrite);
        else
            library = new ShellLibrary(LibraryName,↵
FolderPath, Overwrite);
    }
}
```

The bulk of the code in this case is consumed by setting up the parameters. The first parameter — LibraryName — is a mandatory string that will always be the first parameter. Since the library needs a name, I'm using the ValidateNotNullOrEmpty attribute to tell PowerShell that this must be filled in. If this parameter is null or empty, you will get an error like Figure D.4.

The second parameter in the code is the FolderPath string, which is an optional parameter to set the path of the library. The third parameter is the Overwrite switch parameter, specifying whether to overwrite an existing library.

Once the parameters are specified, then you get into the actual action done by the cmdlet via ProcessRecord. If the FolderPath string is null or empty, the library is created in the default location. Otherwise, it is created in the specified path.

Custom Cmdlets and Advanced Functions

APPENDIX D

FIGURE D.4   Validation error

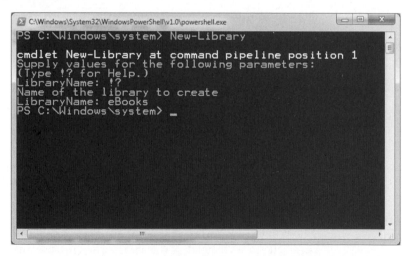

The `HelpMessage` attribute keyword is used for adding the text seen when looking for help with a cmdlet. This appears only as part of the help prompts and does not appear when `Get-Help` is run. Figure D.5 shows this help output.

FIGURE D.5   **HelpMessage** in action

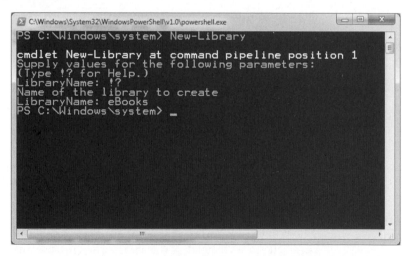

Although the `New-Library` example shows some of the basics of custom cmdlets, there are more things that can be done with a custom cmdlet. If you can add libraries, then you should be able to remove them as well. Since removing a library cannot be undone, it would be helpful to require confirmation from the user before actually removing the library. The following code for a Remove-Library cmdlet will do that:

```
[Cmdlet(VerbsCommon.Remove, "Library", ↵
SupportsShouldProcess = true, ↵
ConfirmImpact = ConfirmImpact.High)]
public class RemoveLibrary : Cmdlet
{
    private string _libraryExtension = ".library-ms";
    private string _defaultlibraryLocation = ↵
    ShellLibrary.LibrariesKnownFolder.Path;
    private string _librarylocation;
    private string _libraryname;

    [Parameter(Mandatory = true, ↵
HelpMessage = "Name of the library to remove", ↵
Position = 0)]
    [ValidateNotNullOrEmpty]
    public string LibraryName
    {
        get { return _libraryname; }
        set { _libraryname = value; }
    }

    [Parameter(HelpMessage = "Location of the library to
remove")]
    public string LibraryLocation
    {
        get { return _librarylocation; }
        set { _librarylocation = value; }
    }

    protected override void ProcessRecord()
    {
        if (base.ShouldProcess("", ↵
"Removing library '" + LibraryName + ↵
"'. This CANNOT be undone.","Removing a Library"))
        {
            if (string.IsNullOrEmpty(_librarylocation))
```

```
                    File.Delete(↵
        Path.Combine(_defaultlibraryLocation, LibraryName) +↵
         _libraryExtension);
                   else
                      File.Delete(↵
        Path.Combine(_librarylocation, LibraryName) +↵
         _libraryExtension);
                }
            }
        }
```

A few things factor into displaying the confirmation message. The SupportsShouldProcess attribute keyword indicates that the cmdlet supports ShouldProcess, which is the method that requests confirmation before proceeding. The ConfirmImpact attribute keyword — new in PowerShell 2.0 — indicates how much of an impact the operation will make, based on what the developer thinks. For this example, ConfirmImpact is set to High since the action removes a file structure and cannot be undone. This keyword should be used only if SupportsShouldProcess is set. By including SupportsShouldProcess and ConfirmImpact, you enable the -whatif and -confirm parameters.

Although these are only a couple of custom cmdlets, you may want to see what other cmdlets can be created to work with these libraries, such as for adding and removing locations to a library, listing the locations in a library, and changing the location of the library's default folder. Be sure to check the online companion site for other custom cmdlets to work with the Windows 7 libraries feature (see Figure D.6). The online examples also cover some of the topics mentioned in this appendix in more detail.

FIGURE D.6   Cmdlets on the online companion

```
[Cmdlet(VerbsCommon.Add, "LibraryLocation")]
public class AddLibraryLocation : Cmdlet...

[Cmdlet(VerbsCommon.Remove, "LibraryLocation")]
public class RemoveLibraryLocation : Cmdlet...

[Cmdlet(VerbsCommon.Get, "LibraryLocation")]
public class GetLibraryLocation : Cmdlet...

[Cmdlet(VerbsCommon.Set, "LibraryLocation")]
public class SetLibraryLocation : Cmdlet...
```

DISPLAYING CMDLET CONFIRMATION WITH CONFIRMIMPACT

Although `ConfirmImpact` allows for the `-confirm` parameter, it does not necessarily mean that the confirmation will appear by default. The trick to getting the confirmation to appear is for your cmdlet to have an equal or higher `ConfirmImpact` value compared to the PowerShell session's `$ConfirmPreference` value, which is `High` by default. For example, if your cmdlet's `ConfirmImpact` is set to `Medium` and you try to run it in your PowerShell session, the confirmation will not appear, because the cmdlet's `ConfirmImpact` is lower than the `$ConfirmPreference`. However, if your cmdlet's `ConfirmImpact` is set to `High`, the confirmation will appear because the cmdlet's `ConfirmImpact` is higher than or equal to the `$ConfirmPreference`. Suppose you use the code for the `Remove-Library` cmdlet and set its `ConfirmImpact` to `Medium`. The following example shows what happens when the `ConfirmImpact` value is higher than the `$ConfirmPreference` value, what happens when the `ConfirmImpact` value is lower than the `$ConfirmPreference` value with the `-confirm` parameter, and finally what happens when `ConfirmImpact` is lower than the `$ConfirmPreference` without the `-confirm` parameter.

Custom Cmdlets
and Advanced
Functions

APPENDIX D

Now that you have an understanding of what it takes to build your own functions and cmdlets, use the examples here as guides for creating your own custom functions and cmdlets. To learn more about distributing your custom functions and cmdlets, see Appendix E.

Packaging PowerShell Extensions

IN THIS APPENDIX, YOU WILL LEARN TO:

hile working with PowerShell, you may become comfortable enough to extend it to meet your business needs. If so, you can develop custom providers, cmdlets, and functions to share with other people. Perhaps you looked at the sample provider in Appendix C or the sample functions and cmdlets in Appendix D and wondered how you could export them to your own machine to work with them.

In PowerShell 1.0, the packaging mechanism for custom extensions was the snap-in. In PowerShell 2.0, modules replace snap-ins. This chapter explores the difference between snap-ins and modules and how to create custom modules. This chapter also shows how to package custom functions for reuse.

Work with Existing Snap-ins

Although snap-ins still work in PowerShell 2.0, they are considered to be the old way of packaging extensions. It was the way to package custom cmdlets and providers in PowerShell 1.0. However, until Microsoft teams and third parties release their snap-ins as modules for PowerShell 2.0, you may sometimes find yourself needing to work with the snap-ins and their related cmdlets in PowerShell.

Snap-ins — including snap-ins for IIS 7.0, SQL Server, and Exchange — have to be installed and registered on the server before you can use them. You may need administrative rights to install a snap-in.

INSTALLING AND REGISTERING A SNAP-IN

Snap-ins need to be installed and registered via `InstallUtil.exe`. This installer program comes as part of the .NET Framework. It helps to create an alias to work with `installutil` from a PowerShell session. To create the alias, use the following command:

```
Set-Alias installutil
$env:windir\Microsoft.NET\Framework\↵
v2.0.50727\installutil
```

To install the snap-in from a PowerShell session with this alias, use the following syntax:

```
installutil SnapInDLLName.dll
```

To see all snap-ins loaded for the current session, use the following command:

```
Get-PSSnapIn
```

Figure E.1 shows some of the snap-ins that come installed with PowerShell.

FIGURE E.1   `Get-PSSnapIn`

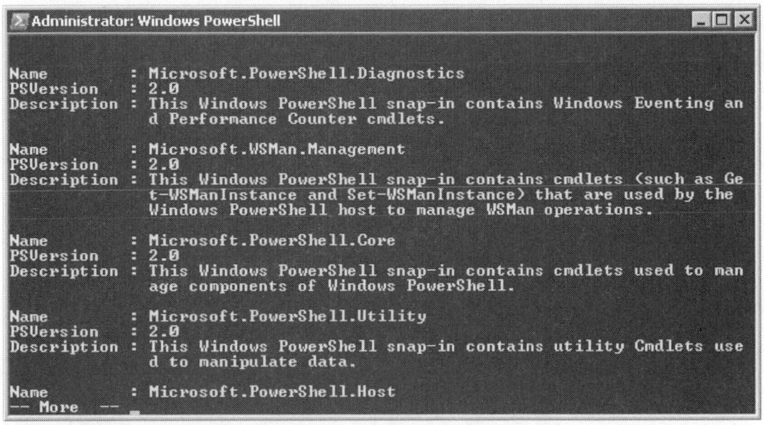

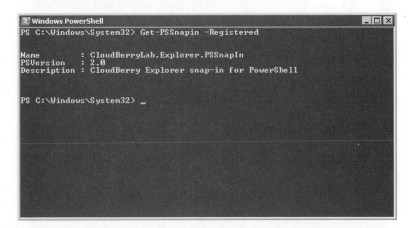

To see all snap-ins registered on the server and not included by the PowerShell installation, use the following command. The example in Figure E.2 shows the CloudBerry Explorer snap-in, used for Amazon S3 cloud management, as a registered snap-in.

```
Get-PSSnapIn -Registered
```

FIGURE E.2   `Get-PSSnapIn -Registered`

To add a snap-in to the current PowerShell session, use the following command:

```
Add-PSSnapIn PSSnapInName
```

Using the CloudBerry example, the command is as follows:

```
Add-PSSnapIn CloudBerryLab.Explorer.PSSnapIn
```

Since snap-ins are used to package extensions, you may want to see what is included in a particular snap-in. To see the contents of a snap-in, use the following command:

```
Get-Command -PSSnapIn PSSnapInName
```

Using the CloudBerry example, the command is as follows:

```
Get-Command -PSSnapIn CloudBerryLab.Explorer.PSSnapIn
```

Figure E.3 shows the output from the previous command.

FIGURE E.3   Get-Command for the CloudBerry snap-in

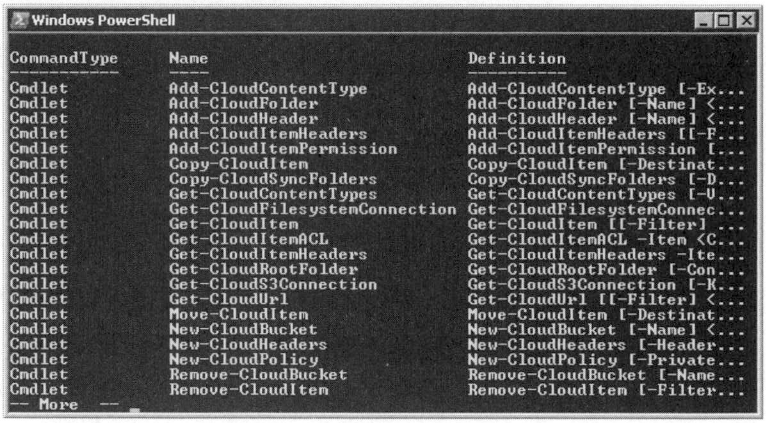

With the advent of PowerShell 2.0, many snap-ins can be treated like binary modules — DLL files that contain cmdlet classes. This means you can import a snap-in rather than installing it on the machine. This also means you can pull in snap-ins without having administrative rights. As long as you know the location of the snap-in DLL, you can try running the following command:

```
Import-Module PathToSnapInDLL\SnapInDLLName.dll
```

Although many snap-ins may load properly this way, there are a few things to keep in mind. For example, a snap-in could set up custom formats or configurations that may not be included via Import-Module. If a snap-in has dependencies, the dependencies will not be included by Import-Module. However, you can fix some of these problems with a file; see the "Manifest File" section later in this chapter.

Create a Custom Module

Modules, introduced in PowerShell 2.0, make it easier to package PowerShell extensions. Chapter 3 discussed how to work with modules. The benefits to using modules rather than snap-ins include the following:

Portability   Modules can be imported by their full paths. This means you can copy modules you commonly use to a portable hard drive, USB stick, or memory card and import them from whichever computer you are working with, as long as it has PowerShell 2.0 installed.

Greater Amount of Supported Members   Snap-ins include cmdlets and providers. Modules include functions, variables, aliases, and more, in addition to cmdlets and providers.

Ease of Import   Unlike snap-ins, modules do not require administrative access to use. Snap-ins had to be installed before use; modules do not have this problem.

With your custom extensions, you should take advantage of these benefits.

Understand Module Concepts

Before building your own module, you should understand what types of modules are available, where modules are stored, how a manifest file works, and how to write help for the module.

Types of Modules

PowerShell modules come in different forms:

- ► Binary modules
- ► Script modules
- ► Manifest modules
- ► Dynamic modules

Binary modules are compiled .NET code assemblies that contain cmdlets. These files have the `.dll` file extension. By default, all cmdlets in a binary module are exported. However, exported cmdlets can be controlled by a manifest file. An example of a binary module is the module created later in this chapter for the Windows 7 libraries provider and cmdlets, as discussed in Appendixes C and D.

Packaging
PowerShell
Extensions

APPENDIX E

Script modules are modules written in PowerShell code. These files use the `.psm1` file extension. Script modules are especially convenient for those who prefer to work strictly in PowerShell and not have to rely on another language, such as C#. Since advanced functions are written in PowerShell, it makes sense to deploy advanced functions via script modules. The script module later in this chapter will be used to deploy the advanced functions from Appendix D.

Manifest modules are modules that take a manifest file, described in the "Manifest File" section later in this chapter, without a root module. These are convenient for loading assemblies, types, and formats — all noted within keys in the manifest file.

Dynamic modules are modules that are not persistent. Think of these as "modules on demand." These modules are created with the `New-Module` cmdlet and are not seen with the `Get-Module` cmdlet, because they are meant to be around for short periods of time.

Module Storage Locations

In addition to knowing which type of module to use, it also helps to know where modules are stored. The `PSModulePath` environment variable stores this information. By default, there are two locations — one in the system folder and one in the user profile. Figure E.4 shows the default module path for a PowerShell 2.0 environment.

FIGURE E.4   The `PSModulePath` environment variable

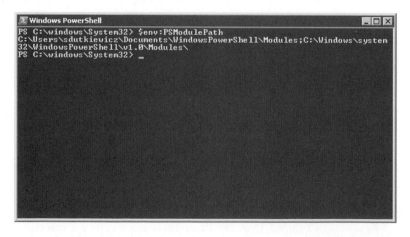

If you have a centralized location for your organization's PowerShell modules, you will want to add it to the `PSModulePath` environment variable. For example, if you store your modules on a server named `central` in a `modules` folder and wanted to permanently update the environment variable, you would update the PSModulePath permanently with the following command:

```
[Environment]::SetEnvironmentVariable("PSModulePath",↵
$env:PSModulePath + ";\\central\modules","User")
```

PERFORMANCE CONCERN WITH PSMODULEPATH

When `Get-Module -ListAvailable` is run, it recursively searches all locations in the **PSModulePath** environment variable. If you add a folder with a lot of files and subfolders, this command will run slower.

Note that you could also update the environment variable with the following command, but it would apply only to the current PowerShell session and any PowerShell sessions spawned from the current PowerShell session.

```
$env:PSModulePath = $env:PSModulePath +↵
 ";\\central\modules"
```

Also note that although these folders can be named however you like, the folder structure should look like this:

► ModuleBase (one of the folders in the PSModulePath environment variable)

  ► Module folder

    ► Module files

Figure E.5 shows an example of this folder structure.

In terms of manifest modules, script modules, and binary modules, the Module folder should typically have the same name as the module.

One other thing to note is that if you are working with modules in the system location, it is advantageous to use Windows PowerShell with administrator privileges, because you need administrator permissions to read/write from the system folders.

Manifest File

The manifest file, also known as a PowerShell *definition file*, uses the `.psd1` file extension. This optional file stores a variety of information about the module, including metadata, dependencies, processing notes, and export restrictions. You can use the `New-ModuleManifest` cmdlet to generate this file. Table E.1 describes the keys in a manifest file.

FIGURE E.5 Module folder structure

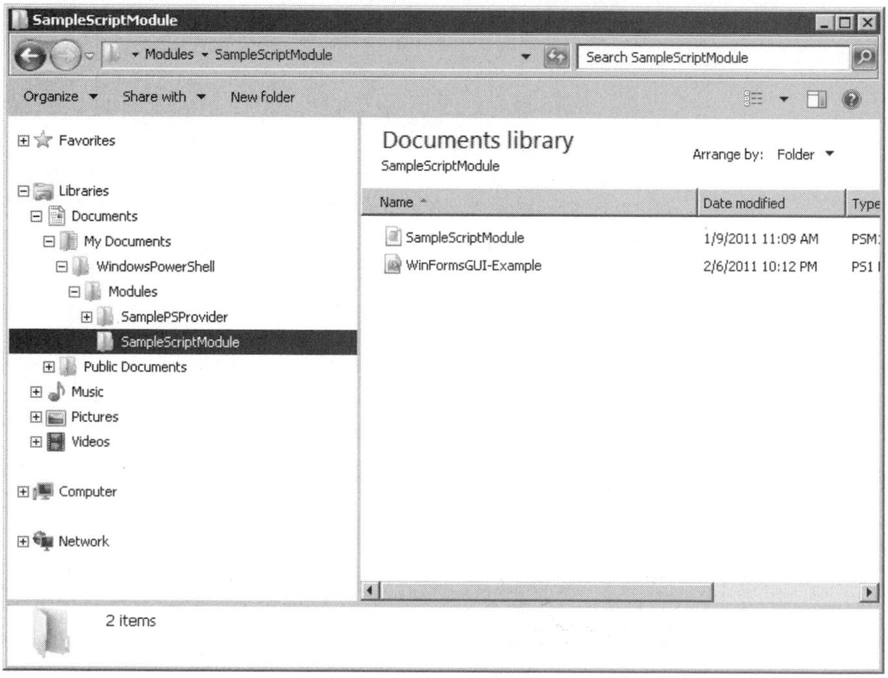

TABLE E.1 Manifest file keys

Name	Description
ModuleToProcess	Name of the root module. This will refer to a script or binary module. If a root module is not specified, the manifest file is considered the root, and the module is then considered a manifest module.
ModuleVersion	Version of the module.
GUID	Unique identifier of the module. If the identifier is not specified, `New-ModuleManifest` will generate its own GUID.
Author	Name of the author(s) of the module.
CompanyName	Name of the company or vendor responsible for the module. If unspecified, `New-ModuleManifest` will default it to `Unknown`.
Copyright	Copyright text for the module. If unspecified, the default value takes the `(c)` *CurrentYear Author*. `All rights reserved.` form.
Description	Description of what is included in the module.

Name	Description
PowerShellVersion	Minimum version of the PowerShell engine. Acceptable values are 1.0 and 2.0. Versions higher than 2.0 are not enforced. This can be left as an empty string (' ').
PowerShellHostName	Name of the PowerShell host required by the module. The host name can be gathered from $host.name. This can be left as an empty string (' ').
PowerShellHostVersion	Minimum version of the PowerShell host. This can be left as an empty string (' ').
DotNetFrameworkVersion	Minimum version of the .NET Framework. This can be left as an empty string (' ').
CLRVersion	Minimum version of the common language runtime. This can be left as an empty string (' ').
ProcessorArchitecture	Processor required by the module. Options include None (used for unknown or unspecified), X86, Amd64, and IA64. If the value is unspecified, the value can be left as an empty string (' ').
RequiredModules	Modules the module depends on. These modules should be in the global scope. Module names can be entered as strings or as a hash table of ModuleName and GUID keys. Note: PowerShell will not import these modules automatically. It just checks that these modules are available. If these modules need to be loaded, use a script to import them and include that script in the ScriptsToProcess list.
RequiredAssemblies	Assemblies the module depends on. PowerShell will load these files before loading types, formats, nested modules, and root modules. Include any DLL files that are needed for formatting and object types.
ScriptsToProcess	Scripts the module depends on. These are run when the module is imported.
TypesToProcess	Type files the module depends on. These files use the .ps1xml file extension. These files define the custom .NET Framework types used in a module. PowerShell processes these types via Update-TypeData when it imports the module.
FormatsToProcess	Format files the module depends on. These files use the .ps1xml file extension. These files define the output of different types, controlling how they display and what they display by default. For example, these format files could force output to display as a table by default. PowerShell processes these formats via Update-FormatData when it imports the module.
NestedModules	Modules nested within the module. These are .psm1 and .dll files that are imported for the module to work with them but may not be exposed to the user. These files can be exposed if the Global parameter is included in the Import-Module line or if their parts are included in one of the …ToExport values. Note: The files will be run in the order they are listed.

(continues)

Packaging
PowerShell
Extensions

APPENDIX E

TABLE E.1 *(continued)*

Name	Description
FunctionsToExport	Functions to export from the module. These are the functions that are available to the PowerShell session or to the module's session state, in the case of nested modules.
	Functions can be named explicitly, or an asterisk (*) can be used to export all functions. If an asterisk is used, all functions, including functions in nested modules, are exported to the PowerShell session.
CmdletsToExport	Cmdlets to export from the module. These are the cmdlets that are available to the PowerShell session or to the module's session state, in the case of nested modules.
	Cmdlets can be named explicitly, or an asterisk(*) can be used to export all cmdlets. If an asterisk is used, all cmdlets, including cmdlets in nested modules, are exported to the PowerShell session.
VariablesToExport	Variables to export from the module. These are the variables that are available to the PowerShell session or to the module's session state, in the case of nested modules.
	Variables can be named explicitly, or an asterisk (*) can be used to export all variables. If an asterisk is used, all variables, including variables in nested modules, are exported to the PowerShell session.
AliasesToExport	Aliases to export from the module. These are the aliases that are available to the PowerShell session or to the module's session state, in the case of nested modules.
	Aliases can be named explicitly, or an asterisk (*) can be used to export all aliases. If an asterisk is used, all aliases, including aliases in nested modules, are exported to the PowerShell session.
ModuleList	All modules packaged in this module.
	Note: PowerShell will not export the files in this list based on this list. This is purely for tracking purposes.
FileList	All files packaged in the module. This can be used to keep track of all files included in the module.
	Note: PowerShell will not export the files in this list based on this list. This is purely for tracking purposes.
PrivateData	Private data to pass to the root module. The data becomes available to the module through the $args automatic variable.

Although the New-ModuleManifest cmdlet may not prompt for all of these keys, you can easily add the missing values to the manifest file by editing the file with a text editor. Figure E.6 shows the New-ModuleManifest cmdlet in action.

Figure E.7 shows part of the generated manifest file opened for editing.

FIGURE E.6   New-ModuleManifest

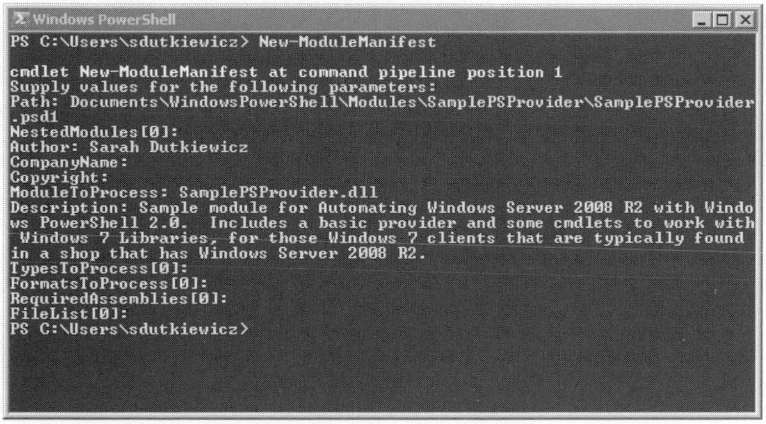

FIGURE E.7   Editing the manifest file

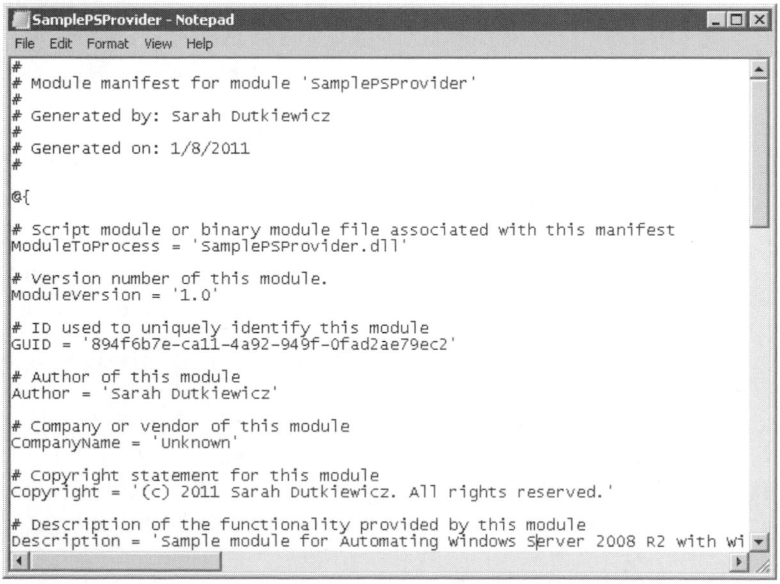

Once you are done editing a manifest, you may want to verify that you entered everything correctly. The `Test-ModuleManifest` cmdlet can verify that the files listed in the manifest exist in the proper paths. Figure E.8 shows what happens when `Test-ModuleManifest` finds problems with a manifest file.

FIGURE E.8   Problems with manifest file

Help File

As stated throughout this book, PowerShell has a great help system. Get-Help is full of descriptions, details, and examples, providing a wealth of knowledge to the PowerShell scripter. When you release your custom extensions, it would be helpful to continue adding to this knowledge base.

The help files are stored in two formats: XML and UTF-8 formatted text files. Help files for cmdlets, providers, functions, and scripts are written in HTML files. Conceptual files — for help topics that start with about_ such as about_ Comment_Based_Help — are saved in UTF-8 formatted text files. Examples of these files are included in the "Build Your Module" section later in this chapter.

The help files have a specific folder and file structure, as shown in Figure E.9.

The help files are imported to a PowerShell session when Import-Module is run. As the previous folder structure suggests, help topics can be tailored to language-specific files. PowerShell will look for the language of the current user first before following the language fallback standards of Windows.

Build Your Module

Now that the building blocks have been laid out, here is the approach you want to take:

1. Identify which type of module to use.

2. Build the module.

3. Determine whether a manifest file is needed. If so, create it.

4. Write the help file.

5. Release for use.

FIGURE E.9   Help file directory structure

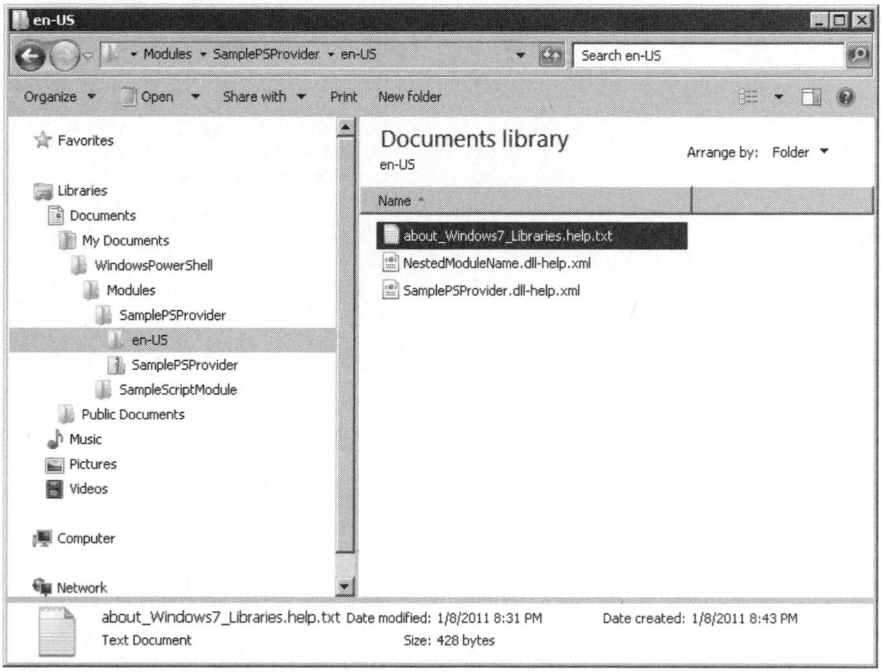

Binary Module Example

In Appendix C, you created a basic provider to work with Windows 7 libraries. In Appendix D, you created custom cmdlets to work with these Windows 7 libraries. Since the provider and the custom cmdlets were written in C#, it seems fitting to package them in a binary module.

The module setup was actually established when you created the new project in Appendix C. As noted in Figure C.7, the project name was SamplePSProvider, which means that when you compile the project, you will get an assembly named SamplePSProvider.dll. Figure E.10 shows the list of all files and references in this project.

Packaging PowerShell Extensions

APPENDIX E

FIGURE E.10 Solution Explorer for `SamplePSProvider.dll`

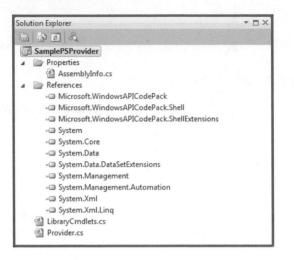

At this point, you can test whether your module will work in PowerShell without having to complete the package. To test the module in PowerShell from Visual Studio 2010, follow these steps:

1. Right-click the project name (SamplePSProvider in this case), and select Properties.

2. From the tabs on the left, click the Debug tab.

3. Update your Start Action setting to Start External Program, and point it to where `PowerShell.exe` is installed.

4. Under Start Options, update the command-line arguments to read as follows:

```
-noexit -command
"[reflection.assembly]::loadFrom('SamplePSProvider.dll') |
import-module"
```

5. Close the Properties screen to save the settings.

Now you can start the debugger and test your module. Figure E.11 shows the debugging PowerShell session.

Notice that the result of `Get-Module` in Figure E.11 shows the `Name` as `dynamic_ code_module_Sa`.... Since debugging is a short-lived process, PowerShell is naming it as if it were a dynamic module. However, as noted in the `ModuleType` column, this is indeed a binary module.

FIGURE E.11 Debugging a binary module

Now that you are in the debug session, you can test the functionality, as described in Appendixes C and D. Once you are done debugging, exit the PowerShell session. Deploy the module as follows:

1. In Visual Studio, go to the Build menu, and select Build SamplePSProvider.

2. Right-click the project name, and select Open Folder in Windows Explorer.

3. Navigate to bin and then the folder with the most recently modified date.

4. Copy the `SamplePSProvider.dll` file and all other DLL files into the `[USER]\Documents\WindowsPowerShell\Modules\SamplePSProvider` folder. Note: If this file structure does not exist, create it.

5. Start PowerShell.

6. Run `Get-Module -ListAvailable`. You should see the `SamplePSProvider` module listed, similar to Figure E.12.

You should be able to run `Import-Module SamplePSProvider` and work with the provider and cmdlets, as documented in Appendixes C and D. If you get an error about not being able to load the module because PowerShell can't find the dependencies, make sure you copied all the DLL files from step 4.

Packaging
PowerShell
Extensions

APPENDIX E

FIGURE E.12 Module deployed

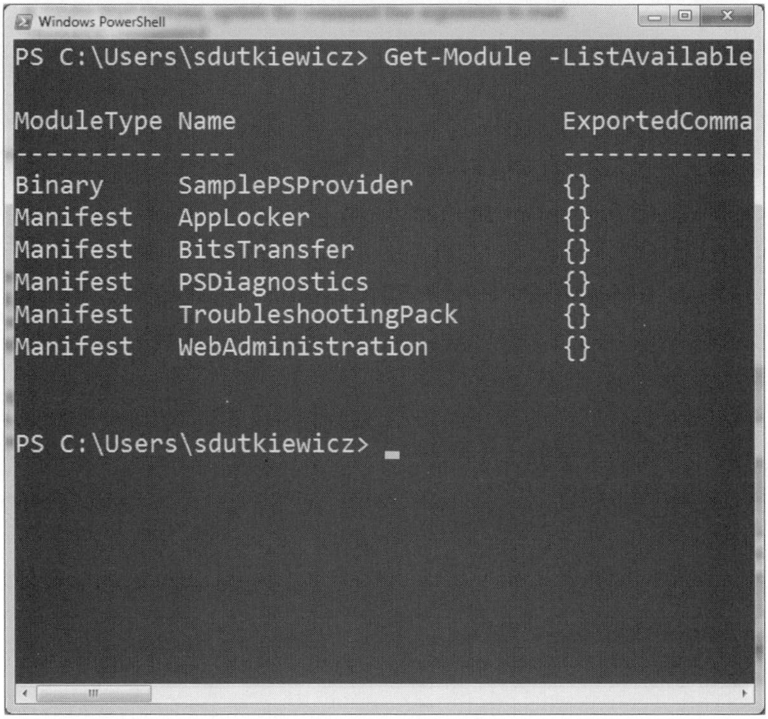

A manifest file can help track these dependencies, so in this case it would be advantageous to have one. For this example, you will reuse the manifest file created earlier in this chapter. To make note of the required assemblies, update RequiredAssemblies to match this:

```
RequiredAssemblies = @(↵
"Microsoft.WindowsAPICodePack.dll",↵
"Microsoft.WindowsAPICodePack.Shell.dll")
```

The last thing you need to do is create some help files for this module. Since libraries are a new concept to Windows 7, you may want to create a conceptual help file:

1. Create an en-US folder in [USER]\Documents\WindowsPowerShell\ Modules\SamplePSProvider.

2. Create a text file named about_Windows7_Libraries.help.txt within this en-US folder.

3. Add the following text:

```
TOPIC
    about_Windows7_Libraries
```

```
SHORT DESCRIPTION
    Describes the capabilities of Windows 7↵
 Libraries.

LONG DESCRIPTION
    This is a sample help file included with ↵
the SamplePSProvider example for ↵
"Automating Windows Server 2008 R2 with ↵
Windows PowerShell 2.0" book.

    For more information on the Libraries feature ↵
included in Windows 7, see:

    http://windows.microsoft.com/en-us/windows7/↵
products/features/libraries
```

4. Save and close the file.

5. If you do not have a PowerShell session already open, start PowerShell.

6. Run `Import-Module SamplePSProvider`.

7. Run `Get-Help about_Windows7_Libraries`. You should see something similar to Figure E.13.

FIGURE E.13 Conceptual help

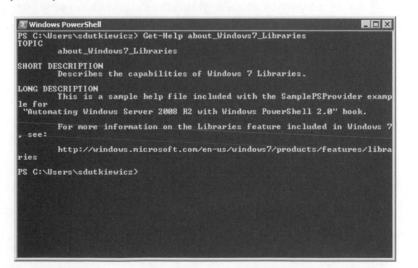

The other type of help file for binary modules is an XML-based help file. The file should be located in the en-US folder (or your native language's folder) and named *ModuleName*.dll-help.xml. For a detailed explanation of the XML layout for cmdlet help files, see the following MSDN article:

http://msdn.microsoft.com/en-us/library/bb525433(VS.85).aspx

Now that the binary module is built, complete with a manifest file and help files, you need to package it to give to others. The easiest way to do this is as follows:

1. Navigate to [USER]\Documents\WindowsPowerShell\Modules\ in Windows Explorer.

2. Right-click the SamplePSProvider folder, and navigate to Send To ➤ Compressed (zipped) folder.

3. Save the filename.

4. Place the ZIP file in a location where your targeted audience can access it.

5. Have them unzip the file into one of their folders listed in their PSModulePath environment variable.

Script Module Example

In Appendix D, you created a function called Get-Function. Since it is already written in PowerShell, it makes sense to package it in a script module. Save Get-Function in a script file with the following file structure: [USER]\ Documents\WindowsPowerShell\Modules\SampleScriptModule\ SampleScriptModule.psm1.

Since you want everything to be exported and do not need to include any dependencies or types or formats, you do not need a manifest file in this case.

Script modules can take advantage of comment-based help. This means you use comments within your code to generate the help file. I have added the comment-based help comments toward the end of this function:

```
Function Get-Function{
    Param(
     # Part or full name of the function
     # Supports wildcards
     [parameter(Mandatory=$true, ↵
ValueFromPipeline=$true)]
     [String[]]
     $FunctionName
     )
```

```
      Get-ChildItem -path function: | ↵
Where-Object {$_.Name -like $FunctionName}
<#
   .SYNOPSIS
   Lists all functions matching a name or wildcard↵
 pattern.

   .DESCRIPTION
   Lists all functions matching a name or wildcard↵
 pattern.

   .INPUTS
   System.String.  Get-Function takes in↵
 a function name or pattern.

   .OUTPUTS
   System.String. Get-Function returns↵
 a string with the extension or file name.

  .EXAMPLE
  C:\PS> Get-Function *
  Lists all functions.

  .EXAMPLE
  C:\PS> Get-Function m*
  Lists all functions whose name starts with "m".

  .EXAMPLE
  C:\PS> Get-Function *port*
  Lists all functions whose name contains "port".

   .LINK
   Get-ChildItem
#>
 }
```

After saving this file, load PowerShell, and run `Import-Module`
`SampleScriptModule`. Once the module is loaded, if you run `Get-Help Get-`
`Function`, you will see output similar to Figure E.14.

FIGURE E.14 `Get-Help Get-Function`

```
PS C:\Windows\system32> Get-Help Get-Function

NAME
    Get-Function

SYNOPSIS
    Lists all functions matching a name or wildcard pattern.

SYNTAX
    Get-Function [-FunctionName] <String[]> [<CommonParameters>]

DESCRIPTION
    Lists all functions matching a name or wildcard pattern.

RELATED LINKS
    Get-ChildItem

REMARKS
    To see the examples, type: "get-help Get-Function -examples".
    For more information, type: "get-help Get-Function -detailed".
    For technical information, type: "get-help Get-Function -full".
```

If you run `Get-Help Get-Function -examples`, you will see each of the
`.EXAMPLE` lines from the earlier code, as shown in Figure E.15.

FIGURE E.15 `Get-Help Get-Function -examples`

```
------------------------- EXAMPLE 1 -------------------------

C:\PS>Get-Function *


Lists all functions.




------------------------- EXAMPLE 2 -------------------------

C:\PS>Get-Function m*


Lists all functions whose name starts with "m".




------------------------- EXAMPLE 3 -------------------------

C:\PS>Get-Function *port*


Lists all functions whose name contains "port".
```

For more information about the different keywords that can appear in comment-
based help, run `Get-Help about_Comment_Based_Help`.

Now that the script module is built, complete with comment-based help, you need to package it to give it to others. The easiest way to do this is as follows:

1. Navigate to `[USER]\Documents\WindowsPowerShell\Modules\` in Windows Explorer.

2. Right-click the `SampleScriptModule` folder, and navigate to Send To ➤ Compressed (zipped) folder.

3. Save the filename.

4. Place the ZIP file in a location where your targeted audience can access it.

5. Have them unzip the file into one of their folders listed in their `PSModulePath` environment variable.

Now that you have seen how to package PowerShell extensions, use these examples as guides for packaging and sharing your extensions with your colleagues or even the PowerShell community.

Building Your Own GUI with PowerShell

IN THIS APPENDIX, YOU WILL LEARN TO:

Command-line scripts are great from an administrative perspective, but the people who may work with these scripts or their output may not necessarily be comfortable in a command-line realm. It would help to create a graphical user interface (GUI) for them to feel a little more comfortable.

Since PowerShell can take advantage of the .NET Framework, GUI development options include Windows Forms (WinForms) and Windows Presentation Foundation (WPF). In this chapter, you will learn the strong points of these technologies and how to use PowerShell to create GUIs with them.

The example GUI gets much of its information from Windows Management Instrumentation (WMI) Win32 classes. You can find more about WMI's Win32 classes here:

```
http://msdn.microsoft.com/en-us/library/aa394084(v=VS.85).aspx
```

Choose Between WinForms and WPF

In terms of creating GUIs in the .NET Framework, the main technology choices are WinForms and WPF. Knowing the strengths and weaknesses of both options makes it easier to decide on the appropriate choice for a particular application.

If your end user is working with legacy applications, there may be a case to write your application with WinForms. This is the older technology compared to WPF, and the look and feel of WinForms controls is very similar to what you would get out of applications written in a Microsoft language before the .NET Framework. If you, as a developer, are more familiar with writing desktop applications in something such as Visual Basic 6, then WinForms should be easy to work with, because many controls are still around in some form in WinForms. If the end user's computer consists of older hardware or running an older operating system such as Windows XP, WinForms may run a lot better than WPF and therefore would be the better choice.

If your end user is more familiar with applications that have been written in .NET or for the newer operating systems such as Windows Vista and Windows 7, chances are that the end user is familiar with a prettier interface. If that is the case, then you may consider leaning toward WPF. Rich user interfaces, easier animations, and better handling of vector graphics are just a few reasons why you would choose WPF instead of WinForms. If you are one of those people who develop for multiple platforms, you may find WPF and its use of the Extensible Application

Markup Language (XAML) more appealing, because XAML is used in both WPF and Silverlight. With that consideration, by going with WPF, your application is one step closer to becoming portable to a web application or even a Windows Phone application.

WHEN TO CHOOSE BOTH WINFORMS AND WPF

You may see that the benefits of each technology could work to your advantage if only you could include both in the same application. There is no "if" about it—you can include both WinForms and WPF in the same application! For example, you may have a WinForms app that could benefit from newer technology. While tossing out the code and starting from scratch sounds tempting, unless you have time in your work schedule to rewrite the whole code, tossing out a complete code base is costly to a business. You might consider replacing small pieces with WPF, if the technology makes sense for the feature you are updating.

Create a GUI in PowerShell

Once you understand the technologies that are available to you, then you can build your application. In this section, you will create a dashboard to look at various attributes of your current machine. This could be useful for monitoring a server's configuration or perhaps be used to obtain information for an inventory database.

The application you create will show the following sections:

Basic System Information   Including domain, manufacturer, model, and name

Hard Drive Information   Including device ID, size, and free space

Memory Information   Including physical memory, virtual memory, process memory, and visible memory

Network Interface Information   Including MAC address and description

Installed Applications   Including version and name

Although you may be familiar with these commands and their output in the command-line environment, there may be formatting and other output issues that could confuse the end user who is familiar with friendly formatting in a GUI. Here are the building blocks you will need for building your GUI.

Building Your
Own GUI with
PowerShell

APPENDIX F

Use the `Win32_ComputerSystem` WMI class to get basic system information:

```
Get-WmiObject win32_computersystem
```

The output should be similar to Figure F.1.

FIGURE F.1 Basic system information

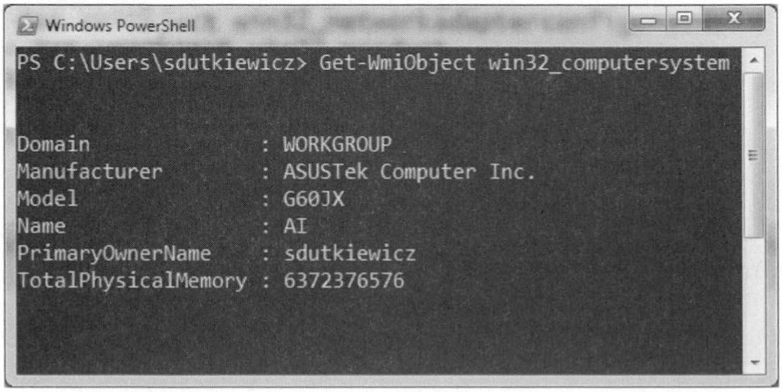

Use the `Win32_LogicalDisk` WMI class to get the hard drive information:

```
Get-WmiObject win32_LogicalDisk
```

The output should be similar to Figure F.2.

FIGURE F.2 List of logical drives

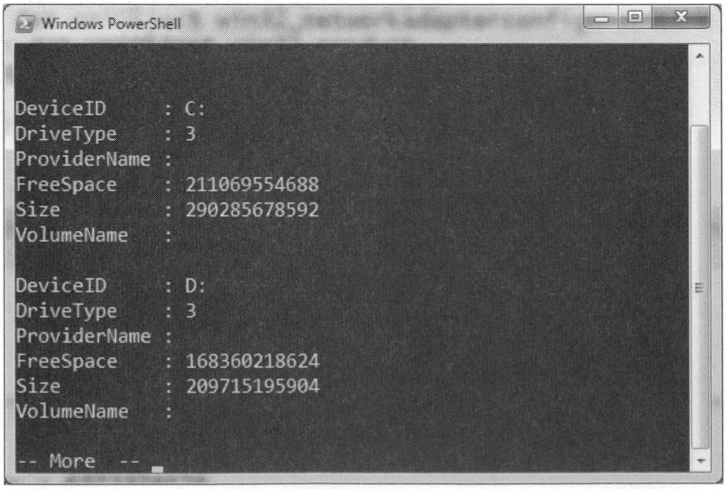

The `Win32_OperatingSystem` WMI class contains a plethora of information regarding a system's operating system, including language, architecture, service pack version, installation date, and memory information. To get the memory information, use the following command:

```
Get-WmiObject win32_OperatingSystem | ↵
Format-List *Memory*
```

The output should be similar to Figure F.3.

FIGURE F.3   Memory information

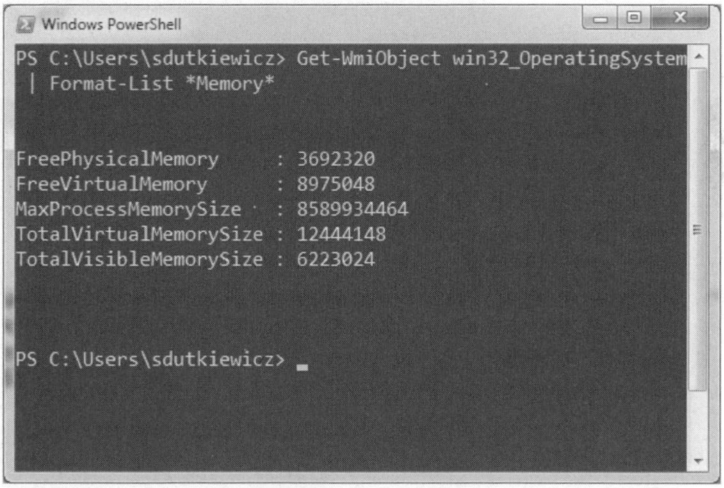

Use the `Win32_NetworkAdapterConfiguration` WMI class to get more information about a system's network interfaces. The following example shows DHCP, DNS, and network address essentials.

```
Get-WmiObject win32_NetworkAdapterConfiguration |↵
Format-List *Address, DefaultIPGateway, IPSubnet, ↵
Description, DHCP*, DNS*
```

The output should be similar to Figure F.4.

Use the `Win32_Product` WMI class to get more information about installed applications. The following example shows how to list all applications installed on a machine that did not come from Microsoft:

```
Get-WmiObject Win32_Product | ↵
Where-Object {$_.Vendor -ne "Microsoft Corporation" }
```

Building Your Own GUI with PowerShell

APPENDIX F

FIGURE F.4 Network interface information

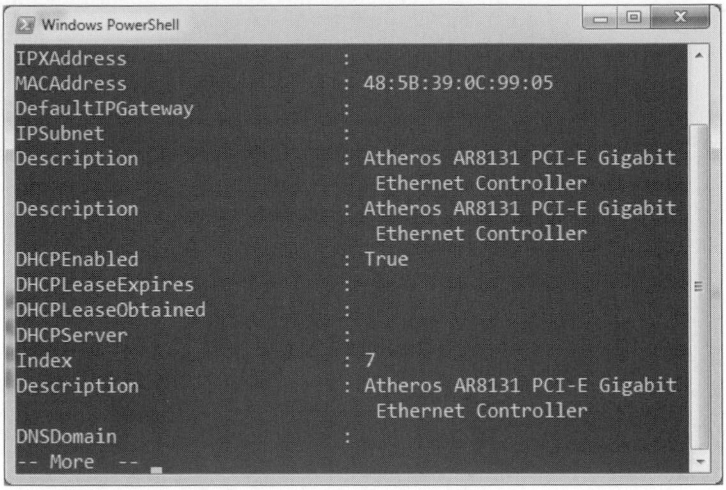

The output should be similar to Figure F.5.

FIGURE F.5 Installed application information

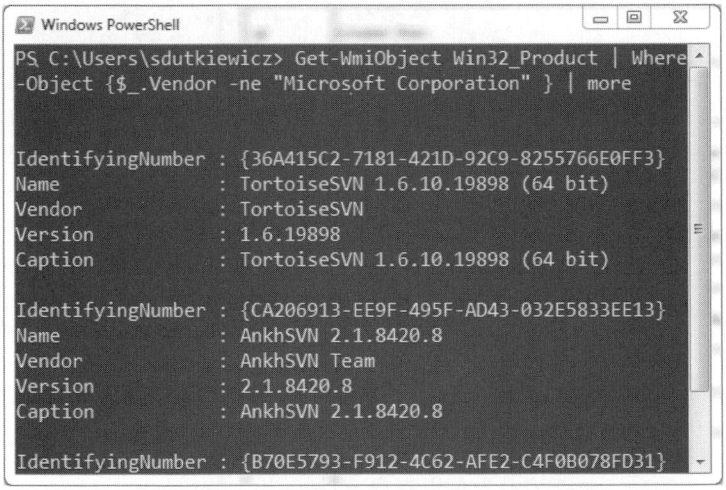

Now that the groundwork is established, let's look into creating a GUI that will display this information for those who are timid in a command-line environment. This GUI will have buttons along the top for each section, with a panel below the buttons to show all the information for that particular section.

Create a WinForms Application

As noted, working with WinForms is a good choice when you need to create a GUI that has a look and feel similar to legacy applications.

The first thing you should do when creating a WinForms application in PowerShell is load the assembly where WinForms comes from — `System.Windows.Forms` — with the following command:

```
Add-Type -AssemblyName System.Windows.Forms
```

Once you load the assembly, you need to create the canvas to work on. To create a WinForms form, use the following command:

```
$form = New-Object Windows.Forms.Form
```

At this point, you have a generic form. To display the form, use the following command:

```
$form.ShowDialog()
```

You should see something similar to Figure F.6.

FIGURE F.6 Default Windows form

Now that a form has been created, you can start adding objects and helper functions to it to create your application. The code for these objects and helper functions needs to be placed before `$form.ShowDialog()`.

Because this application will have buttons with similar attributes, you will want to create a function so that you are not repeating code frequently. For this example, you are using a function called `Create-Button`.

```
function Create-Button([string]$text,↵
[object]$PreviousObject, [int]$height,↵
[object]$container){
    $button = New-Object Windows.Forms.Button
    $button.Text = $text
    $button.AutoSize = $true
    $button.Left = $PreviousObject.Left + ↵
$PreviousObject.Width
    $button.Top = $container.Top
    $button.Anchor = "Left"
    $button.Height = $height
    return $button
}
```

For debugging purposes, you may want to use a MessageBox to display error messages. Use the following function to help prevent writing the same call over and over:

```
function Create-MessageBox ($text){
    [Windows.Forms.MessageBox]::Show($text)
}
```

The results will display in a table for each button. Since the table needs to be generated each time, use a function to generate the output. In the following function, the $output variable is an array of objects with a Name property and a Value property. The $outputpanel variable is the container object that will hold the table.

```
function Create-Table($output, $outputpanel){
    $outputpanel.Controls.Clear()
    $btnContainer = New-Object Windows.Forms.Panel
    $btnContainer.Width = $outputpanel.Width - 25
    $btnContainer.Height = $outputpanel.Height - 100
    $TablePanel = New-Object Windows.Forms.↵
TableLayoutPanel
    $TablePanel.Dock = "Fill"
    $TablePanel.CellBorderStyle = "Single"
    $TablePanel.ColumnCount = 2
    $TablePanel.ColumnStyles.Add↵
((new-object System.Windows.Forms.ColumnStyle(↵
[System.Windows.Forms.SizeType]::Percent,50)))
    $TablePanel.ColumnStyles.Add↵
```

```
((new-object System.Windows.Forms.ColumnStyle↵
([System.Windows.Forms.SizeType]::Percent,50)))
   $TablePanel.AutoScroll = $true
   $output | ForEach-Object {
    $label = New-Object Windows.Forms.Label
    $label.Text = $_.Name
    $label.AutoSize = $true
    $TablePanel.Controls.Add($label)
    $label2 = New-Object Windows.Forms.Label
    $label2.Text = $_.Value
    $label2.AutoSize = $true
    $TablePanel.Controls.Add($label2)
   }
   $btnContainer.Controls.Add($TablePanel)
   $outputpanel.Controls.Add($btnContainer)
}
```

You will want a function to help format each of the results so that they conform to the Name/Value pairs. The following function will loop through the properties for each object and break them down into Name/Value pairs:

```
function Create-ExampleObject ($output){
    $cleanedoutput = $output | ForEach-Object {
       $_ | Get-Member -MemberType NoteProperty↵
| Select Name, Definition | ForEach-Object {
          New-Object PSObject -Property↵
@{Name=$_.Name;Value=↵
$_.Definition.Substring($_.Definition.IndexOf('=')+1)
          }
       }
    }
    return $cleanedoutput
}
```

Since memory and hard drive sizes will be displayed, you will want a function to handle the output formatting. The following function will test the value against known values and append the size abbreviation to the value.

```
function Format-Size($sizeinbytes){
    $formatted = ""
    if ($sizeinbytes/1gb -gt 0){
```

```
        $formatted = ("{0:N2}" -f ($sizeinbytes/1gb)) ↵
+ "GB"
     } else {
        $formatted = ("{0:N2}" -f ($sizeinbytes/1mb)) ↵
+ "MB"
     }
     return $formatted
}
```

Now that the helper functions are in place, you can use those while adding the controls and other functionality.

First up, set some form defaults, including the form caption, the dimensions, and a constant value for button height, because the buttons will be the same size:

```
$form.Text = "WinForms Inventory Example"
$form.Width = 600
$form.Height = 400
$buttonHeight = 30
```

Next, create the panels that will hold the buttons and the output area and add them to the form's controls:

```
$pnlButtonBar = New-Object Windows.Forms.Panel
$pnlButtonBar.Dock = "Top"
$pnlButtonBar.Width = $form.Height
$pnlButtonBar.Height = $buttonHeight
$form.Controls.add($pnlButtonBar)

$pnlOutput = New-Object Windows.Forms.Panel
$pnlOutput.Width = $form.Height
$pnlOutput.Height = $form.Height - $pnlButtonBar.Height
$pnlOutput.Top = $pnlButtonBar.Top + $pnlButtonBar.Height + 20
$form.Controls.add($pnlOutput)
```

Once the panels are created, then the objects that belong in those panels can be created and placed in their respective placeholders. For the button bar, there will be a label with the text *Show:* to give the user an idea that those buttons are there for some reason.

```
$lblShow = New-Object Windows.Forms.Label
$lblShow.Text = "Show : "
$lblShow.Width = 50
```

```
$lblShow.Left = $pnlButtonBar.Left
$lblShow.Top = $pnlButtonBar.Top
$lblShow.Anchor = "Left"
$pnlButtonBar.Controls.add($lblShow)
```

Now that the label is in there to give the user some guidance, you should add the buttons. These buttons will get created using the Create-Button helper function mentioned earlier.

```
$btnSysInfo = Create-Button "System Information" $lblShow↵
$buttonHeight $pnlButtonBar
$pnlButtonBar.Controls.Add($btnSysInfo)


$btnDrives = Create-Button "Hard Drives" $btnSysInfo↵
$buttonHeight $pnlButtonBar
$pnlButtonBar.Controls.Add($btnDrives)


$btnMemory = Create-Button "Memory" $btnDrives↵
$buttonHeight $pnlButtonBar
$pnlButtonBar.Controls.Add($btnMemory)


$btnNetwork = Create-Button "Network" $btnMemory↵
$buttonHeight $pnlButtonBar
$pnlButtonBar.Controls.Add($btnNetwork)


$btnInstalledApps = Create-Button "Installed Apps"↵
$btnNetwork $buttonHeight $pnlButtonBar
$pnlButtonBar.Controls.Add($btnInstalledApps)
```

Once the button bar is created, add one more label with instructions for the end user that will appear when the program loads where the command output would appear:

```
$lblInstructions = New-Object Windows.Forms.Label
$lblInstructions.Text = "Click a button to see more↵
 details."
$lblInstructions.AutoSize = $true
$lblInstructions.Left = $pnlOutput.Left
$lblInstructions.Top = $pnlOutput.Top
$lblInstructions.Anchor = "Left"
$pnlOutput.Controls.add($lblInstructions)
```

Building Your
Own GUI with
PowerShell

APPENDIX F

Now that the objects are created, you need to assign the event handler to each button to handle the Click event. For each button click, you will call out to the respective WMI class and display an identified group of fields. Once the WMI objects are gathered, then they need to be formatted to fit the Name/Value pairs by calling the Create-ExampleObject helper function. Finally, the output gets generated by the Create-Table helper function.

For the system information section, show all fields:

```
$btnSysInfo.add_Click({
    $output = Get-WmiObject win32_computersystem |↵
Select *
    $output = Create-ExampleObject $output
    Create-Table $output $pnlOutput
})
```

For the hard drives section, show only the drives that have a specific size. With those drives, show the total space, the free space, and how full the drive is:

```
$btnDrives.add_Click({
  $output = Get-WmiObject win32_LogicalDisk | Where-Object {$_
.Size -gt 0} | Select Name, FreeSpace, Size | ForEach-Object
{ New-Object PSObject -Property @{Drive=$_.Name;Size=Format-
Size($_.Size); FreeSpace=Format-Size($_.FreeSpace);
PercentageUsed=("{0:N2}" -f (100-(($_.FreeSpace/$_.Size) *
100))) + "%"} }
  $output = Create-ExampleObject $output
  Create-Table $output $pnlOutput
})
```

For the memory section, show all fields containing the word *Memory* from the Win32_OperatingSystem WMI class:

```
$btnMemory.add_Click({
    $output = Get-WmiObject win32_OperatingSystem↵
 | Select *Memory*
    $output = Create-ExampleObject $output
    Create-Table $output $pnlOutput
})
```

For the network section, suppose you are adding MAC authentication to your network security. You would only be interested in connections that have a MAC address. Fields that may be relevant include the connection name and the MAC address.

```
$btnNetwork.add_Click({
    $output = Get-WmiObject↵
 win32_NetworkAdapterConfiguration |↵
 Select MACAddress, Description |↵
 Where-Object {$_.MACAddress -ne $null }
    $output = Create-ExampleObject $output
    Create-Table $output $pnlOutput
})
```

Finally, for the installed apps section, suppose you care only about the application names and respective versions that are installed on the machine, sorted alphabetically.

```
$btnInstalledApps.add_Click({
    $output = Get-WmiObject Win32_Product |↵
 Select Name, Version | Sort-Object -property Name |↵
 ForEach-Object {
        New-Object PSObject↵
 -Property @{Application=$_.Name + " " + $_.Version}
    }
    $output = Create-ExampleObject $output
    Create-Table $output $pnlOutput
})
```

Once all this code is entered, you now have a basic program to display some information about the current machine. Figure F.7 shows the final output.

This example shows a miniscule portion of the Win32 libraries in WMI, and it shows a basic introduction to WinForms in PowerShell. Use this as a guide as you are getting started with writing WinForms applications in PowerShell.

Create a WPF Application

As mentioned earlier, WPF is a good choice when you are developing GUIs for a newer operating system such as Windows 7. The prettiness that is seen in the operating system can be carried on easily in a WPF application.

WPF also allows for the GUI layout to be separated easily from the functionality, using XAML for the GUI and the language of choice as the functionality. In

Building Your
Own GUI with
PowerShell

APPENDIX F

the examples that follow, the GUI code will be stored in a XAML file and read in PowerShell. The functionality for those XAML controls will be written in PowerShell.

FIGURE F.7 Final WinForm output

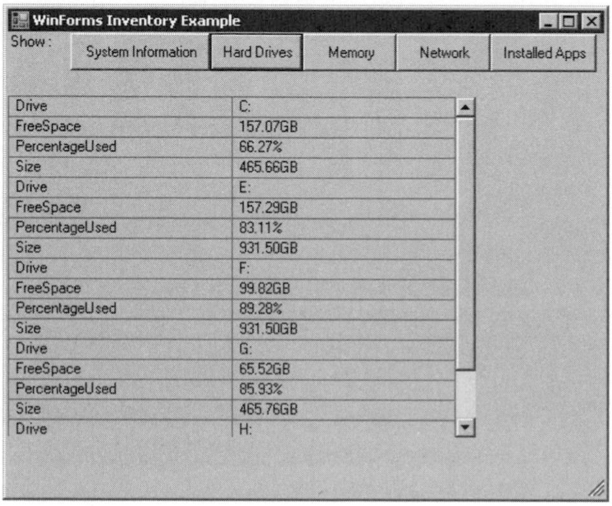

In this section, you will see how to create a WPF application from scratch within PowerShell.

WRITING WPF IN POWERSHELL

Although the following instructions will have you use the Integrated Scripting Engine (ISE), you can also use the PowerShell console to do this. However, when you start a PowerShell console session for WPF development, you need to include the `-STA` switch, because WPF needs to be run in single-threaded apartment (STA) mode. The PowerShell console starts in multithreaded apartment (MTA) mode by default. The ISE, however, starts in STA mode by default and does not need an extra switch when starting.

For more on apartments and threads, see `http://msdn.microsoft.com/en-us/library/ms693344(v=VS.85).aspx`.

To see whether STA is enabled, check that the following value is set to `STA`:

```
$host.Runspace.ApartmentState
```

Since there is a separation between the GUI and the functionality, you should become familiar enough with XAML to know how to work with it. As shown with WinForms, let's take a look at the default WPF form. The XAML for the WPF form looks like this:

```
<Window xmlns=↵
"http://schemas.microsoft.com/winfx/2006/xaml/↵
presentation"
xmlns:x="http://schemas.microsoft.com/winfx/2006/xaml"
Title="Sample WPF Form" Height="150" Width="300">
</Window>
```

For this example, the XAML is stored in D:\MainWindow.xaml.

WRITING XAML FILES

You can download many tools to help you write XAML, including the following:

- ► **Kaxaml**
- ► **Microsoft Expression Blend**
- ► **Microsoft Visual Studio**
- ► **XamlHack**
- ► **XamlPad**

Until you get familiar with XAML and its syntax, it would be easiest to use one of these tools when creating XAML files.

Once the XAML file is created, you can work on adding functionality to the controls. When writing a WPF application in PowerShell, you need to load the WPF libraries:

```
Add-Type -Assembly PresentationFramework
Add-Type -Assembly PresentationCore
```

After the WPF libraries are loaded, you can load the XAML file into a variable with the help of a XamlReader. The code looks like this:

```
$Form=[Windows.Markup.XamlReader]::Load([IO.File]↵
::OpenText('D:\MainWindow.xaml').basestream)
```

At this point, you can display a basic WPF form with the following command:

```
$Form.ShowDialog() | Out-Null
```

You should see something similar to Figure F.8.

FIGURE F.8   Basic WPF form

Now that a window has been created, you can start adding objects to it to create your application. Using the XAML editor of your choice, update D:\MainWindow .xaml with the following XAML:

```
<Window xmlns="http://schemas.microsoft.com/↵
winfx/2006/xaml/presentation"
    xmlns:x="http://schemas.microsoft.com/↵
winfx/2006/xaml"
    Title="WPF Inventory Example" Height="600"↵
 Width="600">
  <Canvas>
    <DockPanel VerticalAlignment="Top"↵
 Grid.Row="0" Grid.ColumnSpan="2">
      <StackPanel Height="30" ↵
Orientation="Horizontal">
        <Label Content="Show:"></Label>
        <Button x:Name="btnShowSysInfo" ↵
Content="System Information"></Button>
        <Button x:Name="btnShowDrives" ↵
Content="Hard Drives"></Button>
        <Button x:Name="btnShowMemory" ↵
Content="Memory"></Button>
        <Button x:Name="btnShowNetwork" ↵
Content="Network"></Button>
        <Button x:Name="btnShowInstalledApps" ↵
Content="Installed Apps"></Button>
      </StackPanel>
```

```
        </DockPanel>
        <Grid x:Name="pnlOutput" Canvas.Top="40"↵
 ShowGridLines="False" Width="550" ↵
HorizontalAlignment="Left" Height="500">
            <Grid.ColumnDefinitions>
              <ColumnDefinition Width="*" >↵
</ColumnDefinition>
              <ColumnDefinition Width="*" >↵
</ColumnDefinition>
            </Grid.ColumnDefinitions>
            <Grid.RowDefinitions>
              <RowDefinition Height="40">↵
</RowDefinition>
              <RowDefinition Height="*">↵
</RowDefinition>
            </Grid.RowDefinitions>
            <Label x:Name="lblInstructions"↵
 Grid.Row="1" Grid.ColumnSpan="2">↵
Click a button to see more details.</Label>
        </Grid>
    </Canvas>
</Window>
```

The previous XAML creates a layout similar to the WinForms application. Make note of the x:Name fields, because you will need to reference them in PowerShell when adding the functionality.

The code for these objects and helper functions needs to be placed before $Form .ShowDialog() | Out-Null.

Using the WinForms example, copy the Create-ExampleObject and Format-Size helper functions. Since these do not necessarily deal with the GUI directly, they can be shared.

The Create-Table helper function needs to be altered. Since you are working with WPF, you will want to reference controls in System.Windows.Controls, instead of System.Windows.Forms. The new Create-Table helper function sets up the WPF Grid control and adds labels to the appropriate grid positions.

```
function Create-Table($output){
    $pnlOutput = $Form.FindName('pnlOutput')
    $pnlOutput.RowDefinitions.Clear()
```

```
    $pnlOutput.Children.Clear()
    $pnlOutput.ShowGridLines = $true
    $rowcount = 0;
    $output | ForEach-Object {
        $rowDefinition = New-Object↵
system.windows.controls.rowdefinition
        $rowDefinition.height = "Auto"
        $pnlOutput.RowDefinitions.Add($rowDefinition)
        $label = New-Object Windows.Controls.Label
        $label.Content = $_.Name
        [system.windows.controls.grid]↵
::SetColumn($label,0)
        [system.windows.controls.grid]↵
::SetRow($label,$rowcount)
        $pnlOutput.Children.Add($label)
        $label2 = New-Object Windows.Controls.Label
        $label2.Content = $_.Value
          [system.windows.controls.grid]↵
::SetColumn($label2,1)
          [system.windows.controls.grid]↵
::SetRow($label2,$rowcount)
        $pnlOutput.Children.Add($label2)
        $rowcount++;
    }
}
```

Now that the helper functions are in place, use them while adding functionality to the UI. Once the XAML is loaded, then you can access the buttons as follows:

```
$btnSysInfo = $Form.FindName('btnShowSysInfo')
$btnDrives = $Form.FindName('btnShowDrives')
$btnMemory = $Form.FindName('btnShowMemory')
$btnNetwork = $Form.FindName('btnShowNetwork')
$btnInstalledApps = $Form.FindName('btnShowInstalledApps')
```

Did you remember the x:Name fields from the XAML? They are what you need to use with the FindName function in order to find controls within the XAML.

After the buttons are in place, you can use the same add_Click code that was used in the WinForms example, because the examples were set up specifically with code reuse in mind. Once the add_Click code is in place, you should have the same functionality and output in the WPF application that you had in the WinForms application. Figure F.9 shows the final output for the WPF application.

FIGURE F.9 Final WPF application

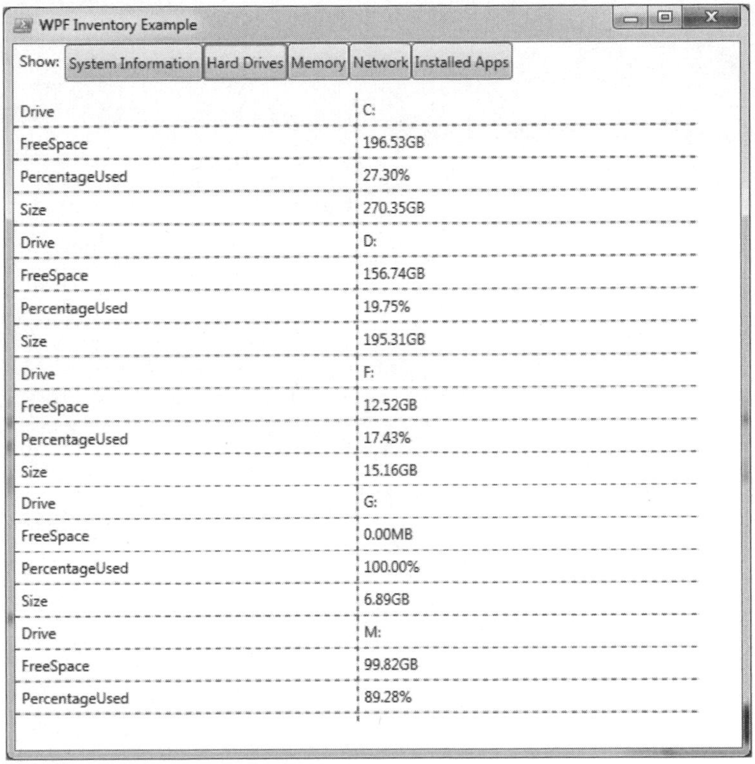

Drive	C:
FreeSpace	196.53GB
PercentageUsed	27.30%
Size	270.35GB
Drive	D:
FreeSpace	156.74GB
PercentageUsed	19.75%
Size	195.31GB
Drive	F:
FreeSpace	12.52GB
PercentageUsed	17.43%
Size	15.16GB
Drive	G:
FreeSpace	0.00MB
PercentageUsed	100.00%
Size	6.89GB
Drive	M:
FreeSpace	99.82GB
PercentageUsed	89.28%

EASIER WPF IN POWERSHELL

Certain tools can make writing WPF in PowerShell much simpler. Some of these tools include the following:

▶ WPK, a module that is part of the PowerShell Pack, is available at: `http://code.msdn.microsoft.com/PowerShellPack`.

▶ PowerBoots, a module, is available at `http://powerboots.codeplex.com/`.

Now that you have seen how to write GUIs from within PowerShell, use these examples as guides for creating GUIs for your own end users. Those who are timid at a command prompt will thank you for taking the time to cater to their preference.

Building Your Own GUI with PowerShell

APPENDIX F

INDEX
· · · · · · · · · · · · · · · ·

Symbols

A